"The River Ran Red"

"But, oh, there was weeping last night at the Homestead!
The river ran red on its way to the sea,
And curses were muttered and bullets whistling,
And Riot was King of the land of the free."

---

from
"A MAN NAMED CARNEGIE"

Co-Editors
Steffi R. Domike
Doris J. Dyen
Nicole Fauteux
Russell W. Gibbons
Randolph Harris
Eugene Levy
Charles J. McCollester
Rina Youngner

Sidebar Contributors
Robert S. Barker
Steffi R. Domike
Nicole Fauteux
Russell W. Gibbons
Archie Green
Randolph Harris
Paul Krause
Eugene Levy
Irwin Marcus
Charles J. McCollester
Kaushik Mukerjee
Theodore B. Sturm
Sharon Trusilo
Joseph Frazier Wall
Don Woodworth
Rina Youngner

Designer
Jo Butz

"The River Ran Red"
HOMESTEAD 1892

David P. Demarest, Jr.
General Editor

Fannia Weingartner
Coordinating Editor

With an Afterword by
David Montgomery

Pittsburgh Series in Social and Labor History

UNIVERSITY OF PITTSBURGH PRESS
Pittsburgh and London

Publication of "THE RIVER RAN RED" was made possible by the assistance of

Mon Valley Media
Pennsylvania Historical and Museum Commission
The Pittsburgh Foundation
Steel Industry Heritage Task Force
United Steelworkers of America

Published by the University of Pittsburgh Press, Pittsburgh, Pa. 15260

Copyright © 1992, Mon Valley Media

All rights reserved

Eurospan, London

Manufactured in the United States of America by Geyer Printing Company, Inc.

Library of Congress Cataloging-in-Publication Data

The River Ran Red : Homestead 1892 / David P. Demarest, Jr., general editor;
    Fannia Weingartner, coordinating editor; with an afterword by
    David Montgomery.
              p. cm. — (Pittsburgh series in social and labor history)
    ISBN 0-8229-3710-7. — ISBN 0-8229-5478-8 (pbk.)
      1. Homestead Strike, 1892. 2. Steel industry and trade—Pennsylvania—
History—19th century. 3. Iron and steel workers—Pennsylvania—
History—19th century. 4. Working class—Pennsylvania—History—
19th century. I. Demarest, David P. II. Weingartner, Fannia. III. Series.
HD 5325.I5 1892.H75   1992
331.89' 2869142' 0974885—dc20   91-50935
                                             CIP

A CIP catalogue record for this book is available from the British Library.

CONTENTS

PREFACE &
ACKNOWLEDGMENTS

The literary conception of this work began around a long table at Michaels—a restaurant in Homestead—in the spring of 1991. Those responsible—listed as the general editor and co-editors—come from a unique combination of backgrounds: two filmmakers, two academics, two labor educators, an art historian, a folklorist, and a community organizer.

Initially our research involved hours of sifting through documents and images at libraries in Pittsburgh and Homestead. Eventually the quest would lead to archival collections in New York City and Washington, D.C. The sheer volume of the material to be discovered, reviewed and transcribed, often from nearly illegible microfilm, could not have been processed without the help of a succession of research associates and transcribers: Caroline Borle, Max Chamowitz, John Dunn, Susan Gross, Susan·Lewis, Sheila Maniar, Monica Mitchell, Pat Ohlin, Ariel Nelson, Rebecca Pillitteri, Matt Ruben, Rhonda Struminger, and Ken Wing. We are grateful to each of them for their part in making this anthology possible.

The creation of this book has been a labor of love, and its publication also has come about through a shared desire to see the story of the Homestead Strike in print. The first financial commitment came from the United Steelworkers of America with the staunch backing of President Lynn Williams. As the successor to the Amalgamated Association which fought the watershed battle in 1892, the Steelworkers can claim a particular connection to the Homestead legacy.

The union's commitment brought others into the project. Janet Sarbaugh shepherded a generous grant through The Pittsburgh Foundation and Jo DeBolt arranged for a substantial contribution from the Steel Industry Heritage Task Force.

Seeing the possibilities of the anthology project, Frederick A. Hetzel, director of the University of Pittsburgh Press, actively encouraged our efforts. He introduced us to Fannia Weingartner who took on the daunting task of creating a coherent manuscript from the reams of articles, letters, poems, and essays we had assembled. She deserves special thanks for her patience in dealing with nine opinionated co-editors.

Our designer, Jo Butz, also deserves enormous praise for integrating such a diverse collection of written and graphic materials. The inventiveness of her design has contributed to this endeavor beyond measure.

Every historical event has its bibliophile or archivist. In Homestead that person is Randolph Harris, a photographer and community organizer who has devoted years to collecting images that tell the story of his adopted hometown. His knowledge of the visual record of the strike and his personal archive offered a firm base on which to build this endeavor. We also thank the other members of the community who shared photos and memorabilia from their personal and family collections with us.

Other people and institutions also have helped make this anthology possible. They include Joseph Belechak and Denise Spang of the Bishop Boyle Center in Homestead where we convened for editorial and strategy sessions; the United Steelworkers and their staff at the Education Center at Linden Hall in Dawson, Westmoreland County, where the editors spent a marathon weekend developing the structure of the book; Mark Brown, industrial historian formerly of the National Park Service; William Gaughan, former U.S. Steel metallurgist and Homestead Works bibliophile; the librarians and staff at the Carnegie Libraries in Pittsburgh and Homestead; the librarians and staff at the Hillman Library of the University of Pittsburgh; the staff of the Philip Murray Institute of Labor Studies at the Community College of Allegheny County; Eileen Flanagan of the Prints and Photographs Department and Corey Seeman of the Archives and Manuscripts Department at the Chicago Historical Society; and Joseph Adams of the Illinois State Historical Society.

A half century ago, the Works Progress Administration commissioned artists to create reliefs and murals depicting the nation at work for public buildings. These works gave Americans a "Living Newspaper" of their history. In the same tradition *"The River Ran Red"* uses words and images to relive a moment of history as recounted by participants and witnesses. The newspaper accounts, magazine commentaries, eulogies, sermons, political statements, court proceedings, and congressional hearings re-create, as no single writer could, the hopes, the terror, and the suffering of July 6, 1892, and the months that followed. As with all such reconstructions of our past, they offer lessons and reflections for the future. ❖

Russell W. Gibbons

INTRODUCTION
by David P. Demarest, Jr.

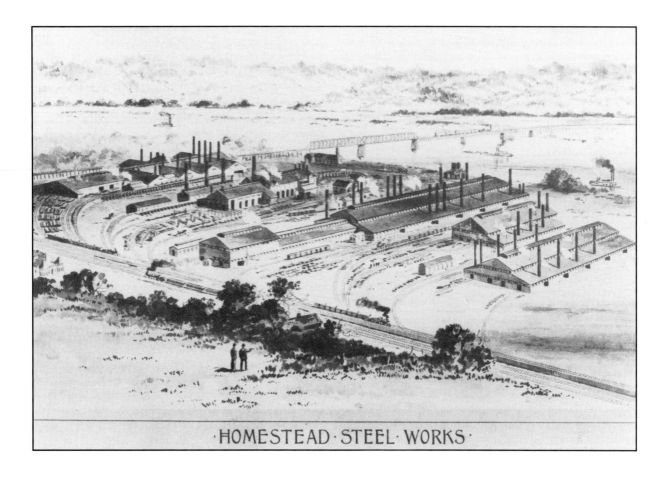

HOMESTEAD · STEEL · WORKS

An 1890 engraving—a company advertisement—displays the 90-acre Homestead Steel Works, purchased in 1883 by Carnegie Bros. & Co. from Pittsburgh Bessemer Steel. The latter had sold the plant for the cost of its investment when it could not settle with the local unions. In the engraving, the original plant, with its 1881 Bessemer shop, is at left center. Across the middle of the picture, the 119-inch plate mill (1890) and the site's first open hearth shop (1886)—both built by Carnegie—stretch out toward the Monongahela River. OH2, the site's newest open hearth complex (1890), is at the near right. Carnegie's engineers were installing—creating—state-of-the-art technology. The company was expanding, buying out rivals.

In the foreground of this 1890 image, two formally dressed gentlemen survey the Works from a shrub-lined hill. Below, in front of them, two trains pass each other, going in opposite directions. The mill buildings, with their prominent smoke

stacks, are deployed in tidy linear masses. Smoke—from the trains, the barges out on the river—makes careful, picturesque plumes. In the background, a third train crosses the Monongahela on the "Pemickey" Bridge. The plant is framed by rail tracks and the river. In this idealized company picture, no steelworkers are visible.

The image of Homestead sent round the world two years later—in July 1892—was starkly different, often lurid. At the center were locked-out workers. Members of the Amalgamated Association of Iron and Steel Workers and their supporters are breaching Frick's fence and rushing to the river bank to stop Pinkertons from landing and taking over the plant. They are firing muskets and cannon at the Pinkertons' barges (the "Pemickey" Bridge, again in the background, now enters history: a famous landmark); they are herding the surrendered Pinkertons through a gauntlet to the train station to be shipped out of town. In addition to the daily newsprint, periodicals like *Frank Leslie's Illustrated Weekly* and *Harper's Weekly* brought other memorable images into homes across America: a cloud of smoke rising from the Pinkertons' burning barges; the Pennsylvania militia marching into town so that Chairman Frick could bring in strike-breaking replacement workers; Alexander Berkman, the anarchist, gun in hand, bursting into Frick's downtown Pittsburgh office in an attempt to assassinate him.

Poets in the labor press commemorated the "Battle of Homestead" with anguished cries of elegy and defiance: "But, oh, there was weeping last night at the Homestead." The mainstream press criticized Andrew Carnegie's apparent hypocrisy. In widely quoted magazine articles published in 1886, he had defended workers' rights to organize in unions and had declared, "Thou shalt not take thy neighbor's job." In a famous editorial, the *St. Louis Post-Dispatch* summed up the public's recoil from Carnegie's failure—he was on his annual vacation in Scotland—to intervene at Homestead:

A single word from him might have saved the bloodshed —but the word was never spoken. . . . "Ten thousand Carnegie Public Libraries" [will] not compensate the country for the direct and indirect evils resulting from the Homestead lockout. . . .

The Homestead Lockout was an instant *cause célèbre* in 1892. Why? Partly at least because journalists—in a process that would become ever more familiar—defined it as an important "news event," offering vivid, popular images, heroes and villains. In a photo taken in late June 1892 (just before the contract deadline with Carnegie Steel), some three dozen national reporters posed on a street in Homestead (see page 158). They were waiting for the pyrotechnics to begin. The Homestead confrontation pitted the world's largest steel manufacturer against one of the country's strongest unions; at issue was the union's survival. That was how journalist Arthur Burgoyne defined the drama:

Against this tremendous power [of the company],—a power equal to the control of 13,000 men and more than $25,000,000 of capital, the [workers] of Homestead were destined to pit themselves in life and death struggle. [Burgoyne, The Homestead Strike of 1892, p. 11]

Contemporary observers—newsmen, people on the streets, the principal actors for both labor and management—were aware that behind the immediate drama lay issues that would affect American life for decades to come. The last quarter of the 19th century was rife with confrontations between an active labor movement and the burgeoning new corporate culture. In Pittsburgh and across the nation—in Baltimore, Chicago, St. Louis—a wildcat railroad strike in 1877 flamed briefly into class warfare; scores of people were killed in the streets as state militias restored order. An era of inner-city armory-building

followed: bivouacs for troops who might be needed to suppress protesting workers. In 1886-87, in Chicago's Haymarket Affair, when police threatened a workers' rally and several were killed or injured by an unidentified bomb-thrower, a wave of political repression followed. Four anarchist leaders of Chicago's workingclass movement were hanged for conspiracy— Judge Elbert Gary (years later, chairman of U.S. Steel) presiding. In Coeur d'Alene, Idaho, at exactly the same time as the Battle of Homestead—in July 1892—locked-out union miners fought strikebreakers and company guards. In this case, the union defeat actually stimulated the Northwest's strong labor movement: the emergence of the radical Western Federation of Miners.

Many of these episodes received detailed, sensational coverage in the press, and sometimes thoughtful analysis. They were understood to be major national events in an era that also initiated a variety of political movements—the Workingmen's Party, the Greenback-Labor Party, anarchism, populism, socialism—in efforts to prevent small farmers and urban workers from being "crucified on a cross of gold" (in William Jennings Bryan's climactic image).

It was this continuing drama of workingclass struggle that drew the national and international press to Homestead in 1892. Most broadly, perhaps, the Homestead Lockout was about democratic citizenship: How would, how should America be governed? Interpreting the Civil War—in which they or their fathers had fought—as a freedom struggle, unionists expressed their politics in metaphors about "freemen," "wage-slavery" and "tyrant" industrialists. They argued that the Fricks and Carnegies of the Gilded Age were establishing a feudalism of corporate control, an aristocracy of wealth that supplanted the American ideals of democracy and participation.

In the 1880s and early 1890s, the town government of Homestead was itself a version of participatory, workers' democracy. In 1892, John McLuckie, an Amalgamated leader, was burgess—the mayor—succeeding "Old Beeswax" Taylor, a long-time regional labor leader and writer; union members made up a majority of the town council. As the historian Paul Krause shows in *The Battle for Homestead* (1992) members of the Knights of Labor and of the Amalgamated Association of Iron and Steel Workers were central in the development of the town's government during the 1880s. All of this changed radically, of course, when Carnegie Steel broke the union in 1892 and blackballed its leaders. For the next half century, every aspect of life in Homestead was dominated by the company and its interests.

In 1892, Carnegie Steel's union-breaking plans relied on advantages that the unionists were unable to match. One was the industry's expanding new technology—an ever-increasing mechanization of the workplace that made it possible to rely on fewer skilled workers per ton of production. The metals craft displaced by steelmaking was iron-puddling—the art by which an experienced and physically strong craft worker—a "puddler"—armed with long-handled tools, rolled and kneaded a ball of molten iron in a literally red hot furnace, while judging by eye the state of its readiness. Comparably awesome jobs existed in steel, but now the major, massive tasks of production were assigned to machines. Steel was not only metallurgically better than iron for many applications—rails, for example—it was mass produced. An iron furnace handled a third of a ton of metal at a time; a Bessemer converter or an open hearth furnace (like those developed at Homestead in the late 1880s) processed many tons of steel.

At Homestead, this change in method and scale of production—often called the "second industrial revolution"—made the craft workers of the Amalgamated Association of Iron and Steel more vulnerable, because more expendable, than a fading generation of iron puddlers had been in their heyday. In a tone of mocking sadness, Arthur Burgoyne describes the Homestead workers' misplaced faith in their skills.

> *It was clearly impossible [so these workers imagined] that men of substance, heads of families, solid citizens of a prosperous municipality could be rooted up, as it were, out of the soil in which they were so firmly planted and beaten to earth by the creature of their labor—for without labor, it was argued, capital would be impotent and valueless. [Burgoyne, pp. 13-14]*

Some 15 years after the strike, historian John Fitch summed up the effects on labor of mechanization in the steel industry:

> *This tendency to make processes automatic has resulted not only in lessened cost with an increased tonnage, but it has also reinforced the control of the employers over their men. . . . Men can learn to pull levers more easily than they can reach the skilled mastery of a position where the greatest dependence is on the man and the least on the machine. Accordingly this development has lessened the value to the employer of all men in a plant and at the same time has made the job of every man, skilled and unskilled, to a greater or less degree insecure. [Fitch, The Steel Workers, pp. 139-140]*

The system by which iron-mill workers in the 1870s (see David Montgomery's *The Fall of the House of Labor,* 1987) decided democratically on work rules and wages was gone forever.

The union's defeat at Homestead in 1892 threw into relief the steel industry's preference for imported cheap labor—mostly from Southern and Eastern Europe, in Homestead especially Slovaks. In the early 1890s, immigrant workers were a distinct minority—though they supported the strike and some joined the union as the Amalgamated extended its mem-

"The Bloody Battle at Homestead, PA. Wednesday's Deadly Conflict Between Pinkerton Men and the Locked-Out Employes," from The Saturday Globe, Utica, New York, July 9, 1892.

bership to build up its strength. The labor movement was often nativist, but some unionists, in the context of Homestead, celebrated the strength of the immigrants:

> The brave Hungarians, sons of toil,
>   When seeking which was right,
> Were killed like dogs by tyrants' hands
>   In the coke districts' fight.
> Let labor heroes all be true—
>   Avenge the **bloody trick**!
> Be firm like steel, true to the cause
>   And conquer Tyrant Frick.
> [See page 124.]

During the low-wage era following the union's defeat, immigrants flooded into the milltowns. They comprised 40 percent or more of the population in Homestead by 1910 and better than 50 percent of the mill's workforce.

In addition to technology and cheap labor, Carnegie Steel had another great advantage in 1892: the law was on its side. True, the charges of murder and treason brought by the company against the strikers—in a calculated effort to disrupt the union leadership—were dismissed by the courts. And true, anti-Pinkerton legislation—already under discussion before July 1892—was passed by the state of Pennsylvania in the wake of the "Battle of Homestead." But in general the law was easily manipulated by company management. The state militia occupied the town, kept strikers off the streets, and enabled the company to resume operations with non-union labor. The right of the company to use its property reigned supreme. In the absence of specific statutes to protect union activity, strikers' efforts to meet and discuss strategy were subject to intimidation and the charge of conspiracy. It would be two generations in the future—during the New Deal of the 1930s—before laws were passed to ensure that workers could elect a bargaining agent, and that a company would be obliged to bargain.

*I*n general, this anthology presents selected period texts and graphics with little or no explanation beyond place and date of original publication. The order is chronological—from the 1880s, through a day-by-day, almost hour-by-hour account of Homestead in the summer of 1892, to a sample of retrospective comments from 1893 to the 1980s. In addition, the book includes a number of brief interpretive pieces by late 20th-century commentators, including the editors of the book.

Obviously this anthology's main intent is to let readers 100 years later "be there"—to hear the voices of the principals, to encounter the events and the actors with the immediacy of a newspaper reader—surprised, shocked, enlightened by the drama. Nineteenth-century journalists wrote with a detailed narrative vigor that is seldom matched in today's daily press. Moreover, the central characters at Homestead, on both the union and company sides, revealed themselves as articulate, charismatic personalities, not only in newspaper accounts, but in letters, business communications, public testimony, and memoirs.

Memorable vignettes abound. Carnegie at the dedication of the Braddock library in 1889: "The first dollar, or the first five hundred thousand dollars I receive from Homestead will be devoted to building such a Library as this." John McLuckie, quoted by the *Pittsburgh Post,* telling a June 19 meeting of 3,000 unionists in the Homestead opera house: "The constitution of this country guarantees all men the right to live, but in order to live we must keep up a continuing struggle." The *Pittsburg Times's* July 1 description of "a gang of about 200 small boys, armed with tin whistles, march[ing] up and down the street in the evening, bearing aloft a full dressed broomstick with the placard 'remains of McBroodie'"—the mill police chief. Frick communicating to Carnegie, July 4, 1892, in the company code. The battle with the Pinkertons, reported in the *New York Herald:* "Like the trumpet of judgement blew the steam whistle of the electric light works at twenty minutes to three o'clock this morning." The New York *World's* headline the day after the battle: "While Blood Flowed Frick Smoked." Alexander Berkman's self-deprecating report (in *Prison Memoirs of an Anarchist*) of his capture after the failed attempt on Frick's life: "'I've lost my glasses,' I remark. 'You'll be damned lucky if you don't lose your head,' an officer retorts." The frightening headlines in the *Pittsburg Press* in December 1892, after the strike has been defeated: "In Humanity's Name. The Press Appeals for Aid for Suffering Homestead. Extreme Destitution in the Unfortunate Borough. Women and Children Who Want for Bread . . . Pride Seals the Lips of Starving Men and Women."

The telling of the story of Homestead through such on-the-scene sources has the virtue of reminding readers how arguable "facts" are—how dependent on who the interpreter is, his politics and vantage point. Who fired the first shot, for example, in the Battle of Homestead—the Pinkertons or the townspeople? The which-side-are-you-on biases of the eye-witness testimony, plus the sheer confusion, suggest it will forever be impossible to know. How many people were killed? The county coroner's record months later showed "ten." But was anyone counting out-of-state Pinkertons? Was the mill shutdown a strike or a lockout? A day-by-day chronicling indicates how such a question depends on the intentions of the parties. In this case, private correspondence reveals Carnegie and Frick plotting to destroy the union over a period of weeks and months.

What a sampling of primary documents, perhaps, can *not* clarify well are certain larger questions of context and interpretation. For example, 1892 was a presidential election year, and the question of whether Amalgamated members should support the Republican Benjamin Harrison or Grover Cleveland, the Democrat, comes up from time to time in the reportage presented here. Traditionally, Homestead had voted Republican in presidential elections—partly because of the Republicans' espousal of the import tariffs that protected steel prices (and thus supposedly steel wages) against foreign competition. Hugh O'Donnell, chairman of the union's Advisory Committee, was a Republican; he emerges in the contemporary accounts as a kind of "business unionist" who in late July tried to negotiate a settlement through private talks with high-placed Republicans in New York. This fruitless effort disgusted John McLuckie, a Democrat, who argued that the McKinley tariff had intentionally exempted from protection the steel billets on which wages were based. The dispute at Homestead probably had the effect of confirming the Republican party as the party of big business and of contributing to Harrison's defeat in the November election. But events also demonstrated that Carnegie Steel would prosper regardless of who won in national politics. As Frick told an interviewer: "If Mr. Harrison . . . the Cabinet, the Senate, and the House of Representatives" all pressured him to settle, he would not "deviate one iota from the lines he had laid out to follow."

Such issues as the tariff, the U.S. presidential race of 1892, the legislative investigations of Pinkertonism, this anthology sums up in sidebars and in the brief chronologies that open each chapter.

*O*ne hundred years later many of the issues raised by the Homestead Lockout and its aftermath still sound familiar. The 1980s and 1990s have replayed questions of how far new technologies (now "high tech") will go in displacing well-paid skilled workers. American industries have again sought out foreign labor—now by exporting work to Mexico, Eastern Europe, and the rim of Asia. Questions of tariffs versus "free trade" are again in the news—though it is now to the Democratic party that both unionists and businessmen turn if they wish to find support for protective tariffs. Meanwhile, the conservative state and federal governments of the 1980s and '90s have made it harder for unions to function: e.g., allowing companies to hire replacement workers during strikes, postponing representation elections.

The Homestead plant itself was closed by U.S. Steel in the mid-1980s, and much of it has since been razed. Beyond the old main gate (now literally a bridge to nowhere), the site of the once proud buildings at the center of the old 1890 engraving is now an empty expanse. In the distance, rising above the desolation, the "Pemickey" Bridge—where the Pinkertons tried to land—is today fully visible from the road: still a monument to labor's struggle. ❖

A 1907 stereograph, "Main entrance to the Homestead Steel Works looking past the office."

About This Book

Variant spellings, especially of proper names, have been retained in the excerpts from primary sources. The two spellings of Pittsburgh—with and without the "h"—were used simultaneously between 1891 and 1911, following an edict from the United States Board of Geographic Names that all place names ending in "gh" should drop the "h." Protests and noncompliance led the Board to revoke this ruling in 1911. Excerpting within a text is indicated by ellipses; the omission of larger sections is indicated by three dots inserted between paragraphs.

Henry Clay Frick, third from left, is next to business partner Andrew Carnegie in this photograph of a group of unidentified friends taken in 1892, four months before the events at Homestead.

EVENTS

1870—Henry Clay Frick is investing in coal and coking near Connellsville, PA.

1875—Andrew Carnegie, already a major figure in the iron business, opens his first steel mill, the Edgar Thomson Works, at Braddock, PA.

1876—The Amalgamated Association of Iron and Steel Workers is formed at a convention in Pittsburgh.

1881—The Pittsburgh Bessemer Company—a competitor of the Carnegie interests—opens a steel mill in Homestead.

1883—Carnegie Bros. & Company, Ltd. acquires a majority interest in the Frick Coke Company.

1883—The Pittsburgh Bessemer Company, troubled by the union, sells its Homestead plant to Carnegie Bros. at the cost of the original investment.

1886—Carnegie, Phipps & Company (a new corporate entity in Carnegie's expanding empire) builds Homestead's first open hearth furnaces—the state-of-the-art technology that will create steel suitable for structural beams and armor plate for the U.S. Navy.

1887—Frick becomes a shareholding partner in the Carnegie companies. Carnegie forces Frick to settle a strike in the coke region on terms favorable to labor so that steel profits can be maintained.

1888—Carnegie breaks the union at Edgar Thomson in Braddock. The plant goes from three 8-hour shifts to two 12-hour shifts.

1889—Frick becomes chairman—the top manager—of Carnegie, Phipps & Company. He negotiates the purchase of the Duquesne Steel Works, which become highly profitable for the Carnegie interests.

1889—At Homestead, the Amalgamated Association successfully bargains a three-year contract (often referred to simply as the "scale"), accepting a sliding wage scale that reflects market prices in exchange for union recognition and the right to regulate working conditions.

1890—In Homestead, "Honest John" McLuckie—a prominent unionist—is elected burgess (mayor) by a nearly unanimous vote.

1890—Senator William McKinley (an Ohio Republican) sponsors a bill that raises import tariffs across the board but exempts steel billets from protection.

1891—Henry Clay Frick employs Pinkertons to crush the latest strike in the coal region, confirming his anti-union reputation.

MARCH 30, 1889 —Excerpted from Andrew Carnegie's dedication of the Library in Braddock, Pennsylvania, across the Monongahela River from Homestead. Many of Braddock's citizens were employed at the Carnegie-owned Edgar Thomson Works in that community.

ADDRESS TO WORKINGMEN

I have said how desirable it was that we should endeavor, by every means in our power, to bring about a feeling of mutuality and partnership between the employer and the employed. Believe me, fellow workmen, the interests of Capital and Labor are one. He is an enemy of Labor who seeks to array Labor against Capital. He is an enemy of Capital who seeks to array Capital against Labor.

I have given the subject of Labor and Capital careful study for years, and I wish to quote a few paragraphs from an article I published years ago:

"The greatest cause of friction which prevails between capital and labor, the real essence of the trouble, and the remedy I have to propose for this unfortunate friction [are as follows]:

"The trouble is that men are not paid at any time the compensation proper for that time. . . . What we must seek is a plan by which men will receive high wages when their employers are receiving high prices for the product, and hence are making large profits; and *per contra*, when the employers are receiving low prices for the product, and therefore small if any profits, the men will receive low wages. If this plan can be found, employers and employees will be 'in the same boat,' rejoicing together in their prosperity and calling into play their fortitude together in adversity. There will be no room for quarrels, and instead of a feeling of antagonism there will be a feeling of partnership between employers and employed. There is a simple means of producing this result, and to its general introduction both employers and employed should steadily bend their energies. Wages should be based upon a sliding scale, in proportion to the net prices received for product month by

month. It is impossible for Capital to defraud Labor under a sliding scale."

Gentlemen, since [my article] you have had a trial of that sliding scale; you are under its operation now.

Never before have my partners and myself taken such pride, such interest, such satisfaction in our business as this year, when, having adopted the sliding scale, we walk through these mills knowing that instead of Labor and Capital standing face to face, jealous and distrustful of each other, we and our workmen are now practically partners, sharing in the present depression of prices together, but also bound to share in the advance in prices which must come sooner or later. This common interest has changed the feelings of my partners and myself to our workmen. You are no longer only employees, you are also sharers with us in the profits of our business, and, sooner than return to the old plan by which Capital and Labor were antagonized, and we had to quarrel every year upon the subject of wages, I would retire from business altogether. As far as I am concerned, I will never again have anything to do with manufacturing unless Labor is given a sliding scale. . . .

The other day I received a letter, dated March 14, from a Homestead man from which I wish to make an extract:

"*Dear Sir*—A tradition prevails that once upon a time you promised to do some thing for Homestead soon. When, or where, or to whom, this promise was made no one can exactly tell. It is enveloped in the mists of antiquity, and commands respect accordingly."

"Do something for Homestead," well, we have expected for a long time, but so far in vain, that Homestead should do something for us. But I do wish to do something for Homestead. I should like to see a Co-operative Society formed there. I should like to see a library there. I hope one day I may have the privilege of erecting at Homestead such a building as you have here; but this letter compels me now to say that our works at Homestead are not to us as our works at Edgar Thomson. Our men there are not partners. They are not interested with us. On the contrary, an Amalgamated Association has for years compelled us to pay one-third more in the principal department of our work, the plate mill business, than our great competitors pay in Pittsburgh. They have compelled us to pay, three times as much per ton as our leading competitors outside of this district, and are driving away our trade in consequence. A few workmen at Homestead make far more than the managers of the works, and the great mass suffer in consequence. . . .

When the labor in the Homestead works, like the labor in the Edgar Thomson, goes hand in hand with us as partners, I trust that able men there will come forward, as they did here, and establish their Co-operative Society, and all I can say in answer to my correspondent is, that anxious as that correspondent may be for something to be done for Homestead, my anxiety to do for Homestead is beyond that of my correspondent. I am only too anxious to do for them what I have done for you, and to do so for all of our works in turn. I know of no better use, I know of no use so just as to apply my wealth for the benefit of the men who have done so much to produce it. This I gladly promise. —The first dollar, or the first hundred thousand dollars I receive from Homestead will be devoted to the building of such a Library as this.

In regard to the concern in which you are now partners with us, in the selection of whose head you have the deepest personal interest, we have been equally fortunate. Mr. Frick began to work like yourselves . . . in the ranks. It is unnecessary for me to speak of Mr. Frick's ability. His career proves that. A railway clerk, at a pittance per month, who creates the largest coke business in the world, and is still on the right side of forty, needs no recommendation from anybody. His career stamps him as a manager and leader of men. I congratulate you upon your chairman. ❖

(facing page) Workers in the rail mill of the Homestead Works during the 1880s. Many of them are holding a turning wrench, a tool of their trade.

AUGUST 1886 —Excerpted from an article by Andrew Carnegie, in **The Forum.**

RESULTS OF THE LABOR STRUGGLE

It has . . . been clearly shown that public sentiment sympathizes with the efforts of labor to obtain from capital a fuller recognition of its position and claims than has hitherto been accorded. And in this expression, "a fuller recognition," I include, not only pecuniary compensation, but what I conceive to be even more important to-day, a greater consideration of the working-man as a man and a brother. I trust the time has gone by when corporations can hope to work men fifteen or sixteen hours a day. And the time approaches, I hope, when it will be impossible, in this country, to work men twelve hours a day continuously.

While public sentiment has rightly and unmistakably condemned violence, even in the form for which there is the most excuse, I would have the public give due consideration to the terrible tempta-tion to which the working-man on a strike is sometimes subjected. To expect that one dependent upon his daily wage for the necessaries of life will stand by peace-ably and see a new man employed in his stead is to expect much. This poor man may have a wife and children dependent upon his labor. Whether medicine for a sick child, or even nourishing food for a delicate wife, is procurable, depends upon his steady employment. In all but a very few departments of labor it is unneces-sary, and, I think, improper, to subject men to such an ordeal. In the case of railways and a few other employments it is, of course, essential for the public wants that no interruption occur, and in such case substitutes must be employed; but the employer of labor will find it much more to his interest, wherever possible, to allow his works to remain idle and await the result of a dispute, than to employ the class of men that can be in-duced to take the place of other men who have stopped work. Neither the best men as men, nor the best men as workers, are thus to be obtained. There is an unwrit-ten law among the best workmen: "Thou shalt not take thy neighbor's job." No wise employer will lightly lose his old employees. Length of service counts for much in many ways. Calling upon strange men should be the last resort.

The results of the recent disturbances have given indubitable proof that trades-unions must, in their very nature, be-come more conservative than the mass of the men they represent. If they fail to evolve the conservative element, they go to pieces through their own extravagance. I know of three instances in which threat-ened strikes were recently averted by the decision of the Master Workman of the Knights of Labor, supported by the best workmen, against the wishes of the less intelligent members of that organization. Representative institutions eventually bring to the front the ablest and most prudent men, and will be found as benefi-cial in the industrial as they have proved themselves to be in the political world. Leaders of the stamp of Mr. Powderly, Mr. Arthur, of the Brotherhood of Loco-motive Engineers, and Messrs. Wihle [sic, for Weihe] and Martin, of the Amal-gamated Iron and Steel Association, will gain and retain power; while such as the radical and impulsive Mr. Irons, if at first clothed with power, will soon lose it.

———❖———

CARNEGIE, FRICK, AND THE HOMESTEAD STRIKE
by Joseph Frazier Wall

*O*n 1 July 1892, the Carnegie Steel Company, Limited came into being. It was the result of the merger of Carnegie, Phipps & Company and Carnegie Brothers & Company. Capitalized at $25,000,000, it was the largest steel company in the world, capable of producing more than half of the total steel production of Great Britain. The flagship of this fleet of steel plants, iron mills and blast furnaces was the recently acquired plant at Homestead, which had been converted into America's largest open hearth steel mill.

Andrew Carnegie and the man whom he had selected to serve as chief executive officer of Carnegie Steel, Henry Clay Frick, were inordinately proud of their creation, but they had selected a singularly inauspicious birth date for their new giant. For on that hot July morning, Homestead lay paralyzed by both strike and lockout, a paralysis that threatened to spread from the newest mill at Duquesne to the oldest at 29th Street in Pittsburgh.

The basic issue was unionization. There were no trade unions in Carnegie's older plants, but unhappily for Carnegie, when he purchased Homestead in the early 1880s at little more than its original cost, he not only acquired the industry's most modern and efficiently designed rail and beam rolling mills, but he also got six highly organized and well-disciplined labor lodges of the powerful Amalgamated Association of Iron and Steel Workers.

Homestead had been a part of Carnegie, Phipps & Company prior to the creation of Carnegie Steel, and in 1889, the steelworkers' union had won a major victory when after a brief strike, William Abbott, president of Carnegie, Phipps, agreed to a three year contract which gave to the union most of its demands. In the spring of 1892, labor had confidently expected the company to renew the same contract. Now, however, Homestead would be part of a much larger Carnegie organization, headed by a new chief executive officer, and Henry Clay Frick was no William Abbott. He was generally regarded as the most implacable foe of organized labor within the industry, a reputation which he had deservedly earned in the coal fields of Pennsylvania.

Frick was determined that in 1892 there would not be a repetition of Abbott's panicky yielding to labor. Frick intended to offer the union a new contract whose terms would be so unfavorable that it would be rejected out of hand. Frick did not intend to negotiate. It was either take it or leave it, and if the union left it, as Frick was sure it would, he would go on to deal with the workers on an individual basis. Unionism in the Carnegie Steel empire would be eliminated.

Frick's position was clear. What was less certain was Andrew Carnegie's position. Although Carnegie held no office in the new company he had created, not even membership on the board of directors, he did hold 55 percent of its capital, and quite clearly, the company was his to direct. He held the script for the show firmly in his own two hands, and he could scrutinize and criticize every gesture made, every line spoken, on this impressively large new stage.

As he faced the inevitable show-down with labor in the spring of 1892, Frick could not be sure what that script handed down from on high would be, for there were two distinct Carnegie personalities at conflict with each other within the same individual. There was first, the idealistic Carnegie, the child of radical Scottish Chartism, who had drawn his political philosophy from the teachings of his father and his maternal grandfather, Tom Morrison. This was the Carnegie who had written Triumphant Democracy, who had bought a chain of newspapers in England to beat the drum for egalitarian republicanism, who had stood by Abbott in 1889 in the latter's concessions to labor, and who, most alarmingly, had written two articles in Forum magazine upholding the right of labor to organize and decrying the use of strikebreakers.

But there was also the other Carnegie, the aggressive, hard-headed businessman who had built out of Andrew Kloman's small iron forge in Allegheny the world's greatest steel company. This Carnegie was always worrying about costs, always wanting more profits, not to dispense in dividends but rather to reinvest in the company to make it ever larger. Would it be the Carnegie who wanted to be loved, or the Carnegie who wanted to be powerful who would prevail in the summer of 1892? Of one thing Frick was certain. It must be either Frick or the union—one or the other would go.

Frick needed to have no fear as to which Carnegie would decide the issue. Given the alternatives of losing face or losing Frick, Carnegie did not hesitate in giving his chief

Thaddeus Mortimer Fowler's lithograph of "Homestead, 1902." The Pemickey Bridge, upper left, locates the Homestead Works in relation to the community along the river. By 1892, the rural village of 1881 had become an industrial boom town. In the decade after the strike, the plant expanded and many new immigrants swelled the population of greater Homestead to 18,000.

executive the carte blanche *the latter demanded in dealing with the union. On May 4, before leaving for his annual summer sojourn in Scotland, Carnegie dashed off a brief note to Frick: "We all approve of anything you do, not stopping short of approval of a contest. We are with you to the end."*

With this note in hand, Frick could direct operations as he saw fit. As expected, his contract terms were rejected by the union. Frick refused to bargain further. Instead, he called upon the Pinkerton Detective Agency to bring in 300 guards to secure the closed Homestead plant and to allow the entry of strikebreakers who could put the mills into operation. So the stage was set for the tragedy of Homestead.

When he told Frick he would "approve of anything you do," Carnegie did not anticipate any great trouble. "Of course you will win," he wrote to Frick on June 10 from

Scotland, "and win easier than you suppose, owing to the present condition of the market." Certainly Carnegie never imagined that there would be blood shed on the banks of the Monongahela, that Homestead would in the years to come serve as a symbol to American labor of the injustice and perfidy of the "bosses," or that he himself in spite of—or perhaps especially because of—his noble words on the rights of labor and his benevolent gifts of libraries and art museums would become to both liberals and conservatives the supreme hypocrite of his age, even more despised by labor than was Frick, who had directed the operations. "You can't trust any of them" was the moral the workers drew from Homestead. It was better to confront a Frick with a hard heart than a Carnegie with a false tongue.

In the years that were to follow Carnegie tried to recover what he had lost at Homestead by shifting

all the blame on to Frick, by insisting that if he had only been on the scene there would have been no importation of Pinkerton guards, no massacre, and no strikebreakers. In time he would create his own version of Homestead which bore little relation to reality. "I have one comfort," he was to write his good friend, British statesman William Gladstone, "self-approval." It is doubtful, however, that he had even that. Twenty years later, he would write in his autobiography, "Nothing I have ever had to meet in all my life, before or since, wounded me so deeply. No pangs remain of any wounds received in my business career save that of Homestead. It was so unnecessary." These lines, at least, have the ring of absolute veracity in his otherwise largely imagined account of what had happened on those July days a century ago in a place which had once borne the name of Amity Homestead. ❖

H.C. FRICK

H.C. Frick, the manager of the Carnegie Steel Company, is a young man still— the youngest of Pittsburg's millionaires, probably, and certainly the brainiest. He was born in December, 1849, in Fayette County. His first business experience was obtained at a very early age in A. Overholt's whisky distillery, but when he was barely twenty-one he was already interested in a coke-making plant, and before long he had embarked as an operator on his own account. He made his first big strike about 1872, when, having built a branch railroad from Broadford to Mt. Pleasant, he sold it to the Baltimore and Ohio Railroad at a handsome profit. The money that he made in this deal he immediately invested in coal land and additional coke plants. By January, 1882, the coke interests held by him and E.M. & Walton Ferguson had reached such a magnitude that Carnegie Brothers & Co. paid $1,500,000 for a half interest in them. Mr. Frick then bought the Standard Coke Works, J.M. Schoonmaker's plant, and the Connellsville Coal and Coke Company's works, bringing the whole property up to between 20,000 and 25,000 acres of Connellsville coal land, while later purchases bring the holdings of the Frick Company to upwards of 35,000 acres of the very best coal. The company has nearly 10,000 coke ovens, which in a busy time produce about 16,000 to 18,000 tons of coke daily.

On the death of David A. Stewart in December, 1888, Mr. Carnegie, recognizing the great business ability of Mr. Frick, offered him an interest in the firms of Carnegie Bros. & Co., and Carnegie, Phipps & Co., which Mr. Frick accepted and paid for. He at once was made chairman of Carnegie Bros. & Co., and when all the Carnegie interests were consolidated, the other day, Mr. Frick became chairman of the new company, and the active head of an immense business. Mr. Frick married Miss Childs, of a well-known Pittsburg family, some years ago, and they have two children, who share with them a beautiful home in the East End, the most popular suburb of Pittsburg. Mr. Frick is of a forceful, self-reliant nature, and in previous conflicts with labor organizations has shown a determination to carry his point at all hazards. ❖

Henry Clay Frick, 1890s

(left) **H.C. Frick Company, like many mining companies, paid part of their workers' wages in "scrip," which could only be used to buy merchandise in the company store.**

(above) **This 1912 photo of Marguerite, an H.C. Frick mining site in Westmoreland County, displays the rigid layout of the typical company town. The company store is to the right; the coke ovens to the left.**

Excerpted from U.S. Senate Report No. 1280, testimony given November 23, 1892, by H.C. Frick on the H.C. Frick Coke Company's labor relations.

FRICK TESTIMONY

Q. When did the labor troubles begin with you in your business, and from which class of labor, that is the native or foreign labor, did complaints begin and continue?

A. The first strike of any importance that I remember occurred in 1886, in the coke region. It began on the 16th of January, 1886. The principal cause was for the reason that we refused to allow the women, the wives of foreigners then in our employment, to assist their husbands on the coke yards. In 1885, I think it was, the State of Pennsylvania passed a law prohibiting the employment of women. While we had never employed any women, never had a woman's name on our pay roll, yet the wives of these foreigners would go to work with their husbands and assist them. As these men did piecework, we paid them for what piecework they did. On the State passing this law, which went into effect on the 1st of January, 1886, we issued an order that women should not go with the men to work. This caused the strike—it was the start of the strike. After the strike was once started other questions arose. Finally, on or about the 22nd of February, 1886, we conceded an advance to the workmen of 10 per cent. I think all resumed work. After making that concession they worked but a short time until they wanted something more, and we had continual trouble up until

April 29, 1887, when, after having granted almost everything they asked and reaching a point where we could make no further concessions, we finally got the labor unions to agree to leave the demand they made at that time to arbitration. We selected three men to represent us, the labor union selected three to represent them, and those six selected Mr. John B. Jackson, of this city [Pittsburgh], as the seventh man. The case was of course submitted to him, he rendered a decision refusing the workmen the demand they made. They immediately struck against the award. That strike continued until the 27th of July, I think, that same year. In the meantime the Frick Coke Company granted the demands. The other operators, however, fought the strike out and won. Then after that date, we will say the 27th of July, the Frick Coke Company, who owned a large number of ovens in the region, were paying 12 ½ per cent more wages than the other operators in the same region. That continued, I think, until February, 1890, when a general scale was agreed on covering wages in the Connelsville [sic] region and when other operators commenced to pay the same. The agreement then made expired on the 10th of February, 1891. At that time, after repeated conferences, we were unable to agree upon a new scale, and I think it was in March of that year after, as I say, repeated conferences, and being unable to agree with our workmen, we posted notices stating just what wages we would pay. Our employes refused to accept it, and we began to introduce new workmen. Our experience had been such with organized labor that we could place no reliance on the agreements they made with us, and we concluded that we would end the thing once for all, and determine whether we had a right to employ whom we pleased and discharge whom we pleased. That strike lasted, I think, until the latter part of May of that year, at which time we succeeded in starting our works with what is called "nonunion workers," and from that time until the present we have had no trouble. Our men have been contented and happy. We have not been bothered with the labor agitator and with committees asking all sorts of concessions.

————————❖————————

THE COKE REGION

by Eugene Levy

*U*nderlying the pre-eminence of Pittsburgh as an iron and steel center was the nine-foot-thick "Pittsburgh" seam of coal. The expansion of steel production owed much to the river and rail transportation networks that were well developed by the 1890s, but it is doubtful that Pittsburgh and its mill towns would have come to dominate steel-making in the United States until World War I, had it not been for the region's superior coking coal.

Despite many technological changes over the past 150 years, then, as now, baking coal in an oven for one to three days drives off various chemicals in the form of gases and leaves behind coke, a porous but solid material, 85-90 percent carbon. Coke's physical and chemical qualities make it ideal for use in iron-making blast furnaces. Coke will physically support the many tons of iron ore dropped on it in the furnace; it burns long and

hot, refining the ore to produce molten "pig" iron. Molten pig iron, in turn, is an essential ingredient in most steel-making processes.

The best of the coking coal lay east to southeast of Pittsburgh in what would soon come to be called, after a prominent town at its center, the Connellsville Coke Region. Extending for some 50 miles across Westmoreland and Fayette counties, this region dominated coke production in the United States from the 1870s through the 1910s.

Coke ovens in late 19th-century America were not located in massive centralized facilities near steel mills, like the coke-producing technology of today. Early mine owners built row after row of dome-shaped

brick ovens, the interior of each some eight feet high and twelve feet in diameter, next to the coal mines that provided the necessary raw material. The Coke Region in 1900 had 22,000 "beehive" ovens, producing just over 10 million tons of coke annually (about half of the nation's output) with much of that tonnage going into Pittsburgh's blast furnaces.

Local entrepreneurs around Connellsville began making coke in beehive ovens in the 1840s, but demand grew slowly until after the Civil War. By the mid-1860s the rapidly expanding steel industry needed more and more iron, one of its basic ingredients. The iron-making blast furnaces in turn needed coke. Demand escalated and coke production soon took off. Capitalists from around the country sought area coal lands, but by the late 1870s Henry Clay Frick, a local boy, had emerged as the dominant force in the industry. Twenty years later, the H.C. Frick Coke Company, by then a part of Carnegie Steel, produced about two-thirds of the Region's coke.

Initially miners from around Pittsburgh and from eastern Pennsylvania made up most of the Coke Region's labor force. By the late 1880s, however, an increasing percentage of workers were recent immigrants, many of them from Southern and Eastern Europe. Whether "Americans" or "Hunkies,"

most workers and their families lived in "patches," isolated settlements scattered across the rural landscape where the houses, as well as nearly everything else, were built and owned by the mining company. Frequently the mine and the patch shared the same name: Mammoth No. 2, United No. 1, Mutual, Leisenring No. 3, Leith. At Mammoth No. 2, a modest-sized H.C. Frick patch, the families of the miners and coke-yard workers occupied approximately 60 double frame houses facing the mine shaft, the company store, and 199 beehive coke ovens belching acrid smoke day and night.

Living conditions ranged from ill-built shanties to 12-room houses for the mine superintendents, but the typical residence was a double house, each side with two rooms downstairs, two rooms upstairs, and an outhouse in the back yard. In good years (and times were frequently not good in a cyclical industry such as coal mining) most workers made about $20 a month, from which came rent of $6 to $7, the cost of food and clothing from the company store, and coal for

cooking and heating. H.C. Frick patches were probably the best maintained (and the most paternalistic), but everywhere in the Coke Region it was a hard-scrabble existence with the mine owners and their superintendents masters of the scene.

Many of the mining operations in the immediate Pittsburgh area employed union workers, but the Coke Region proved difficult to organize, dominated as it was by one company. Union organizers made some small gains after several strikes in the late 1880s. Frick then took a firm stand, and by 1891 he could declare his company free from all union agreements. In testimony before a sub-committee of the Judiciary Committee of the U.S. Senate on November 23, 1892, Frick proudly maintained, "We had a right to employ whom we pleased and discharge whom we pleased." Frick's success in beating back efforts to organize his coal and coking operations provided a ready model in the campaign to drive the Amalgamated Association of Iron and Steel Workers from all of Carnegie Steel, Homestead included. ❖

(facing page) Workers pulling coke from a row of beehive ovens, with the tools of their trade—rakes, leveling bars, shovels—close at hand, c. 1890s.

(right) H.C. Frick's Union Supply Company operated company stores at most of the Frick mine sites. This one, shown in 1895, was at Broadford.

JANUARY 30, 1886 —Reprinted from **Harper's Weekly.**

RIOTS OF COKE DRAWERS.

Although strikes have become more and more frequent, the number that causes riots constantly becomes less, for every year more disputes between employers and the employed are settled by arbitration or by mutual concessions, and even when both parties remain stubborn, the strikers are so well cared for by their unions that the strongest temptation to do violence is removed. But the Hungarian laborers in the coke region near Pittsburg, Pennsylvania, have no union, will make no concessions nor think of arbitration, and their violence recalls the temper of the strikers at Pittsburg in 1877. Three years ago they were brought to the coke ovens to take the place of native laborers who made a strike, and they have learned too well the method of their predecessors.

There are in this region 12,000 coke ovens, at most of which Hungarians and Poles, men and women, are employed. They receive twenty-seven cents per wagon for digging coal, and from fifty-five to sixty cents per oven for drawing coke. They asked for an increase of five cents per wagon and per oven, which the owners refused to grant, and claimed that they were unable to grant. On January 18 many of the Hungarians stopped work, and the strikers were reenforced during the next three or four days, until 3600 ovens were shut down, and 5000 men were idle. They immediately began to do deeds of violence. On the 19th, 200 Hungarians and Poles, led by Steff Stanex, a gigantic miner, who was the most daring spirit among the strikers, all armed and many intoxicated, marched with banners, to the music of a fiddle and of a washboiler as a drum, made an attack on the Alice Coke-works near Connellsville, drove the workmen away, pulled open oven fronts, and did what damage to property they could.

From Mount Pleasant southward there is a continuous line of ovens for twelve miles, at nearly all of which Hungarians were employed, and at several of them riots were caused by the drunken strikers. At the Morewood mines there was an encounter between the 300 armed followers of Steff Stanex and a posse of special officers. The Hungarians, men and women, armed with revolvers, clubs, and knives, resisted arrest. A pitched battle ensued. As many as a hundred shots were fired. Several men were badly beaten, a number were wounded, and one was killed. The hills above the works were covered with native workmen, women, and peaceful miners, who collected to witness the battle. The Hungarian women fought with their husbands and brothers, and after they were driven into their houses they continued to shoot. At several other places the strikers marched to music, sometimes of a drum, sometimes of a bass-viol, threatening violence. A company marched through the streets of Scottdale armed with fence rails, clubs, pick handles, crowbars, and such rude but dangerous weapons, and made raids on the dram-shops, many of the women as well as the men becoming drunk. At another place, the Donnelly and Diamond works, a riot occurred in which five Hungarians and three Americans were fatally wounded. A negro man at one settlement, without provocation, fired at a procession, which forthwith became a mob, and gave him a beating that will prove fatal.

These Hungarians are the most difficult class of laborers to manage when they are peaceful, or to pacify when they are enraged. Few of them speak English. They live here in the same squalid fashion as in Hungary. They know nothing of American life or manners, or of the courts, or of working-men's rights. Their only idea of carrying a point is of carrying it by physical force. Many of the men have

done service as soldiers, and they know how to fight, and are not afraid to resist officers of the law. Indeed, they have no other notion of an officer than as of an enemy in war.

There are employed in this Connellsville coke region as many as 6000 laborers, exclusive of miners. The most of them are coke "drawers," and their labor consists simply of filling the ovens with coal, and after it has become coke of drawing it from the ovens. It is not skilled labor, and the only serious result of a strike of coke drawers, beyond a brief period of idleness at the ovens, is the damage done by the violent strikers.

The danger in such a case is the danger of a fight, and not of the strike itself. The disturbance has demonstrated that the employers who brought the Hungarians to take the place of native or naturalized laborers that commanded higher wages are not likely to profit by the experiment. The loss of property and of profits during the interruption of work, and the expense that will be involved in gradually substituting other workmen for the violent Hungarians, even if the wages are not increased, will equal the savings in the wage account since they came, to say nothing of the loss of a dozen lives. The owners of these coke ovens have a monopoly, no product of such excellent qualities as fuel for furnaces being obtainable elsewhere as in this limited territory.

————— ❖ —————

(facing page) **This detail of Charles Graham's wood engraving "Among the Coke Furnaces of Pennsylvania,"** Harper's Weekly, *January 30, 1886, shows a curved row of beehive ovens, probably near Connellsville. The women, wheeling barrows of coke to waiting railroad cars, are in ethnic dress. Their presence in the coke yards aroused public indignation.*

ANOTHER FRIGHTFUL ACCIDENT AT THE MILL.

The History of the Homestead Steel works of Carnegie, Phipps & Co., is marked with a large number of frightful accidents, not to speak of innumerable minor mishaps. That of last Saturday, wherein one man lost his life and seven others received more or less serious injuries, and still others narrowly escaped a similar fate, was scarcely less terrible than many recorded in the past. Not withstanding the labor saving devices of improved machinery and the increased skillfullness of the workmen, there is no guarantee that such catastrophes will not be repeated, again and again at the mill.

The following account by one of the workmen employed in the Converting department, explains just how the accident occurred.

When the blast is put on, it forces a terrific blaze containing particles of the molten steel, out against an iron shield. In the course of a few hours there is an accumulation of metal on the shield or wall which of course is quite heavy and must be removed at frequent intervals, otherwise it would fall, which it did in this instance. The accumulation is called the "skull." Passing somewhat under the shield is a pressure pipe leading from the hydraulic ram to the converter or vessel. It is the pressure of water in the ram and pipe that controls the movements of the vessel, as well as the many cranes in the converting department. When the "skull" fell, it struck the pipe referred to, causing the pressure to escape. Released from control, the vessel containing molten metal tipped over and emptied into the pit below where it came in contact with moisture, resulting in a terrific explosion. The metal was scattered in all directions, some of it striking the opposite wall seventy feet away. It is not surprising that many workmen were burned. Indeed the great wonder is, that more were not fatally burned. The list is long enough however.

———❖———

Charles Graham's wood engraving, "Making Steel at Pittsburgh—The Bessemers at Work," Harper's Weekly, *April 10, 1886. This image of the Bessemers at the Edgar Thomson Works in Braddock became the signature image of 19th-century Pittsburgh industry. Graham was the first artist to present Pittsburgh mill workers as dignified and serious men engaged in dangerous work.*

JUNE 1, 1892 —Excerpted from an article, "Steel Wonders," by Harry B. Latton in an issue of **The Pittsburg Times** *devoted to promoting local industry.*

THE HOMESTEAD PLANT

It is elements of genius, skill, and experience combined together with unlimited confidence in the future of the country and millions of capital that has made the great steel works at Homestead, owned by Carnegie, Phipps & Co., Limited. It was the skill of the practical men of this mill which produced a grade of steel possessing tensile strength 43 per cent greater than any open-hearth or Bessemer metal heretofore made. It was due to research and the expenditure of vast amounts of money by this firm that enabled the National Government to commence the construction of a navy which is already creditable to the nation. Some achievements already accomplished which but recently were declared impossible by eminent metallurgists have warranted the declaration that "nothing is impossible."

This plant, which now comprises 600 [actually around 90] acres with 87 acres under roof, was only commenced in 1880. As in other concerns in the galaxy of Carnegie enterprises, Mr. Carnegie is the senior partner. Until recently, Mr. William L. Abbott was chairman, but he retired April 1 to enjoy a season of rest and was succeeded by Mr. H.C. Frick. The duties of the office of Vice Chairman devolve upon Mr. H.M. Carry, one of the best metallurgists and practical steel men in the country. The secretary, Mr. Otto H. Childs, is also thoroughly practical, and possesses a capacity for business which has long ago placed him to the front rank. I.C. Phipps, a nephew of Henry Phipps Jr., is treasurer. Like Mr. Carnegie, Mr. Henry Phipps Jr., whose interest ranks only second to the first named, does not take active part in the management.

Of the operating department, Mr. John A. Potter is superintendent, and has entire charge of the conduct of the great mill. He is a young man, only a few paces in the thirties, but has the experience of a veteran, having lived in iron and steel atmospheres on both sides of the water.

THE PRODUCT OF THE PLANT

There are no blast furnaces here, although the firm owns the Lucy furnaces in Pittsburg. This plant produces plates of various character, boiler, armor, etc., beams and various shapes of structural material. The buildings are all constructed of soft firebrick, roofed and trussed with steel. The hoisting apparatus of the plant consists of numerous hydraulic cranes, some of which will raise and deposit anywhere within the arc of the circle which it describes a weight of 200 tons—equal to eight car loads. Think of a lifting monster capable of taking up as much weight as eight cars carry. It is marvelous. The pressure in the water chambers of these cranes is 600 pounds to the square inch. One man handles the largest with the same ease that an engineman draws the throttle of his engine. The amount of water required to operate these and other appliances in the mill, feed the boilers, etc., is 7,000,000 gallons per day.

MAKING ARMOR PLATE

The process of making armor plate—and this is now with additions recently completed the largest in the world—is perhaps the most interesting process. Furnaces known as open hearth are used to melt and prepare the metal in this work. There are in one furnace department eight open hearth furnaces, each having a capacity of 80 tons, though 25 tons is seldom exceeded. The contents of these furnaces may, if desired, be run into one casting or ingot. If an armor plate is to be made, it is cast in the pit near the furnaces. This pit is a large circular area below the surrounding surface. All the armor for a vessel is made according to pattern. The entire portion of a vessel to be armored is constructed of wood, and is virtually cut up in sizes to suit the plates. Each piece represents the portion of the vessel upon which the plate will rest. In miniature these pieces would resemble cutup puzzles. Then patterns, referred to above, for the plates are made, and when a plate is finished it must fit exactly to the wooden facsimile of the portion of the vessel for which it is intended. If a bolt head protrudes through the side of the vessel, the facsimile piece will show it, and the plate must be cut or indentured at precisely the right place to fit over the bolt head. An ingot is cast in sand molds in the pit, and from it the

SCIENTIFIC AMERICAN

[Entered at the Post Office of New York, N. Y., as Second Class matter. Copyright, 1892, by Munn & Co.]

A WEEKLY JOURNAL OF PRACTICAL INFORMATION, ART, SCIENCE, MECHANICS, CHEMISTRY, AND MANUFACTURES.

Vol. LXVII. No. 9.] [Established 1845]   NEW YORK. AUGUST 27, 1892.   [$3.00 A YEAR.]

1. Working of armor plate rollers. 2. Graduated wheel and scale rods for gauging the plate. 3. Largest ingot ever produced in America. 4. Hydraulic shears for trimming plates. 5. An ingot leaving furnace. 6. Pump house and river landing.

THE CARNEGIE WORKS, HOMESTEAD, PA.—ROLLING THE GREAT STEEL ARMOR PLATES.—[See page 132.]

This cover illustrates various steps in the process of manufacturing armor plate at the Homestead Works. Published by the patent agents Munn and Company of New York, the magazine often promoted the agency's corporate clients.

(Homestead Plant, continued)

plate is made. When the steel is ready, the open hearth furnaces are tapped, and streams of molten steel run into the mold; and the ingot is made. The weight varies from 20 to 100 tons. It is then stripped, taken from the the metal mold while still hot and is transferred on a special car to the press shop. This car has a capacity of 150 tons, five times that of the average freight car. At the press shop, two large cranes that could lift an ordinary house take this mountain of metal and put it in a furnace where it is heated. When the ingot is in proper condition, it is lifted from the furnace, placed on the big car, and is carried to the Armor rolling mill. It is a mill so vast that mere figures are powerless to convey a full appreciation of its size. An entire foot of steel weighs over 600 pounds. In an ingot weighing 30 tons there are 120 cubic feet and 200 cubic feet in a 50 ton ingot. These great rolls flatten and widen the ingot until it has reached the desired size. It is then taken again to the press shop where any rough or ragged ends are cut off by a hydraulic press of 2,500 tons capacity. It will shear a plate of steel six inches or a foot thick as quickly as a hungry tramp will cut a tenderloin steak.

The plate is then placed in a furnace to be tempered. When that process is completed, it is removed and placed into a bath containing 100,000 gallons of oil, where it is allowed to cool. After cooling, it is again put in a furnace and brought to a red heat, called annealing, thence is placed in an annealing pit and covered with ashes and sawdust and allowed to remain 12 or 18 days. At the end of that time the plate, over which so much time and hard work has been spent, is carried to the great armor plate machine shop, a vast building, larger than machinery hall at the Pittsburg Exposition building. Here is a collection of the most gigantic planers, drills, presses, saws, lathes, and tools that was ever made. Some of the planing machines weigh 200 tons.

GOVERNMENT INSPECTION

Upon the arrival of the plate in this shop, the Government Inspector selects his physical tests. If found perfect and up to contract the plate is then finished, a branch of work exceedingly important, for every part of the plate, even if it is to be destroyed the first hour of service, must be made according to design without the variation of a fraction of an inch. When a group of from 10 to 20 plates are ready for shipment, the Government Inspector checks at random for another test. If it stands the test, the plate is sent to the testing ground at Indian Head, and then it is set up and fired at by the highest power guns. If this plate does not stand the test, the entire group is rejected and thrown upon the contractor's hands.

At no time in any melting department of the mill is a heat made without analysis. With a laboratory the finest in the State, with chemists and metallurgists whose skill is unsurpassed, a uniform product precisely as desired is assured. The chemists analyze all the raw materials to be used. Exhausting tests of every character are constantly being innovated.

But there are other mills. The armor plate department of the Homestead works is only a part. The beam and structural mills are to an unprejudiced, practical steel man, works of art. Mr. Potter lifts his hat to the great new beam mill each morning and shakes hands with himself. This mill, and some planes and forges in the armor plate department, all in operation, stand where tulips grew last fall.

THE BEAM MILL
In order to better explain the beam mill, it should be mentioned that a cogging mill is necessary to prepare the ingot for the beam mill. These mills, separate or combined, are the largest in the world. The cogging mill is called 40 inch. That is, it will take a bloom weighing 15 tons and roll it down to any desired size for either beam shapes or forge blooms. One remarkable feature is the hot saw in connection with the cogging mill. This saw will go through a bloom 24 inches square as quickly as a circular saw will go through a strip of wood. If beams are being made, the cogging mill reduces the big ingot to beam shape, and then it is carried automatically on driven rolls to the structural rolls, operated by an engine developing 5,000 indicated horsepower at 75 revolutions per minute. The fly wheel of this engine weighs 100 tons. At the structural rolls, a beam 35 inches wide by 100 to 120

feet long can be made. From these rolls it continues its course to the saws, where it can be cut to any desired length. After being sawed, the beam starts backward and goes through the process of fitting, punching, and finishing, and finally goes to the depressed shipping track, upon which the top of a gondola rises even with the level of the ground. Here is a hydraulic crane which will take a beam from any point within the crane's radius and deliver it to the desired place. So rapidly is the work of making beams prosecuted that frequently when ready for shipment, they are still hot.

Besides the eight open hearth furnaces mentioned in connection with the armor plate mill, there are eight other furnaces of the same kind from 30 to 40 tons capacity. Near by is the plate mill, which rolls to any desired size and to the width of 120 inches. It was probably not mentioned that the armor plate mill can roll 100 ton ingots, and that it has the largest shears in the world, 54 by 54 inches which cut steel of any thickness with the greatest of ease.

The new Bessemer department is equipped with four 18 foot cupolas, vessels in which iron is melted before it is run into the converters. There are two 12 ton converters. Everything in this department is operated automatically, with hydraulic pressure. The capacity of the department without crowding is 20,000 of ingots for beams, channels, T's, and other structural material per month. The old Bessemer mill has been changed to a large refractory house for the grinding of clays, mixing, and other uses.

THE PERFECT SYSTEM
Throughout the entire plant the most perfect system prevails. The yards are gridironed with railroad tracks to facilitate the transportation of raw or finished material, or material in process of completion. Nineteen locomotives of all sizes are required to handle the traffic. The plant has at the most convenient point, shops for repairing and turning rolls, in which there are 10 lathes; machine shops in which are employed 30 machinists and their helpers. The blacksmith shop, with forges, steam, hammers, etc., keeps 25 men busy. Repairs to gas and steam and water pipes and required connections

demands the constant employment of a dozen men. There are carpenters, tinners, pattern makers and mechanics of every branch employed.

When it is realized that this plant produces so many kinds and shapes of material, it is easily understood that the utmost care is required on the part of the management and that much skilled labor is required. The open hearth furnaces require 32 skilled melters, one for each furnace for each shift. It must not be forgotten that this mill never stops except a few hours on Sunday. The eight rolling mills require 10 skilled rollers, and so on.

The entire plant is lighted with electricity. The system comprises 300 arc and 2,200 incandescent lights. An important use to be made of electricity is to replace numerous small engines with electric appliances. Contrivances called buggies that transfer ingots, billets, or slabs to and from heating furnaces are operated by engines. Electricity will give the engines used in this and several other capacities a long rest.

The office building of the company is a large Gothic brick and stone structure standing on an eminence overlooking the entire plant. Here are the business quarters of Superintendent Potter and his assistants, draughtsmen, and engineers, the large accounting, and other offices.

Further removed from the mill are eight handsome residences built for the operative managers, and a handsome club-house for the accommodation of guests and officers. The firm has also erected 40 other houses for their better class workmen. All the 3,500 employees appear contented. They are paid on the sliding scale based on the ceiling price of billets for the term of three months preceding. The minimum selling price, however, is fixed at $25.

From a little village a few years ago, Homestead has grown to a borough of nearly 12,000 inhabitants, chiefly supported by the great Homestead Steel Works.

———❖———

AMALGAMATED ASSOCIATION OF IRON AND STEEL WORKERS
by Sharon Trusilo

*E*ight lodges of the Amalgamated Association of Iron and Steel Workers represented the views of skilled millmen at Carnegie's Homestead Works in 1892. Like other Amalgamated locals, the Homestead lodges suffered from craft and personal jealousies, and consequently, did not always agree with the decisions of the National Lodge or its leaders. At the same time, they were not usually labeled the union's First District "troublemakers."

Comprising eight districts nationally in the early 1890s, the Amalgamated Association was strongest in Western Pennsylvania and the Ohio Valley. It was one of 50 national and international unions that formed during the 1860s through the mid-1870s and one of nearly a dozen of these unions that survived until 1880. Wage cuts, unemployment, and the resulting hard living conditions incited organized labor to strike and demonstrate frequently during the late 1870s and early 1880s. Ironworkers, like men in other trades, believed that the tight labor market would insure the success of their attempts to unionize.

Over a 15-year period before 1873, skilled millmen formed obscure, short-lived, local unions. By 1873, however, more than 4,200 skilled millmen were organized into three comprehensive national ironworkers' unions: the United Sons of Vulcan (1858, reorganized in late 1861 in Pittsburgh, but not particularly successful before 1870); the Associated Brotherhood of Iron and Steel Heaters, Rollers and Roughers of the United States (1865, reorganized in 1872 in Chicago); and the

Iron and Steel Roll Hands' Union (1870, reorganized in 1873 in Chicago).

All three unions experienced only marginal success, since their planning seldom went beyond immediate problems and each union often lacked both income and membership. The onset of a five-year depression in 1873, however, changed the attitudes of ironworkers, particularly union leaders. Officers realized that singly each union was ineffectual. Their organizations' strike histories demonstrated that the lack of cooperation among unions limited bargaining power while draining already depleted treasuries.

Arguing that the rationale for amalgamation—the advancement of union members' social and economic status through mutual aid and job security—was already written into each union's constitution, the leadership succeeded in gaining support for the founding of the Amalgamated Association of Iron and Steel Workers of the United States. The new union, organized in Pittsburgh on August 4, 1876, outlined three basic goals in the preamble to its constitution: the reestablishment of a prosperous iron trade, job security, and the opportunity for workers' advancement through the improvement of their "moral, social and intellectual condition."

The Amalgamated's officers had anticipated manufacturers' hostility and public resentment, but believed that a strong, nonviolent union would serve as the best weapon against their opponents since it would counter claims that the Amalgamated threatened national

peace and prosperity. However, the officers also encountered vacillating attitudes about amalgamation among ironworkers. As the number of skilled crafts eligible for membership—wire-drawers, hammerman, millwrights, pitmen, etc.—increased in the 1880s, craft tensions and personal rivalries escalated.

In 1882 there were several strikes for union recognition and to establish a sliding scale with the manufacturers. The major wage scale strike began in Pittsburgh in June, spread to Ohio Valley mills, and ended with the union's defeat in late September. After the strike, the Amalgamated tried to reorganize the local lodges by craft. This temporarily eased tension. But the sliding scale issue continued to exacerbate craft animosities throughout the 1880s. It generated convenient rationalizations for violations of any work rules that blocked the advancement of one man or a particular group of workmen. By the end of the decade, officers admitted a need to suppress craft conflicts that detracted from the Amalgamated's solidarity and therefore were detrimental to the union's bargaining position.

In an attempt to diminish the appearance of division, Amalgamated officers convinced union members to align with the new American Federation of Labor in 1887. The Amalgamated thus strengthened its position as an individual union and became part of the power structure of the American Federation of Labor by the end of the 1880s. The growth of the union from 3,755 members organized into 111 lodges in 1877 to 20,975 members in 291

JUNE 1892 —Excerpted from the preamble to the Constitution of the Amalgamated Association of Iron and Steel Workers.

AAISW PREAMBLE

Year after year the capital of the country becomes more and more concentrated in the hands of the few; and, in proportion, as the wealth of the country becomes centralized, its power increases and the laboring classes are more or less impoverished. It therefore becomes us as men who have to *battle* with the stern realities of life, to look this matter fair in the face. There is no *dodging* the question. Let every man give it a fair, full and candid consideration, and then act according to his honest convictions. What position are we, the Iron and Steel Workers of America, to hold in our society? Are we to receive an equivalent for our labor sufficient to maintain us in comparative independence and respectability, to procure the means with which to educate our children and qualify them to play their part in the world drama?

"In union there is strength," and in the formation of a National Amalgamated Association, embracing every Iron and Steel Worker in the country, a union founded upon a basis broad as the land in which we live lies our only hope. Single-handed we can accomplish nothing, but united there is no power of wrong we may not openly defy.

Let the Iron and Steel Workers of such places as have not already moved in this matter, organize as quickly as possible and connect themselves with the National Association. Do not be humbugged with the idea that this thing cannot succeed. We are not theorists; this is no visionary plan, but one eminently practicable. Nor can injustice be done to anyone; no undue advantage should be taken of any of our employers. There is not, there can not be any good reason why they should not pay us a fair price for our labor, and there is no good reason why we should not receive a fair equivalent therefor.

To rescue our trades from the condition into which they have fallen, and raise ourselves to that condition in society to which we, as mechanics, are justly entitled; to place ourselves on a foundation sufficiently strong to secure us from encroachments: to elevate the moral, social and intellectual condition of every Iron and Steel Worker in the country, is the object of our National Association. ❖

---

lodges in 1892, indicates the extent of the Amalgamated's influence among skilled iron and steelworkers, primarily in the Ohio Valley. Craft tensions, as much as societal ones, resulted in discrimination against blacks and "green hands." Any man other than a son or brother who had not worked in the trades under union rule had a hard time getting a job in a mill.

The four years of the union's greatest prosperity and success, from late 1888 through early 1892, paralleled its influential years in the American Federation of Labor. As one of the Federation's five major unions in membership size, and consequently in number of delegates to annual conventions, the Amalgamated helped to shape and direct that organization's policies. The Amalgamated's national secretary, William Martin, concurrently served as a vice-president in the American Federation of Labor from 1888 through 1890.

By the late 1880s, however, the Amalgamated had become preoccupied with preserving the security of the status quo. Ambitious proposals —such as worker-ownership of a rolling mill—were suppressed. New members were less willing to risk immediate material gains for future prospects than long-time members.

The majority of the 253 delegates to the Amalgamated's 22-day convention in 1890 were first-time representatives. They cared less for executive opinions and reports about the daily operation of the union than for committee work regarding the sliding scales connected with their own lodges' craft interests. The convention evolved into a parliamentary battleground where special interests always superseded collective ones. The delegates' focus on wage scales reflected the preoccupation of the union's general membership at the beginning of the 1890s—a tunnel vision that effectively neutralized the Amalgamated Association during the watershed crisis at Homestead in 1892. ❖

Excerpted from U.S. Senate Report No.1280, testimony given November 24, 1892, by William Weihe, puddler and President of the AAISW.

WEIHE TESTIMONY

Q. State to the committee the character of the work of the high-priced men so that we can get an idea why they are paid, whether the work is dangerous, specially skilled, or what there is about it that commands such high wages? —**A.** A roller has charge of a train of rolls; that sometimes requires 10, or 12, or 15 men under him. He is held responsible for the machinery, not in dollars and cents, but as a skilled mechanic. He has to be able to judge whether the iron is hot enough, or whether it is rolled perfect; he must know how to set the iron to the gauge required, or size desired, and must always give information to those under him what their duties are in producing material. The manager generally goes to the roller and asks him, if there is any change in size, what is best to be done, and consequently the roller is the highest paid man in that department. Of late years they have invented machinery that reduces the skill to a certain extent. At one time it was very hard to get good rollers because they were not apt to have the machinery in as perfect condition as they are getting it now.

Q. Have his wages been reduced in proportion to the increase in the efficacy of the machinery? —**A.** In the Carnegie Steel Company they have. They have some mills that the rollers formerly received the same price as they did in iron mills, but the 23-inch and the 33-inch mills were reduced three years ago on account of the improvements that were made and the increased capacity.

Q. What was reduced? —**A.** The wages of the men. The roller received 70 cents per ton, and paid his labor. There was a reduction of some 30 per cent on that job at that time, on account of the improvements that were made and the increased capacity. . . .

Q. Now, what next? —**A.** The heater. He has charge of the furnace; must see that the iron and steel is properly charged,

and must know when it is hot enough to take out and roll, and is held responsible for the heating of it. If he does not understand his business thoroughly he may scorch it or burn it, and the loss of the billet, weighing all the way from 50 pounds to 2,000 tons, according to whatever train the iron is to be heated on, is a serious loss to the firm, and consequently these men receive higher pay than the ordinary workman.

Q. Now, take the next. —**A.** The laborer is under him. He has charge of certain duties around the furnace, looking after the grate and the cinders. His wages are less than the heaters', because the skill required of him is not as great as the heaters.

Q. Taking month by month, year by year, how much time do that class of men use in their works when the mills are going on regularly? —**A.** That depends upon the method upon which they are working. Some work on an eight-hour system; others, again, work on the twelve-hour system.

Q. In either case, how many days, in the course of a year, would they probably work? —**A.** Well, they may run two hundred and fifty up to two hundred and seventy-five days.

. . .

Q. And do the lower grades of skilled workmen work more days in the course of a year than the higher grades? —**A.** They work more days than the tonnage workers. The heaters, rollers, and others are tonnage workers, and the blacksmiths, machinists, and others are the day workers, and they work more days in the year, on account of the repair work they often have to look after.

Q. Now, going back to the actual amount of day's wages, what would be a fair average day's wage for the highest grade of skilled workmen in the steel mills? —**A.** In some mills they would make more than others, the average—do you mean the tonnage workers?

Q. I mean the rollers. For example, take the rollers? —**A.** In the Carnegie Steel Works at Homestead the average wages of rollers for the past twenty-three months—that is, before the 1st of July—I think was $7.60 [per day], that is of one train. The 119-inch train in the mill is the highest paid train. The heaters earn so much less, and others in proportion.

Q. How do you account for the fact that the average is only about $7 when the highest amount of wages is $12 and upwards? —**A.** That was, I suppose, based on the Carnegie Company's run during the month of May. They ran the mill at its fullest capacity, and I have no doubt gave the men the best of orders in order to get a great tonnage. They had a greater tonnage in May than they ever had before, by having heavy sizes, running the mill every minute they could possibly run it, and so they got a great tonnage for that month, but I am speaking of the average for the twenty-three months.

Q. That is what I wanted to get. What would be the average for the lower grades of skilled workmen? —**A.** Some, perhaps, make $3, $2.50, some $2, and some are paid by the hour, perhaps 14 cents an hour. The average I would not be able to give exactly. I think there were over 1,600 men that ran less than $2 a day in the Carnegie Company.

Q. Do you mean that 14 cents an hour applies to the lower grades of skill? —**A.** No, the ordinary grade of labor.

Q. My question related to the lower grades of skilled labor, the day workers. —**A.** It may run from $2 to $3 per day. There may have been some few over that, but I think very few.

Q. What, approximately, is a fair day's wage in the iron and steel industry, taking $1.40 as the lower for the unskilled workmen and the higher priced $12 and upwards for the skilled, all throughout? —**A.** I don't think it would be above $3. I think that is about it. You mean the highest and lowest?

Q. Yes.—**A.** I don't think it would be above $3.

Q. What, in your judgment, is the best way of settling disputes concerning wages between employers and employés? —**A.** By both getting together and reasoning the matter over and talking upon questions that are brought before them. That finally will bring good results. That has been our experience in the last ten years. Get together, through conferences, committees on both sides. It has brought good results up to this year. Of course there may be times when both parties become somewhat heated, but when it comes down to the question of right or wrong it is very seldom they have disagreed. ❖

TECHNOLOGICAL CHANGE AND WORKERS' CONTROL AT HOMESTEAD

by Charles J. McCollester

*T*he 1892 Battle of Homestead took place during a period of rapid technological and organizational change in the American iron and steel industry. The rolled structural steel made at Homestead would alter the face of American cities by making skyscrapers possible. Its alloyed steel armor plate would make the United States the world's leading naval power. The Homestead Works were a technological wonder of the time, the American answer to the giant Krupp works at Essen, Germany, boasting an output 50 percent higher than that of any other mill in the world.

The changes from small-batch iron puddling to large-scale steel production, however, put the workers and their organizations at a disadvantage. The steel magnates like Frick and Carnegie increased the scale and pace of production by introducing mechanical and engineering improvements that increased productivity while reducing the role of labor.

Steel is iron containing enough carbon (.1 to .5 percent) to be hardened by sudden cooling, but not enough to make it brittle like cast iron. Malleable iron, made in small furnaces by puddling, required constant handling and attention by an individual worker or teams of workers—in processes called boiling, rabbling (stirring), balling, squeezing, rolling, and shearing. Steelmaking, by contrast, relies on the metallurgical changes happening inside the furnace rather than as a result of skilled manipulation by a worker. Modern steelmaking grew out of an increased ability to obtain high temperatures and precisely adjust the chemistry of the heat to obtain the exact characteristics of metal desired. The imperative of large-scale production was to increase the continuity and automation of the process—which involved producing pig iron in a liquid form (in the blast furnace), transferring the iron to a furnace where it was purified and chemically adjusted to become steel, and then casting it into ingots that were not allowed to cool until rolled into finished products.

Steel began to challenge iron's 3,000-year domination only with the invention of the Bessemer furnace, patented in England in 1856 (William Kelly of Pittsburgh was a rival claimant to a similar process). By 1870, the Bessemer furnace was solidly established, producing 300,000 tons worldwide that year. In the mid-1870s the most advanced Bessemer technology was installed by Holley and Jones at Carnegie's Braddock mill. By 1881, the Braddock plant itself was producing over 200,000 tons of Bessemer steel a year. Bessemer furnaces

These 10-ton Bessemer converters were installed in the Homestead Mill shortly after the strike. The one on the left is "in blow." The blast of air rid the molten pig iron of excess carbon and converted it into steel.

Homestead Mill, Open Hearth #2. Molten steel would be transported by an overhead crane and funneled through a "pony" ladle to cast 90-ton ingots in the pit below. These would eventually be rolled into armor plate.

The Carnegie Company had only a few open hearth furnaces in 1892; by 1910 it had 60 and produced far more open hearth than Bessemer steel. This is most likely Open Hearth #4 built c. 1906. Men watch from above as the molten steel is tapped.

produced about 25 tons of low carbon steel in about one hour from tap to tap.

While Bessemers ruled at Braddock and were also constructed at Homestead, the latter became primarily an open hearth shop. The Siemens-Martin open hearth furnace that had been developed in England and France was originally an acid technology that did not effectively remove phosphorus. With the installation of open hearths in 1886, Homestead introduced a technology that produced the first commercial "basic" steel. Basic lining materials (dolomite, limestone) produced a primarily limestone slag, tying up the phosphorus and thus producing a superior steel.

Open hearth steel production was a very slow process compared to Bessemer, taking from 8 to 12 hours to produce a heat. However, furnace size could be greatly increased (it averaged 50 tons at Homestead in the 1880s) and separate batches could be processed to the same metallurgical specifications so that giant castings could be made from combined pours. In the year preceding the strike, Homestead claimed a world record casting of 250 tons and in 1892 rolled a 72-ton ingot. The open hearth's major advantage over the Bessemer was that harmful impurities, such as sulphur and phosphorus, could be more easily removed, and alloyed steel could be developed for specialized products, such as armor plate, boiler plate, and flange steel. These characteristics of the open hearth process opened the prospect that crucial decisions could be made by engineers or by chemists in a metallurgical laboratory rather than by skilled workers wresting iron from ore by fire, muscle, and experience.

Homestead also distinguished itself by the size, organization, and improvement of material-handling equipment like overhead cranes, hoists, charging machines, and buggies. Continuous production with sequenced material-handling mechanisms reduced the need for teams of experienced workers acting in concert at critical moments of a dynamic process. Three-high rolls provided continuous rolling; hydraulic tables raised plates for continuous passage back and forth between the moving rolls; a massive 363-foot cooling table for the 119" plate mill conveyed slabs to the shears, without laborious handling and stacking. By 1892, virtually all the mills at Homestead were mechanized and continuous. Visitors would watch in awe as monstrous machines, dubbed Leviathan and Behemoth by the workers, withdrew giant slabs from flaming furnaces, expertly transporting them with no human hand visible in their operation.

Another technological factor was the promise of electrical power, which was being pioneered at the nearby Westinghouse plants. While steam power still dominated at Homestead in 1892, electricity promised new ways to automate production and eliminate labor. Indeed, in 1893, the 23- and 33-inch mills were completely remodeled with electrically operated machinery, doubling production while reducing the number of workers. Furthermore, George Westinghouse's success in developing valve and transmission systems for natural gas in 1884 allowed Homestead's open hearths to be gas fired. This eliminated the need for coal-handling facilities requiring large labor gangs. On the eve of the 1892 conflict, large gas fields in which Carnegie held an interest were discovered near Pittsburgh, guaranteeing continued cheap energy for the Homestead open hearths.

Technological changes provided the context within which Carnegie and Frick believed they could defeat the Amalgamated Association in its Homestead stronghold, thus eliminating any interference from the union in the company's radical reshaping of the production process.

Until 1892, the union exerted considerable control in the workplace, determining which skilled workers were hired and promoted, the way jobs were allocated, and how work was paced. It made decisions about the production process, including the quality of pig iron that should be used and the quantity of scrap. Since steel wage rates evolved directly out of former iron pay scales, wages tied to steel tonnage escalated with the rapidly increased production. Company sources claimed that the top skilled tonnage workers could make $10 to $15 a day. Sunday work, other than maintenance, was virtually abolished at Homestead. While open hearth departments generally worked 12-hour-turns (including some periods of low activity), roll shops were down to 10, and the Bessemer departments were working three 8-hour shifts. The pressure in union shops was for shorter hours and overtime pay. The question was how much of the new productivity was the company willing to return to the workers in wages and benefits?

As events at Homestead would illustrate, wage disparities among groups of workers caused tensions. Mechanics, who manufactured and erected the machinery that the tonnage men operated, might make only a third or a quarter of the top tonnage rate. Laborers—increasingly Slavs and Hungarians—earned even less. Ultimately, however, the mechanics and the laborers supported the Amalgamated leadership, looking to the union as the source of their prosperity and protection. ❖

Excerpted from U.S. House of Representatives Report No. 2447, testimony given July 14, 1892, by John Alfred Potter, General Superintendent, Homestead Works.

POTTER TESTIMONY

Q. Will you describe to the committee what each class of those workmen do, the methods by which they perform their labor; not in perfect detail, but so as to give us a general idea, beginning, say, with the rollers, and so on through? —**A.** Well, the rolling at Homestead is different from what it is at any other mill. Our organization at Homestead is made up so that it takes the responsibility from the rollers. In the first place, our rollers are not responsible for the men, as they do no hiring or discharging of men. We have superintendents in each department to attend to those duties. In some other mills, the roller has charge of a certain number of men whom he pays out of his salary, but that is not the case at Homestead. We pay each man. The rollers' duties vary on each mill at Homestead. On the plate mill, where the rollers are in question, which is known as the 119-inch mill, there the roller receives the piece of steel on his table in the slab form, probably 4 or 5 inches thick and of different dimensions.

He has before him a sheet which tells him the size of the plate which must be made out of that slab. He then manipulates that through the mill, passes it through the rolls different times until he has reduced it to the proper width and proper thickness, and then it goes through a different process of being sheared into proper dimensions. The roller is responsible for the work done on his mill in this way: he has to gauge that piece of steel to see he gets the proper thickness and that it is also gauged to the proper dimensions.

Q. You say that the workmen in that mill can turn out twice the product by reason of the improved machinery? —**A.** Yes, sir.

Q. Than any other mill in the world? —**A.** Yes, sir; of the same character.

Q. What do you mean by the same character? —**A.** The same class of mill.

Q. Well, if there is no mill like it in the world there is no other same class? —**A.** That is right.

Q. The labor cost of turning out that product at that mill would be one-half

Excerpted from U.S. House of Representatives Report No. 2447, testimony given July 14, 1892, by H.C. Frick.

FRICK TESTIMONY

Q. Mr. Potter, the general manager of your mills, stated a few moments ago that owing to the improved machinery in your mills at Homestead, you were able to turn out 50 per cent more product with 50 per cent less labor in certain lines. Do you indorse that statement? —**A.** I think that is substantially correct, in one department.

Q. In other words, with the use of that machinery one man does the work that four men did formerly? —**A.** I think that is correct.

Q. Which department is that? —**A.** I think he had reference to the 119-inch plate mill, with the assistance of the other department, the 32-inch slabbing mill.

Q. Can you state independently of other costs the labor cost of producing a ton of steel billets? —**A.** I could get those figures for you, but I think I will have to decline to give them to you.

Q. You decline to give all the cost to you or your company, but upon what ground do you decline to give the labor cost separate from the other? —**A.** Well, I do not think we should be asked to give away those details of our business.

Q. You asked the Government for a duty to compensate between the difference in the American labor cost and the foreign labor cost; then upon what principle, receiving from the Government a protection which is ostensibly and avowedly for that purpose, do you decline to give the information upon which that legislation is based? —**A.** We did not ask the Government for such protection.

Q. You did not? —**A.** No, this concern did not.

Q. You are greatly misrepresented then if you did not. The press misrepresents you very much.

———❖———

what it would be anywhere else where they are paying the same wages?— **A.** I do not know whether that is so or not.

Q. Does not that follow as a necessary result? —**A.** Not under our system. We pay two mills for reducing the plate; other mills take the ingot direct and roll it into the plate in one mill. In our case, as I have explained to you, we cast the ingot, 12 tons in weight, and we roll it down on one mill.

Q. Now, you are going away entirely from the question. You stated that with your machinery there the men could turn out twice the product, and I ask the simple question whether, if that is true, the labor-cost of that product would not be one-half of any other mill having the same rate of wages? —**A.** I do not think it would.

Q. Well, that is all then; that answers the question. What kind of machinery is there which increases the facility of labor? —**A.** Automatic machinery, hydraulic, etc.

Q. Is that the machinery of which there is no mill possessed? —**A.** We use hydraulic machinery to a greater extent than any other mill.

Q. Then the use of machinery actually reduces the cost of the product does it not? —**A.** Well, it should do it; that is what we want it to do.

———❖———

Excerpted from an exchange with a puddler in **The Iron Puddler** *by James J. Davis, published by Grosset & Dunlap, New York, 1922.*

MAN IS IRON TOO

"For twenty-five minutes while the boil goes on I stir it constantly with my long iron rabble. A cook stirring gravy to keep it from scorching in the skillet is done in two minutes and backs off blinking, sweating and choking, having finished the hardest job of getting dinner. But my hardest job lasts not two minutes but the better part of half an hour. My spoon weighs

Puddlers needed tremendous strength to stir the molten iron and lift the finished "balls," which could weigh up to 200 pounds.

twenty-five pounds, my porridge is pasty iron, and the heat of my kitchen is so great that if my body was not hardened to it, the ordeal would drop me in my tracks.

Little spikes of pure iron like frost spars glow white-hot and stick out of the churning slag. These must be stirred under at once; the long stream of flame from the grate plays over the puddle, and the pure iron if lapped by these gases would be oxidized—burned up.

Pasty masses of iron form at the bottom of the puddle. There they would stick and become chilled if they were not constantly stirred. The whole charge must be mixed and mixed as it steadily thickens so that it will be uniform throughout. I am like some frantic baker in the inferno kneading a batch of iron bread for the devil's breakfast.

'It's an outrage that men should have to work like this,' a reformer told me.

'They don't *have* to,' I replied. 'Nobody forced me to do this. I do it because I would rather live in an Iron Age than live in a world of ox-carts. Man can take his choice.'" ❖

The forging press handled 90-ton ingots. They were heated in the furnace, behind on the right, and held in place by the Porter Bar, foreground. The press could exert 10 to 12 thousand tons of pressure and reduce the thickness of an ingot to 20 inches. This armor plate would then be sent to the rolling mill for final reduction.

E V E N T S

JANUARY 1892–John Potter, Superintendent of the Homestead Works, initiates contract negotiations with the Amalgamated Association. The current contract will expire June 30.

FEBRUARY–The company proposes reducing the market-price minimum for the sliding scale to $22 per ton and cutting skilled workers' tonnage-based wages. The union wants to maintain the current minimum of $25 per ton.

MAY–Early in the month Carnegie leaves for Great Britain, where he will stay until the end of the year.

MAY–The company adds the demand that a new contract end December 31 rather than June 30.

MAY 29–Frick, following written instructions from Carnegie, presents an ultimatum to the union: Accept terms by June 24, or the company will run non-union.

JUNE–The company builds a high wooden fence, topped by barbed wire, around the Homestead mill.

JUNE 2–Frick writes to the Pinkerton Detective Agency to prepare a force of 300 guards to deal with "the trouble we anticipate" when the company re-starts non-union on July 6.

JUNE 19–Delegates to the annual convention of the Amalgamated Association in Pittsburgh attend a mass meeting in the Homestead opera house. John McLuckie addresses the crowd.

JUNE 23–In its last negotiating session, the company and the union fail to agree.

JUNE 24–Several hundred Slav workers form an Amalgamated lodge and vote unanimously to follow the union's directives in case of a strike.

GATHERING STORM

"Of course you will win," –Carnegie to Frick

2

Excerpted from **Homestead,** *Chapter II, by Arthur G. Burgoyne, a Pittsburgh journalist who covered the strike as it was happening. Originally published by Rawsthorne Engraving and Printing Company, Pittsburgh, 1893.*

OPERATION OF THE SLIDING SCALE

The Homestead scale was prepared early in the spring [1892]. In January, the superintendent of the mill, Mr. Potter sent for the joint committee of the local lodges and requested that the men prepare a scale. It was not the policy of the Carnegie firm, Mr. Potter said, to leave the way open for a strike. If there were differences of opinion between employer and employees, the proper method of settlement was by arbitration, and it was, therefore, advisable that the scale should be presented early, so as to leave ample time for an amicable adjustment of disputed points.

For three years previous, the men had been working under what was known as a sliding scale, an expedient which at the time of its adoption was regarded as a sure preventive of strikes. This scale established as the basis on which wages were to be determined, the market price of steel billets, in the manufacture of which the Carnegie Company was extensively engaged. When the price of billets went up, wages were to go up correspondingly, and when the price of billets went down, wages were to be correspondingly lowered. $25 a ton was agreed upon as the minimum. If billets were quoted below that figure, there was to be no further depression of wages. In other words, the men and the firm were practically in partnership, increased profits to the latter meaning increased earnings to the former, unless the bottom fell out of the market, in which case it became the duty of the stronger partner to protect the weaker.

The circumstances under which this equitable compact was made are of interest in so far as they exhibit the very different temper of the Carnegie Company towards its men in the past from that which marked its line of conduct after Mr. Frick was placed at the helm.

In January, 1889, the men, who had been working under a yearly scale, quarreled with the firm over the terms proposed for the ensuing year and a strike was declared. William L. Abbott, a man of comparatively mild and liberal disposition, was then serving as chairman. Mr. Abbott undertook to break the strike, and when the men resorted to riotous conduct, called upon the sheriff of the county for aid. The sheriff, Dr. Alexander McCandless, an official who enjoyed great popularity, and possessed the courage and tact essential in such an emergency, went promptly to the scene with a force of deputies recruited for the occasion. At the first encounter with the mob, the deputies let their courage ooze out at their fingers' ends and fled from the town.

The sheriff, nowise disheartened . . . took the best possible means of ending the trouble by constituting himself a mediator between the Carnegie firm and the strikers. Through his efforts a conference was arranged, and peace was restored through the adoption of the famous sliding scale, with the understanding that it would hold good until June 30, 1892. Mr. Carnegie, then absent in Europe, professed to be much pleased with the amicable settlement arrived at and the incidental guarantee of peace for three years to come. . . .

When Superintendent Potter, in January, 1892, spoke to the men about a new scale, he gave no hint of the prospect that the firm contemplated sweeping away the beneficial arrangement which had so long governed their earnings. . . .

The shadow of Mr. Frick loomed up gloomily in the background . . . but there was really no occasion to think of shadows when the genial Potter presented himself as the very embodiment of sunshine. [His] ideas . . . bore the special brand of Mr. Carnegie [who] was on record as being opposed to the use of force in settling disputes between capital and labor.

———❖———

25

Two documents reprinted from **The Inside History of the Carnegie Steel Company**, *Chapter 2, by* **James Howard Bridge**, *originally published by* **The Aldine Book Company, New York, 1903.**

Carnegie sent this notice to Frick, who did not post it. As a result the workers remained uninformed of Carnegie's stand.

ANDREW CARNEGIE,

5 West 51st St.

New York, April 4, 1892.

N O T I C E
TO EMPLOYEES AT HOMESTEAD WORKS.

These Works having been consolidated with the Edgar Thomson and Duquesne, and other mills, there has been forced upon this Firm the question Whether its Works are to be run 'Union' or 'Non-Union.' As the vast majority of our employees are Non-Union, the Firm has decided that the minority must give place to the majority. These Works therefore, will be necessarily Non-Union after the expiration of the present agreement.

This does not imply that the men will make lower wages. On the contrary, most of the men at Edgar Thomson and Duquesne Works, both Non-Union, have made and are making higher wages than those at Homestead, which has hitherto been Union.

The facilities and modes of working at Homestead Works differ so much from those of steel mills generally in Pittsburgh that a scale suitable for these is inapplicable to Homestead.

A scale will be arranged which will compare favorably with that at the other works named; that is to say, the Firm intends that the men of Homestead shall make as much as the men at either Duquesne or Edgar Thomson. Owing to the great changes and improvements made in the Converting Works, Beam Mills, Open Hearth Furnaces, etc., and the intended running of hot metal in the latter, the products of the works will be greatly increased, so that at the rates per ton paid at Braddock and Duquesne, the monthly earnings of the men may be greater than hitherto. While the number of men required will, of course, be reduced, the extensions at Duquesne and Edgar Thomson as well as at Homestead will, it is hoped, enable the firm to give profitable employment to such of its desirable employees as may temporarily be displaced. The firm will in all cases give the preferences to such satisfactory employees.

This action is not taken in any spirit of hostility to labor organizations, but every man will see that the firm cannot run Union and Non-Union. It must be either one or the other.

Andrew Carnegie to Henry Clay Frick from England.

COWORTH PARK, SUNNINGDALE, BERKS.

June 10, 1892.

As I understand matters at Homestead, it is not only the wages paid, but the number of men required by Amalgamated rules which makes our labor rates so much higher than those in the East.

Of course, you will be asked to confer, and I know you will decline all conferences, as you have taken your stand and have nothing more to say.

It is fortunate that only a part of the Works are concerned. Provided you have plenty of plates rolled, I suppose you can keep on with armor. Potter will, no doubt, intimate to the men that refusal of scale means running only as Non-Union. This may cause acceptance, but I do not think so. The chances are, you will have to prepare for a struggle, in which case the notice [*i.e.* that the works are henceforth to be non-union] should go up promptly on the morning of the 25th. Of course you will win, and win easier than you suppose, owing to the present condition of markets.

ANDREW CARNEGIE.

JULY 8, 1892 —Excerpted from an article, "Frick Explains," in the Pittsburgh Commercial Gazette. *See pages 94-95 for further excerpts.*

Three Points of Difference.

"There were three points upon which we differed. The skilled workmen in the Amalgamated association work under what is known as a sliding scale. As the price of steel advances the earnings of the men advance; as the prices fall their earnings decrease in proportion. While there is no limit to an advance of earnings on the scale, there is a point at which the decline stops. It is known as the minimum, and the figure heretofore has been $25 per ton for 4x4 Bessemer billets. We believe that if earnings based on the selling price of steel can advance without limit, the workmen should be willing to follow the selling price down to a reasonable minimum, and so this figure was finally fixed by the Carnegie Company at the rate of $23 instead of $25.

"The reason for asking this upon our part was that the Carnegie company had spent large sums of money in the introduction of new machinery in the Homestead plant, by means of which the workmen were enabled to increase the daily output, thereby increasing the amount of their own earnings. We had originally asked a reduction to $22, but

subsequently agreed to compromise the rate at $23. The Amalgamated association was unwilling to consider a reduction below $24 on steel billets, notwithstanding the fact that the improved machinery would enable their members, even at $23, to earn more than is paid in other Amalgamated mills. This was the first point at issue.

A Change Proposed.

"Under the present Amalgamated system the date of the expiration of the sliding scale is June 30, annually. We asked that this date be changed to December 31 (same as at Edgar Thomson), for the reason that the change would permit us to take our estimate upon the wages we must pay during the year, beginning on January 1, so that we would be able to make contracts for the year accordingly. This point the Amalgamated association refused to accede and demanded the old date. The third proposition was the reduction in tonnage rates in those departments in the mills where the improvements I have spoken of have been made and which enable the working men to increase the out put and consequently their earnings. Where no such improvements had been made, there was no request upon our part for a reduction in tonnage rates. In other words, we asked no reduction in tonnage rates, the skilled workmen would make more money than they did when the scale of 1889 went into effect.

"As a rule the men who were making the largest wages in the Homestead mill were the ones who most bitterly denounced the proposed revision of the scale, for out of the 3,800 men employed in every department only 825 were directly affected by this reduction. . . ."

———❖———

The 128-inch, three-high Lauth mill, bought in the late 1890s from Bethlehem Steel, exemplifies the Carnegie Company's policy of upgrading technology.

Excerpted from U.S. House of Representatives Report No. 2447, testimony given July 13, 1892, by John McLuckie, steel worker, Burgess of the Borough of Homestead.

McLUCKIE TESTIMONY

Q. Where do you live? —**A.** Homestead.

Q. Do you hold any official position there? —**A.** I am burgess of that borough.

Q. How long have you held that position? —**A.** This is my second term, this year, 1892.

Q. How long have you lived in Homestead, Pa. —**A.** Over five years.

Q. What business have you been engaged in? —**A.** I am a steel worker.

Q. Do you mean you worked in the mills of Carnegie, Phipps & Co., at Homestead? —**A.** Yes, sir.

Q. What particular kind of work did you do? —**A.** In the converting department.

Q. How long have you worked there? —**A.** Ever since I came to Homestead, five years ago last May.

Q. Do you belong to the Amalgamated Association of Iron and Steel Workers? —**A.** I do, sir.

Q. About what wages have you earned and received for the work you have been doing there? —**A.** I can not say, but I suppose it would average, probably, $2.25.

Q. About how much per month? —**A.** Perhaps $55.

Q. Do you know anything about the contract under which skilled workmen have been working for that company for some considerable time past? —**A.** The late steel contract? . . . After considerable trouble . . . the scale was signed [in 1889] and our wages were based on 4 by 4 inch billets. That proposition was made and examined by the officials of the association of which I have the honor of being a member and we concluded it was [as] safe to base the wages on that as on anything on the list. The productive capacities of the mills of the United States at that time were quite limited, and it was protected by the tariff as well as any other article. After going to work feeling assured we had a safe basis upon which we could depend, the McKinley bill came in and reduced—as you will discover by an examination—the tariff upon that identical article upon which our wages were based and raised the tariff on every other article, such as plates, beams, and structural iron. It increased the protection as far as other products, plate etc., was concerned and decreased the tariff on the identical articles on which our wages were based, and that is the reason I say it is a gigantic conspiracy assisted by vicious legislation to wrong the workman of what he is entitled to, a fair day's pay for a fair day's work.

Q. You think that the less the tariff the less the wages? —**A.** You are cross examining me, and you are a judge and lawyer and—

Q. No, I am simply a man and a member of this committee. I understood you to say the conspiracy consisted in the McKinley

bill reducing the duty upon this particular article of steel, and that depressed wages? —**A.** It did.

Q. So, then, it would be true—**A.** I said it did on this particular article.

Q. Why did it on this particular article? —**A.** Because it was part of this conspiracy to furnish material.

Q. How could a conspiracy reduce the price of an article of that sort; a conspiracy of Maj. McKinley and Mr. Frick, I suppose? —**A.** To reduce our wages.

Q. For that reason the higher the tariff upon an article which you make the better your wages? —**A.** Not always, sir.

Q. Well, in this case? —**A.** Look here, we did not get anything.

Q. But in this case you regarded the law to be a conspiracy to reduce your wages by reducing the tariff? —**A.** Simply because our wages were regulated by the selling price of that article, and by their reducing the value of the article it reduced our wages.

Q. You understand by reducing the tariff you were paid less wages directly or indirectly? —**A.** In this case lower wages were paid.

Q. It gave them an excuse to do it.
A. It was to their interest at the time.

Q. I do not know anything about that. Let me get a further idea. You thought a conspiracy existed; of whom did that conspiracy exist; who were the parties to that conspiracy in your judgment? —**A.** I think the Pacific Railroad people were connected with it.

Q. Who else? —**A.** The Carnegie and H. C. Frick interest.

Q. Who else? —**A.** I do not know; it is a pretty hard question.

———❖———

Excerpted from U.S. House of Representatives Report No. 2447, testimony given July 13, 1892, by William T. Roberts, steel worker.

ROBERTS TESTIMONY

Q. Where do you live? —**A.** I live in Pittsburg.

Q. Are you well acquainted with Homestead? —**A.** Yes, sir.

Q. Do you work at the Carnegie Works there? —**A.** I will be up there two years next September.

Q. In what department? —**A.** In the armor plate department.

Q. Are there any facts you wish to state? And, if so, state them. —**A.** I heard the question debated here this morning in regard to the expiration of our scale. It seemed to me that almost everyone who talked upon the matter evaded the vital point in the matter. I can state a reason why we object to ending the scale in the winter time, and that is, that the burnt child dreads the fire. We know from past experience—at least, I do—that when winter time comes around and our contract ends in the winter—I do not know that the Carnegie firm would do it, but I know people who have stood just as high in the estimation of the working people of

this country who have done it—they take that opportunity at that time of the year to starve us into submission. They have done it on every occasion. We, as working people, have fought for this principle we have got in the organization, until to-day every manufactory in the United States, with the exception probably of one or two, those run by nonunion, are willing at all times to sign our scale from one summer month to another. In the winter time when they throw us idle there is always a class in this country known as "snow birds" who never work in the summer time. They crowd our mills in the winter time, and we are almost crowded out in the winter time by those people whom no manufacturer can employ in the summer, but they are always ready and willing to do this work in the winter time, after we have labored all through the summer, and they ought not to require of us that when we come to the winter months these idlers should drop in there to take our places and then after all the damage has been done and spring comes on and we have been out four or five months that we should be compelled to go back and work for the wages this rabble has made for us.

———❖———

(facing page) John McLuckie

Reprinted from U.S. Senate Report No. 1280, Exhibit C. in testimony given November 23, 1892, by H.C. Frick.

Exhibit C.
Pittsburg, PA., June 2, 1892

Dear Sir: I am in receipt of your favor of the 22d.

We will want 300 guards for service at our Homestead mills as a measure of prevention against inteferrence [sic] with our plan to start the operation of the works on July 6, 1892.

The only trouble we anticipate is that an attempt will be made to prevent such of our men, with whom we will by that time have made satisfactory arrangements, from going to work and possibly some demonstration of violence upon the part of those whose places have been filled, or most likely by an element which usually is attracted to such scenes for the purpose of stirring up trouble.

We are not desirous that the men you send shall be armed unless the occasion properly calls for such a measure later on for the protection of our employés or property. We shall wish these guards to be placed upon our property and there to remain unless called into other service by the civil authorities to meet an emergency that is not likely to arise.

These guards should be assembled at Ashtabula, Ohio, not later than the morning of July 5, when they may be taken by train to McKees Rocks, or some other point upon the Ohio River below Pittsburg where they can be transferred to boats and landed within the inclosures of our premises at Homestead. We think absolute secrecy essential in the movement of these men so that no demonstration can be made while they are en route.

Specific arrangements for movement of trains and connection with boats will be made as soon as we hear from you as to the certainty of having the men at Ashtabula at the time indicated.

As soon as your men are upon the premises we will notify the sheriff and ask that they be deputized either at once or immediately upon an ontbreak [sic] of such a character as to render such a step desirable.

Yours very truly,
H. C. Frick,
Chairman.

Robert A. Pinkerton, Esq.
New York City, N.Y.

The arrows added to this map of industrial Pittsburgh (1908) show the route the barges would follow after taking on the Pinkerton guards at Bellevue.

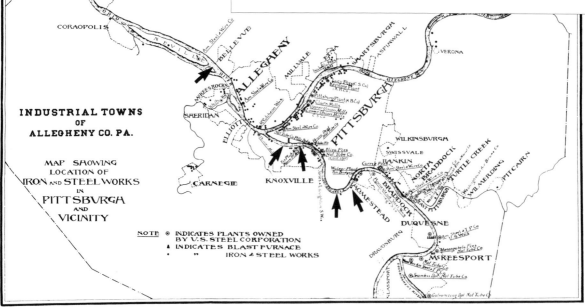

INDUSTRIAL TOWNS
OF
ALLEGHENY CO. PA.

MAP SHOWING
LOCATION OF
IRON AND STEEL WORKS
IN
PITTSBURGH
AND
VICINITY

NOTE ⊚ INDICATES PLANTS OWNED
BY U.S. STEEL CORPORATION
▲ INDICATES BLAST FURNACE
• " IRON & STEEL WORKS

FEAR OF A STRIKE.

————

Ominous Outlook at the Great Carnegie Steel Works at Homestead.

————

ULTIMATUM GIVEN BY THE FIRM.

————

It Demands Heavy Reductions For All Tonnage Workers.

————

ALMOST CERTAIN TO BE REJECTED.

————

Developments now indicate that Homestead will be the scene of a great conflict between capital and labor. The Carnegie Steel Company stands on the one side, and over 4,000 workingmen under the protection of the Amalgamated Association on the other.

The scale of wages which has been in force three years expires on June 30. In 1889, when this scale was signed, there was a short but very lively fight, which [was] ended by Sheriff McCandless acting as mediator and bringing representatives of the two sides together after all negotiations had been dropped. At that time it was the avowed intention of Carnegie to run the mill non-union, but this year their tactics have been very different.

Early in January Manager J. A. Potter sent for the various committees and informed them that the company desired no shutdown this summer, and in order to avoid [this] desired to discuss the next scale before the Amalgamated convention met. They desired to so arrange matters that the plant could run right along after the usual shutdown of July 1. This desire arose, of course, from the heavy contracts on hand from the government for iron plate, besides other orders. The management said, however, this conference was only to apply to four depart-

NO SIGN OF A STRIKE YET.

————

Improvements at the Homestead Mills Accounted For by the Manager.

————

CONSERVATIVE MEN FEAR NO TROUBLE.

————

Hot Heads Still Are Insisting That a Fight Will Be Made.

————

A COMPROMISE SCALE PREDICTED.

————

At Homestead, the Carnegie, Phipps & Co. steel mills are running as though a strike, or anything like a strike, was not in the shape of possibility. The men are all hard at their regular work, with the exception of the delegates to the Amalgamated convention. But a strike is no remote possibility. It is regarded by many as a very likely termination to the wage question which is soon to be settled between the two factors in this dispute. The more conservative steel workers and the salaried employees of the company seem to think that serious results and disputes will be averted. It is thought that the disputants will finally be able to come together and fix a scale that will be signed by both parties. The scale that the Carnegie company has prepared has not yet been brought before the association, and when it is will be referred to the scale committee.

John A. Potter, a superintendent of the Carnegie, Phipps & Co. Homestead mills, said: "I don't know anything about any trouble here and I don't think there is going to be any. Our mills are running full turn and we have orders ahead that will keep us busy for a year at least. Our men get good pay and make money, in fact, they are better paid than in most places. I don't think they intend to strike. We are making no preparations for a strike as we don't apprehend one. We bought some new ground and are fencing it in, as we have done with all our grounds. That talk about the barbed wires at the top of our fences being charged with electricity is bosh.

"We are employing about 3,600 men, and they are all good workmen. In case they should refuse to sign the scale by June 24, we will have no trouble, but talk it over with them and advise them. Our scale is very reasonable, and not materially lower than the present one. We do not intend to employ non-union men, and have never thought of it. I think that our men will sign the scale."

———❖———

ments—the armour plate mill, the 119-inch plate mill and the two open hearth departments. In the other mills changes in machinery are under way, or in con-

templation, which render it impossible to draw up a scale at the present time which would apply to the same departments in a few months.

———❖———

JUNE 7, 1892 —Excerpted from **The Pittsburgh Post.**

WILL BE A FIGHT TO THE FINISH

————————

Manufacturers and the Amalgamated Association Will Have Trouble.

————————

SWEEPING REDUCTIONS CONTEMPLATED.

————————

THE CONVENTION OPENS THIS MORNING.

In face of the fact that the Republicans at Minneapolis will this week resolve that under the beauties of the protective tariff system the manufacturing interests of the country are experiencing unparalleled prosperity, the iron and steel manufacturers are preparing to ask an enormous reduction in the wages of their men. The members of the Amalgamated Association of Iron and Steel Workers are fortifying themselves for the most desperate struggle known in the organization's history. There can be no mistaking the situation; the manufacturers are determined upon a general reduction of wages, and the association is just as determined that it will not stand the proposed cut.

The great convention of the Amalgamated Association opens to-day in Turner hall, Forbes street, and will continue in session at least a week. Its membership includes 60,000 iron and steel workers. It is beyond question the most powerful independent labor organization in the world, and every movement of the manufacturers seems to confirm the belief long entertained that they aim at its destruction in the coming conflict. For weeks and months the cloud has been gathering, and every mill man and every man connected with the office forces of the manufacturers shrugs his shoulders and gives signs of the impending danger when asked about the situation.

————————❖————————

JUNE 25, 1892 —*Excerpted from the* National Labor Tribune.

AT THE CONVENTION.

Canton, O., June 15.

Editors National Labor Tribune:

At the present convention of the A.A. of I. and S.W., now being held in Pittsburg, I missed quite a number who were at the last one.

I noticed that there were fewer old men in the convention this time than last. In fact I may say that I saw no old men there at all, the oldest man among them being in the prime and vigor of manhood, while predominating the convention were the bright young men of the craft. Earnest, vigorous, aggressive, yet the steadfast purpose which seemed to be easily read on every countenance would indicate that there is a conservatism sufficient to balance the aggressive radicalism that must and cannot help but crop out in such meetings.

In looking over the past and reviewing the work of conventions held heretofore, I cannot help but think that ever since the formation of the Association no convention has had the responsibility placed upon it this one has; never has there been such a crisis before the organization, as the present. It therefore behooves every delegate who wishes to see the organization a success to weigh well every vote he casts. It also behooves every member of the organization to have the greatest patience with whatever is done at the convention. . . .

The Carnegie Company have wiped out organization in the Edgar Thomson works at Braddock; have prevented organization being established in the Duquesne; under the management of Mr. Frick they have wiped out organization in the coke regions, and if they make up their minds to wipe it out at Homestead, who shall say them nay? They have already made arrangements to turn the works into a penitentiary, according to an account in the Sunday papers of Pittsburg, and to prevent those in from getting out and those out from getting in, have built up a fence nine feet high, and have put their lines of barbed wire fence around the top, and have arranged them so they can be charged with electricity, and wo [sic] be to any man who dares take hold of the wire to peep over the fence either from the outside or in.

O'Malley

———❖———

Frank Leslie's Illustrated Weekly, July 14, 1892. Bird's-eye view of the Homestead Works in full operation.

JUNE 18, 1892 —*Excerpted from* The Local News, *Homestead.*

———

—A disturbance at the steel works on Wednesday evening, in the shape of a fight between James Gibson, a steel-worker of Munhall, and John Caddy, a watchman on the P.,V.&C. railroad, caused considerable excitement in Homestead and was construed by many persons and most of the Pittsburg papers to have direct bearing on the wage situation. The facts of the case, tersely told, are these: Since the high fences have been built on either side of the P.,V.&C. railroad, by Carnegie, Phipps & Co., watchmen have been placed at the places where the railroad enters between the fences, and the duty assigned them was to prevent persons from walking on the tracks. John Caddy was one of these, and on Wednesday when Gibson started to walk up the track, Caddy stopped him, telling him to go the other way. This Gibson refused to do and words brought on blows, in which Gibson was getting the best of the fight, when Yardmaster James Dovey ran in and caught Gibson, whether to separate the combatants or to hold Gibson while Caddy assaulted him, as some say he did, is not known, but while Gibson was in this disadvantageous position, Watchman Caddy belabored him severely with a club. Gibson at last broke loose and came to Homestead, where his wounds were dressed. In the meantime the fight attracted a crowd, who pursued Caddy down the P.,V.&C. railroad toward town. By this time Gibson had arrests sworn out for both Dovey and Caddy, and that calling for Caddy was placed in Constable Jury's hands, who arrested Caddy and placed him in the lock-up to await a hearing on Monday evening before Squire Geltner (?). Dovey was also arrested and gave bail for a hearing at the same time. On Thursday Caddy also furnished bail for his appearance. It is said Superintendent Potter became bailsman for Dovey.

———❖———

JUNE 20, 1892 —Reprinted from
The Pittsburgh Post.

HOMESTEAD WORKMEN FIRM.

They Will Unitedly Refuse to Sign the Reduced Scale of the Company.

GREAT MASS MEETING YESTERDAY.

Addresses of the Leaders Counsel Firmness and Moderation.

McKINLEY HIGH TARIFF DENOUNCED.

A mass meeting of the delegates to the seventeenth annual convention of the Amalgamated Association and the employees in Carnegie's steel mill at Homestead was held in that place yesterday morning in the Eighth avenue opera house, with about 3,000 men present. The meeting had been called for 10 o'clock, but long before that time the men began to form in groups earnestly discussing that one great theme that was nearest their hearts. At 9:30 the large opera house was comfortably filled, and at 10 o'clock the house was packed from pit to gallery, and the aisles and hall were jammed with those who were glad to get standing room. The mass meeting was the all absorbing attraction, and the churches were but poorly attended.

The Excelsior band of Homestead was on the stage and played many national airs as the great concourse of men were gathering.

. . .

Burgess John McLuckie of Homestead . . . [asked]: "What brings you here this morning? Is it idle curiosity, or is it a real tangible reason beyond? The cause of this wage trouble is not generally understood. We were persuaded to vote the Republican ticket four years ago that our wages might be maintained. As soon as the election was over a widespread feeling on the part of manufacturers toward the reduction of wages was exhibited over the land. As soon as the McKinley bill was passed the article in the production of which we work was the only article that suffered a reduction. It is Sunday morning and we ought to be in church, but we are here to-day to see if we are going to live as white men in the future. The constitution of this country guarantees all men the right to live, but in order to live we must keep up a continuing struggle. This is the effect of the legislation and nothing else. The McKinley bill reduced the tariff on the four-inch billett, and the reduction of our wages is the result. You men who voted the Republican ticket voted for high tariff and you get high fences, Pinkerton detectives, thugs, and militia."

Mr. B. Maverek, an official in the Pittsburgh Slavanic [sic] order, was introduced. He addressed the Poles, Hungarians and Slavs present in their own languages, explaining the object of the meeting and allaying that excitement and misapprehension under which they were laboring. Mr. Maverek's talk lasted about 10 minutes.

———❖———

JUNE 21, 1892 —*Reprinted from*
The Pittsburgh Post.

CARNEGIE MAKES A POINT.

————

Manager Potter Signs the Homestead Mechanics.

————

BIG SURPRISE FOR THE AMALGAMATED.

————

The Committee's Action May Not Be Supported.

————

STEEL SCALE BEFORE THE CONVENTION.

————

"Mills from the River," by Orson Lowell,
published in **McClure's Magazine,**
June 1894.

The Carnegie Steel Company gained a victory yesterday at Homestead, which gives them a decided advantage in the coming contest with the Amalgamated Association. With a stroke of his pen Manager Potter signed 1,000 men, enlisting their services for a period of three years, strike or no strike. These men are termed mechanics and although they do not belong to the Amalgamated Association, the news that they had sworn fealty to the Carnegies carried alarm into the ranks of members of the Amalgamated Association here.

The men who placed their signatures to the wage agreement through committees appointed from the different department comprise all the engineers, machinists, blacksmiths, boilermakers, pipe-fitters and their several helpers; pattern makers, carpenters, tinners, painters, riggers, coppersmiths and foundrymen, with assistants, numbering in all, when all departments are full, nearly 1,000 men.

The agreement signed by them dates from yesterday, and declares that they shall work under the same condition and at the same wages as paid at present for a period of three years.

This means that should every man of the Amalgamated Association strike on July 1 the ponderous machinery and purely mechanical work of the great mills will go on, as every mechanic has sworn to stick to his post.

———❖———

(above) In the Carrie Blast Furnace, incorporated into the Homestead Works in 1898, the molten iron reached temperatures of 2500 degrees Fahrenheit. The workers tapping the furnace were engulfed by the heat.

(left) A membership card for Acme Lodge, one of eight AAISW lodges in Homestead.

From U.S. House of Representatives Report No. 2447, July 12, 1892, in H.C. Frick testimony.

June 22, 1892

Mr. Wm. Weihe, Pres't,
    Amalgamated Association of I. & S.W.,
        Pittsburg, Pa.

Dear Sir:—
    Our Superintendent at Homestead, Mr. Potter, advises that a Committee from your Association waited on him last night and asked for a conference tomorrow at 10 o'clock, and that if satisfactory to us to advise you to-day. We beg to say that we will be glad to meet you and a committee with full power to act for those of our Homestead employes who are members of your association tomorrow at this office at 10 o'clock.

                Yours very truly,
                    H.C. Frick,
                    Chairman.

JUNE 24, 1892 —*Reprinted from* **The Pittsburgh Post.**

AMALGAMATED SUSTAINED.

The Slavs met Tuesday night and effected a temporary organization, which will soon be made permanent by the forming of a large lodge of laborers of that nationality.

It was moved that all wage workers at Homestead steel works abide by the decision of the Amalgamated convention in regard to their scale, and that they stand and fall with the association. This motion prevailed amid intense enthusiasm.

Three delegates were appointed on the conference committee which meets with the Carnegie company this morning. On motion all tonnage men retired from the room, and then behind closed doors and under no influence the men ratified the night's proceedings.

The mechanics denounced the signing of Potter's scale and asked that the signees appear before them and tell them why they did it.

The Amalgamated convention was called to order at the usual hour yesterday morning, but no business was transacted and an adjournment was again taken in order to allow the wage committee to continue their work in getting up their report. The Homestead scale is not yet completed, but it is said the details will be arranged in time for the proposed conference with the Carnegie officials to-day. Some concessions it is said will then be made on both sides. It is pretty well settled that this morning a conference will be held between General Manager Potter of the Carnegie steel works and the steel conference committee, during which it is expected that definite action will be taken on the Homestead scale.

———❖———

JUNE 24, 1892 —*Excerpted from*
The Pittsburgh Post.

NO COMPROMISE IN SIGHT

———

Threatened the Hun.

During the evening M.P. Maverek, the Hungarian, who had addressed the Slavs on Sunday Morning at the mass meeting and also on Tuesday evening at their temporary organization, and who is charged with having sold out his knowledge to Superintendent Potter for a raise in his wages from $1.75 a day to $2.50, stepped into the hall and said that he wanted to go to the platform and set himself at rights with the men. He told a Post reporter that he was innocent of the charges of duplicity and that he had not sold himself to Potter, nor had he revealed anything of their proceeding to that gentleman. When the men became aware of Maverek's presence great excitement prevailed. That worthy, [finding] that he would have no chance to make any explanation, started to leave the hall. Just as he got to the door a burly mechanic, Rotrough by name, stopped him, saying, "What are you doing here?

You're the fellow who turned spy on the Slavs and gave everything away to Potter." The Hungarian, now white with terror as he was jostled about by a rapidly increasing crowd, muttered that he had an explanation to offer; that if he had done what was said of him, he would want to be killed. "You won't want long, " was meaningly told him by a person in the crowd, "You are just the kind of fellow that will be killed. You'd do well to watch yourself."

At this point cries of "Throw him into the street" were heard, and it looked like these suggestions would be put into practice when a policeman stepped into the crowd and dispersed it. He had little difficulty in doing this, however, as the Amalgamated men were not going to suffer any row to spoil the pleasure of the evening.

———❖———

At this stage the prospect for a satisfactory readjustment of the Homestead steel scale is in many respects reassuring and confirms the predictions given in these columns in former issues. The speedy settlement of the iron scale during the week is to be regarded as a favorable indication of what may be accomplished with the steel scale. At the very first conference held, on Thursday, between the Amalgamated Association committees and representatives of the steel manufacturers, the first figures presented as a scale basis were on the part of the firm $22.00 per ton for four inch billets and on the part of the steelworkers, $25.00. After strongly arguing their claims, pro and con, each side conceeded [sic] something and upon adjournment, the difference between them was only one dollar. It may take many conferences and some time to come to a final agreement, but so far, a disposition has been manifested to reach an acceptable conclusion, which certainly augurs well.

———❖———

(facing page) "Main Street in Hungarian Colony," from Frank Leslie's Illustrated Weekly, *July 14, 1892. Immigrants from the Austro-Hungarian Empire were generally referred to as "Huns" and "Slavs," but most were ethnic Slovaks, not Hungarians.*

VERY QUIET AT HOMESTEAD.

———

Tonnage Men Preserving Discreet Silence.

———

LEADERS OPPOSE ANY MASS MEETING

———

Hardly Possible for a Strike to Be Averted

———

BOTH SIDES PREPARE FOR TROUBLE

Anti-Scab Tactics.

A Post reporter overheard a group of tonnage men discussing plans of opposition should non-union men be run into the works. One plan was the use of balloons, by means of which bombs could be dropped right into the mill. But this was only wild scheming, yet it goes to show the feeling of the men in regard to this possible exigency. They say the mill shall never be run by non-union labor, and one man declared: "My job means my life, and any fellow that takes my job tries to take my life and then his won't be safe." The Carnegie company have, in addition to their high fences and water plugs, watch towers and electric lights, and have arranged everything so that the mill and its grounds present much the appearance of a fort or stockade.

No railroad trains will stop at the mills after June 30. The long new platform, recently laid by the P., McK. & Y. R. R. will not be used for landing non-union men. The point has been gained by the Amalgamated Association. No trains will stop at any other than the regular stations, and the men claim that this will give them the chance of conferring with any non-union men that the firm may try to put in the mill. They are confident, if they have this opportunity, that no men will enter the mills, as the arguments that would be used on such an occasion would doubtless be very convincing to newcomers.

The leaders state that no rioting will be countenanced and that every measure and discipline will be used to insure its utter suppression.

———

Very Quiet at Homestead.

Last night 600 Slavs banded themselves together in a labor organization of that nationality, which is said to be a lodge of the Amalgamated Association. Maverek, the Hungarian, who has been charged with playing the spy among the Slavs has in a large measure exonerated himself. He stated Thursday night, at the reception of the delegates, that he was approached by the managers of several departments and charged, and even threatened, to take this course. He was taken into Mr. Potter's office and still further worked on. He took a better job at increased pay, but he did not sell his soul to the firm. The men generally believe him to be telling the truth.

———❖———

JUNE 28, 1892 —*Reprinted from* The Pittsburgh Post.

LOOKS LIKE WAR

————

The Homestead Mill Owners Are Making Ready Their Defenses

————

DETECTIVES SAID TO BE COMING

————

Two Suspected Pinkertons Run Out of Town Yesterday.

. . .

The preparations for an actual siege at the Homestead steel and iron mills exceed anything of the kind ever heard of before. The company, judging from all outward appearances at least, are getting ready to withstand violent attacks. This would seem to argue that, in spite of declarations a couple of weeks ago that the firm was not contemplating the employment of non-union labor, this was the very thing they were going to do, and in anticipation of violence on the part of the men in that event, were preparing to carry the day their own way in spite of opposition. The great fences that surround the mill are stronger than any fences one ordinarily sees. They are in reality massive board walls, and strung along the top are two wicked rows of jagged barbed wire. At each of the gates immense fire plugs have also been placed with an enormous water pressure in each. In all of the dark places and exposed portions of the mills are lights of 2,000 candle power each, which have been placed, so that when the strike commences, in the words of the Bible, "there will be no night there."

THE GREAT LIGHTS

These search lights are nothing more than gigantic magic lanterns. The bridge over the railroad tracks which connects the old city farm grounds, recently purchased by the firm, and the mill enclosure has [sic] not been considered conspicuous enough by the firm, hence they have placed in it an arc light which will reveal the presence of anyone who would try to cross it at night. Port holes with ugly mouths grimly look out upon the peaceful valley from the mill, fort, barricade, stockade or whatever the Carnegie plant at Homestead could be called to-day, and silently bear witnesss that they are there, not for the peaceful purposes of steel manufacture, but for struggle and fight.

This open preparation for attack has a demoralizing influence upon the men, who have been preparing to conduct a strike, if there be any, peaceably and without violence. They do not relish the red rag of defiance flung right into their faces, and hence the talk of opposition grows. The leaders are not giving away the plans of the tonnage men, and it is more than probable that few besides the leaders know anything about the course that will be pursued in event of a strike. Burgess McLuckie of Homestead is an Amalgamated man himself, and his influence in preserving the peace will be very great among his brother workmen. But the coolest of the men do not deny that there will be grave trouble if the firm attempts to introduce into the mills non-union or scab labor. . . .

STRANGERS RUN OUT

Yesterday a little incident occurred at Homestead that created a great deal of excitement. Strangers had been noticed lounging about, and it was reported that they were Pinkerton men, also that several of the Coal and Iron police who had patroled the coke regions during the late strike, were in the city. A committee of men was at once appointed to look up the suspected strangers. The two men were found in a saloon. The workmen walked up to them and demanded their business.

"Oh, we are only here looking around. We have a little private business to attend to," said one of the men.

"You are only looking around, are you?" queried Carney, one of the committee. "Well, the best thing you can do is to get out and do your looking around from some other seaport."

The strangers protested that they were only looking into their private affairs.

"I know you," broke in another member of the committee, "I saw you both several years ago. I worked at Joliet then, and you watched the mills there during the strike. Get out."

The fellows were given half an hour to leave town but did not consume one-half that time in reaching a train. They were followed to the train by a crowd of hooting men and boys. Word was received last night that at least 300 Pinkertons and members of the Coal and Iron police will be here Thursday next. It is believed that if trouble ensues here, the company will order down all the men who served as policemen during the coke strike, and that a few Pinkertons will be added. . . .

A man was punched in the head Saturday night in a Homestead barroom for saying: "I'm not going to depend on the Amalgamated Association for my living." This illustrates how high the feeling runs there at present. A mechanic, and a man who usually knows what he talks about, was overheard saying that the Homestead firm was going to shut down their mill for repairs for two weeks from July 1, and are hence not in any hurry to sign with the men. Many tonnage men are not fearing a strike, but are counting on the outside interference of Pittsburgh businessmen and capitalists accomplishing for them a compromise.

HOW THE FOREIGNERS STAND

The workmen yesterday received more encouragement from the laborers. A committee of foreigners waited on the several lodges of the Amalgamated Association and informed the officers that they had decided to stick by the organization to the last man. Several hundred of these foreign workmen, comprising the better element of Slavs and Hungarians, met last night and voted unanimously to strike when ordered, and to remain out until they were again permitted to go to work by the Amalgamated Association. The spokesman of the party made a clear statement of what his countrymen expected to do should trouble arise. He said they all realize they must have a head. They were too radical, and as a result suffered the worst. He asked that a representative American workman be appointed to take charge. Their request was complied with, and the laborers were told off into six squads. Over each squad there was placed a cool-headed, conservative American, whose actions will be guided by orders from higher officials, and whose orders the foreigners have sworn to obey.

JUNE 29, 1892 —*Excerpted from* The Pittsburgh Post.

Ready for Battle

_____

The Warlike Preparations at Homestead Are Going on Steadily.

_____

ALLEGED SCABS ARE BOUNCED.

_____

A Mill Shut Down, but the Men Not Discharged.

_____

Scale Signed at M'Keesport.

_____

A stranger came to Homestead yesterday and one of the first men he spoke to was a tonnage man. He asked where he could get good lodging and board, as he was going to work in the mills. The Amalgamated man was about to direct him to a place when he asked the unknown when he was going to work. The man replied that the firm had engaged him to start to work on July 1, promising him a steady job. At this juncture several other iron and steel workers happened along and the crowd took the man in charge and rushed him toward the river, telling him they had a good place for customers like him. They hustled him into the ferry, when the Pittsburgh side was reached he was assisted, more dead than alive from terror, out of the skiff and warned to keep away.

A two-page spread in Frank Leslie's Illustrated Weekly, *July 14, 1892, included these two vignettes, "Under suspicion," expressing the townspeople's fear of spies, and "Sample of the fence around the works." The gun openings revealed the company's willingness to resort to violence.*

PRE-LOCKOUT POLITICS IN HOMESTEAD

by Irwin Marcus

*T*he power of the workers at Homestead rested not only on their skills and the strength of the Amalgamated Association of Iron and Steel Workers, but also on their involvement in the community. Churches and fraternal associations linked town residents and skilled workers as they worshiped together and organized social affairs including picnics, parades and singing societies. Iron and steelworkers and their sympathizers also played active roles in politics.

Two issues had highlighted the election of 1890 in the Pittsburgh area. In the congressional races the tariff issue dominated the debate as the Republican party supported a protective tariff as beneficial to the whole country. Democrats enlisted opponents of high tariffs in their ranks by depicting high tariffs as helpful to special interests. Workers and their supporters called on manufacturers to share the bounty they were reaping from the tariff and sought to persuade advocates of protectionism to link the tariff to unionism. In a very lively campaign, the Democrats amassed large gains in the congressional election and held a substantial majority in the U.S. House of Representatives. In the state races, especially the contest for governor, the Democrats hammered on the issues of honesty in government and the maintenance of popular government. Robert E. Pattison, the Democratic nominee for governor, toured the state and spoke in behalf of clean government and against the spoilsmen. The Republicans interjected the tariff issue toward the end of the campaign, but Pattison won a narrow victory aided by Democratic majorities in most large cities. He also carried the town of Homestead by a narrow margin. The Pittsburg Press responded to Pattison's statewide victory with glee and offered an overstated assessment of its significance as "a moral revolution in Pennsylvania politics of transcendent importance." ❖

THE WAGE QUESTION IN POLITICS.

REDUCTION OF 20 To 60%

B. Harrison—"For Heaven's Sake Don't Quarrel Now!"

(left) **The Pittsburgh Post,** *June 28, 1892.* **A dwarfish Benjamin Harrison tries to avert a conflict between labor and capital which might ruin his chances for renomination to the presidency.**

Excerpted from U.S. Senate Report No.1280, testimony given November 24, 1892, by William T. Roberts, steel worker.

ROBERTS TESTIMONY

Q. State your name, age, residence, and occupation. —**A.** William T. Roberts; age, 36; residence, Pittsburg; occupation, heater.

Q. Where are you employed? —**A.** Prior to the 1st of July in the employ of the Carnegie Company, at Homestead.

Q. How long have you been in the employ of that company? —**A.** Very nearly two years.

Q. What rate of wages were you receiving? —**A.** I was paid by the ton, receiving about the third rate of wages in the department I was working in, averaging about $3.50 to $4.00 per day.

Q. Were your wages affected by the strike that occurred in July last? —**A.** Yes, sir; in the first place they were.

Q. In what way? —**A.** About the middle of last February, I think it was—I didn't pay any particular attention to the time, because I didn't think anything further than a mere getting together of the men and the firm would result—we were sent for to the office and were told we were expected to meet the firm, and make some arrangements for preparing a scale to govern us in the future. I myself was the first on the scale to be reduced. And the second proposition they had made to us—you understand the high-priced men on the mill were left off altogether. They were going to deal with him by giving him a salary, and making his position better than before. Then the heater was marked on our scale, $3.04 a hundred tons. I was marked $3.11, and was reduced on their proposition to $2.13, and when we commenced to talk the matter over I says "Why have these reductions been made in this particular? Why have I been reduced to $2.13?" After talking the matter over, Mr. Potter allowed they may not have known as much about my work as they should have, but to let it go, that they would fix it all right; but he says to me "It is no use of you people coming back here unless you come back here with some authority to act. We understand that your association is liable to throw off anything that you may do, and unless you can come back here prepared or with the authority to make reductions where reductions are necessary, it is no use of your coming back." I went down again to the men, and told them I thought the best thing they could do was to give me and the committee power to go and do the best thing we could; that I thought the company was preparing for a strike, and to run without us, and unless they gave me power to make arrangements I thought there was going to be trouble. The men saw the force of it, because prior to that day they had been building high fences and grating up our sewers, and we have very large sewers, and building this high fence around there, and everybody commenced to look suspicious. They had electric search lights on the hill, and one down by the river. Finally the men agreed to let me go down and do the best I could. I notified the superintendent of our department that I had that power, that I had the privilege of coming up there and making any arrangement that would be satisfactory to them. Moreover I told them, "You can tell your people we are willing to make any reductions where they can show any reductions are necessary. We want to settle it without trouble; don't want a strike."

The superintendent of our mill seemed satisfied with that, and he told me that he immediately reported to the people in the office. After that we never heard anything more from the firm until the 29th, I think it was the 29th of May, when we were sent for to the office to talk the matter over, and were presented with Mr. Frick's ultimatum. I don't know just how it was worded, but I think in the report of the Congressional committee there is one of them in there. There was also a letter from Mr. Frick, stating his object in sending it, and he stated that "Unless this scale is accepted by the 24th of June we intend to deal with our men individually." I turned back to the office, and I says to Mr. Potter, "Do you think this is fair; do you think this is giving us a chance to talk the matter over?" I says, "You people, when I was here last, told me if I would come back with power to make a scale, that you were willing to enter into negotiations and try and arrange the thing in an amicable manner." "I can not help it," says he. "It is Mr. Frick's ultimatum." I says, "John, I don't think that is a square deal, in getting our men to give me the privilege of making an arrangement with your people." That simply cut off all conference with the Carnegie firm. We had no more chances to confer with them. I left the mill on the 30th of May. I worked on the 30th. I went to the convention after that, and I left my address so the superintendent of our department (who claimed that he was satisfied in his mind that we would have a conference with the firm) would telephone me to come up at a moment's notice. The notice never came, and on the 23rd we sought a conference with the firm, which lasted but a few minutes. We didn't do much with them.

Q. When did you go out of the mill on strike? —**A.** Our scale expired on the last day of June, and they themselves shut the mill down on the 29th, I think. ❖

(facing page) Robert E. Pattison, Governor of Pennsylvania, 1891-1895, as depicted in **Harper's Weekly,** *July 23, 1892.*

JULY 1, 1892 —Excerpted from an article, "Resting on Arms," *in* The Pittsburgh Post.

The Situation of the Combatants at Homestead Last Night.

————

WORKMEN HAVE THEIR PLANS LAID.

————

Evidently a Finish Fight Against Organized Labor.

————

MORE FIRMS SIGN THE SCALE.

————

. . . A great mass meeting was held in the Fifth avenue opera house yesterday morning at ten o'clock. Every amalgamated man in Homestead was present, and all mechanics and day laborers who could get off were also on hand. The great hall was jammed full. Edward Richards was chosen chairman and W. L. McConegley secretary. The object of the meeting was to discuss the present state of affairs, the outlook and general plans of action. The utmost enthusiasm, good feeling and unanimity prevailed. As soon as the meeting was called to order by Chairman Richards some of the men suggested that it be conducted behind closed doors, and that all visitors and reporters be requested to retire. This stand was opposed by others, who held that the meeting should be open to the world, as they had nothing to conceal, and wanted the true state of affairs made known. On the motion it was decided that the meeting be made public.

APPEAL TO THE PRESS.

The report from the executive committee was then offered. Before reading it the chairman asked the members of the press present to give a fair and impartial account of the proceedings of the meeting and of the situation in Homestead. He said some of the newspaper articles had been one-sided and misleading. He stated that the articles had not always appeared in certain of the papers as they had been written. The report of the executive committee, which met in the Hotel Anderson, Pittsburgh, on Wednesday last, was then read. The general situation had been thoroughly canvassed, and it was resolved to ask the mechanical department to come out with the Amalgamated and stand by them. It was recommended that joint committees from each of the eight lodges be appointed and instructed to wait upon the mechanics and ask them to come out with the Amalgamated on July 1.

The chairman spoke of the report that had been published some days ago to the effect that 700 or 800 of the mechanics and day workers had signed the scale offered them by the firm. He also stated that the report had been found to be untrue when it was hunted down. He said the author was discovered to be a young man acting in the capacity of government armor plate inspector. This statement was greeted with the greatest uproar. Shouts of derision and cries of "lynch him," "run him out of town," and "hang him," were heard in the confusion. The chairman soon restored order, however, and cooler heads counseled the men to let the fellow alone to the reflections of his own conscience.

ABOUT THE CONFERENCE.

The result of the conference committee with the firm, which had been held some days since, was presented. It said when the committee came to settle on the minimum scale price that only Messrs. Frick and Potter were present with them. The firm demanded a reduction from $25 to $22, and when the men refused this Frick and Potter withdrew to allow them to confer among themselves. When the committee had agreed to come down from their price only Mr. Potter returned to the room and that gentleman, hearing what their decision was, said Mr. Frick had decided to let the matter drop, but as they had made a concession of $1 he would see Mr. Frick again. On Mr. Potter's second appearance he told the men Mr. Frick had also conceded $1, but that the scale must terminate December 31, 1894, instead of June 30, 1895. The men did not agree, and then Mr. Potter withdrew his concession of $1, and the conference committee in turn withdrew their concession and left without any terms at all in common between them. The chairman said: "Were we right?" and the 3,000 men present with one voice responded, "Yes, yes." At the mention of Mr. Frick's name in the report yells of disapproval, hisses and groans went up.

The following resolution was presented: "Whereas, So many members of the Amalgamated Association have been in the habit of leaving Homestead during former strikes, be it therefore

"Resolved, That should any member do this during the coming trouble without sufficient excuse for doing so, the Amalgamated Association consider him no longer one of them, and refuse to work with him."

HOW NEWS WILL BE GIVEN OUT.

This resolution was adopted unanimously without discussion. A motion that a press committee consisting of six men be appointed, and that all news should be given the press through this committee and that it should be authoritative and that no other members of the Amalgamated Association be permitted to give out information prevailed. Frank Verbullion,

Slav, then told his fellow countrymen what had been done at the meeting.

At this juncture in the proceedings a member stepped forward and stated he had received authoritative information that a body of 300 rollers, under the guise of being Pinkerton men, would leave Philadelphia en route for Homestead in the evening. The men were to be brought to Homestead, and under this disguise they hoped to gain entrance into the mill. When this announcement was made at first there was dead silence, but only for a moment, and then the uproar broke loose. One man yelled: "Let them come; we'll roll them," and various other threats were made. The meeting then adjourned, while the Amalgamated men went into secret executive session.

PLANS FOR A FIGHT.

It was learned that the plans for definite and decided action were taken in case a fight should be necessary. The leaders were chosen, and it was decided how they were to be handled. Every preparation for active warfare was made. During this secret meeting men arose and pledged their lives to the cause. One aged iron worker cautioned the men to be temperate, telling them that they would lose their power if they lay around the streets drinking and carousing. He ended with this touching appeal:

"I have but one life to lose, and that is already far spent, but I am willing to sacrifice it for my little home." Others spoke of how Frick was trying to break up the Amalgamated and to bring the men down to the straits in which the coke workers had been reduced, where it was necessary for father, mother and children to work in order to live even very poorly. They alleged that he had ground down his men in his various non-union mills and was now turning his attention to Homestead. Several of the leaders who are non-drinkers spoke and appealed to the men to be sober and quiet.

———❖———

JULY 1, 1892 —Excerpted from The Pittsburg Times.

SITUATION AT HOMESTEAD.

———

The Men Meet and Are Determined to Stand by Their Demands—The Mills Now Practically Deserted.

———

The strike or lock-out was finally inaugurated on the part of the 4,000 Homestead mill workmen yesterday, who at 10 o'clock held a monster mass meeting in the Grand Opera House of that borough, and appointed committees to be in charge of the trouble. . . .

The mechanics and laborers who have been working were yesterday evening met at the mill gate by a delegation of the Amalgamated people, who in a formal speech, asked them to remain away from the mill after last night. The majority readily complied and returned to get their tools, but one, more venturesome, cried out: "What if we don't want to come out!"

"Come out anyway, or if you don't you'll have to be a rapid runner," was the reply of the crowd.

This settled the matter and the men quietly came out with their tools, and the mill was dark at 9 o'clock, save for the lanterns of the vigilant watchmen.

A gang of about 200 small boys, armed with tin whistles, marched up and down the street in the evening, bearing aloft a full dressed broomstick, with the placard "remains of McBroodie [mill police chief]." This style of warfare evidently did not please the crowd of millmen, one of whom snatched the effigy from the standard bearer, while the small army scattered in dismay and gave vent to their infantile derision by derisive shouts from the opposite side of the street.

———❖———

The mill shaped children's lives from the 1880s to the closing of the plant in 1986. Detail from stereograph taken in 1907.

EVENTS

JUNE 28—The company shuts down the armor plate and open hearth departments, locking out some 800 men.

JUNE 29 am—At a meeting in the Homestead opera house, 3,000 steelworkers unanimously support the negotiating committee's rejection of the company's final offer. An Advisory Committee is chosen (with members from all eight Amalgamated lodges) to supervise activities during the lockout/strike. The Committee sets up headquarters in the Bost Building at Heisel Street and Eighth Avenue.

JUNE 29 pm—The laborers walk out of the steelworks in support of locked-out workers. The company closes the entire Homestead Works —a day before the contract runs out and declares it will no longer recognize the union. Altogether, 3,800 men are locked out.

JUNE 30-JULY 5—The Advisory Committee organizes the workers into military-like units to guard the mill and keep watch for an infiltration of replacement workers or Pinkerton guards. The burgess closes the saloons, and the Advisory Committee cuts down the effigies of Frick and Potter that have been strung up around town.

The Modern Baron With Ancient Methods.

The World, July 1, 1892. Although it was Henry Clay Frick who ordered construction of the wood fence rumored to be electrified and defended with water jets and guns, this New York cartoonist held Carnegie responsible. Whereas the national press focused on Carnegie, the local press focused on Frick.

LOCKOUT

"The thunder of an awful silence pervades. . . ."

3

JUNE 30, 1892 —Excerpted from The Pittsburgh Post.

IT IS A LOCKOUT.

The Carnegie People Forestalled the Employes at Midnight.

Notices of Discharge Posted.

About 3,800 Men Are Thereby Thrown Out of Employment.

The News Quietly Received.

They Set About Making Plans For the Campaign.

At 12 o'clock last night every department of the immense Carnegie steel works at Homestead was shut down, throwing about 3,800 men out of employment. The men received notice of the shut-down quietly, as they had been fully prepared for it by the following notice posted up in many places throughout the great works:

"All employes of the several departments will report to the office on Saturday next, July 2, when they will receive their full pay."

This notice is simply a notice of discharge. It has been the custom of the Carnegies, and all other mills, to discharge their men on the night of the expiration of the yearly contract. The men had declared positively that they would strike at the date of the expiration of the yearly contract. This term of expiration was to occur either at 6 o'clock this morning, or at 6 o'clock this evening, just as the authorities decided. At midnight the firm cleverly forestalled the men, and flatly declared a shut-down. Instead of being a strike then at the great steel works, the action of the firm has made it a lock-out.

ALL ARE FULL OF ANXIETY.

The Situation at Homestead Causes Nervous Strain—More Preparations For Trouble.

As the time for the expiration of the scale at Homestead approaches the excitement quickens to a white heat. Many of the men are becoming very nervous under this trying ordeal. An undivided sentiment exists, now that the firm has unmistakably shown its hostile attitude and determination to attempt an extermination of the amalgamated, in favor of a strike that shall be a strike. All expectation of an amicable settlement seems to have vanished, and nothing is now thought of but preparation for the trial that seems bound to come.

There is quiet in Homestead, it is true, but it is like the quiet of a town under military surveillance. It is impossible for a stranger to set foot in the town without his presence being noted right away. And that newcomer who can give no satisfactory explanation had better not go to Homestead in these uncertain times. While the firm is making vast and complete preparations for defense, the tonnage men and their comrades are apparently doing nothing at all to indicate that they will be the aggressors.

(right and facing page) The front page of The World, *July 1, 1892, carried these sketches of the provocative fence topped with barbed wire that the company erected around the Homestead Works. The workers' response to "Frick's Fence" was predictably hostile.*

JULY 1, 1892 —Excerpted from **The Pittsburg Dispatch.**

JAMES McNEALLY

James McNeally, in the dim and misty past, posed as one of the blue-coated guardians of public peace and private property in Pittsburg. The company promised him a position. This is his story of what followed: He reported at the office and asked if there was any existing trouble, and they replied no. He then came down town, and being a stranger here, the Investigating Committee wanted to know of him and his business here, which he refused to satisfactorily answer. A crowd soon gathered around him and they proceeded to search him, and in his coat pocket was found a handy billy. He was asked if he had any more weapons about his person to which he answered, that it was none of their business.

An Invitation to Homestead.

They made a closer search and brought to light a big revolver and also a letter, a facsimile of which is given below. He was taken at once to the borough bastile and locked up and an information was made against him before Squire Kuhn for carrying concealed weapons. He was given a hearing Tuesday evening and admitted his guilt. Appended is a copy of the letter found in his pocket:

> CARNEGIE PHIPPS & Co., LIMITED,
> HOMESTEAD STEEL WORKS,
> J. A. POTTER, SUPERINTENDENT.
> MUNHALL P. O., JUNE 28

Mr. James McNeally, ex-Police Officer, Pittsburg, Pa.:

DEAR SIR —Please come up to my office tomorrow. Wish to see you. Yours truly,
J. A. Potter, Superintendent.

McNeally pleaded guilty. This morning Constable Stewart escorted him to Pittsburg jail. When the worthy constable saw that a crowd of more than a thousand men and boys were waiting at the station to greet his prisoner he wisely avoided a scene by walking his man to Howard station, two miles below here.

———❖———

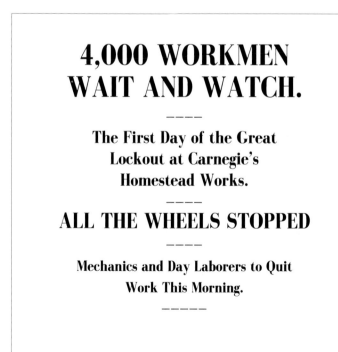

4,000 WORKMEN WAIT AND WATCH.

————

The First Day of the Great Lockout at Carnegie's Homestead Works.

————

ALL THE WHEELS STOPPED

————

Mechanics and Day Laborers to Quit Work This Morning.

—————

JULY 2, 1892 —Reprinted from
The Local News, *Homestead.*

The Fort that Frick Built

Twix Homestead and Munhall

If you'll believe my word at all

Where once a Steel Work's noisy roar

A thousand blessings did out-pour

There stands today with great pretense

Enclosed within a white-washed fence

O wondrous change of great import

The mill transformed into a fort.

————

The alliterative phrase, "Fort Frick" is a new and suggestive name for the steel works. The existing condition of things at the works is believed to have been brought about primarily through the direction of Mr. Frick, and the use of his name in the rechristening is perfectly natural. But the other part of the name is perhaps the more suggestive portion. The fence that has been thrown about the works is eleven feet high, and upon top of that, with six inches of space between are three lines of barbed wire firmly secured to boards every few feet which extend eighteen inches higher than the fence. This fence has been white washed, and is the most conspicuous thing to be seen at the works. In fact it is about the only thing to be seen inasmuch as it totally hides the view of the passer by. It is very formidable looking and suggests a fort indeed. "Fort Frick" will go down in history.

————❖————

JULY 2, 1892 —*Excerpted from*
The World, New York.

HARRISON STEPS IN.

————

This Carnegie Trouble Must Be "Patched Up at All Hazards."

————

THE IRON FIGHT ON AND THE REPUBLICANS RUB THEIR EYES.

————

The President's Patronage Awaits the Arbitrator.

————

The Men Gird Up Their Loins for Fight—A Member of the Carnegie Firm Kicks a Workman Severely—Pickets Four Miles Out from Homestead and a River Patrol on Constant Watch—A Demonstration Which Shows How Non-Union Men Will Be Met—The Whistle of Warning Is Heard for the First Time—It Is a False Alarm, but the Temper of the Men Is Shown—The Carnegies Claim They Have the Situation in Hand.

[SPECIAL TO THE WORLD.]

WASHINGTON, D. C., July 1. —Chris Magee, the Pennsylvania Republican boss, has had a number of conferences with the President this week. He has left for Pittsburg with an important commission from Mr. Harrison.

From excellent authority it was learned to-night that the President had become alarmed over the object lesson in Protection furnished at Mr. Carnegie's mills at Pittsburg and had directed Mr. Magee to carry the message to the mill-owners that the trouble must be patched up at all hazards.

Mr. Magee was told, according to this authority, that upon his success in effecting a peaceful settlement would depend the President's favor in the distribution of Federal patronage in Pennsylvania.

Republican Benjamin Harrison, president of the U.S. since 1889, faced another election in November 1892. He was an ardent supporter of the protective McKinley tariff.

HEADQUARTERS ADVISORY COMMITTEE,
A. A. OF I. & S. W.

HOMESTEAD LODGES,
3D FLOOR,
BOST BUILDING,
Cor. 8th Ave. & Heisel St.

HOMESTEAD, PA., July 2, 1892.

MR. E. F. WOOD,
        Assistant Supt. Homestead Steel Works:
        It has been noticed that the gas has been lighted in the Limestone Furnace No. 2, Open Hearth. It has caused considerable excitement among our men. There is a great number of men who, on account of its being pay day, cannot be held in check. If the gas is not turned off we cannot be responsible for any act that may be committed.

                Respectfully submitted,
                ADVISORY COMMITTEE.

(left) The Advisory Committee, suspecting that strikebreakers were working in the plant, sent this letter.

(facing page) **Frank Leslie's Illustrated Weekly,** *July 14, 1892. A vignette of the pleasure-tug, "Annie," patrolling the river for signs of Pinkertons or strikebreakers. The actual mill site is closer to the river level than the artist indicates.*

A NIGHT ALARM.

____

How the Locked-Out Men Are Prepared to Fight.

[SPECIAL TO THE WORLD.]

PITTSBURG, Pa., July 1. —Three sharp toots from the big new whistle of the town electric light works sounded the first alarm in the fight between Andrew Carnegie's big protected steel mill and the 4,500 workmen whom he has locked out. It was at 9:30 o'clock to-night.

A breathless man covered with perspiration rushed into the headquarters of the Amalgamated Association. He had rowed across the Monongahela River from Rankin, had run from the landing to the hall, and brought the report that the Baltimore and Ohio Railroad's night express, due in twenty minutes, was loaded with non-union men.

In two minutes the whistle signalled the fact to the men of Homestead, who rushed from every direction for the landing.

The steam-yacht Edna, manned by members of the Advisory Committee and commanded by the commodore in charge of the river patrol, returned the whistle signal to the town.

In less time than it takes to tell it almost scores of skiffs pushed out in the darkness and one thousand men landed on the opposite bank of the river, where they surrounded the station. There was no noise and no undue excitement. The men acted like trained soldiers.

Hugh O'Donnell, Chairman of the Advisory Committee of Fifty and the successful leader of the strike of 1889, sat by The World reporter in the stern of the Edna as she steamed across.

"DON'T LOOK FOR A BATTLE."

"Don't look for a battle," he said in answer to the reporter's question. "Every one of our men is whispering to himself the watchword 'hands down'." You will see no pistols or clubs or stones. We will simply surround these strangers, whether they be 'black sheep,' workmen or Pinkerton detectives and very gently but very firmly push them away from this locality. If they are content to move in the direction of Pittsburg, well and good. If they choose to resist they may be forced to the river bank. We have flat boats there, which such people may cast themselves adrift in, if they don't care to listen to reason."

The express arrived and stopped but the alarm turned out to be a false one.

The occurrence serves as an illustration of the way in which the trouble is being handled. The Organization of the men is perfect. The Advisory Committee appointed by the eight lodges of the association is in complete control of affairs. It meets morning and evening, and members of the committee are at Bost Hall, on Eighth avenue, every hour of the day and night.

As many of the 4,500 locked-out men as can be handled are on picket duty at every possible point of entrance to the works. They are divided into two squads, one for the day and the other for night duty, each under command of a captain and two lieutenants.

The river front for three miles is patrolled by the Edna and men in skiffs. Fifty men are encamped at Rankin, where the railroad bridge, which carries the P., Mck. and Y. tracks across the river into the works, has its terminus.

The country is thoroughly picketed and patrolled for four miles in every direction from the big steel mill. No stranger is allowed to remain in town until his credentials have been proved satisfactorily. Committees meet every regular passenger train upon its arrival. ❖

JULY 2, 1892 —Headline from The Pittsburg Dispatch.

AWAITING THE FOE

————

One Thousand Homestead Employes Prepare to Receive Non-Union Men.

————

GUARDING THE RAILROAD

————

Misled by a Rumor That 200 Workers Were to Arrive Last Night.

————

QUICK RESPONSE TO AN ALARM.

————

River Front, Stations and the Works Thoroughly Picketed.

————

GOOD PROSPECTS FOR FUTURE PEACE

Excerpted from U.S. House of Representatives Report No. 2447, testimony given July 14, 1892, by John Alfred Potter, General Superintendent, Homestead Works.

POTTER TESTIMONY

Q. Will you tell the committee when you first saw the disturbances? —**A.** Well, the first disturbance we had probably took place in the mills while the mills were running the last three or four turns. Each morning we woke up we would find our effigies hanging through the works.

Q. When you say "our" whom do you mean? —**A.** Mr. Frick and myself.

Q. They had you hung up in effigy there? —**A.** Yes, sir. I sent the officers and my private clerk to tear one down which I learned was Mr. Frick's effigy. The mills were still in operation, and as he tore it down and he walked into one department they turned the hose on him and hooted at him.

Q. They washed him down? —**A.** Yes, sir; washed him down. The morning of July 1 as I went to go to work I found the office gate was surrounded by probably 20 or 30 men. I stood and watched the proceedings and saw some of my foremen, none of my superintendents, but all of my foremen were stopped and intimidated or turned back with some little argument. I finally went there and had to walk around several men to get into the gate. ❖

As company chairman, Frick instituted regular Tuesday luncheon meetings to improve communications among his superintendents. John Potter may well have been present when this photo was taken, probably in the 1890s.

JULY 9, 1892 —Excerpted from the National Labor Tribune. *The story predates the dramatic events of July 6, but since the paper appeared on a weekly basis it was not published until after the confrontation.*

THE HOMESTEAD LOCKOUT

The first day of the Homestead lockout came a day before it was expected, a day before the expiration of the old agreement, hence was as much of a violation of the agreement as would have been a strike 24 hours before the close of the month of June. To what this shutdown was due we are not informed, but the inference is that the action of some of the men in hanging in effigy, within the mill, the leading active member of the Homestead company had something to do with it. It would be well if the men who are inclined to this sort of enthusiastic display would suppress themselves, and thus aid the Association to a sensible contest that would keep the sympathies of the public with the workmen. From the outstart the public has been on the side of the wage workers, and it is important that this condition should continue. But such will not be the case if the locked-out workmen do not do all in their power to conduct their contest in good temper. There is nothing to be gained by the "effigy" way of running business, and there is much to be lost by continuance of it. The lockout has not yet developed into an occasion for bitterness, and may not, except the company introduce a Pinkerton guard. Exhibitions of the "effigy" style probably do not hurt the feelings of Mr. Frick. More than likely he congratulates himself on such, as so many indications that the men are wasting their energies on nonsense that would better be devoted to deliberate holding out for their scale. If the firm should vary the contest by hanging in effigy some of the principal members of the A.A. of I. & S.W., the public would come to the conclusion at once that the firm had not the capacity to conduct a scale fight to a successful termination. But though the public does not expect that degree of quietness from several thousand men that is expected from the officials of an industrial corporation, yet it regards as weakness any noisy demonstrations, and it has confidence only in quiet conduct. In the Pittsburg district this is the case more especially, for the reason that the public has had experience of the results of turmoil in labor strikes. That public has paid some millions of dollars for property destroyed in the railroad strike of 1877, and it is not in the humor to commend anything that tends toward further destruction of property. The courts have decided that the county wherein occurs destruction of property by mob must pay the value of the property destroyed. The courts have not only decided this principle of law, but the people of Allegheny county have had to go down into their pockets year after year to pay such bills, and just so soon as they shall get an inkling of the probability of another bill of this sort against them, so sure will the parties at fault have opportunity not only to say farewell to public sympathy, but to get a full measure of public condemnation. These remarks apply as well to Mr. Frick's management as to that of the Homestead workmen, for he knows full well that the introduction of the Pinkerton guard would be the worst possible provocation to disorder.

———— ❖ ————

Meant for Mr. Frick.

The Pittsburg Dispatch, *July 4, 1892. The Advisory Committee removed effigies of plant officials in an effort to maintain calm.*

This view of Homestead from Myron R. Stowell's "Fort Frick" or the Siege of Homestead, evokes the stillness that hung over the smokeless town during the lockout.

JULY 2, 1892 —*Reprinted from* **The Local News,** *Homestead.*

—The thunder of an awful silence pervades in the vicinity of the steel works. In the region of Munhall, that community in which for three years the hum of the ponderous machinery has reverberated and almost caused the very earth to tremble, is now ominously silent; where the escape of steam from an hundred exhaust pipes has filled the air with a continuous blast; where the rolling mills kept up a mimic and perpetual cannonading, all is silent. Going upon the hill above Sir John Munhall's lovely residence, and looking down into the mill yard, a beautiful scene lies before us. Spread out on its broad expanse is the property owned by the Carnegie Steel Company, and for a greater part covered by their mammoth works. It lies there, a monster, sleeping. How different from its waking moment! Where there were ordinarily hundreds now there is not a single puff of smoke or steam.

———❖———

Reprinted from **The Inside History of the Carnegie Steel Company,** *Chapter 14, by James Howard Bridge, originally published by The Aldine Book Company, New York, 1903. Speech by Hugh O'Donnell, Chairman of the Advisory Committee, in response to the lockout.*

O'DONNELL ON THE HOMESTEAD BATTLE

"The Committee has, after mature deliberation, decided to organize their forces on a truly military basis. The force of four thousand men has been divided into three divisions or watches, each of these divisions is to devote eight hours of the twenty-four to the task of watching the plant. The Commanders of these divisions are to have as assistants eight captains composed of one trusted man from each of the eight local lodges. These Captains will report to the Division Commanders, who in turn will receive the orders from the Advisory Committee. During their hours of duty these Captains will have personal charge of the most important posts, i.e., the river front, the water gates and pumps, the railway stations, and the main gates of the plant. The girdle of pickets will file reports to the main headquarters every half hour, and so complete and detailed is the plan of campaign that in ten minutes' time the Committee can communicate with the men at any given point within a radius of five miles. In addition to all this, there will be held in reserve a force of 800 Slavs and Hungarians. The brigade of foreigners will be under the command of two Hungarians and two interpreters."

JULY 2, 1892 —Excerpted from an article, "Eighty Thousand Men Out,"
in **The New-York Times.**

THE BIG STRIKE AMONG THE IRONWORKERS IN FORCE.

—————

. . . It's evident that there is no "bluffing" at Homestead. The fight there is to be to the death between the Carnegie Steel Company, limited, with its $25,000,000. capital, and the workmen.

The Carnegie Steel Company gave formal notice to-day, through its Secretary, that the Homestead Mill is to be operated as a non-union plant and that no expense is to be spared to gain this point.

The Secretary [F. T. F. Lovejoy] said: "The mills at Homestead have been closed for repairs, and will remain closed for two or three weeks. About the 15th or 20th of July it will be published and posted that any of our old employes may return to work and must make application by a certain day as individuals. All who do not apply by the time stipulated will be considered not to desire to work, and their places will be filled by new men.

"It is in the work of giving new men the places of the old employes that will cause the real conflict. The strikers will offer no violence so long as the mills stand idle, but when new employes are brought to the mills the old men will seek to persuade their successors to leave, and, failing in this, will attempt to dislodge them.

"It will be easy to get new men into the mills, for one of the Vanderbilt lines passes directly through the property, and the men may easily be set down there.

"Only 280 of the 3,800 men employed in the Homestead Mills are affected by the new scales. The wages of only that number are changed, and the remainder are to receive the same wages as at present. But so strong is the loyalty of the men to their organization that nearly all of the employes have decided to fight for the 280.

"We made the scale to suit trade and mechanical conditions, and gave no thought to the political cause or effect nor to the tariff, and hereafter we will have nothing to do with trade organizations."

In addition to this the Carnegies put forth a statement in justification of its position. In this it is claimed that the reduction offered is due to trade conditions, and that with the improved facilities that have been supplied to the workmen they will be able to make as much money as under the old scale.

It is conceded that the proposed change in the time of the expiration of the scale from July 30 [sic, June 30] to Dec. 31 is not so favorable to the workmen, because they cannot fight so hard for what they consider their rights in Winter as in Summer; but it is argued that it is important to know what the cost of production will be before contracts are made, and that for this reason the change is made.

The statement of the Secretary has added to the bitterness at Homestead. That of the firm is regarded as a skillful juggling with figures. The workmen are convinced that an acceptance of the Carnegie scale means a reduction in wages of from 20 to 60 per cent, as well as the abolishment of their organization, and they are prepared to fight to the end.

There was no disturbance at Homestead to-day, save a dispute between the manager for the Carnegie Steel Company, Mr. Potter, and a workman. It ended by Mr. Potter kicking the workman and running for his life.

The workmen have the mill and the whole town in a state of siege. Committees have been appointed to patrol the river stations and all entrances to the town. Night and day their beats will be patrolled and official reports sent to the Advisory Committee.

The first reports from those in command of the different points were received this evening, and it was shown that not one outside workingman attempted to enter. A large number of skiffs have been secured to patrol the rivers on either side of Homestead, and the steamer Edna is at the command of the men.

The Chairman of the Strike Committee said to-night: "We now have our organization perfect. We will be in touch with every city and hamlet in the United States, and will be enabled to hear the moment a train of men for the mill leaves other cities. The Advisory Committee has visited all the saloons and requested that the sale of liquor be restricted and that mobs be not allowed to gather.

"The saloonkeepers have complied with our request, and if called upon to do so will close their places. One of the first acts done by our committee was the cutting down of all the effigies which for several days have graced the telegraph poles."

The only counter-move thus far made by the Carnegies has been to increase the force of watchmen in the mills. It is reported to-night that an attempt will be made before morning to land 300 mechanics in the mill by the river entrance in order to make necessary repairs. The strikers, to prevent this, have the river bank lined with 600 men, and any attempt of the mechanics to land will provoke an ugly fight.

———❖———

Excerpted from U.S. Senate Report No.1280, testimony given November 24, 1892, by William Weihe, puddler, President of the AAISW.

WEIHE TESTIMONY

Q. Are you connected with any labor associations or unions? —**A.** I have been president of the Amalgamated Association for nine years, and my term expired on the 1st of November, this year. To give you an idea, the object and motive of the association has been for years to get the cost of labor as nearly uniform as possible, where the work is similar. By having the various representatives from various iron and steel works together in one body you can get an expression of the price paid and everybody agree upon a price for each mill that comes as near as possible to the same cost, so as not to have any disadvantage, or give any manufacturer an advantage unless he has improved machinery. The association never objects to improvements. If there are improvements that do away with certain jobs they make no objection. They believe in the American idea that the genius of the country should not be retarded.

Q. How large a per cent of the men engaged in the Carnegie company works were affected by this proposed reduction? —**A.** In the four departments, as I have seen by the papers, somewhere between 325 and 330. I think that was about the amount they gave.

Q. And how large a number of men were employed in all departments? —**A.** In the neighborhood of 3,800.

Q. Then it affected less than 10 per cent of the entire number? —**A.** At that time.

Q. Was the action of the other men who were not affected due to an apprehension on their part that in time their wages would be reduced, or did they take that action out of sympathy with the men whose wages had been reduced? —**A.** All tonnage workers knew, if the departments it did affect would have consented to the reduction, that their wages after July 1 would have been in the same position.

Q. So that, as a matter of fact, the action taken by them was in the line of self-defense, rather than from sympathy for the men whose wages had been directly reduced? —**A.** That the company intended to reduce; yes, sir. ❖

JULY 3, 1892 —Excerpted from **The World,** *John McLuckie, steel worker and Burgess of Homestead, talking to a reporter.*

DO NOT PROPOSE TO BE BULLDOZED

"We do not propose that Andrew Carnegie's representatives shall bulldoze us. We have our homes in this town, we have our churches here, our societies and our cemeteries. We are bound to Homestead by all the ties that men hold dearest and most sacred. The Carnegie Company has imported men of all nationalities in places that are east of us and west of us and south of us. They never have imported a man into Homestead, and by ____ [sic] they never will. We shall not permit it.

"At the present time the men in the mill at Homestead are not receiving higher pay than prevails elsewhere. The wages of most of them are one third lower than at the mills of our competitors. The reduction of the wages proposed in the scale submitted by Mr. Frick means that the employees in the Homestead mills will receive on pay-day from 12 to 42 percent less than they have been receiving. The result of our acceptance of this scale would mean a cessation of public improvements in Homestead, a material reduction of the prosperity of the town, and in a great many cases individual hardship. It would be a blight upon Homestead.

WORKMEN ONLY ASK JUSTICE
"Our people here are hard-working, peaceable, quiet, progressive. There is not a better class of people in any town of this state. There has been but one arrest recorded in Homestead during the past month. We are asking nothing but our rights, and we will have them if it requires force to get them. . . .

"Andrew Carnegie may beat us in this struggle, but if he does he beats himself. These mills have large contracts for architectural ironwork to be used in the Worlds Fair buildings at Chicago. They also have contracts to furnish ten miles of elevated railway to be used in connec-

William Weihe, President of AAISW, from Harper's Weekly, *July 23, 1892. Arthur G. Burgoyne described him as "...six feet and a half of sound sense, /A brawny colossus quite free from pretense./With Capital's cohorts he copes without fear,/And they say, in his way, he is really sincere."*

(Bulldozed, continued)

tion with the Fair. Last Monday the Illinois Central Trades Assembly, which represents 60,000 workmen, passed resolutions that not a single beam of timber of non-union workmanship should enter these buildings.

TO BE ADDRESSED BY ADLAI STEVENSON

"Next Sunday Gen. Adlai E. Stevenson has been invited to speak to the members of Illinois Trades Assembly. He will have an audience of at least fifteen thousand people.

"The Worlds Fair Commissioners from Pennsylvania [include] Gov. Pattison,—[His] course in sending the militia to their armories during the great coke strike in the Frick mines makes us believe that he will be equally fair with our workmen in Homestead. We have a united people, and I think that we can keep those mills idle till Mr. Carnegie's representatives decide to put us to work again."

———❖———

From Henry Clay Frick's Letterpress Book, Clayton Corporation, Archives, Pittsburgh. A cable and a letter:

CODED CABLE

July 4, 1892

CARNEGIE, MORGAN, LONDON.

SMALL POND PONY PLUNGE REPAIRING POND PONY CHOKE WATCHMAN ARRIVE PLUNGE MORNING BOARD. EARLY.

LETTER

July 4, 1892

Robert A. Pinkerton, Esq.,
New York City,

My Dear Sir;

I am just in receipt of your favor of the 3rd. In reply would say, that we have all our arrangements perfected to receive your men at Ashtabula, and to conduct them to Bellevue Station, a few miles below this City on the Ohio River, where they will be transferred to two boats and two barges. This will likely be done tomorrow night at 11 oclock. The boats and barges are manned with reliable men, and will at once start for our Homestead works, and should arrive there about 3 oclock on the morning of the 6th. The boats are well provisioned, all the uniforms etc. that you have had shipped to the Union Supply Company, are on board the boat. There will also be on board the boats the Sheriff's Chief Deputy who will accompany and remain with your men.

We have taken all possible precaution to keep the arrangements quiet, but, of course, it is more than likely that we will not be successful in this.

Yours Very Truly,

Chairman.

IN MILITARY STYLE,

————

Complete System of Organization Adopted by Homestead Workers.

————

EVERY POINT GUARDED.

————

Told Off Into Three Divisions With a Commander Over Each.

————

A SIGNAL STATION ARRANGED.

————

Official Denial That Any Furnaces Had Been Lighted.

————

POTTER LEAVES FOR A PLEASURE TRIP

————

The Pittsburg Dispatch, *July 4, 1892,*
"Discussing the Situation on Sunday."
The Advisory Committee discouraged
gatherings to discuss contract negotia-
tions for fear that they would end in
angry demonstrations.

The people of Homestead spent a very wet Sunday yesterday. It was none of your new fangled poetic summer showers, but a genuine old-fashioned drizzle, which transformed the dust-carpeted streets into rivers of sticky, yellow mud. It flooded the camps of the men detailed to watch the silent works and made life a moist and heavy burden for the little gang of humanity within the white-washed confines of the steel works. The weather forced the populace to remain indoors, and it proved to be a damp, dull and unprofitable day.

The deep-chested champions of organized labor rested in their tents, smoked countless tobies and talked over the situation. To them the one redeeming feature of the day was the morning meeting of their recognized leaders, the Advisory Committee. The 50 members of the committee gathered in conclave shortly after 9 o'clock in the morning, and it was long after noon when they opened the door of their council chamber.

Established a Signal Station.

The most important task accomplished by the committee yesterday was the erection and furnishing of a signal station.

This is located on the roof of the headquarters. The tower commands a full and unobstructed view of Fort Frick and the surrounding country. With the aid of a fieldglass the man in the signal tower can gaze over the ramparts and take a leisurely survey of what is going on in the enemy's camp. During the day he can signal by a system of variously colored flags to the pickets stationed on the hills across the river, at night a strong flash light will be used. The river patrol will send up rockets when necessary and will also make a liberal use of colored fire. That hoarse-voiced steam whistle at the electric light works will be reserved for special occasions, but in great emergencies it will sound the general alarm.

Mr. V. F. Wood, the assistant superintendent of the Homestead works, was located yesterday. He said: "There is no truth in the report that the fires have been lighted in the limestone furnaces in the open hearth department. Saturday morning the regulations which control the pressure of natural gas in the furnace pipes failed to work properly and I ordered the escaping gas to be ignited in order to avoid accident.

————◆————

DE-FENCE AT HOMESTEAD.

(above) The Advisory Committee used the third floor of the Bost Building on the edge of the mill site as its headquarters during the strike. A telegraph office set up on the first floor became a center for the press. This appeared in Frank Leslie's Illustrated Weekly, July 28, 1892.

(left) This cartoon from The World, July 4, 1892, expresses this newspaper's view that the McKinley tariff was at the root of the Homestead conflict.

JULY 5, 1892 —Reprinted from **The Pittsburg Dispatch.**

STARTLED BY RUMORS

————

Homestead Workers Excited by a False Alarm of Invasion.

————

AN OLD LADY DOES GUARD DUTY

————

The Fourth of July Spent in a Pleasant, Patriotic Manner.

————

PONTOON BRIDGE ACROSS THE RIVER

————

Peace reigned at Homestead yesterday. There was but one little flurry this afternoon, but it did not last long and turned out a farce. The people have devoted themselves to the celebration of the day in picnics, excursions and shooting of fireworks. Last night the town was alive with rockets and Roman candles. The great works up the river were dark and silent, and the guards of the Amalgamated Association make their rounds and keep their watch [sic].

At about 3 o'clock yesterday afternoon two excited men ran to the headquarters of the workmen and said that 50 black sheep, with their trunks and bags on their backs, had entered the town and were coming up the avenue. Within 10 minutes 500 of the Association had gathered and had moved rapidly to the foreign settlement, where a line was formed. Every street about the location, where strangers were supposed to have entered houses, was guarded by a cordon of men. This line ran from City Farm lane along Third avenue to McClure street, and as soon as the district was surrounded the leaders made a thorough search of the houses. The truth was soon discovered. Ten Hungarians, who had decided to leave Homestead, had taken their baggage upon their backs and started from their boarding houses for the river. They had been accompanied to the McClure street ferry by a crowd of relatives and friends, and had crossed to the Baltimore and Ohio. It was this throng which the two runners had seen and which had caused the alarm.

A Very Determined Old Lady.

There were some odd incidents connected with the scare. As one of the leaders of the men was returning from the search he met, standing at the mouth of an alley, an old lady, whose hair is white and whose form is bent by the weight of gathered years. Her eye flashed as she straightened up and cried out: "The dirty blacksheep; did you get them? I have guarded this point well." With that she displayed a long and heavy black-jack, whose thong was passed about her wrist and grasped with a firm hand, which she could have wielded with telling effect. "I believe that the woman could win this strike for us," said one of the Association chiefs to-night.

The workmen expect soon an effort to throw non-union men into the mills under strong guard. One reason they expect this is that Manager Potter and many of the superintendents have gone away on the excuse that they are taking advantage of the shut-down to enjoy summer vacations. It is said that over 100 superintendents of the many departments have gone away within the last three or four days. Instead of seeking rest and peace in the seclusion of some sylvan hunting or fishing resort, they have, as a rule, gone to the various large cities of the country, where non-union workmen could be secured, if anywhere. It is noted that Manager Potter has gone to the company's iron mines near Duluth, where there are brawny men by the hundred.

(Startled, continued)

Pontoon Bridge Across the River.
Notwithstanding this scattering of the agents of the Carnegie Steel Company, the officers of the Amalgamated Association are not in the least dismayed. This fact is evidenced by their every word and act. The organization of the men is now almost perfect. The watch duty is divided into three turns and the entire town, the river front and the neighborhood of the mills are thoroughly patrolled. The headquarters on Eighth street are never closed, day or night, and there the watchmen regularly report. The system of signals to call men from their homes has been so well arranged that within ten minutes a pontoon of skiffs can be thrown across the Monongahela river, either to intercept and board a steam boat, or throw a large body of men to the other side of the river.

The good order preserved by the thousands of idle workmen here is a marvel to the stranger coming into the city. The score of saloons were all open to-day and the streets were crowded with people. Yet none of the saloons did a heavy business, and last night not a really drunken man was to be seen on the streets. Many of the men yesterday went to Pittsburg and there enjoyed the Fourth at Schenley Park or at ball games, many others attended the picnics of St. Mary's Catholic Church in a beautiful grove outside of the borough. When the celebrators returned they made no perceptible ripple on the surface of affairs. The three borough policemen had little or nothing to do. The citizens sit about their shops and discuss politics and labor questions, and complain of the sensational reports sent out about excitement and turbulence. Still they all admit that no man can tell when the crisis will come.

Developments Expected To-Day.
Yesterday Charles K. Bryce, who was fire marshall of the old Volunteer Fire Department, assumed charge as fire chief under the borough reorganization. He is a capable and prompt man, and the citizens have confidence in his ability to protect the town from any accidental conflagration or work of incendiarism. The pressure on the hydrants is so great

---

JULY 5, 1892 —Reprinted from **The Pittsburg Dispatch.**

CAN'T BUILD MEN-OF-WAR.

————

Naval Circles at Washington Worried by the Lockout at Homestead—Armor Plate Needed for the New Cruisers—Hoping for a Speedy Settlement.

————

Naval officials are much concerned over the labor trouble at the works of Carnegie, Phipps & Co., according to a dispatch from Washington, D.C. The firm are already much behind with their contract for supplying armor for the new vessels of the navy. Navy officials can see nothing but further delay as long as the strike continues. The situation is especially embarrassing at this time from the fact that nearly all the vessels are approaching a stage when work upon them will have to be stopped unless there are early deliveries of armor plate.

One of the inducements that led the department to place a contract with them was the expectation that their simple method of rolling plates would facilitate the delivery of material for the new ships, and although the delay has been longer than anticipated, the department was beginning to congratulate itself that the most trouble was over when the news came of the shutting down of the works.

Fortunately the strike will not seriously delay work on the battle ships unless it should continue for an extended period. A few weeks ago the department arranged an exchange of plates between the two armor contractors whereby the diagonal and some of the side armor plates of the battle ships which were most urgently needed will be made by the Bethlehem works in exchange for other class of armor that can be more easily made by Carnegie, Phipps & Co. The monitors and other armored vessels will therefore be more seriously affected by the strike than the battleships, which latter Secretary Tracy intends to push to completion even at the expense of other vessels.

Carnegie's contract with the department calls for 6,000 tons of armor, aggregating in cost nearly $4,000,000. Not one-tenth of the armor has yet been delivered. The company will not suffer any in the way of penalties for delay, as it has always been the practice of the department to waive any claim on this account where the delay is the result of labor troubles. The department officials cannot believe that the company will be long in reaching an agreement with their men for the reason that any prolonged cessation of work would not only mean an immediate loss, but might jeopardize their chance of getting an additional contract for from five to ten thousand tons of armor soon to be let by the Navy Department.

———❖———

---

that engines are not needed, and a stream can be thrown nearly 90 feet high or over 200 feet horizontally.

It is expected that there will be an important development to-day, but the leaders last night would not give a hint as to its nature.

Homesteaders were much relieved when they learned that the two barges being loaded with provision at Pittsburg were not intended for Homestead, but for the Beaver Dam.

———❖———

Excerpted from U.S. House of Representatives Report No. 2447, testimony given July 13, 1892, by Hugh O'Donnell, heater, Chairman of the Advisory Committee organized to oversee all matters at Homestead during the strike.

This portrait of Hugh O'Donnell, sketched "from life in his pleasant home," appeared in The World, *July 17, 1892. He had been a stringer on a newspaper and served as a spokesman to the press for the Amalgamated Association.*

O'DONNELL TESTIMONY

Q. I do not assume that you have had connection with any illegal transaction at all, but I want to say to you in advance that if any question which we propound to you should call for an answer which in your opinion would subject you to a prosecution or anything of that kind you need not answer it. I do not assume you have of course, but I just give you that precaution, which is but right. —**A.** I am not afraid of that at all.

Q. What position do you hold in connection with the skilled laborers formerly employed at Homestead in this State, if any? —**A.** I am simply a member of W.T. Rober[t]s Lodge, No. 125, Amalgamated Association of Iron and Steel Workers.

Q. Have you been a worker yourself in Homestead? —**A.** Yes, sir; for the last six years nearly.

Q. Have you recently held some other position in connection with the troubles which have occurred there? —**A.** Yes, sir, chairman of the advisory committee.

Q. Who compose that committee? —**A.** Members of the eight amalgamated lodges, representing so many departments.

Q. What work have you been performing? —**A.** Heater in the 119-inch plate mill.

Q. What is the extent of your experience in that kind of work in that mill? —**A.** In that mill I have been a millworker since I have been 17 years of age. I commenced in the sheet mill.

Q. How long have you been engaged in it? —**A.** I have been engaged in that mill for five and a half years, or about that time.

Q. In that mill up there? —**A.** Yes, sir; I commenced in that mill when the mill first started and grew up with it.

Q. After the shut down of the mills did the workmen who had been employed theretofore exercise any control over them in respect to keeping anybody out and looking after the property or any sort of supervision, and, if so, to what extent within your observation? —**A.** To this extent, that there was a mass meeting held, and there was quite a large number there. For instance there is a mechanical department there, that is, mechanics, blacksmiths, and others who are purely incidental to the production of a ton of steel, and we called a mass meeting.

Q. They were not affected by this? —**A.** No; they were not affected by the scale at all. We called a mass meeting and we considered the matter, and a resolution was passed there that they remain out with us until such time as we arrived at an agreement with the firm. Immediately after the mass meeting all the lodges—the meetings are secret to a certain extent, as all business transactions are mostly—the eight lodges had a joint meeting and they deliberated upon the crisis at hand and they there elected a certain number from each lodge—assuming they had the responsibility, each of the eight lodges was empowered to appoint five members of an advisory committee. That was a committee constituted an advisory committee. Then this action was taken. Members were appointed to this committee by each lodge. I was appointed by our president, with several others, and we organized ourselves into an advisory committee and I was elected chairman of that. This advisory committee got headquarters. We knew if we went on strike there we had quite a number of irresponsible people and there would be others coming from a distance, and we appointed subcommittees and we placed men around the works to guard them; not around the fence, but on the outside to keep outsiders, wholly irresponsible people, from doing any damage. ❖

EAST–EUROPEANS IN HOMESTEAD

by Paul Krause

The first immigrants from Eastern Europe began arriving in Homestead in 1881, not long after the steel works opened. During the next 11 years, many of these immigrants, along with their "Anglo" (British, Irish, and native-born American) colleagues, actively sought to reconcile the various tensions that might divide the working community of Homestead. Although the town was tainted by some of the Nativist bias that pervaded Western Pennsylvania, Homestead proved exceptionally hospitable to the East-European immigrants. The combined influence of unions, with their firm commitment to worker solidarity, along with local religious and political traditions, encouraged the general acceptance of Homestead's newest citizens as brothers in labor.

Curiously, however, scholars have ignored—or been blind to—the exceptional history of the East-Europeans in Homestead. Historians have on the whole applied the general rule of xenophobia to their understanding of the community; in so doing, they have misrepresented important facts of immigrant life and interethnic collaboration. Indeed, in the entire corpus of writing on Homestead, there are but few references to the nationality of the East-European workers. Following the practice codified by The Pittsburgh Survey, most historians have incorrectly used the term "Slavic" in describing Homestead's East-European residents.

There is, however, no single "Slavic" people, and no single "Slavic" language; in Homestead, prior to the Lockout of 1892, most East-European immigrants were, in fact, Slovaks—Slovaks who brought with them their own dreams for modest material comfort and independence that was summed up in the expression "za chlebom."

The full Slovak idiom, "ist' za chlebom," means to seek livelihood or employment, but literally, the expression translates as "going for bread." Za chlebom was essentially the slogan of Homestead Slovaks, and it encapsulated the simple material desires of these new "Americans." In the end—that is, in the Homestead Lockout of 1892—these desires were not so different from those of Anglo-American steelworkers who rallied with their Slovak brothers to protect a shared right to earn, as the constitution of the Amalgamated Association of Iron and Steel Workers explained, "a fair day's wages for a fair day's work."

To be sure, the East-European and Anglo steelworkers of Homestead came from different worlds. However, beginning with the town's first great labor dispute—the Homestead Strike of 1882—East-European and Anglo joined together to protect what they conceived of as their common rights in the mill and town. In this strike, interethnic solidarity was fostered by the leaders of the Irish National Land League, an organization dedicated to securing industrial independence for American workers and political independence for Ireland.

Among the members of the Homestead branch of the Land League were Joseph Rosinski and his brother Simon, two Polish-American steelworkers who later became small businessmen. It seems likely that Homestead's first Slovak immigrants—steelworkers Pavel Olsav and Juraj Terek—also belonged to the league and helped

A Slovak family in national dress around 1900.

their co-workers secure victory in the bitter 1882 strike.

Like thousands of other Slovaks who came to Pittsburgh beginning in the early 1880s, Olsav and Terek grew up in the region of the Hapsburg Empire where a variety of economic, political, and demographic forces had created rapidly growing numbers of landless agricultural laborers. In search of livelihood such workers moved from village to village, from the countryside to the urban centers of Hungary and, finally, from Hungary to North America. Zemplin Province, the birthplace of Olsav and Terek, was the principal source of Slovak emigration: between 1879 and 1901, almost 33,000 Zemplincania left the province. (This figure represented an astounding 77 percent of the province's population.) Zemplin was the home of many of the first Slovaks who came to Greater Pittsburgh. Like the 16 year-old Olsav, Terek left his home a young man, an experience common to most Slovak immigrants.

Olsav and Terek soon were joined in Homestead by two young women from their home region who, after crossing the Atlantic, found work as domestic servants in New York City until they made enough money to continue on to Homestead. One of the women, Susanna Tirpakova, married Olsav shortly after her arrival. The other, Anna Terekova—probably Terek's sister—married another immigrant, Jan Span, who was destined to play an important role in Homestead's Slovak community.

In the ten years following the arrival of Olsav and other pioneer Zemplincania, the East-European settlement in Homestead grew to over 1,000 persons. (A handful of Galician Jews, Magyars, and Italians also lived in the town prior to the Lockout of 1892.) Like Pavel and Susanna Olsav, most of the immigrants came from the provinces of north-central Hungary and were Roman Catholics. Some, however, were neither Slovak nor Roman Catholic, but like steelworker John Hornak, Carpatho-Rusyns who had been raised in the Byzantine Rite Catholic Church. Smaller numbers of Protestant Slovaks and Catholic Poles also settled in Homestead. Yet the East-European settlement constituted a unified community, as the overwhelming majority of its members worked and worshiped together, lived in the same neighborhood, and joined the same fraternal benefit societies.

In Homestead, the focal point of East-European religious life was St. Mary's Church, organized by Irish-American Catholics in 1881. From the beginning, though, St. Mary's was not a typical "Irish" parish. For East-European Homesteaders who came to the town in the 1880s attended mass, baptized their children, and prayed for their departed in the same sanctuary and with the same priest who ministered to the Irish Catholics of the town. Only after 1891, when the first Slovak parish in Greater Pittsburgh was organized in Braddock, did Homestead Slovaks venture beyond the town to fulfill their spiritual needs.

While East-European steelworkers and their families worshiped with the families of many leading Irish-American steelworkers, they looked to their own for leadership in religious life as well as in the world of work. Nearly every child born to East-European parents, for example, had East-European godparents; it was, in fact, Pavel and Susanna Olsav and Jan and Anna Span who were the Homestead Slovaks most often chosen as godparents and witnesses for East-European baptisms and weddings. Olsav and Span, along with Michael Masley and several other Slovaks who arrived in Homestead in 1883, also provided leadership in other areas of the religious and institutional life of the East-European community.

Span, the owner of a butcher shop by 1890, and Masley, a grocer, were key figures in the fraternal life of the East-Europeans. Together, they helped organize Homestead Lodge No. 26 of the First Catholic Slovak Union, the leading fraternal benefit society of Slovak immigrants. Masley served as the first president of the "First Hungarian Slovak Sick Benefit Society of Saint Michael the Archangel," named after the patron saint chosen by the Slovak parishes of Braddock and Homestead. The East-European steelworkers of Homestead chose Olsav as the unofficial leader of Lodge No. 26.

In the Homestead Steel Works, Olsav and virtually every other East-European immigrant was employed as a "laborer." It was these workers who were responsible chiefly for loading and stoking the furnaces and moving raw and finished materials between the mill and the yard. The friendly taverns in or near the East-European settlement in Homestead's second ward provided the men with their chief recreation after a hard day's work. The backroom of one such establishment, owned by Vincent Waasilefski, occasionally served as a meeting place for East-European women, too. But the handsome billiard tables in the front room at Waasilefski's were the big draw for the men; Anglo-Irish workers joined East-Europeans in this, the town's finest pool-hall.

In the Homestead Lockout of 1889, the entire East-European community mobilized itself to resist Carnegie's first great effort to eliminate unionism from the Homestead Steel Works. During the lockout, steelworker John Elko, a Slovak immigrant, was killed while on patrol for Pinkertons and "scabs."

Thousands of his Anglo co-workers turned out for his funeral, and their union—which won the lockout—pledged to support Elko's widow for as long as she remained in Homestead. Three years later, on July 6, 1892, when Carnegie Steel again moved against Homestead unionism, Pavel Olsav and other East-European Homesteaders ran to the front line of the town's defense to reaffirm a solidarity that Homesteaders took for granted.

In the battle with the Pinkertons, Joseph Sotak and Peter Fares, both Slovak immigrants, were shot and killed. Fares was carrying a loaf of bread to his position when he was caught in the gunfire. As he lay dying, he shook the loaf at the Pinkertons. "You cannot take this from our mouths," were his last words. ❖

Excerpted from U.S. Senate Report No. 1280, testimony given on November 24, 1892, by William Weihe, puddler, President of the AAISW.

WEIHE TESTIMONY

Q. Have you found that there are among the workmen in these large establishments a few restless, mischief making men who incite the other men to acts of violence, and urge them to make demands upon their employers that are unjustifiable? —**A.** Well, it may be that there are some few, but as a body they are not, especially where the men are organized. The teachings, laws, and rules of the organizations prevent anything of the kind. Questions of that kind are discussed in the lodge room, and it is generally the rule that the better class belongs to the organizations, and through them others that have different ideas, radical ideas, are held down.

Q. So far as your observation has extended, from which class, the native or the unnaturalized foreigners, do most of the troubles emanate? —**A.** Well, it depends upon what class of foreigners you would place them in. There is a certain class of foreigners not accustomed to the English language and who very often have their own ideas of what has taken place in the country they have come from, and would perhaps feel like doing in this country things that are not peculiarly American—such as the Hungarians, Slavs, and perhaps Polanders. There is a certain class of foreigners that come here and make good citizens, and I don't think there would be any difficulty with them. It is that element not accustomed to the English language, or to the laws, rules, and usages, that makes trouble.

Q. So that you would apprehend more trouble on the part of the nationalities you have suggested than from either natives or foreigners from other countries than those you have named? —**A.** That is, I believe the Americans, as a rule, are always willing to listen to reason, and to abide by anything that is fair and just. My experience has been that when men have been educated up in the various classes of their work they are willing to discuss matters of that kind with their employers, and if it can be shown through the fluctuations in the markets that certain things should be done, they are willing to abide by it, if they can be convinced in that way. With the foreigners, such as I have mentioned, it is very difficult to do that. ❖

The #2 Lodge of Ruthenians (Carpatho-Rusyns) at Homestead. Ethnic associations served a social function and provided insurance for their members.

YOUR SUMMER TRIP.

Do not fail to choose your hotel from the excellent list published to-day. You will find it a great assistance.

JULY 6, 1892 —Excerpted from **The Pittsburg Dispatch,** *detailing events of the previous day.*

WENT BY RAIL, BACK BY BOAT.

Protection Demanded From Sheriff McCleary by Manager H. C. Frick.

DEPUTIES AT HOMESTEAD

Are Met by the Workmen and Sent Home on the Steamer Edna.

The Sheriff Issues a Proclamation—Formal Dissolution of the Advisory Committee of Fifty—Borough Business Men Want an Injunction Upon the Officers—Governor Pattison Telegraphed for by the Workers—Secretary Lovejoy Says Repairs Will Be Commenced at the Works Within a Few Days—Hopes Still Entertained of a Peaceful Settlement.

The events at Homestead yesterday were the call of the firm to the Sheriff for protection, the effort, in a small way, of the Sheriff to respond, and the expulsion of the Sheriff's deputies from the borough by the iron-bound organization of the workmen.

Great anxiety awaits the developments of to-day. Both sides seem to feel that the crucial test has come. Sheriff McCleary does not yet say that he gives up the contest, but he does say that he cannot tell what action he will take. On his action to-day much depends. His action yesterday was all that he could take upon

Drawings from **The Pittsburg Dispatch,** *July 6, 1892.*

the moment, because he sent his entire office force, as far as it could be spared, to Homestead. After a lively experience, they were returned to the city. The Sheriff says he can find no extra deputies, but that he will do what he can to preserve the peace.

A Call Upon Sheriff McCleary.

The call from the firm, on which action was taken yesterday, is as follows:

Dear Sir—You will please take notice that at and in the vicinity of our works in Mifflin township, near Homestead, Allegheny county, Pa., and upon highways leading thereto from all directions, bodies of men have collected who assume to and do prevent access to our employes to and from our property, and that from threats openly made we have reasonable cause to apprehend that an attempt will be made to collect a mob and to destroy or damage our property aforesaid and to prevent us from its use and enjoyment. This property consists of mills, buildings, workshops, machinery and other personal property. We therefore call upon you , as Sheriff of Allegheny county, Pa., to protect our property from violence, damage and destruction, and to protect us in its free use and enjoyment.

CARNEGIE STEEL COMPANY, LIM.,
H. C. FRICK, CHAIRMAN
CARNEGIE, PHIPPS & Co., LIM.,
H. C. FRICK, CHAIRMAN.

The Sheriff's Visit to Homestead.

In response to the appeal from the Chairman of the Carnegie Interests Sheriff McCleary, accompanied by ex-Sheriffs Gray and Cluley, reached Homestead shortly after 9 o'clock yesterday morning. They made their way to the headquarters of the Amalgamated Association on Eighth Avenue, and requested a private conference with the Advisory Committee. Their request was granted, and at 10 o'clock the three Pittsburgers filed into the private office of the committee and met face to face the 50 men who up to that time had managed the affairs of the locked-out men. Addressing himself to

sburg **Dispatch.**

YOUR SUMMER TRIP.

Do not fail to choose your hotel
from the excellent list published to-day. You will find it a
great assistance.

JULY 6. 1892—TWELVE PAGES. THREE CENTS.

the Chairman of the committee Sheriff McCleary said: "Mr. Chairman and gentlemen of the Advisory Committee: The Carnegie Steel Company has called me in my official capacity as Sheriff of Allegheny county to protect the property and buildings of the company, located here. I thought that it would be a wise move to come here this morning and personally look over the ground."

The Officer of the Committee.

The Sheriff's terse speech created a decided situation. He was requested to retire for a few moments. The committee spent a quarter of an hour behind the closed doors and then the chairman made this answer to the Sheriff: "The Advisory Committee is not only ready but anxious to assist you in preserving peace and protecting property hereabouts. In proof of which we now offer any number of men, from 100 to 500, to act as your deputies. They will serve without pay and will perform their duty as sworn officers of the law; even though it could cost them their lives. Furthermore, the committee will give bond of either $5,000 or $10,000 for each man, no matter how many, that they will do their duty."

The Sheriff, after devoting ten minutes to allow meditation replied: "Gentlemen I thank you for this offer and perhaps in the near future I will accept it, but just now I prefer to have my own men and I will send 50 deputies to Homestead this afternoon."

Escorted Around the Silent Works.

At this juncture one of the committeemen suggested that it would not be a bad idea to have the Sheriff and his two assistants inspect the plant and its environments. The suggestion was acted upon at once and an escort committee was quickly appointed. In charge of this committee Sheriff McCleary left the hall and walked around the works. It required something more than an hour to show him everything and it was close on to noon when the party returned to headquarters and re-entered the Council chamber.

The Sheriff was then politely asked to give the committee his view of the situation. "I see no signs of disorder anywhere," he said, "and, I must say that I think there is no necessity of having deputies here, nevertheless, I must perform my duty and I will send the men." When the Sheriff concluded he was again asked to leave the room.

The Advisory Committee then held a Secret session that lasted for over an hour.

The Advisory Committee Dissolved.

Then followed the dramatic climax of their episode. The door of the committee room suddenly swung backward on its hinges and those in the great outer hall were asked to enter. When the Sheriff and his party crossed the threshold they found the 50 members of the Advisory Committee gathered around a long table. On this table were heaped piles of official looking documents. In the center of the group stood the Chairman. He said:

"Sheriff McCleary, the last meeting of the Advisory Committee has just been concluded. We, as members of that committee, have, after due deliberation, re-

Dissolving the Advisory Committee of Fifty.

solved to formally dissolve this committee, and we have asked you in here in order that you may witness the spectacle. The Advisory Committee from now on will not be responsible for any disorder or any lawless act perpetrated either in Homestead borough or Mifflin township. Do you understand—our responsibility ceases from this very moment. I now declare the Advisory Committee to be dead."

All the Records Destroyed.

Then a strange thing happened. Hardly had the final words passed the lips of the speaker when each member of the committee unfastened from the lapel of his coat his badge of office and tossed it on the table. The odd bits of narrow ribbon formed a crimson mound in the center of the table.

Scarcely had this been done when the piles of official documents were carefully laid in the open grate. The Chairman borrowed a match from a bystander and struck it on the iron fender. Carefully shading the tiny flame with his hands, he bent over and ignited the papers. The hungry flames caught the solid pages of manuscript, and as the grate is new and the draught was strong, the official archives of the committee were soon reduced to a smouldering mass of blackened ruin.

The Chairman turned to the sheriff and said: "You have seen all; have you anything further to say to us?"

Sheriff McCleary replied: "Gentlemen, I have nothing more to say. Good afternoon."

The Sheriff Returned to Pittsburg.

Then, with a low bow to the Chairman, the sheriff backed out of the room. He was followed by his two deputies. The trio hurried down the narrow stairway which leads to the street, and after a brief consultation walked rapidly down Heisel street. When they arrived at the river bank a red-faced man in a leaky skiff offered to row them across the river for a quarter a head, and his proposition was quickly accepted. The three officials were

(Went by Rail, continued)

landed at Salt Works Station shortly after 2 o'clock, just in time to catch a Baltimore & Ohio train bound for Pittsburg.

After their guests had departed the labor leaders held another secret consultation, and after it was all over sent this telegram to their legal counsel in Pittsburg.

HOMESTEAD, PA., July 5.

To W. J. Brennan, Esq., Pittsburg, Pa.:

The Citizens of Mifflin township ask for a temporary injunction to restrain the Sheriff from sending deputies to the Homestead Steel Works, situated in Mifflin township. We believe that it is a move calculated to cause unnecessary disturbance.

Expect an Injunction This Morning.

This telegram was signed by three well known citizens of Mifflin township, but the leaders declined to make public their names.

Mr. Brennan made no reply to this telegram. It is believed that he will apply to court this morning for the injunction.

The news that Sheriff McCleary had determined to send armed deputies to the works and that the all-powerful Advisory Committee had of its own accord dissolved created intense excitement in Homestead. Men gathered at the intersections of the streets and in low tones discussed the situation. The general tone of this sidewalk criticism was conservative, but there were many men who said that if the imported deputies attempted to enter Fort Frick there would be trouble.

THE DEPUTIES' RECEPTION.

Two Thousand Men Await the Officers' Arrival at Munhall With the Sheriff's Proclamation— Escorted to Head-quarters Under Guard— Keeping Back the Crowds.

It was between 5 and 6 in the afternoon when the evening express showed up at Homestead station. Before the train had come to a full stop a man jumped from the platform of the rear car and announced to the little group of watchers that there were ten armed deputies aboard the train. "They are bound for Fort Frick," shouted the man as he worked his way through the crowd, "and they are going to get off at Munhall."

According to the railroad people the time from Homestead to Munhall is exactly six minutes, allowing a stop of one minute at City Farm, which is midway between the two stations. The express was on time and didn't stop more than three minutes at Homestead, yet when it pulled up in front of Munhall station a crowd of fully 2,000 men were massed on the road-bed and platform. Among the first passengers to alight was a tall man with a stubby silver gray mustache and the form of an athlete. Close at his boots were 9 able bodied and determined look-

Escorting Deputies to Headquarters.

ing men. The man with the silver gray mustache was Sheriff McCleary's right hand man, Deputy Sheriff Samuel H. Cluley. His companions were Deputy Sheriffs Herbert Thomas, Samuel Young, Thomas Houck, J. L. Evans, Harvey Towny, R. T. Newell and William Dittrich and Messrs. Robert Johnson, William Dersam and George Bailey.

Sheriff McCleary's Proclamation.

Deputy Sheriff Cluley had with him the following proclamation, issued by sheriff McCleary. It was posted at conspicuous places throughout Homestead, and was read with much interest by the locked-out workmen:

PROCLAMATION—TO WHOM IT MAY CONCERN.

Whereas, It has come to my knowledge that certain persons have congregated and assembled at and near the works of the Carnegie Steel Company, Limited, in Mifflin township, Allegheny county, Pa., and upon the roads and highways leading to the same, and that such persons have interfered with workmen employed in said works obtaining access to the same, and that certain persons have made threats of injury to employes going to and from said works, and have threatened that if the owners of said works attempt to run the same the property will be injured and destroyed.

Now, I, William H. McCleary, High Sheriff of said county, do hereby notify and warn all persons that all acts enumerated are unlawful, and that all persons engaged in the same in any way are liable to arrest and punishment.

And I further command all persons to abstain from assembling or congregating as aforesaid, and from interfering with the workmen, business, or the operation of said works, and in all respects preserve the peace and to retire to their respective homes, or places of residences, as the rights of the workmen to work, and the right of the owners to operate their works will be fully protected, and in case of failure to observe these instructions all persons offending will be dealt with according to law.

WILLIAM H. McCLEARY,
High Sheriff of Allegheny County.
Office of Sheriff of Allegheny County,
July 5, 1892.

Received by an Immense Throng.

The travelers were quickly recognized by the assembled populace, but there was no shouting or hooting. The crowd closed in on the deputies when the train had pulled out, and before they could realize the purpose of the men Deputy Cluley and his professional brethren were engirdled by a solid wall of surging humanity. For a single moment not a word was uttered and then a man who is prominent in the councils of the locked-out men stepped up to the deputies and said: "Gentlemen, what is your business here?"

Cluley, who had remained marvelously cool during this episode, answered: "We are deputy sheriffs and our instructions are to proceed to the Homestead Steel Works with all possible speed."

"You fellows will never get to the gates alive," shouted someone in the crowd, and his words were cheered by his comrades.

Here the man who had first spoken raised his hand and shouted: "Order, boys, order; these gentlemen are now in

Receiving the Deputies at Munhall.

our care and you must protect them from the unthinking mob."

The March to Headquarters.

This well-timed speech had a marvelous effect on the crowd. When the leader ordered that a path be cleared those in front fell slowly back and a narrow lane was cleared. Then the spokesman of the assembled wage-earners turned to the deputies and simply said: "Follow me or I will not be responsible for what may happen."

"Move on; we will follow you," replied Cluley, and then the march to headquarters was begun. First came half a dozen of the leaders, headed by the chairman of the old Advisory Committee; close behind them walked the deputies, and at the heels of the deputies was the rear guard composed of 20 men who are prominent in labor circles. The little procession formed in single file and walked between the walls of swaying humanity with measured tread. The marshal of the procession wisely chose the most direct route from Munhall station to headquarters hall. Passing through a narrow side street he turned into Eighth avenue and headed directly for the hall.

It was a nerve-straining march from start to finish. With every step the crowd grew in proportions, and when half the distance was covered the head of the line was confronted by another crowd which surged down the broad avenue with solid ranks. "What's the trouble? Have the infernal scabs arrived?" was the query of the leader of the second crowd as he confronted the marshal of the advancing column.

Arrived Safely at the Hall.

"No, no," replied the quick-witted individual, "it was a false alarm, and I want you to turn about and return immediately to your posts."

This equivocation worked beautifully. The men turned in their tracks and, all unconscious of the fact that a group of deputies were close in the rear, hurriedly retraced their steps. At last this great restless throng arrived in front of the unpainted walls of the headquarters, then it halted and spread out until the neighboring streets and lanes were filled to overflowing. Slowly the deputies and their escorts made their way to the side entrance of the hall. When they had claimed [sic] the stairway and found themselves in the big smoke-seated [sic] room, they breathed sighs of genuine relief. They were men of nerve and undoubted courage, but the tremendous strain to which they had been subjected had told on them, and they did not hesitate in acknowledging that they were very glad to be where they were.

OFFICERS SENT HOME.

The Deputies Decide They Are Powerless to Force Their Way to the Works and Willingly Accept an Invitation to Return to Pittsburg.

The deputies had been given their choice of either accepting free transportation back to Pittsburg or remaining in Homestead and taking the consequences. . . . It was finally decided to hustle the men aboard the steamer Edna and carry them by the water route to Glenwood village. The second and final stage of the journey to Pittsburg could easily be made by the Glenwood and Pittsburg car line.

"WE NEVER SLEEP" —THE PINKERTON NATIONAL DETECTIVE AGENCY

by Kaushik Mukerjee

*B*efore the summer of 1892, the Pinkerton agency had already garnered a reputation as the enemy of workers across the nation. Unionists, journalists, and politicians alike joined in condemning the activities of Pinkerton's armed guard service in labor disputes. And not without reason, for their mere presence frequently added the spark that led to an explosion of violence.

Allan Pinkerton, founder of the agency, had emigrated from Scotland in 1842. Like Carnegie, he had been a Chartist in his youth. He established a cooperage business in the vicinity of Chicago, but became a part-time detective after he discovered and exposed a counterfeiting ring. In 1850 he opened a detective agency, providing watchmen and guards for banks and businesses and , eventually, detectives employed to prevent mail and railroad robberies. Strong abolitionist sympathies involved Pinkerton and his operatives in pro-Union activities during the Civil War, and he credited himself with thwarting an early attempt to assassinate President Lincoln in Baltimore. His sons, William and Robert, worked in the agency and, after their father's death in 1886, carried it forward with great success. By 1893 there would be regional offices in Denver, Boston, Kansas City, Portland, St. Paul, and St. Louis.

The massive expansion of American industry and business during the last quarter of the 19th century on the one hand, and severe recessions on the other, exacerbated tensions between labor and management. Violent clashes erupted over wages, working conditions,

and the employment of strikebreakers during work stoppages. Many businessmen believed that standard law enforcement, in the form of the county sheriff system operating under the aegis of local government, did not provide the kind of protection they needed when faced by angry workers during a labor dispute. Consequently, they turned to private protection agencies. Pinkerton's was one of the most successful.

The earliest record of Pinkerton involvement in a labor dispute dates from 1866, when the agency provided guard service during a coal miners' strike in Bradwood, Illinois. Thereafter, the agency supplied guards to coal, iron, and lumber concerns in Illinois, Michigan, New York, and Pennsylvania in cases of protracted and often violent strikes. Especially well known is the agency's suppression of the Molly Maguires, a secret organization of Irish-American miners in the coal fields of Pennsylvania, in the late 1870s.

The agency was also active in attempts to suppress the 8-hour-day movement in Chicago during the 1880s and in combating strikes at the McCormick Reaper Works there, as well as during the Iron Molders Lockout in Troy, New York, in 1883-84, the New York City's Long-

shoremen's strike of 1887, and the Burlington Railroad strike of 1888, among others. In July 1892, while engaged at Homestead, the agency was also involved in suppressing a miners' strike in Coeur d'Alene, Idaho, where a Pinkerton detective had infiltrated the union and had succeeded in being elected recording secretary.

According to testimony before the U.S. Senate Investigative Committee that convened after the Homestead affair, the agency's "Preventive Patrol" offered armed and uniformed guards to business proprietors for the protection of their property from "disaffected or striking employees". An additional service was provided by the "daily written report" which informed patrons of any "irregularities or occurrences" observed by guards or detectives on duty.

This description of rather "routine" activities, however, did not accord with the way labor organizations viewed the Pinkertons. In the words of John McBride, an early president of the American Federation of Labor, "They have awakened the hatred and detestation of the workingmen of the United States, and this hatred is due not only to the fact that they protect the men who are stealing the bread from the mouths of the families of the strikers, but to the fact that as a class they seem rather to invite trouble than to allay it."

The companies employing agencies like Pinkertons saw things differently. Robert Pinkerton gave their view when he stated, "every large strike has shown that these labor organizations will murder and destroy property out of sheer wantonness and revenge." What would transpire on the banks of the Monongahela on that early July morning of 1892 would suggest that the reality lay somewhere between these two extreme views.

The story of John W. Holway offers a Pinkerton guard's view of what happened in Homestead. A 23-year old student in Chicago, Holway had originally been employed as a watchman for the agency. He later accepted the assignment in Homestead for $15 a week plus expenses. Testifying before the U.S. Senate Investigative Committee assembled to examine the use of armed private guards by businesses, Holway gave a grim account of his experience en route to and upon arriving at Homestead (see page 81). His testimony indicated that many of the guards were poor or unemployed men who had turned to the agency for the promise of a steady income. The majority were in every way unprepared for what awaited them.

Henry Clay Frick, who had written to the agency as early as June 2, 1892, in anticipation of trouble at Homestead, had previously used Pinkertons in labor disputes in the coke region. Confident that he had defeated unionism there, he now engaged the agency to help him eradicate the influence of the Amalgamated Association of Iron and Steel Workers at the Homestead Works. ❖

(right) William A. Pinkerton and Robert A. Pinkerton sojourning at Hot Springs, Arkansas.

William A. Pinkerton in his Chicago office. On the wall, far right, hangs a portrait of his father Allan, founder of the agency.

Frank Leslie's Illustrated Weekly, *July 14, 1892. During the lockout both sides were on the alert. The company trained a searchlight on the river, while the workers patrolled it in small boats to prevent the landing of strikebreakers, known as "black sheep."*

E V E N T S

JULY 5, 10-11 pm—*Approximately 300 Pinkerton guards (most of them hired for this job only) arrive by train at Bellevue, just down the Ohio River from Pittsburgh. They embark on two barges—the "Monongahela" and "Iron Mountain"—that have been outfitted as living quarters.*

JULY 6, 2:30 am—*Strikers on watch in Pittsburgh spot the barges as they start up the Monongahela and telegraph a warning to Homestead. A steam whistle alerts the town and thousands of men and women rush to the river banks.*

JULY 6, 4 am—*As the barges approach the company's landing wharf, the crowd breaks down a section of the "Fort Frick" fence and runs along the bank inside the mill, yelling at the barges.*

JULY 6, 5-6 am—*When the Pinkertons try to disembark, shooting breaks out from both the shore and the barges (witnesses cannot agree on who fired first). There are casualties on both sides, including the Pinkertons' captain.*

JULY 6, 6-8 am—*The tugboat "Little Bill" leaves the scene to take the wounded Captain Heinde to a hospital. The townspeople barricade themselves*

along the shore. The barges remain stranded at the landing.

JULY 6, 8 am-6 pm—*The crowd tries a number of tactics to dislodge the Pinkertons from the barges: firing a Civil War cannon, pouring burning oil on the river, throwing dynamite. Nothing works; a stalemate ensues.*

JULY 6, 6 pm—*The Pinkertons agree to surrender. Despite a guarantee of safe passage to the railway station, they are forced by the crowd to "run the gauntlet" and are badly beaten.*

JULY 7, 1 am—*The Pinkertons are returned by train to Pittsburgh.*

THE BATTLE

"Watch the river. Steamer with barges left here."

4

JULY 6, 1892 —Reprinted from the **Pittsburgh Commercial Gazette.**

EXTRA.

5:30 O'CLOCK A. M.

PINKERTONS AT HOMESTEAD.

—————

A Barge Containing 300 Passes Lock No. 1 at 2:15 A. M.—They Find a Warm Reception.

A telephone message from Lock No. 1 said that 300 Pinkerton detectives passed there at 2:15 A. M. on a model barge, towed by the Steamer Little Bill, for Homestead.

A telegram from Homestead received at 3 o'clock this morning stated that news of the Pinkerton force passing Lock No. 1 was received at Homestead at 2:30 A. M. Instantly the town was alarmed and thousands of men, women and children lined the river banks. Many of them were armed with clubs and revolvers.

At 4 A. M. the barges were in sight of Homestead, but had not reached the landing.

The Amalgamated scouts here had first information of the departure of the barges and sent word to the leaders at Homestead.

There was an exciting scene in the Postal Telegraph office at Homestead when the news arrived. The office was quickly filled with armed men. The operator thought for a moment he was to be attacked.

4:45 A. M.—The Pinkerton men have landed at the mill. The crowd has torn down a half a square of the fence and is pouring through the gap.

Immediately on the landing of the Pinkertons a pitched battle occurred.

Shots were fired by the men on the shore and the Pinkertons replied. Five of the Pinkerton men fell and two of the strikers were wounded.

(above) Illustrated American, *July 23, 1892. The Pinkerton landing site as seen from the Pemickey Bridge.*

(right) Frank Leslie's Illustrated Weekly, *July 14, 1892. Men, women, and children run past the company office building to meet the Pinkerton barges.*

JULY 6, 1892 —Excerpted from the St. Louis Post-Dispatch.

BLOOD FLOWS.

—————

Labor and Capital in Deadly Conflict at Carnegie Mills.

—————

Battle Between Pinkerton Guards and Striking Workmen.

—————

Five Men Known to Have Been Killed on Each Side.

—————

Twenty Others Carried From the Field Badly Wounded.

—————

Cannon and Winchesters the Weapons of Warfare.

—————

The Guards Driven Off But Fighting Continues.

—————

GOV. PATTISON REFUSES TO CALL OUT THE MILITIA.

—————

Perilous Position of the Pinkertons Penned Up in Barges Between Two Fires—Strong Probability That the Homestead Mills May Be Burned to the Ground—A Truce Shot Down by the Strikers—Graphic Story of the Battles on the Bank of the Monongahela—Names of the Men Who Fell.

HOMESTEAD, Pa., July 6. —Capital and labor have clashed at Homestead, and the town is red with blood. Never in the bloody history of riots in this vicinity, save the great rail road riots of 1877, has there been such carnage and such a battle.

The 300 Pinkertons who came in a boat to Homestead in the early morning have desolated many a heart and their shots have aroused such desperation that it is safe to say that before the men would now allow the mill to be operated by non-union men they would burn it over their heads.

The story of this battle is hard to tell. In the dark mist of early morning, when the town was quiet, the rumor of the arrival of a boat-load of Pinkertons reached Homestead. The word was sent along the line and the streets in almost an instant were crowded with men, women and children, hurrying in the direction of the works landing. Some were only half clad. On the maddened mass rushed, some to return without even a tear in their eyes; others to part forever on the battle grounds. Mothers stood with babes in their arms wondering what would be the result if the Pinkertons made an attempt to land. The most horrible forebodings have been realised and there are many homes in distress, many mothers, fathers, sisters, brothers and sweethearts with tears running down their cheeks, mourning the loss of some one who fell by the bullets from that boat. The landing of that boat will ever be remembered at Homestead and for generations to come the fathers will tell their children of the bloody battle of Monongahela.

———❖———

JULY 7, 1892 —*Excerpted from the* New York Herald.

DAYLIGHT CALL TO ARMS

_____

The First Shot Fired When The Pinkertons Attempted To Land.

_____

[By Telegraph To The Herald.]

HOMESTEAD, Pa., July 6, 1892. —Like the trumpet of judgement blew the steam whistle of the electric light works at twenty minutes to three o'clock this morning. It was the signal for battle, murder and sudden death, though not one of the thousands who heard and leaped from their beds to answer its signal dreamed of how much blood was to flow in response to its call. . . .

It was the signal agreed upon to rouse the town upon the approach of the invaders, were they "black sheep," Sheriff's deputies, "Pinkertons," or soldiers. Four nights before it had blown a false alarm when a boat of Hungarian "black sheep" were said to be on their way up the river. Then it had been a sharp blast. Now, as if in earnest protest that the people would not be called from their beds in vain, its blast was made terrifying in its volume and duration. Ten minutes before the news had come over the wires from a faithful scout in Pittsburg that the two barges, Iron Mountain and Monongahela, which had lain since Sunday at Manchester, were going up stream under tow of the steamer Little Bill and that 300 of the hated Pinkertons were on board.

There was no method, no leadership apparent in the response to the blast from the light works. It was the uprising of a population. In every house along the steep side street running up from the river bank lights gleamed before the great blast was ended, and before its echoes died men were stumbling out of the doorways into the light of the morn and the noisy flare of the natural gas street lamps.

Not men alone, but women, too; women armed with clubs as they joined the throng which streamed up the Pennsylvania and Pittsburg and McKeesport tracks picking its way with a fleet footedness born of long practice over the ties.

MOTHER FINCH'S BATTLE CRY.

The leader of the women, a white haired old beldam who has seen forty strikes in her long life, strode to the front, and brandishing the hand billy which she always keeps about her house for just such emergencies, shrieked aloud, "the dirty 'black sheep,' the dirty 'black sheep.' Let me get at them. Let me get at them." This was Mrs. Finch, the leader of the Amazons whenever this dark dahomey land of labor goes to war. High and shrill and strong for her years as the voice of the lustiest fisherwoman who marched on Versailles, it rose in the night air and a hundred voices answered it, "Good for you, Mother Finch. Damn the black sheep. We'll send them home on stretchers. Hell will be full of new pictures in the morning."

These were some of the answers to Mother Finch's shrill battle cry. Empty mouthings of a foolish mob going to war against hopeless odds of arms and discipline, the cries seemed then terrible as the charging cry of the black fanatics of the Sudanese desert.

LEADER OF THE MEN.

Not less strange than the leader of the women was he who seemed to be more than any one else the leader of the men. This was Billy Foy, a middle aged Englishman, who for a long time was the leader of the Homestead corps of the Salvation Army. All the fervor of his wild religious training, spent hitherto in emptiness in denouncing the intangible devil and the invisible powers of evil, seemed to find a long looked for object upon which to wreak its will. The man had been longing for a chance for years to grapple with the powers of darkness in bodily form. Now it was coming—coming

From the 1893 edition of Homestead *by Arthur G. Burgoyne. This rendering of the Pinkerton barges and the tugboat "Little Bill" was probably based on newspaper sketches.*

up the river to rob him and his mates of their very homes and beds.

The men of peace, the advisory committee men, the diplomats, the amateur lawyers who had guided the affairs of the lockout, were present, some of them, but not conspicuous save in urging their fellows to avoid bloodshed. As the crowd neared the hated high board fence which Superintendent Potter had erected in the fatuous belief that it would keep out the mob when its blood was up, it split in half. Those who were of peaceful intent followed the railroad track up through the works, feeling their way in the dark over the ties of a high trestle. Those who meant business, headed by Billy Foy and Andrew Souljer and others, made for the river bank, where the barges would land.

. . . Into the yard, stumbling over ingots and billets, swarming about cupolas and ringing loud defiance with their clubs and their heels against the armor plates meant for the country's defence, now the bone of bloody contention among countrymen, went the mob, wild with warlike delight over their easy victory. . . .

READY FOR BATTLE.

Then in the dark, angry mass of men which lined the banks beneath the pump house were little glints of light, which showed that a hundred hands had been into a hundred hip pockets and came out with six chambered revolvers full of death in each. Still no movement was made as the deck hands tied the steamer up to the little landing. The crowd was waiting for the Pinkertons, the rims of the slouch hats they could see now and then on the bulwarks of the barges. Down went the gangplank from the steamer, and then at its further end appeared the figure of a man whose hated blue uniform and badge could be made out in the gray light of five o'clock of a July morning.

Billy Foy marched resolutely to the foot of the gang plank, followed by half a dozen other men. "Now, men," cried the Pinkerton captain, for it was he, "we are coming ashore to guard these works and we want to come without bloodshed. There are three hundred men behind me and you cannot stop us." The clear ringing voice of the brave captain—for brave he was and faithful to his duty to the last

moment of his life—had hardly died away when a high pitched, excited voice, the voice of a man possessed by a controlling power, in whose hands he is but a crazy puppet, shouted back, "Come on, and if you come you'll come over my carcass." It was Billy Foy, the Salvationist, gladly accepting his chance, which had come at last, to grapple with powers of darkness in bodily form.

The Pinkerton captain carried a cane in his hand. For answer to the challenge he slashed at the Salvationist's head. Vain now was the shout of the calmer leaders: —"Keep back, men! Keep back! There will be bloodshed!" Vain was precept or example or aught else to direct power in the path of peace.

THE FIRST SHOTS.

Two shots rang out in answer to the blow. One came from behind the Pinkerton captain. The Salvationist rolled, writhing on the landing with a bullet through his body. He grappled with powers of darkness and they had done him nigh to death. The other shot flashed from among

Frank Leslie's Illustrated Weekly, *July 14, 1892.*
"The Repulse of the Pinkerton Barges at the Landing."

(Call to Arms, continued)
the crowd on the bank and the Pinkerton captain fell back into the arms of his men. Then for the first time the slouched hats behind the bulwarks of the barges took a hand. A row of rifles gleamed an instant from the side of the shoreward vessel, and in an instant more a sheet of flame ran all along her clumsy hulk from stem to stern. Bad marksmanship has saved a hundred lives here today. The volley, which one would have supposed would have broken the backbone of the riot and blown the hopes of the mob to hold the mill out of their very existence, only dropped two men. One was Andrew Souljer, the other an unknown Hun.

Dozens of others may have been and probably were slightly injured, but only two dropped. One of the chief men of the advisory committee, whose two arms were raised in an appeal to the crowd to retire in good order, felt a burning feeling all along his outstretched thumb and looking at it saw that its flesh had been neatly barked by a rifle bullet. A little

better practice and one of the brainiest organizers in the Amalgamated Association would have been a lump of clay. Here was the Pinkerton men's one chance of the day, and here it was lost owing to the confusion caused by the loss of their captain.

BROKE IN A PANIC.
The crowd for a moment was panic stricken. Up the hill it broke in a wild hunt for cover. One fellow who had been flourishing a revolver in dramatic fashion dropped it and scrambled up the bank on his hands and knees. But when they reached the shelter of the mills the men found that they were not followed. The Pinkerton men sent a message to the physician at the City Farm to attend their fatally wounded leader and those among themselves who had sustained slighter casualties. Then they put off their landing until seven o'clock.

It was a fatal error. The mob was in for bloody war now, and the delay was utilized by them with effective generalship.

While the steamer was making ready to start for Braddock with the dying captain and the wounded men, Homestead was scouted for arms. Homestead is a place where arms abound. There is good shooting along the Monongahela, and nearly every family has some sort of firearm, a musket, a shotgun or a sporting rifle. By the time that the Little Bill was under way for Braddock, the mill yard was a series of rifle pits. The bridge trestles and girders and heaps of scrap iron and half open doors of the various mills and shops were filled with men, and around the numerous little offices lurked dozens more skilled in the use of arms and bearing them in their hands.

Not one of them, from the smooth faced boys, who seemed to prevail in numbers, to huge mustached old steel workers who had drawn Carnegie's pay for half their lives, had any more compunction about killing a "Pinkerton" than they had about stamping on a mill rat. Nor were small arms all the preparations that Homestead had for the invad-

THE COMPANY'S STATEMENT.

———————

OFFICIAL DOCUMENT ISSUED BY THE CARNEGIE STEEL CO.

PITTSBURG, Pa., July 6 — The Carnegie Steel Co. (limited) has given out the following statement to the press:

"Our Homestead Steel works were on July 1 taken possession of by a mob, which was immediately thereafter organized by the local representatives of the Amalgamated Association of Iron and Steel Workers, and all our mechanics, mill men and even foremen and superintendents of departments were forcibly denied admission thereto. We were also notified by a self-styled advisory committee that no fires would be permitted at the works lest the men become excited to further unlawful acts. This continued until yesterday when we called upon the sheriff of Allegheny County for protection and assistance in regaining possession of our property. The Sheriff went to Homestead and on his return sent deputies to the works and posted a proclamation ordering the men to disperse. His deputies were routed and his proclamations torn down. The Sheriff then, through his chief deputy, attempted to take three hundred of our watchmen, who were sent to the works by boat last night. These men were met more than a mile below the works by an armed mob of Amalgamated men, who followed them to the river bank and fired rifles and revolvers at the boats. This shooting was continuous for twenty-five minutes before one shot was returned from the boats, which was not until the boats were tied up at our landing. On the arrival of the boats the mob tore down a large portion of the fence about the works and filled the bluff above the landing, keeping a continuous fire and wounding three of our watchmen. Then, and not until then was the fire returned, resulting, we are advised, in some loss of life. The mob was so large as to prevent the landing of the guards, who are at this time in the boats, awaiting orders from the authorities. We are not taking any active part in the matter at present, as we cannot interfere with the Sheriff in the discharge of his duty and are now awaiting his further action."

———————❖———————

ers. The borough has two brass cannon within its borders, said to be the property of the Grand Army of the Republic. . . .

CANNON OPENS FIRE.

Soon after the brass cannon opened from the other bank. The first and only death it caused was in the ranks of the friends of the men who fired. This was Silas Wain, a young fellow, who, with his brother, was standing near the boiler house of the works. A three pound ball, aimed too high by the amateur gunners across the stream, flew far above the roofs of the barges, and the boy's corpse, a mangled mass of bloody flesh, was stretched in the dust of the mill yard. Stretchers were in active requisition for the wounded by this time and the undertaker's wagon was plying about the yard to give its grewsome [sic] care to the dead. . . .

———————❖———————

Frank Leslie's Illustrated Weekly, *July 21, 1892.*
"The Fight Between the Strikers and the Pinkertons."

*Hugh O'Donnell, President
of the Advisory Committee.*

HUGH O'DONNELL

Hugh O'Donnell, one of the most conservative men here, was seen by your reporter when depicting the early morning scenes; he wept as numbers of men gathered around to hear the story. It certainly was a sight as the cannons and guns pealed forth their thunder.

O'Donnell said: "At the first shrill shriek of the Water-works whistle a messenger rushed to my house and dragged me out of bed. In a half dressed condition I rushed to the scene, and on the way met Capt. O. O. Coon of the Sixth Regiment, and John Flynn. With these men I went right to the front, standing on the river bank with 8,000 men who were shouting and yelling and eager for the fray. I could scarcely be heard. Capt. Coon then took an elevated position, and with a giant's strength shouted to the men: 'For God's sake put down your guns and look to the protection of your families.'"

ATTEMPT TO BURN THE BARGES

When the boat Little Bill, which brought the barges to Homestead, was seen coming down the river to get her convoy again a large United States flag was flying from her masthead. The appearance of the boat was a signal along the river front for renewed activity both on and off the barges. "She's coming to take the barges away," was the cry raised on the shore. As the boat came nearer it was seen that she carried a squad of armed men who were lined up inside next to the Homestead Mills. When opposite the converting department the men on the boat opened fire on those on the shore.

For ten minutes firing continued, the Pinkertons on the barges joining the men on the boat in the shooting. The men on the bank returned the fire from behind the furnace stacks, which they used as a shield. So warm was the fire from the shore that the men on the boat were driven to cover. Several men on the boat were seen to fall and it is certain that they were wounded. No one on shore was injured by the firing from the boats.

The Little Bill made an attempt to tie up with the barges but this was futile, owing to the shower of bullets from the shore, and the tow boat passed down the river leaving the occupants of the barges in very uncomfortable quarters.

———❖———

Captain Rodgers Repeats the Tale of the Ill-Fated Expedition.

The day following the Homestead riots Captain Rodgers, owning the tow-boats the Tide and the Little Bill, gave the following statement concerning his connection with the expedition and its disastrous results up the Monongahela: "On the 25th of June, Mr. H.C. Frick sent for me and made arrangements for the transportation, on a date to be thereafter given, of 300 or more men, with their subsistence, from a point not then determined on the river to the Carnegie works at Homestead. He said they were to act as watchmen in the works and that they would be under the direction of the sheriff of the county.

"On Tuesday, July 5, early in the day, I got orders from Mr. Frick to send my boats to Davis island dam to meet a train that would arrive there between 10 and 11 o'clock with these men on board. I was also notified from Mr. Frick that a deputy sheriff would meet me at the dam to take charge of the expedition.

"I went down with our two small tow-boats, each in charge of a barge, and arrived at the dam about 10 o'clock. Was there met by Mr. Joseph H. Gray, who had a letter of introduction to me, stating he was to accompany me as a deputy sheriff. We had to wait half an hour for the arrival of the train on the Ft. Wayne road with the men on board. I did not count them, but was told by those in charge there were 300. They seemed to be a nice-looking set of men and intelligent, well-dressed and behaved. They seemed to be under the charge of four men who acted as captains. The men talked freely of going to Carnegie to act as watchmen and seemed to have no idea of being

Excerpted from U.S. Senate Report No. 1280, testimony given November 18, 1892, at Chicago by John W. Holway, student, employed as a Pinkerton guard.

HOLWAY TESTIMONY

Now I could not tell by looking the men over who was experienced and who was not, but there were 30 or 40 men who had been in previous strikes, always in Pinkerton's employ, so far as I could learn, who had charge of our squad who held the titles of sergeants, just as in a military organization. These men were the chief actors down there at Homestead. They were the men who, after the captain had left us, kept us from being killed. If not for their presence I believe all the men would have jumped overboard. There were some G. A. R. [Grand Army of the Republic] men among them; there was quite a number. There were also regular detectives. During this firing there was a second battle. I was out of sight, but there were cracks of rifles, and our men replied with a regular fusilade. It kept up for ten minutes, bullets flying around as thick as hail, and men coming in shot and covered with blood. These detectives were about the only men that kept us from being killed. They had a restraining influence upon the rest of us. A good many of the men were thoroughly demoralized. They put on life-preservers and jumped under the tables and had no control over themselves whatever. Through the rest of the day there was this second battle when the strikers started the firing. There seemed to be sharpshooters picking us off. At first they fired straight at us, but after awhile they fired through the aisles on the side, and they would shoot men who thought they were safe. The bullets would come, zip, and you would hear some man yell, and you would know they were not cautious. There were sharpshooters picking us off all day, and about 12 o'clock barrels of burning oil were floating around the bank to burn us up, to compel us to go on the wharf and there shoot us down, but they didn't succeed because the oil was taken up by the water, and at about 1 o'clock a cannon was fired by the strikers.

Now, this cannon we supposed, directly we heard it, was fired to hit us below the water line and sink our boat, but the cannon did not hit us at all hardly. It was kept up all the afternoon. There was one shot came through the roof around me, through some cots, struck the wall and bounded out there, and one man picked it up. It was an iron ball, about two and a half inches in diameter. It tore a hole in the roof, but didn't do any harm except to make our men panicky, and there was an awful spirit of panic there, worse than the firing, because it demoralized the men. At about 3 o'clock we heard something; we thought was a cannon, but it was dynamite. Afterwards I learned it was worse than a cannon; sounded like a very large cannon. It partially wrecked the other boat. A stick of it fell near me. It broke open the door of the aisles, and it smashed open the door, and the sharpshooters were firing directly at any man in sight. That was about 3 o'clock. Most of the men were for surrender at this time, but the old detectives held out and said, "If you surrender you will be shot down like dogs; the best thing is to stay here." We could not cut our barges loose because there was a fall below, where we would be sunk. We were deserted by our captains and by our tug, and left there to be shot. We felt as though we had been betrayed and we did not understand it, and we did not know why the tug had pulled off and didn't know it had come back. ❖

(Captain Rodgers, continued)

engaged in a work of danger. On the way up from Davis island dam they seemed more intent on getting something to eat and bunking than anything else. Two-thirds of the men were asleep until the firing on the boats commenced near Homestead.

Everything was quiet at the lock and nothing seemed of an unusual character until we were within about two miles of Homestead when we heard many whistles blowing, which impressed us with the idea we were expected. As we neared Homestead daylight was breaking and we could see the crowd gathering on the Homestead shore. . . .

"The first crowd attacked and tried to stop our tying up and putting out a stage plank. As they came it was something like a charge over the river bank, with the evident intent to get on the barges. They got on the stage and were met by the Pinkerton men. One young man threw himself flat on the stage when Captain Hines [Heinde], of the Pinkerton corps, went forward to push him off. His lying there looked like a piece of bravado, and the others were trying to crowd in over and pass him. While another Pinkerton man was endeavoring to keep the crowd back with an oar, the man lying on the landing stage fired the first shot at the captain—I mean the first shot that did any damage—wounding him in the thigh.

"We then put out our stage, and the firing ceased with the exception of an occasional shot until we left to go to Port Perry with the wounded. Our time and theirs the next two hours was spent in taking care of the wounded.

"The arms that the Pinkerton men had were sent in advance, and were put on the boats with other stores before they arrived. On the way up, after the firing commenced, they unpacked the arms, and were engaged in it during the firing.

"About our going to Port Perry, owing to the condition of Captain Hines, who would have bled to death, and others of the wounded, it was thought we should take them where they could get medical aid. The captain is an intelligent, cool and courageous man, and it would have been better all around had he not been stricken down. He merely said to me, 'I don't feel like lying here and bleeding to death.' There were five others beside the captain, one of whom died before he got to the hospital. . . ."

———❖———

Excerpted from U.S. House of Representatives Report No. 2447, testimony given July 14, 1892, by Charles Mansfield, Homestead citizen, former newspaper reporter.

A vignette from Edwin Rowe's 1892 broadside, "Great Battle of Homestead." Descriptions of the battle indicate that the workers used steel beams and plates as barricades, not the crates pictured here.

MANSFIELD TESTIMONY

Q. Were you at Homestead or in that vicinity on the morning of the 6th day of this month? —**A.** Yes, sir.

Q. Did you see a boat or barges containing Pinkertons and others come to the wharf near the works? —**A.** Yes, sir.

Q. Did you see them attempt to land? —**A.** Yes, sir.

Q. Where did you first see the boat? —**A.** The first time—I went down with this crowd to the river bank and I arrived just near the electric-light plant when I heard whistles blowed—no, I heard whistles blowed which waked me and I got up, dressed, and went down to the river bank outside the mill, and the first I saw of the boat was when it was coming up the river below the town.

Q. Are you a laborer; do you work down there? —**A.** No, sir; I am employed in a real-estate office in Homestead. Previous to that time I worked for a local newspaper as reporter and had charge of their news route, and my business was to notice these things for the purpose of assisting the people on that paper to get a correct account of it.

Q. Did you hear any firing before you went to the river? —**A.** No, sir; I was there before the firing was done. I was there when the whistles were blowing, and it was some time about 2 o'clock; probably 3; it was early in the morning, and I could not say exactly now, and the boat did not come until after that.

Q. Where were you when you heard the first firing? —**A.** Standing on the river bank between the company's fence and Dixon street along the river bank.

Q. Before the crowd had entered the works? —**A.** Oh, yes, sir.

Q. Did you see any who fired? —**A.** No, sir; it was impossible to see them, as it was dark; it was early in the morning, and there was a very large crowd, and to say who did the firing would be a thing no person could speak of truthfully.

Q. I am not asking you what particular persons did, but do you know which way the firing was? —**A.** Yes, sir; the first firing was done outside of the mill probably, and from where I was standing I could see the flashes in the air. They were fired generally most in the air. I did not see any firing done in the direction of the boat.

Q. The firing was from the bank? —**A.** Yes, sir; into the air.

Q. You went along with the crowd up to where the boat landed? —**A.** Yes, sir; I did not go up with the first rush.

Q. When you got there did you see the men on the boat attempt to land? —**A.** Yes, sir; after the crowd run up I went up behind them and stood at the corner of the pump house to be out of range. I did not want to get hurt at all, and I stood there and saw the firing.

Q. Who commenced the firing? —**A.** The firing was off the boat first. From where I stood the boat was tied above the pump house, and I stood at the corner of the brick pump house, the new one the machinery is not in yet, and from that corner I saw them fire off the corner of the boat. The fire was from the boat first, and a man fell.

Q. Did a man on shore fall? —**A.** Yes, sir; I did not know who he was at the time, but I learned afterwards. ❖

FOUGHT ALL DAY.

————

Twelve Dead and Many Wounded in a Fight at Carnegie's Mills.

————

FIRST FRUIT OF THE IRONMASTER'S RESOLVE TO CRUSH HIS MEN.

—————

A Force of Armed Pinkerton Men Attempted to Take the Works.

—————

TWO THOUSAND WORKMEN WITH GUNS AND DYNAMITE RESISTED.

——————

Oil Fired on the River to Burn the Detectives' Boats.

———————

The Pinkerton Men Were Taken in Barges from Pittsburg to Homestead in the Night—Their Arrival at Dawn the Signal of War—The First Shot Fired by a Workman—Then the Pinkertons Fired a Volley. Which Was Kept Up Between the Men on Shore and the Men on the Barges—For Twelve Hours the Fight Was Kept Up Between the Men on Shore and the Men on the Barges—Cannon Were Used by the Workmen—Finally the Pinkertons Surrendered—They Were Forced to Run a Gauntlet and were Horribly Beaten—Women and Boys Joined in the Brutal Work—The Barges Were Then Burned—Gov. Pattison Has Refused Militia Until the Sheriff Attempts to Restore Order—The Sheriff Has taken the Prisoners to Pittsburg—There Is Talk of Lynching There.

———————

WOMEN SPUR ON THEIR HUSBANDS.

Five or six hundred women who had rushed to the mill-yard added to the excitement by their frenzied shouts and adjurations to their husbands and brothers to "Kill the Pinkerton: Sink their barge: Shoot them down!"

They began to weep and wail loudly when they saw the blood-stained garments of the dead and wounded. It was a matter of the greatest difficulty to get the women out of the mill-yard, but this was finally done, and those of the men who had guns at home rushed off to get them.

The sun had just risen and the day dawned fair and cloudless. The barges lay at their moorings like two long, immense coffinboxes. They are known as "model barges" and are used for carrying perishable freight up and down the river, sometimes behind and sometimes ahead of the tug.

THE MONONGAHELA A VERITABLE FORT.

They are about 140 feet long, 32 feet wide and 12 feet from water line to roof. The deck is entirely inclosed by double planking 2 ½ inches thick on the sides and 4 inches thick on the roof.

Port-holes large enough to admit the barrel of a gun had been bored at frequent intervals in the side of the Monongahela.

When the Pinkertons were driven to the interior of their floating fortress these port holes were made use of.

Sharpshooters from the ranks of the Homestead workers took up positions in the mill-yard wherever a pile of coal, or small building, or freight car afforded protection, other sharpshooters were on the piers of the railroad bridge about three hundred yards distant. On the Braddock side of the river, 400 yards from the boat, men lay behind ties and hastily thrown-up breastworks, and sent bullets into the side of the barge whenever one of the occupants showed any part of his body.

A CANNON ON THE SHORE.

A small brass cannon belonging to the local Grand Army post and known as "Griffin's pet," was secured by some of the mill men and taken across the river in a skiff.

From a position, near the big stone pier of the railroad bridge "Griffins's pet" sent iron slugs into the sides of the Tennessee. Sixteen of these murderous slugs constituted a charge for the "pet."

A PARLEY PREVENTED BY A VOLLEY.

Along about 7 o'clock, when the most conservative of the leaders had done their best to allay the feverish excitement among their men an attempt was made to hold a parley with the Pinkertons.

No sooner had the workmen shown their heads within range of the Winchester rifles than a volley of bullets from the barges showed that no arbitration or truce was desired on that side. The sharpshooters resumed their steady work and the cannon kept on booming.

The Homestead men set about devising other means for getting rid of the intruders. They were well protected on the banks by a long, high pile of soft coal and several buildings, including the water tank, pumping station and the brick house where the natural gas mains for the mill are connected with the supply pipes.

The Pinkerton detectives seemed to be in an invulnerable position. The cannon across the river was doing scarcely any executions, and very few bullets got through the thick sides of the barges.

A warfare in which the sharpshooters took the principal part was kept up in a desultory sort of way for two or three hours. During this period two most lamentable casualties occurred. Andrew Striegel, one of the young mill workers, shot himself in the neck while handling his revolver and was instantly killed.

The men who were handling "Griffin's Pet," on the other side of the river, had extreme difficulty in sighting their piece because of the bullets which flew thick and fast around them from the barge. One of their shots fell into the water many feet short of the barge, and when the next was fired the brass gun was elevated and the deadly slug flew away over the barge and among the workmen on the bank.

Silas Wayne, who worked in the open-hearth furnace, was struck in the neck by one of the slugs and killed. His flesh was horribly lacerated and he presented an awful appearance as he lay bleeding on the ground. Two other workmen were injured by the flying slugs but not seriously.

About 10 o'clock the brass gun was brought across to the Homestead side of the river and was run into the gas house. A hole was knocked in the brick wall, and through this the piece would crane upon the bows of the two barges.

SHOT DOWN NEAR "THE WORLD" CORRESPONDENT.

At 10:30 o'clock as *The World* reporter stood near the open-hearth furnace, a man with a rifle standing outside not ten foot away received a bullet in his breast and fell to the ground. He had ventured out from the protection afforded by the iron sides of the mill in his over-anxiety to get a shot at the men who had killed and wounded his friends in the early morn.

He was carried into the mill, his wounds roughly dressed, and loving hands bore him to his home, where a physician attended.

There is no hospital in Homestead, and all of the wounded among the workmen were taken to their own home except George Rutter and Lawrence Loughlin, who were carried to Pittsburg on a special locomotive and went into the hospital there.

———❖———

A vignette from Edwin Rowe's 1892 broadside, "Great Battle of Homestead," depicting the Pinkerton surrender.

From "Fort Frick" or The Siege of Homestead by Myron R. Stowell, 1893. The surrender of the Pinkertons.

FULL SURRENDER.

————

The Pinkerton Detectives Marched From the Barges Defeated.

————

WORKMEN ALLOWED THEM LIFE.

————

But Heaped all Sorts of Indignities on the Prisoners.

————

COMPELLED TO RUN A GAUNTLET.

————

They Were Kept Prisoners in the Rink Until Late Last Night.

————

THEN STARTED TO PITTSBURGH.

————

Full Story of the Determined Attack on the Boats.

————

WAS NO RESISTANCE IN THE AFTERNOON.

At 4 o'clock in the afternoon President Weihe of the Amalgamated Association appeared within the mill yard in the rear of the fortifications. A great crowd surrounded him, and after considerable difficulty the big man obtained sufficient quietness to address the men. He stated to the men that there had been too much bloodshed and begged them to stop and think. He said that the sheriff had requested him to use his influence in permitting the men in the barges to leave without further molestation. Shouts of "No! No!" rang out upon all sides.

While President Weihe was speaking he was interrupted continually by the sharp crack, crack of the rifle, and at intervals by deafening explosions of dynamite. Mr. Weihe counseled the men to think of the future. By permitting those men to go away it would prevent the militia from coming into Homestead. There were cries of "Let them go! Let them go!" and "No! No!" Continuing Mr. Weihe said the sheriff had promised him that if their men were sent off without further trouble that there would be no more Pinkertons come into Homestead.

ARRIVALS FROM PITTSBURGH
While he was yet speaking an incident at the barges drew away his auditors. A company of millworkers from the Southside, Pittsburgh, were marching into "Fort Frick" headed by the United States flag and a tenor drum. Many of the newcomers were armed. They were warmly greeted. When the excitement had somewhat subsided, one of the leaders of the Homestead men, taking the flag in his hand, mounted upon a car and commanded silence. The great crowd took off their hats and gave him a lusty hurrah. The leader of the Amalgamated men said he had been requested by President Weihe to once more entreat the men to desist from their firing and allow the besieged men to depart in peace. This was greeted by shouts of "No! No!" and "Yes! Yes!" variously intermixed. He begged the men to show the world that they were gentlemen, and notwithstanding the great injury and wrong done them, to forbear. The men were disposed to listen and many shouts of "Let them go" began to be heard. The speaker, who was Hugh O'Donnell, said a boat would come up flying a white flag, and there would be men whom they would know, and they must let it come up and take its barges away. The men cried out "No, no; let the Pinkertons lay down their arms and march out." The man asked how they would convey word to the barges. Some said "Go down yourself," others said, "Appoint a committee." Volunteers were called for, and several responded.

At this juncture a great shout arose from the rifle pits, to which the crowd rushed. Two men on the boats had stepped out on the front in full view, holding up their hands. A hundred guns were leveled at them, but there were cries all around, "Don't shoot," "Don't shoot." One of the Homestead men rushed down the steep bank and leaped upon the boats. He exchanged a word or two with the men on the boat, and then turning drew from his pocket a white handkerchief and waved it.

————❖————

JULY 7, 1892 —Reprinted from
The World, New York.

PICTURE OF THE SURRENDER.

————

The Captured Pinkertons Forced to Run the Gauntlet—Clubbed and Beaten.

HOMESTEAD, PA. July 6, —After the capitulation men and women from all directions by the hundreds started for the mill-yard. The Pinkerton men were to be brought ashore and excitement ran high.

In the mean time Jack Clifford, a steel worker, walked up the gang-planks and tried to stop his comrades from coming aboard. He knew their temper and feared for the results, but he delayed the raid for a moment only. The mob started for the boat, . . . and took complete possession. They ran like wild men about the edges and in a twinkling of an eye filled the cabins of both boats from both ends.

————

THE PRISONER TREMBLED.

The Pinkerton guards shook like the traditional aspen leaf. They huddled in groups in the corners and waited for death. Of mercy they expected none, but they were pleasantly disappointed.

They were jostled about, kicked and cuffed and sworn at but their lives were spared, although rougher treatment was in store for them at the hands of the main army of the mob still left on the river bank.

Broken windows and doorways and bedding, with which the boats were stocked for a siege, were thrown overboard, and about thirty rifles were confiscated by the steel workers. The rest of the arms and ammunition were taken charge of in the name of the Amalgamated Association, to be delivered at a point not made public.

Then the march of the prisoners to the shore and through the quarter of a mile of mill-yard to Munhall station of the Pittsburg, Virginia and Charleston Railroad was begun. The Pinkerton men were brought ashore singly and in couples. They walked unmolested down the gang-plank and up the bank. True, they were jeered, called "scabs" and cursed, but not a hand was raised against them.

The Mob Thirsted For Revenge.
At the top of the bank they found themselves in a narrow passageway between two huge piles of rusty pig-iron. When they emerged, it was to enter a lane formed by two long lines of infuriated men who did not act like human beings. They were frenzied by the long day of fighting and bloodshed. Their own relatives and comrades had been shot down and they thirsted for revenge. They had no thought for the rules of modern warfare. Surrender did not end all with them, and as the Pinkerton men, everyone with a satchel in hand, came in view they jumped upon them like a pack of wolves.

Beaten With Clubs And Guns.
The men screamed for mercy. They were beaten over the head with clubs and the butt ends of rifles. You could almost hear the skulls crack. They were kicked, knocked down and jumped upon. Their clothes were torn from their backs, and when they finally escaped it was with faces of ashen paleness and with the blood in streams rushing down the backs of their heads staining their clothes. It ran in rivulets down their faces, which in the melee they had covered with their hands.

They ran like hunted deer panting and screaming through the mill yards.

That they might be distinguished from the men on the bank so that none would get away they were forced to walk with uncovered heads. For a distance of 600 yards or more a regular gauntlet was formed and through this the Pinkerton men walked, ran or crawled as best they could. The first to leave got only hoots and jeers. Then with open hands the men who formed the gauntlet began to strike them on their uncovered heads. The leaders were unable to do anything with the crowd and soon clubs were introduced. This was in the mill-yard near the end of the gauntlet. There the rule was when you see an uncovered head hit it.

"Murder, murder!" shrieked the frightened ones, as the blows rang on their heads.

"Men for the love of God have mercy on me; don't kill me," pleaded a gray

(facing page) This dramatic depiction of the enraged citizens of Homestead— men, women, and children—subjecting the Pinkertons to the gauntlet provoked strong reactions across the country.

headed man from whose head and face was flowing blood from many wounds.

Their hats, their satchels and even their coats were taken from them and either torn to pieces or carried off. The police force of the steel workers tried to save them, but it was no use.

When a man reached the top of the bank he would receive a blow from a club which would knock him down. When he got up he always ran and blows from clubs and fists rained on his unprotected head.

One young fellow, with blanched face, saw what was awaiting him and he burst into tears. Dropping onto his knees he begged for mercy, but he was soon raised to his feet by kicks from all sides. Then he started to run and as he did a blow from a blood-stained club laid him low. Two men ran to him and escorted him safely through the rest of the line.

————

LED LIKE LAMBS TO THE SLAUGHTER.

————

One of the Pinkerton Men Says They Did Not Know Their Destination.

PITTSBURG, PA. July 6. —Several Pinkerton men managed to avoid the second gauntlet at Homestead and lose themselves in the crowd waiting for the 6:30 p.m. train to Pittsburg. The baggage car of this train was filled with cots, in which rested the wounded men taken off the boats, and the open doorway of the car revealed their identity and brought out cheers at every station on the ten-mile journey to Pittsburg.

A wounded Pinkerton man occupied a seat with a *World* correspondent. He was as pale as a ghost and panting with a chest wound of some kind.

When charged with being a Pinkerton guard by the correspondent he admitted it in a terrified whisper. The train was filled with sympathizers of the strikers and the cheers at every station increased his terror.

He exhibited a pair of calloused hands and said he was a mechanic—a maker of organ bellows at Chicago. He did not

even know the name of the river on the banks of which the all-day battle had been fought. He said: "One hundred and twenty-five of our men came from Chicago, the balance from Brooklyn, New York and Philadelphia. We did not know our destination. We were engaged as private watchmen, but we did not know we were to be used to shoot down honest workingmen, for we are workingmen ourselves and sympathize with the strikers now that we know the truth.

"We arrived in Pittsburg last night. We boarded the boat at midnight. The real cause of our engagement was not made known to us until we were in sight of the steel mill. Then it was too late. We were pushed ashore and the shooting commenced. We did not fire the first shots.

"It was not long until the steamer Little Bill which towed us to Homestead moved out in the stream and started up the river. Our captain took the wounded on board and said he would return later, but he never came back and we were left without a leader all day, held in a slaughter pen near the shore. There was no chance to escape. The barge without motive power stood an easy target for the men on shore. It was riddled with bullets.

"All our men were not armed. Those who had rifles used them. They shot through the windows. They were desperate. It was a case of being shot to death on one side or drowning on the other.

"We were hopeless, and we resolved to sell our lives dearly."

————❖————

THE LABOR TROUBLES AT HOMESTEAD, PENNSYLVANIA—ATTACK OF THE STRIKERS AND THEIR SYMPATHIZERS ON THE SURRENDERED PINKERTON MEN.—DRAWN BY MISS G. A. DAVIS, FROM A SKETCH BY C. UPHAM.—[SEE PAGE 47.]

Excerpted from U.S. Senate Report No. 1280, testimony given November 18, 1892, in Chicago, by John W. Holway, student, employed as a Pinkerton guard.

HOLWAY TESTIMONY

At about 4 o'clock some one or other authorized a surrender, effected by means of a medical student, who studies at the eclectic college over here, the most intelligent man on board for that matter, a Freemason. He secured a surrender. I don't know how he secured it by waving a flag. We secured a surrender. What he wanted was that our steam tug pull us away, but instead of that the strikers held that we should depart by way of the depot.

That surrender was effected, and I started up the embankment with the men who went out, and we were glad to get away and did not expect trouble; but I looked up the hill and there were our men being struck as they went up, and it looked rather disheartening. I had a telescope satchel in my hands and went about half way down to the mill yards without being hurt, when three fellows sprang at me and knocked me down twice and one said, "You have killed two men this morning; I saw you." I dropped my satchel, and I think these men were probably thieves; I put them down for thieves. I supposed there was not going to be any more crowds, but in front of the miners' cottages there were crowds of miners, women, etc., and as we all went by they commenced to strike at us again, and a man picked up a stone and hit me upon the ear; I saw him throw it, and it glanced off, and right ahead I saw some thieves I judged to be from Pittsburg. One had a slung [sic] shot, and he would hit a man upon the ear and if he had a satchel he would drop it. I got on further toward the depot and there were tremendous crowds on both sides and the men were just hauling and striking our men, and you would see them stumble as they passed by. I tried to get away from the crowd; I had no satchel, so I put my hat on and walked out of the line of Pinkerton men, but some one noticed me, and I started to run and about 100 got after me. I ran down a side street and ran through a yard. I ran about half a mile I suppose, but was rather weak and had had nothing to eat or drink and my legs gave out, could not run any further, and some man got hold of me by the back of my coat, and about 20 or 30 men came up and kicked me and pounded me with stones. I had no control of myself then. I thought I was about going and commenced to scream, and there were 2 or 3 strikers with rifles rushed up then and kept off the crowd and rushed me forward to a theater, and I was put in the theater and found about 150 of the Pinkerton men there, and that was the last violence offered me.

That evening I was told we were going to be arrested for murder and put in jail. We were pulled over to Pittsburg and kept there all night. Next morning we pulled out for New Jersey. The train went as fast as it could, because they expected mobs of strikers at Harrisburg and different places would assault us; it ran as fast as it could to New Jersey — Jersey City; we reached there about one o'clock that night. ❖

From Henry Clay Frick's Letterpress Book, Clayton Corporation Archives, Pittsburgh.

CABLE

July 7, 1892.

CARNEGIE,
    MORGAN, LONDON,

SMALL PLUNGE, OUR ACTIONS AND POSITION THERE UNASSAILABLE AND WILL WORK OUT SATISFACTORILY.

GIVEN TO SCHOONMAKER OVER LONG DISTANCE TELEPHONE TO BE SENT FROM NEW YORK.

Harper's Weekly, *July 16, 1892. The German sign on the building, variously called the Opera House and the Rink, means "Harmony Singers Hall."*

JULY 8, 1892 —Excerpted from the St. Louis Post-Dispatch.

THE PINKERTON REMNANT

About 5 o'clock their ammunition began to run out, and a proposition for an unconditional surrender was breached. One man opposed the idea strenuously, but finally the rest of the men decided to run up the white flag. Finding that sentiment was going against him, the man who opposed surrendering became more vehement than ever and said that he would not surrender; that death was preferable to crawling ashore like whipped dogs and that he for one would fight it out to the end. According to the men telling the story there were sharp shooters aboard the barge and one of them said to the man who preferred death to surrender "Your — if you don't agree to come in, I will blow your — brains out." The reply was: "I will not come and I'm going to fight it out or die."

Turning to the opening in the end of the boat the man asked for the way. In his hand was a Colt revolver. Toward the end of the boat he suddenly raised the pistol to his head, pulled the trigger, and fell back on the deck dead, his brains oozing out on the already blood-soaked boards. This tragedy coming so fast upon so many others took the last particle of courage out of the detectives and they at once surrendered.

———❖———

JULY 9, 1892 —Excerpted from The Local News, *Homestead.*

A Good Riddance.

About one o'clock in the morning, a special train arrived from Pittsburg on the P.V. & C. railroad to convey the Pinkertons out of the town.

Sheriff McCleary, President Weihe and others were on the train and assisted in getting the men from the opera house to the cars. They were with difficulty persuaded that they would not be harmed. The crowd assembled at the doors was not large or demonstrative. Hugh C. O'Donnell addressed them and requested that they would extend safe conduct to the prisoners on their way to the cars. He was assured of this and the men were as good as their word; for the rabble had disappeared at that late hour. The Pinkerton's [sic] came out two by two and marched quietly to the cars, escorted by the workmen. Not the least harm was offered them, but when they had boarded the train and it was starting off, a ringing shout went up all around. The train proceeded to Pittsburg, and during the morning and forenoon were sent eastward. They have reason to long remember Homestead.

———❖———

THE HOMESTEAD RIOTS

. . . The Pinkerton men disembarked, and were placed under guard, and moved toward the jail. The leaders were in earnest in their promises to protect their prisoners, but they were powerless to do so. The progress toward the jail was like running the gauntlet. Men, boys, and women broke through the guards, and stabbed and clubbed the disarmed prisoners. Stones were thrown at them as they staggered hurriedly along. It was cruel and cowardly business this, and scarcely a single man of all those who surrendered escaped unhurt.

The jail was too small to hold the prisoners, and a neighboring hall was was used both as prison and hospital. Later the sheriff took possession of the prisoners, and had them conveyed to Pittsburg. The mob was left in charge of the works. During the day the sheriff telegraphed to the Governor of Pennsylvania, saying that he had not the power to maintain the peace, and asking for military assistance. The Governor replied that he would not call out the militia until all the resources of the local civil authorities had been exhausted. The sheriff called upon all good citizens to help him suppress the disorder, but not more than sixty men responded to the call.

It is not known certainly, when this paper goes to press, what the casualties amount to. But there were six workingmen killed and seventeen wounded. Of the Pinkerton men two were killed and more than two hundred wounded. Mr. Frick, in behalf of the Carnegie Company, says that the company is taking no hand in the matter, but will hold the county responsible for any damage to the property. The men employed by the Pinkerton agency were employed, however, for the Carnegie Company. Mr. Andrew Carnegie is in Europe, and was at Braemar, Scotland, the day the fight occurred. He was said to be very much excited and distressed. The riot has been mentioned both in the United States Senate and House of Representatives. In the latter body a resolution was offered instructing a committee to investigate and report the cause of the trouble.

———❖———

JULY 7, 1892 —*Reprinted from the* Pittsburgh Commercial Gazette.

THE OTHER SIDE.

____

The Stories Related By the Wounded Pinkerton Detectives.

____

They Did Not Know the Task That Was Ahead of Them—Hired to Do Guard Duty—Only Crackers to Eat for Two Days.

____

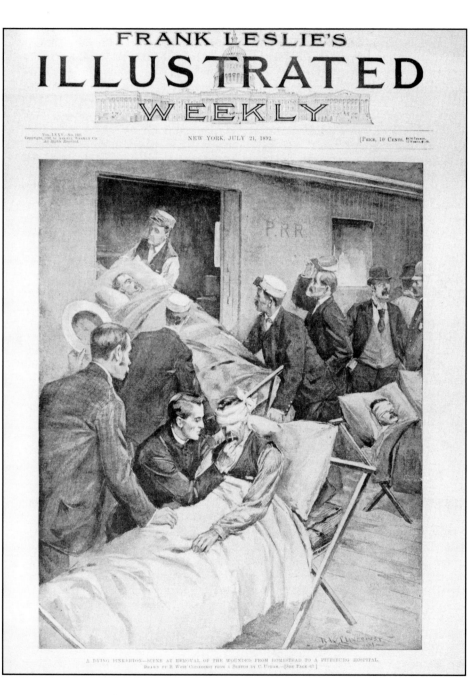

FRANK LESLIE'S
ILLUSTRATED
WEEKLY

NEW YORK, JULY 21, 1892. [PRICE, 10 CENTS.

A DYING PINKERTON—SCENE AT REMOVAL OF THE WOUNDED FROM HOMESTEAD TO A PITTSBURG HOSPITAL.
Drawn by B. West Clinedinst from a Sketch by C. Upham.—[See Page 47.]

The 7 o'clock train on the Pittsburgh, Virginia & Charleston road yesterday evening was an object of great curiosity as it came into the city bearing among others several of the wounded Pinkertons, who had surrendered an hour before under desperate conditions. The report that preceded the train's arrival was to the effect that five of the seven dead Pinkerton men had been taken from the barge and placed on the train, and it was this that raised curiosity to the highest pitch. When the trains pulled into the Union station there was a great mass of people crowded about the building and approaches attracted by the two ambulances from the West Penn Hospital. This was the first indication that the five men were not dead as reported.

As rapidly as possible they were removed from the train to the hospital and given attention. All were seriously wounded, but only one was in serious condition. That was a man named Connors of Montgomery street, New York, who was known as "Mike" in the party. He had been shot in the arm about 6:30 yesterday morning and had lain in the barge all day long, during the many attempts to destroy it, without attention. His comrades were too busy trying to defend themselves to do anything for him, and last night when he was taken to the hospital the wound in the arm and a badly-torn side were so bad that the surgeons said that from the manner in which his vitality was ebbing he could hardly last until morning. The wound is in the upper arm and ran blood in a stream for most of the day.

The Other Wounded Men.

The other Pinkertons of the party were Ed R. Spear, No. 182 Oak street, Chicago; Charles Snatherham, No. 918 West Madison street, Chicago; Pat Groff, No. 197 Ontario street, Chicago; Ed McGovern, No. 144 Bridge street, Philadelphia; John R. Credvall of New York, who said that his address was anywhere in the United States. He and Ed McGovern are experienced men in the Pinkerton service, and Credvall is an attache of the Pinkertons' New York office. McGovern has been in their service for some years and has done service in all the big strikes in the eastern cities. Criknell [sic] was shot through the left hand, McGovern and Spear are shot in the leg, and Groff is badly wounded in the back, Snatherham was thrown over a lot of lumber on the barge and badly bruised about the back.

All of them are brawny looking fellows, but were of one opinion, namely, that they had enough of Pinkerton service. Curiously not one of the Pinkerton men except Crulvale [sic] knew the destination of the parties that left New York, Philadelphia and Chicago on Monday night and arrived in Pittsburgh on Tuesday night. Spear is a rather intelligent man, who nursed his lacerated leg with a smile and made humorous comments on the affair. In answers to questions he said:

"No, we did not know where we were going when we engaged. We were asked to do guard duty somewhere and the impression was given that the work was in Kansas City. We were not told that, but it was the general impression in the party. No: I can't say what road we came in on or where we were transferred to the flatboat. I know it was late at night and that there was no sign of houses. I did not take any notice of what the barge was like at the time, but about dawn, as we approached the landing, I saw that it was a perfect trap and could not have been worse for the purpose. Each man was assigned to a certain duty as soon as we boarded the boat, and I was put in charge of the rifles. There were about 401, and probably 325 men.

Overawed by Numbers.

"It was about 6 o'clock, I should judge when the barge was run in to the landing and preparations were made for leaving the boat. As we came into view we saw that the banks were swarming with men, and before we got started they opened fire. We replied the same way, and a hot skirmish took place for several minutes. All we could do was to keep under cover, for we were greatly outnumbered and were prevented from landing by the force that held the approach to the mill grounds and each man acted for himself. It was simply a matter of choice in the manner of dying either by fire, by water or bullets, and one way was certain. We could make no defense, as we were simply targets, and thought that surrender was the best thing to do. All we had to eat was a few crackers and a little coffee, and were a little weak at the end of the second day. I had been living on tobacco since Tuesday morning."

His Worst Experience.

McGovern said that the eastern contingent expected that the Carnegie works was the objective point, but that none of the party dreamed that the situation was bad. "Yes, I have had plenty of experience," said he, "but this is the worst. I was in the New York Central strike and other big ones, but this one beats them all. It was an awful day. By God, but those men did shoot. I never saw and heard so many missiles in all my life. These men are terrible. I never saw anything like it and don't want to see the like again."

———— ❖ ————

WERE THEY SWORN OFFICERS?

PITTSBURG, Pa., July 8. —The statement as to whether or not the Pinkertons were sworn as deputies are very conflicting. Sheriff McCleary says they were not, but the Carnegie people insist that they were. E. P. Spear of Chicago who is at the West Pennsylvania Hospital confirms the statement of the Carnegies. The latter admits that he was with the party but asserts that he did not administer the oath to them. This question will be an important one in settling the question of responsibility.

Sheriff McCleary was to-day shown the interview with H. C. Frick, in which he says that the Pinkerton men were sent to Homestead with the full knowledge of the sheriff and that ex-sheriff Gray was authorized to deputize the Pinkertons in case of trouble. Replying to this, Mr. McCleary said: "I knew the men were going to Homestead and knew that Col. Gray was going with them. I did not know the men were armed and once for all I want to state that Col. Gray was not authorized to deputize them. I want to say for them and for the last time that they were not deputized with my knowledge or consent. Col. Gray has said himself that he did not deputize the Pinkertons and I do not believe he did."

———— ❖ ————

JULY 9, 1892 —*Excerpted from* The Pittsburg Leader.

BILLY PINKERTON.

————

Insists That He Had an Understanding with Sheriff McCleary.

————

The Guards Signed Contracts and Knew What Was Expected of Them at Homestead . . .

————

CHICAGO, July 9. —"[W]e had a tacit understanding with Sheriff McCleary that every one of our men was to be sworn in as deputy. At the time the boat was attacked McCleary's chief deputy, Gray, was with our men.

"What intention had he in view, being with the men, if he was not going to make them his subordinates? Had he raised his voice and ordered the men to fight for the Sheriff of Allegheny county the mere act would have made them deputy sheriffs. The only reason our men were not sworn in as deputies when the fight occurred was the sheriff's violation of his promise and his official oversight."

"How about the story that your men were engaged and sent to Homestead under false pretenses, the men being given to understand that they were to be watchmen in a rural town?" he was asked.

"That is the worst kind of rot, and I can prove it. The reported interview with one of the men published in a number of papers is a pure fake. Do you suppose I have been in this business all these years to let a fool, like that fellow alleged to have been interviewed must have been, get the best of me on a business proposition?

"Each and every man signed a black and white contract, in which his duties were outlined to a letter before he left on the train. All of those stories about taking the men from town to town in order to confuse them and throw them off of the real terminus of the journey are falsehoods."

————❖————

Excerpted from U.S. House of Representatives Report No. 2447, testimony given July 13, 1892, by Joseph H. Gray, who accompanied the Pinkertons being transported on the barges.

GRAY TESTIMONY

Q. Were you authorized by the sheriff to go as deputy sheriff to take charge of those men? —A. No, sir; I was there to protect and preserve the peace.

Q. Well, describe your journey up there. —A. Before we arrived there Mr. Potter, the superintendent of the Carnegie Company, was called into —

Q. Was he on the boat? —A. He was; yes, sir, he was called into the cabin and Capt. Hinde [Heinde] and another Pinkerton officer, and we gave them some instructions that in case of any trouble under no consideration were they to fire their guns unless in self-preservation, and not until some person was wounded or killed of their party. They went back to the barges, and when we came in sight of Homestead whistles began to blow there, some miles away, and some steamboat lying at the wharf, and all through the town, and there was a firing on the wharf, a promiscuous firing of small arms, pistols, etc. We ran on up past the crowd, and there was some fog on the river, but we could see a congregation of people on the river banks, and we were going pretty rapidly. When we got up pretty well and as we were nearing the shore I commenced to hear balls rattle against the boat fired by small-arms, but before we passed into the Carnegie place—there is a fence running down to the river dividing it from the line—there was a ball came through the pilot-house. I examined the glass, and I concluded that that was a rifle ball. Another struck the whistle and another struck the smoke stack, and we had a good deal of firing of that kind. When we got in near the shore these people followed us up pretty rapidly, and when they struck the fence they could not get through, so they tore it down, and therefore we gained on them and were ahead of them all the way to the landing. I could see the crowd coming, and when we reached the landing they came down through the mill property in a large number. When we came to the bank the captain asked Mr. Potter to send a couple of men out to assist them in tying the boat, which he did. Capt. Rodgers came and Mr. Potter and he sent some person out to protect him when he was tying the boat, and immediately upon his going to tie his boat they commenced coming down over the embankment and to the water's edge, and very soon thereafter commenced firing.

Q. Who commenced the firing? —A. The mob on the bank.

Q. Had the gang plank been put out? —A. I could not say that. I was on the upper deck of the boat and could not see over the top of the barge, and I could not say what the men were doing on the front of the barge.

Q. Up to that time had any Pinkerton men or any person on the boat or barges fired? —A. Not a gun.

Q. You swear that the firing began from the crowd on the shore? —A. I do most positively. No gun was fired from that boat until after there had been very considerable firing from the front. ❖

FRICK EXPLAINS.

He Tells the Cause of the Trouble and of Efforts to Settle.

POINTS IN DISPUTE.

By Improved Machinery Introduced Wages Will Not Drop.

DAILY OUTPUT INCREASED.

A Compromise Offered on the Original Proposition Was Refused— He States the Proposed Equalization of Earnings Only Affects 325 Out of 3,800 Men and They Earn the Most Money—The New Scale Does Not Affect 15,000 Workmen in the Other Carnegie Establishments.

Mr. H.C. Frick, chairmen of the Carnegie Steel Company, Limited, yesterday consented to talk on the situation at Homestead for the first time since the trouble at their extensive plant.

Mr. Frick's office was besieged by Pittsburgh newspaper men and correspondents for outside papers all day. It was impossible for him to see each separately and he preferred not to see them all together. He finally selected George N. McCain of the Philadelphia Press as his medium of communication. That gentleman at once procured a stenographer and the following is a verbatim report of the interview:

What Mr. Frick Said.

"The question at issue is a very grave one. It is whether the Carnegie Steel Company or the Amalgamated association shall have absolute control of our plant and business at Homestead. We have decided, after numerous fruitless conferences with the Amalgamated officials in the attempt to amicably adjust the existing difficulties, to operate the plant ourselves. I can say with the greatest emphasis that under no circumstances will we have any further dealing with the Amalgamated association as an organization. This is final. The Edgar Thomson works and our establishment at Duquesne are both operated by workmen who are not members of the Amalgamated association with the greatest satisfaction to ourselves and to the unquestioned advantage of our employes. At both of these plants the work in every department goes on uninterrupted; the men are not harassed by the interference of trade union officials, and the best evidence that their wages are satisfactory is shown in the fact that we never had a strike there since they began working under our system of management."

. . .

Why the Works Were Closed.

"Finding that it was impossible to arrive at any agreement with the Amalgamated officials, we decided to close our works at Homestead. Immediately the town was taken possession of by the workmen. An advisory committee of fifty took upon itself the direction of the affairs of the place; the streets were patrolled by men appointed by the committee, and every stranger entering the town became an object of surveillance, was closely questioned, and if there was the slightest reason to suspect him he was ordered to leave the place instantly under a threat of bodily harm. Guards were stationed at every approach to Homestead by this self-organized local government. Our employes were prohibited from going to the mills, and we, as owners of the property, were compelled to stand by powerless to conduct the affairs of our business or direct its management.

"This condition of affairs lasted until Tuesday, when I appealed to the sheriff of Allegheny county, stating the facts as I have outlined them. The sheriff visited Homestead, and talked with the advisory committee. Its members asked that they be permitted to appoint men from their own number to act as deputy sheriffs; in other words, the men who were interfering with the exercise of our corporate rights, preventing us from conducting our business affairs, requested that they be clothed with the authority of deputy sheriffs to take charge of our plant. The sheriff declined their proposition, and the advisory committee disbanded. The rest of the story is a familiar one; the handful of deputies sent up by Sheriff McCleary were surrounded by the mob and forced to leave town, and then the watchmen were sent up to be landed on our property for the protection of our plant."

Why Pinkertons Were Employed.

"Why did the Carnegie Company call upon the Pinkertons for watchmen to protect their property?"

"We did not see how else we would have protection. We only wanted them for watchmen to protect our property and see that workmen we would take to Homestead—and we have had applications from many men to go there to work—were not interfered with."

"Did you doubt the ability of the sheriff to enforce order at Homestead and protect your property?"

"Yes, sir; with local deputies."

"Why?"

"For the reason that three years ago our concern had an experience similar to this. We felt the necessity of a change at the works; that a scale should be adopted based on the sliding price of billets, and we asked the county authorities for protection. The workmen began tactics similar to those employed in the present troubles. The sheriff assured the members of the firm that there would be no difficulty; that he would give them ample protection and see that men who were willing to work were not interfered with. What was the result? The posse taken up by the sheriff—something over 100 men— were not permitted to land on our property; were driven off with threats of bodily harm, and it looked as if there was going to be great destruction of life and property. That frightened our people. . . .

"The facts concerning the engagement of the Pinkerton men are these: From past experience, not only with the present sheriff but with all others, we have found that he has been unable to furnish us with a sufficient number of deputies to guard our property and protect the men who were anxious to work on our terms. As the Amalgamated men from the 1st of July had surrounded our works, placed guards at all the entrances and at all avenues or roads leading to our establishment and for miles distant there from, we felt that for the safety of our property and in order to protect our workmen it was necessary for us to secure our own watchmen to assist the sheriff, and we know of no other source from which to obtain them than from Pinkerton agencies, and to them we applied."

"We brought the watchmen here as quietly as possible; had them taken to Homestead at an hour of the night when we hoped to have them enter our works without any interference whatever and without meeting anybody. We proposed to land them on our own property and all our efforts were to prevent the possibilities of a collision between our former workmen and our watchmen. We are to-day barred out of our property at Homestead and have been since the 1st of July. There is nobody in the mills up there now; they are standing a silent mass of machinery, with nobody to look after them. They are in the hands of our former workmen."

"Have the men made overtures for a settlement of the difficulties since this trouble commenced?"

"Yes, sir. A leading ex-official in the Amalgamated association yesterday, when this riot was going on, called on the sheriff and I am informed asked him to come down to see me, stating that if he could get a promise that we would confer with the representatives of the Amalgamated association looking toward an adjustment of this trouble, that he would go to Homestead and try to stop the rioting."

Refused to Confer.

"Did you consider his proposal?"

"No, sir. I told the gentleman who called that we would not confer with the Amalgamated association officials. That it was their followers who were rioting and destroying our property, and we would not accept his proposition. At the same time this representative of our former workmen said they were willing to accept the terms offered, and concede everything we asked except the date of the termination of the scale, which they insisted should be June 30 in place of December 31."

"What of the future of this difficulty?"

"It is in the hands of the authorities of Allegheny county. If they are unable to cope with it, it certainly is the duty of the governor of the state to see that we are permitted to operate our establishment unmolested. The men engaged by us through the Pinkerton agencies were sent up to Homestead with the full knowledge of the sheriff and by him placed in charge of his chief deputy, Col. Gray, and, as we know, with instructions to deputize them in case it became necessary. We have made an impartial investigation and are satisfied beyond doubt that the watchmen employed by us were fired upon by our former workmen and friends for twenty-five minutes before they reached our property, and were fired upon after they had reached our property. That they did not return the fire until after the boats had touched the shore, and after three of the watchmen had been wounded, one fatally. After a number of the watchmen were wounded and Capt. Rodgers, in charge of the towboat, at their request had taken the injured away, leaving the barges at our works unprotected, our former workmen refused to allow Capt. Rodgers to return to the barges that he might remove them from our property, but fired at him and fatally wounded one of the crew."

. . .

The Political View.

"How do you regard the present trouble at Homestead from a political standpoint? What effect will it have as a tariff issue in the political campaign of the coming fall?"

"We have never given a thought as to what effect our affairs might have on either of the political parties. We cannot afford to run our business and run politics at the same time. It would prove very unprofitable if we were to trim our sails to meet political issues. At the same time I may say it is not a matter in which the protective tariff is involved, and every intelligent man, whether he be manufacturer or employe, is aware of the fact. It is, however, a question as to whether or not the proprietor or its workmen shall manage the works?

"We did not propose to reduce the earnings of our employes below those of other Amalgamated men in other mills. As I have said, we have put in improved machinery which other mills do not possess, it increased our output and increased the earnings of our men. We asked that a reduction be made in these departments so that the earnings of our employes would be on a par with other workmen in other Amalgamated mills. It is not a question of starvation wages, for you will please bear in mind the fact that the proposed equalization of earnings affects only about 325 out of 3,800, and they are the ones who earn the most money in our establishment. It has no effect upon the wages of more than 10,000 other employes engaged in our establishments at Duquesne, Braddock, Pittsburgh, Beaver Falls and in the coke region."

MR. FRICK EMPHATIC.

————

No Man Who Fired a Shot Will Be Employed at Homestead.

Mr. Frick said yesterday that they had done all in their power to avert the calamity which had occurred. The workmen had made the fight, and if there ever was a chance of their being employed in the mills again, such a hope was entirely lost now. Not a man, he said, who had been known to raise a rifle or revolver in the bloody fight of Wednesday morning would ever be employed in his Carnegie works again. They would maintain the stand they had at first taken. They would not be dictated to, and non-union men would fill all the places of those who saw fit to start the battle. By this is meant that no man openly asserting his affiliations with any union will be employed.

————❖————

WHILE BLOOD FLOWED FRICK SMOKED.

————

He Refused to Listen to Peace Overtures from President Weihe.

————

[OFFICIAL TO THE WORLD.]

PITTSBURG, PA., July 6 —One of the coolest men in Pittsburg today, so far as appearances went, was H. C. Frick, President of the Carnegie Steel Company (Limited). While the men whom he had locked out and the men he had employed to force an entrance into the mill were killing each other at Homestead the steel king sat in his magnificently furnished office and smoked cigars, gave orders to subordinates or chatted with visitors. To some of the latter he was cool and stern.

"The time for conferences ended on the 24th of June. I will see no person who represents the Amalgamated Association."

This was his curt message to William Weihe, President of the Amalgamated Association, who asked for a conference early this morning.

Weihe was ready to yield anything for the sake of peace, and if Frick had consented to see him half the trouble at Homestead today might have been averted.

To a newspaper man who called, Mr. Frick said nonchalantly:

"The matter is out of our hands now. We look to the sheriff to protect our property. The men upon our properties now are not strikers, they are lawbreakers. We are conveying to the sheriff all the information in our possession regarding the situation and he must take responsibility of action."

"How about the military?"

"The matter of calling out the militia is also in the hands of the Sheriff. He alone can decide at what point the disorder passes beyond the control of the civil power."

"Will you hold any conferences with representatives of the workmen?"

"I will hold conferences with nobody. The matter, as I have said, is out of our hands and the supremacy of the law is the only question involved. The officers of the law are the proper persons to deal with that."

The dapper official of the Carnegie Steel Company washed his hands of responsibility with these words:

"I was very sorry to hear of the disturbance at Homestead. We are entirely out of the deal now so far as protecting our interests up there are concerned. The matter now rests entirely with the Sheriff, and to him we look for protection of our property."

Mr. Frick will not admit that he believes himself to be in any danger, but notwithstanding this, it is known that he was guarded in his office to-day and that his residence is guarded to-night.

Before leaving his office this evening Mr. Frick again reiterated to personal friends his determination to win the strike at any cost.

When H. C. Frick, of the Carnegie Steel Company was advised of the surrender of the Pinkerton detectives and of the subsequent actions of the men workers, he displayed no emotion whatever. He remarked that his firm in no way would be responsible for the damage and that everything would be charged to Allegheny county, and when asked what his future course would be he replied that the plant would be run according to the firm's wishes and that no terms but theirs would be countenanced.

———❖———

This photograph by B.L.H. Dabbs became a symbol of the Pinkertons' defeat. The strikers attempted to set fire to the barges several times during the battle but failed. The **Pittsburgh Commercial Gazette** *reported that after the surrender, "two or three men . . . were seen to pass inside the outer barge bearing a torch. . . . The fire spread rapidly and twilight now being about ended the entire river front was lit up, while 2,000 throats shouted: 'Hurray for Homestead.'"*

JULY 8, 1892 —*Excerpted from the* St. Louis Post-Dispatch.

SENATOR PALMER'S POSITION.

———

THE MILLMEN WERE RIGHT IN RESISTING THE PINKERTON INVASION.

WASHINGTON, D.C., JULY 8. —The position taken by Senator [John] Palmer of Illinois, in the discussion of the Homestead riot in the Senate yesterday, is variously commented on by men here. The Senator was bold in his declaration that the millmen were right in resisting the Pinkerton invaders.

Mr. Palmer said that the presence of the Pinkerton armed force at Homestead was in contempt of the authority of the State of Pennsylvania. Its manner was mocking and insulting. It was difficult for American citizens (whether they were in the right or in the wrong) to submit to be driven by an armed force. He confessed that every impulse of his mind tempted him to say that he should dislike being driven (even though in the wrong) by a power which might happen to be in the right. He maintained, however, that those citizens of Homestead were right. He maintained that, according to the principles of law, which should hereafter be applied to the solution of these troubles, they had the right to be there. That made it necessary for him to assert that these men had a right to employment there. They had earned the right to live there. Those large manufacturing establishments would have to be, hereafter, regarded as political establishments in a modified sense, and their owners would have to be regarded as holding their property subject to the correlative rights of those without whose services their property would be utterly valueless. That only conceded to them a right to a reasonable profit on the capital invested in their enterprises. He maintained, furthermore, that these workingmen, having spent their lives in that peculiar line of service, had the right to insist on the permanency of their employment and that they had a right to insist also upon a reasonable compensation for their services. He maintained that at the time of the assault on these people at Homestead they were where they had a right to be. They were on the ground which they had a right to defend. They were conducting themselves in the line of their rights. Manufacturing establishments were public institutions, just as railroads were. They were public because they worked for the public, because they employed the public and because the men in their service became unfit for other service. While conceding the right of the capitalists to control their property and to a reasonable regard for their investment, he claimed that the laborer has the right to permanent employment during good behavior. Of course, the laborer was compelled to submit to the chances of business. Where profits were small the parties would have to divide the loss; and where they were large they would have to be divided. That (he maintained) was the law to-day, business law was the perfection of reason.

——— ———

JULY 14, 1892 —Excerpted from **Frank Leslie's Illustrated Weekly.**

THE HOMESTEAD TROUBLES.

The deplorable occurrences at Homestead, the seat of the great steel-producing industry, have produced a widespread impression throughout the country. It is well in considering them to bear in mind the precise facts in the case. The great Carnegie works employ some five thousand five hundred operatives. For some time past there have been disagreements between the men and their employers as to the wages scale. Recently, when the expiration of a contract which has been observed for the last three years was close at hand, the operatives proposed a scale of wages for the coming year. The association of employers also submitted a scale which involved some decrease in the wages paid per ton. To this the men made objection that it was unjust, and refused their assent. Thereupon the association named a day when their scale must be accepted, and that day having passed, discharged its men, shut down its works, and prepared to defend them against attack. The difference between the scale proposed and the scale asked by the men was a dollar per ton.

With a view of protecting their works, the association of employers called upon the sheriff for a posse of watchmen, and an attempt was then made to introduce a force of two hundred Pinkerton men to guard the premises. Upon approaching the works these were assaulted with arms and a battle ensued, as a result of which a number of persons on both sides were killed and many others were wounded. The Pinkertons were compelled to capitulate, and were finally removed from the scene under the protection of the constabulary. These are the bare facts in the case.

There can be but one opinion among right-thinking men as to the course pursued by the workmen. It was indefensible. Every workman has the right to work or not to work, as he may choose. He may quit work if the wages are not satisfactory, and may employ peaceful means which do not invade the rights of others to protect his interests. But he cannot go one step further. It is the right of the Carnegie company to manage its own business. It is its right to employ such men as it may choose, and to pay them such wages as they may be willing to accept. It has a right to demand the protection of the State in the full and free enjoyment of its property and the unmolested prosecution of its business. It may be that in this case a compromise of the difference between the company and its workmen would have been advisable, but it was, as to its own interests, the sole judge as to the course which should be pursued. When the workmen undertook to prevent the placing of the property under the care of such watchmen as the managers had selected, they were guilty of an inexcusable outrage. It is said, indeed, that these workmen had offered themselves to guard the premises, but it was for the employers to accept or reject their proposition according to their estimate of the properties of the case. It is said that the introduction of the Pinkerton detectives was injudicious and calculated to aggravate the employés, the ready answer is, that in the failure of the regular officers of the law to give necessary protection there was no other resource left than the employment of an outside force. It is the sheerest nonsense to say that employers in this country may not protect themselves against anticipated or actual assault, within the limitations of law, by such agencies as they may elect.

The simple fact is that for days law was at defiance in and about the Homestead works. Mob violence was rampant and supreme. Property of immense value was exposed to the fury of an angry and tumultuous mob. It goes without saying that the cause of labor is not strengthened by such invasions of individual and propertied rights. Labor has rights which are as sacred as the rights of capital. They ought to be, and in every civilized community will be maintained. But this will be done by the orderly processes of the law, backed by the force of enlightened public opinion, which in this country is, in the last analysis, the determining factor in every controversy involving essential principles. The workingman who seeks with a rifle in his hands to enforce his own view as to whom the employer shall employ, or the wages he shall pay, does infinitely greater harm to the just interests of labor than the imperious capitalist who uses his power, in violation of justice and fair play, to oppress and degrade those in his service. ❖

Harper's Weekly, *July 16, 1892. The smoking ruins of the barges.*

Excerpted from U.S. House of Representatives Report No. 2447, a sworn statement by William A. and Robert A. Pinkerton, followed by testimony given July 22, 1892, in Washington by Robert A. Pinkerton.

PINKERTON TESTIMONY

WASHINGTON, D.C., *July 22, 1892.*

To the Judiciary Committee of the House of Representatives:

You have asked us to appear before you and testify in regard to the business conducted by us under the name of Pinkerton's National Detective Agency. The present inquiry by your committee arises from the recent deplorable events at Homestead, in the State of Pennsylvania, and we are informed that a statement on our part of our connection with strikes and of the general method of carrying on this branch of our business will aid the committee in its investigation.

The agency was founded in 1850 by the late Allan Pinkerton, and during the last twenty years it has frequently furnished private watchmen to protect the property of individuals and corporations during strikes. The men employed by us in this strike work are selected with great care and only after a full investigation of their characters and antecedents. Not a single incidence can be cited where we have knowingly employed unreliable or untrustworthy men, or where any of our watchmen have been convicted of a crime. Moreover, we have seldom allowed our watchmen to carry arms for the purpose of protecting property and life unless they were authorized by the proper legal authorities or sworn in as deputy sheriffs. Our men have never wantonly or recklessly fired a single shot in any of these strikes, and have only used their arms as the last extremity in order to protect life. We have consistently refused to permit our watchmen to bear arms without special legal authority or as deputy sheriffs even when on private property, and we had no intention of varying from this rule in the Homestead strike.

When first requested to send watchmen to protect the Homestead plant and property of the Carnegie Steel Company, Limited, we refused to do so unless all our men should be sworn in as deputy sheriffs before going to Homestead. We were then assured that the sheriff of Allegheny County, Pa., knew that our men were going to Homestead to act as watchmen and to guard the property of the company and protect its workmen from violence. We were further assured that the sheriff had promised, immediately upon any outbreak or disturbance, to deputize all our watchmen as sheriff's deputies if it became necessary for the protection of life and property. On that condition only did we consent to furnish about three hundred watchmen. A large number of these men were our regular employés, who could be thoroughly trusted for integrity, prudence, and sobriety. The remainder were men whom we employed from time to time or who were known and recommended to us. They did not go into the State of Pennsylvania as an armed body or force, and we should not have permitted or assented to this. There was no intention or purpose whatever of arming them until they were on the property of the company at Homestead and until and unless they had been sworn in as the sheriff's deputies.

The Sheriff's Chief Deputy Gray accompanied our men, being on the tug towing the barges, and it was distinctly understood that he had authority to deputize them in case of necessity. The boxes containing the arms and ammunition were shipped from Chicago and were to be delivered at the Homestead yards. The instructions to our men were that they should not be armed unless previously deputized by the sheriff. As a matter of fact, the boxes on board the barges were not opened and the arms and ammunition were not distributed until after the strikers had commenced firing on the watchmen and it became evident that it was a matter of self-defense, for life or death. Klein had been murdered by the strikers and about five other watchmen shot and wounded before our men began their fire in self-defense. Even then it was impossible to attempt to shoot those firing at the barges, because the strikers made a breastwork for themselves by placing women and children in front and firing from behind them. Not a single woman or child was injured by our men.

When our men surrendered, the leaders of the strikers solemnly promised full protection to property and life. They know that our men surrendered because the wounded required attention and for the purpose of saving further loss of life. After the surrender all our men, including the wounded and helpless, were brutally beaten and robbed by the strikers, and the leaders made no real or honest effort to protect them. Our men were robbed of watches, money, clothing, in fact, everything, and then mercilessly clubbed and stoned. Conners, unable to move or defend himself, was deliberately shot by one of the strikers and then clubbed. Edwards, also wounded and helpless, was clubbed by another striker with the butt end of a musket. Both died, and subsequently another watchman became insane and committed suicide as a result of the fearful beating after having surrendered. All our men were more or less injured. The acts of the strikers, after our men surrendered, would be a disgrace to savages. Yet, because done in the name of organized American labor, sympathy, if not encouragement, is shown for such deeds by part of the press and by political demagogues.

We do not shirk responsibility for any of our acts in this or any other strike. The coming murder trials ought to bring out the truth and uphold the law. Our actions will then be shown to have been legal from beginning to end. Whatever may be the present

Illustrated American, *July 23, 1892.*
The hulks of the barges.

prejudice against our agency, we shall patiently wait the sober reflection of the country in the confidence that the enormity of the wrong and outrage done to our men at Homestead will be ultimately recognized, although the example will in the meantime have caused incalculable injury to the community.

We were advised by our counsel, Messrs. Seward, Guthrie & Morawetz, of New York, that we were not violating any law of the United States or of the State of Pennsylvania; that our acts were lawful; that we had the right to employ and send men to Homestead to act as watchmen; that if they were attacked they had the right to kill, if absolutely necessary for self-defense; that they had the right to bear arms on the premises of the Carnegie Company in order to protect life and private property whether or not they were deputized by the sheriff of Allegheny County; that we had the right to ship arms from Chicago to the Carnegie yards at Homestead for the purpose of arming our men if and after they were deputized by the sheriff; that in view of the attack on the barges our men had the right to bear arms and to defend themselves, and that all their acts in firing in self-defense from the barges, after the attack on them, were legally justifiable under the laws of the United States and of the State of Pennsylvania.

Yours, respectfully,

Wm. A. Pinkerton,
Robert A. Pinkerton.

Q. How many human lives have your employés taken since your agency first entered upon the business of supplying men to protect the property of corporations and employers against so-called "strikers," or to make effective so-called "lockouts?"

A. During the twenty years that we have been engaged in this strike work, not a single instance can be cited where our men have fired upon the strikers except as a last extremity in order to save their lives. During these twenty years three men have been killed by our watchmen in these strikes, up to the time of the Homestead affair. In each instance our men were sworn in as deputy sheriffs or peace officers, and whenever tried have been acquitted.

Q. It seems to me there is an inconsistency in your statement. You say that your men are armed for the purpose of defending themselves, and yet you say they are not to defend themselves until after they are fired upon. Now, down in my part of the country it is generally too late for a man to defend himself after he is fired upon; he is generally hors de combat afterwards?

A. There is quite a difference between where you live and up here, although the law may be the same.

Q. Then they are not as good shots here as they are down there?

A. No, I do not think they are. In fact, if the firing at Homestead had been done to kill there would have been a great many more people killed than there were. I have no doubt if the men had wanted to use those arms they would have obtained possession of that yard, but they would have had to sacrifice a great many more lives to do it.

Q. There is one other question I wanted to ask you. Knowing the hostility of the Knights of Labor people and organized labor generally to your force, and knowing that in all probability sending your men to Homestead would result in collision, why did you send them there without the authority of the officers of Allegheny County, and without stipulating that they should be qualified as officers before they approached the Homestead works?

A. I stipulated that as far as possible. I had no reason to know that our men would go and be assaulted; we supposed our men would be landed on that property without assault. ❖

Excerpt from U.S. House of Representatives Report No. 2447, testimony given July 13, 1892, by John McLuckie, steel worker, Burgess of the Borough of Homestead.

McLUCKIE TESTIMONY

I do not wish this little affair at Homestead to be considered a war between labor and capital. That was a war, if it could be so styled, between laboring men because these Pinkertons and their associates were there under a consideration; they were there under pay, and the person who employed that force was safely placed away by the money that he has wrung from the sweat of the men employed in that mill, employing in their stead workmen to go there and kill the men who made his money. ❖

Scribner's Magazine, *March 1896. Orson Lowell based this painting on several photographs taken at the time of the battle.*

JULY 8, 1892 —*Reprinted from the* St. Louis Post-Dispatch.

MY LORD OF CLUNY CASTLE

To the Editor of the Post-Dispatch:

Lord Cluny of Cluny Castle, Scotland, and Earl of Homestead, Pa., U.S.A., has spoken. He spoke in a tone of thunder, and in a language not to be misunderstood.

He loudly and forcibly proclaims to the inhabitants of his adopted country that "vested rights," no matter how wrongfully gotten, under all and any circumstances must be protected; that the Declaration of American Independence is a delusion and a snare; that we, who by the grace of God and the help of the deluded and bought voters, gained the upperhand, are the only ones who have any rights whatsoever; that we, who by unjust laws have the power to fleece the voting cattle in order to be enabled to make free gifts of churches, libraries and drinking fountains, are the "real stuff;" that we, who live by the sweat of other people's brows, are competent only to enact laws which insure tranquility, order and that peace of mind necessary to a quiet and uneventful existence in this vale of tears.

Lord Cluny has proven that protection protects, and then again it does not.

Protection protects the Earl of Homestead, but in one instance at least it failed to protect his hirelings, who being an outgrowth of our advanced Christian civilization, are more to be pitied than condemned.

"My lord" has seen fit to throw his gauntlet at those who produced for him the colossal fortune which he legally enjoys, and when they manfully resist to further furnish campaign boodle for the re-election of the recipient of a barrel of old Scotch, the author conclusively proves that "triumphant Democracy" is a huge swindle.

UNCLE TOM.

Lines on the Homestead Riots

Wednesday, July 6th, 1892.

NIGHT HAS cast its darkened mantle
  O'er the vale and mountain steep,
And the birds have ceased their warbling—
  In their nests they softly sleep.

By the moonbeam's glimmering radiance
  Forms are seen like phantoms bright,
Gliding to and fro with anxious
  Watchings through the lonesome night.

All along the river, sentinels
  Pace its banks with searching eye,
Ready to convey the signal,
  Should the foe be lurking nigh.

Whilst their vigilant task pursuing,
  Distant sounds break on the ear,
Wafted by the gentle breezes
  O'er the moonlit waters clear.

Look! it is the "Little Billy!"
  See! the barges are in tow;
Sound the alarm, it is the enemy;
  Let the Homestead people know.

Quick along the wires flashing
  Speeds the message of alarm :—
"To arms! To arms! prepare to meet them;
  Make resistance—every man!"

Ready to obey their leaders
  Thousands rush with maddened haste,
'Till they reach the place of landing,
  Where, in line, each man is placed.

Then speaks out a voice stentorian :
  "Men, remember, don't shoot first;
If 'Pinkerton' should force a landing,
  Bear the consequence they must."

The air is rent with cheers defiant
  As the barges heave in sight;
Every man is nerved for action,
  Should the foe persist to fight.

The barges reach the fatal landing
  Where the "warnings" are exchanged
By both leaders; each in turn
  The situation well explained.

Heedless of the doom awaiting,
  The leader gave his men command :—
Ready, march!" each man obeying,
  Made their first attempt to land.

Then a fierce and deadly conflict
  Throws a shadow o'er the scene;
Flash on flash, in quick succession,
  Mark the enemy's lines between.

The Pinkertons in scattered numbers,
  Are driven back in quick retreat;
Thrice they charge to gain the workshops—
  Thrice they suffer sad defeat.

All day long the conflict rages;
  Night has brought its saddened tale;
In the morn lips red and rosy,
  Closed in death lies cold and pale.

Weeping mourners o'er their loved ones;
  Pitying eyes, tear-filled with grief;
Sympathizing hearts, with gracious
  Offerings seek to lend relief.

Thus a day of strife has ended,
  Which in memory shall recall
Scenes that ne'er can be forgotten
  Long as stands "Carnegie Hall."

THREE CENTS A COPY.

Unknown Source

JULY 6-8—According to the Pittsburgh Commercial Gazette, nine Homestead workers and five Pinkertons were killed in the battle, or were "fatally injured." Months later in Homestead, Arthur Burgoyne states that making a list of the dead has proved a "difficult matter." He defers to the coroner's record: seven workers, three Pinkertons.

JULY 7—Hundreds attend the Methodist service for John Morris and hear Rev. J.J. McIlyar denounce the Pinkertons as a "blot on civilization and a disgrace to this country." Led by the Golden Eagle band and accompanied by "a body of Amalgamated men formed up in fours," the funeral processions for Morris and Slovak worker Peter Farris join and together climb the hill to the cemeteries above the town.

JULY 7—In the evening, several men from Pittsburgh who are distributing Anarchist pamphlets are hustled out of town by Homestead officials.

JULY 8—Eulogizing Thomas Weldon, a roller in the mill who was "killed by the accidental discharge of a gun," Catholic priest Father Bullion argues that workers have "a right to expect permanent employment in a company such as Carnegie Steel."

JULY 8—In Harrisburg, a committee of Homestead citizens, including the Amalgamated Association's Hugh O'Donnell, meet with Governor Pattison and urge him not to send troops to Homestead. Union personnel have restored Frick's fence, and are guarding the perimeter of the mill and controlling access to the town. The saloons remain closed.

JULY 10—Interviewed in Scotland about the bloodshed at Homestead, Andrew Carnegie declares: "I have nothing whatever to say. I have given up all active control of the business."

This cartoon from The World, *July 7, 1892, was one expression of the outrage at the forces arrayed against the "American" workmen at Homestead. Carnegie wears a diamond stick pin.*

The funeral cortege for John Morris and Peter Farris, as depicted in The Pittsburg Dispatch, *July 8, 1892.*

5

Reprinted from **Bread and Roses,**
by **Milton Meltzer,** *published*
by Facts on File, Inc.,
New York, 1991.

FATHER WAS KILLED BY THE PINKERTON MEN.

'Twas in a Pennsylvania town not very long ago
Men struck against reduction of their pay
Their millionaire employer with philanthropic show
Had closed the work till starved they would obey
They fought for home and right to live where they had
     toiled so long
But ere the sun had set some were laid low
There're hearts now sadly grieving by that sad and bitter
     wrong, God help them for it was a cruel blow.

CHORUS
God help them tonight in their hour of affliction
Praying for him whom they'll ne'er see again
Hear the poor orphans tell their sad story
"Father was killed by the Pinkerton men."

Ye prating politicians, who boast protection creed,
Go to Homestead and stop the orphans' cry,
Protection for the rich man ye pander to his greed,
His workmen they are cattle and may die.
The freedom of the city in Scotland far away
'Tis presented to the millionaire suave,
But here in Free America with protection in full sway
His workmen get the freedom of the grave.

CHORUS
God help them tonight in their hour of affliction
Praying for him whom they'll ne'er see again
Hear the poor orphans tell their sad story
"Father was killed by the Pinkerton men."

JULY 8, 1892 —*Excerpted from* The World, *New York.*

IN THE HOUSES OF MOURNING.

―――――

Burial of the Victims of the Pinkerton Bullets at Homestead.

―――――

[SPECIAL TO THE WORLD.]

HOMESTEAD, PA, July 7 —The "Dead March" sounded through the streets of Homestead all this afternoon. The solemn, mournful music moaned and wailed for the dead who are gone.

The sun shone brightly in the valley. Under its blazing glances the morning glories withered and the earth was white with heat. Long lances pierced the Virginia creepers that cling about the brown cottages. In four of them the pencils of light showed the black caskets of those who yesterday fought for their bread and their homes.

Widows of the day, to whom the sombre robes were unreal, watched the undertakers place the bodies in their coffins. The children, with white, awed faces, spoke in whispers and looked about them fearsomely.

In and out flitted the neighbors, giving their sympathy in whispers and firm pressure of hands.

There was no loud wailing and lamentation. The grief is too deep for that and underneath it all is something sterner, something that is awful, soul compelling.

PETER FARIS'S LATE HOME.

There is a little, two-story, red-brick house along the railroad track. Peter Faris lived there with his brother. Peter was big and brawny. He had a broad, flat, square face with stiff, mouse-colored hair like his brother, only his brother has many more wrinkles in his forehead than Peter had. There was a carpet on the floor in the front room. The mirror of the bureau was turned in the wall. There was a casket in the room and a brass candlestick with five burning candles stood upon it. It was a plain casket with no name on it, only the words "At Rest." Peter's Testament, in which he had scribbled his name in many places was upon the casket. All the morning the big brother with his seamed face, bent over the coffin, moaning and kissing the glass which covered the face. It looked as Peter looked yesterday, only there was what looked like a clot of blood on the smoothly shaven upper lip. It was the little round hole which the Pinkerton bullet made as it sped into Peter's brain yesterday during the second attack.

WHERE JOHN MORRIS LIVED.

A dozen blocks away on Ninth avenue is the little brown cottage, with a peaked roof and a patch of green grass in front, where John M. Morris lived. There was a mother there, a tiny little woman, and sisters and a brother to mourn with the young wife. There was no pleasanter home in Homestead, no home more respected. And those who came with their sympathy whispered that he had died as heroes died, and for an instant the suffering ones would forget their grief.

These two men were buried today, the first of those whom the Pinkerton bullets caused to be placed in the earth. No King, no man of great renown ever received higher tribute from those who knew him than did these workmen. . . .

THE MOURNERS.

Upon the two front seats were those who loved John Morris better than all the others. His mother, a little round wrinkled woman, leaned her head upon the shoulder of her youngest son, a youth of fourteen, who is taller than she. No curious eyes could pierce the veil which covered the face of the wife. She sat on the second seat and all the while held in the strong clasp of the hand of her brother, whose drawn face and blazing eyes half frightened those about them. There were two sisters on the front seat. One held a baby in her arms, and while the minister was speaking the little one crowed and laughed, thinking in its babyish way it was all in good fun.

Upon the platform a woman sat before a little pipe organ, upon which she played softly. Six men and a tiny little woman made up the choir. The faces in the audience grew more soft as "Rock of Ages" filled the church. . . .

THE SERMON.

A square, strong figure has the Rev. J.J. McIlyar. His face is round and sturdy; his jaw is square; his mouth like a straight line. Above the massive forehead his gray hair is thin. A famous fighter is the Rev. McIlyar. He was a fighting Democrat during the war. Throughout western Pennsylvania he is known as a man who fears nothing and who never knows defeat.

When he arose to speak it was with the air of a man who was about to say something important and who had thought it over carefully. He said that he officiated at many funerals. In the army he had spoken the last words over famous generals and the lowest private. Since then he had officiated at the funerals of those who occupied the highest walks in life and the humblest. Yet in all his long experience he had never been called to serve on an occasion so sad as this, which had been inflicted upon a peaceful and prosperous community, and it seemed to him so unnecessary, so uncalled for, that human life should be taken under the circumstances.

There had been a difference between employees and employers in the plant located in the town about the wage scale. The employers demanded that the new scale should expire on Dec. 10, 1894. This more than the difference in wages was objected to by the men because the scale must expire at the time most expensive for living and when it is impossible to get other employment.

After many conferences the employers laid down a law like that of the Medes and Persians. During all this time the work was going on. Strangely enough, before the old scale ran out the mill was closed down. During all this time perfect peace reigned in Homestead. There was no drunkenness, no fighting, no outbreak. The men desired no war and no disturbance.

EFFORTS OF THE MEN FOR PEACE.

"The Sheriff came here. He was met peaceably. He was treated gentlemanly. He was offered 300 to 500 men to protect the works. These men would be sworn in as deputy sheriffs to serve without pay. They would give bonds for any amount for the faithful performance of their duty. He said he preferred to furnish his own men.

"He was escorted from Homestead. All had been quiet, and all remained so.

"On the evening of July 4," continued Rev. Mr. McIlyar, "when the citizenry of this peaceful town were quietly enjoying the lovely summer evening, there was floating down the Ohio River to a secluded spot below Allegheny City two boats prepared for war. They had on board guns, pistols, provisions, beds, everything necessary for a siege. The people of this town were ignorant of it.

"The employer had taken the matter . . . into his own hands. He went to New York and employed Pinkertons. One hundred and fifty men there were in charge of the Homestead plant. A friend there informed the men here. In the night, clandestinely, the gunboats were towed up the river. In the morning, when the fog was heavy, they anchored themselves in the most convenient position at the plant.

THE PREACHER ASKS A QUESTION.

"What would you have done had this crowd of Pinkerton men, this gang unauthorized by law to take the place of militia and police, not recognized as a defense corps, come upon you?"

The preacher had shot this long question at his audience as if words were the only things his cloth permitted him to shoot. A grim smile played faintly about the corners of the men's mouths. The women's faces began to look hard.

"Somebody employed these men, of course," the preacher went on. "They didn't come without orders. This brought on the difficulty. These hired fighters attacked the men of this quiet, peaceful, order-loving community, and the men of Homestead defended themselves. This blessed man lying here; this mortal man, an affectionate husband, sober and industrious, gentlemanly in manner, was killed because a conflict provoked by the Pinkerton clan made it necessary for him and his fellow-workmen to protect their homes and families. . . ."

LAST LOOK AT THE DEAD.

. . . There was no wild scene when the family said goodby to Morris. The women were like the men in their sorrow: They have suffered much. They know how to bear suffering.

The coffin was placed in the hearse again, the line reformed, and there was a funeral procession such as the iron regions have never seen.

To the slow music of the dead march hundreds upon hundreds of men, four abreast, marched along in stern silence. Other men and many women stood along the line of the march. No one seemed to talk. It was very still. There was only the shuffling of the feet and the mournful cadence of a funeral march.

Slowly up the hill a long line of men moved along. After them came scores of carriages. There were a few women in these, but very few.

THE FUNERAL OF FARIS.

Halfway up the hill they met another funeral procession. It was that of Peter Faris, the brawny young Slav. Five hundred of the 8,000 [sic] of his nationality at Homestead followed the body.

The two processions of one long line wound around the country road up the steep hill to the cemeteries, a mile and a half away. The fierce sun beat upon them. Along the route in a dozen places women stood in their front yards with pails of cold water which they offered to the thirsty ones in line.

It was all a labor of love. It was in no perfunctory spirit that these men followed the bodies to their graves, but because they were men whom they had loved.

WHERE THE BODIES WERE BURIED.

A narrow lane divides the Catholic and the Protestant cemeteries. Upon a knoll of velvet green, the highest point in the Protestant cemetery, John Morris was buried.

In the Catholic cemetery over the hill and near a ravine, there is a little corner. There are few graves in the Catholic cemetery, but in this corner the mounds of earth are close together with scarce a foot of space between them. On small wooden crosses names and dates are rudely written.

It was in this part of the cemetery that John [sic] Faris was buried. He was one of the laborers of Homestead, as is his

Allegheny County, ss.

An Inquisition indented, taken at Homestead Borough, before Ward Pyle, in the County of Allegheny, on the 23 day of July August A. D. 1892, before me, BUFFER McDOWELL, Coroner of the County aforesaid, upon the view of the body of _Silas Wain_ then and there lying dead, upon the oaths and solemn affirmations of six good and lawful men of the County aforesaid, who, being sworn and affirmed, and charged to inquire, on the part of the Commonwealth, when, where, and how, and after what manner the said _Silas Wain_ came to his death, do say upon their oaths and affirmations aforesaid, that the said _Silas S. Wain_

And so the Jurors aforesaid, upon their oaths or affirmations, as aforesaid, say that the aforesaid _Silas Wain_ for the cause aforesaid, in manner and form aforesaid, came to his death, and not otherwise.

In Witness Whereof, as well of the aforesaid Coroner, we, the Jurors, have hereunto put our hands and seals, on the day and year, and at the place above mentioned.

Cornelius Asbury [SEAL.]
John Bush [SEAL.]
C. Shlegel [SEAL.]
Buffer McDowell [SEAL.]
S. D. Fleitz [SEAL.]
R. H. Moorhead [SEAL.]
H. Davis Miller [SEAL.]

REMARKS:

Allegheny County, ss.

An Inquisition indented, taken at S. Ward Pittsburg, in the County of Allegheny, on the day of July August A. D. 1892, before me, HEBER McDOWELL, Coroner of the County aforesaid, upon the view of the body of _T. J. Owens_ then and there lying dead, upon the oaths and solemn affirmations of six good and lawful men of the County aforesaid, who, being sworn and affirmed, and charged to inquire, on the part of the Commonwealth, when, where, and how, and after what manner the said _T. J. Owens_ came to his death, do say upon their oaths and affirmations aforesaid, that the said _T. J. Owens_

And so the Jurors aforesaid, upon their oaths or affirmations, as aforesaid, say that the aforesaid _T. J. Owens_ for the cause aforesaid, in manner and form aforesaid, came to his death, and not otherwise.

In Witness Whereof, as well of the aforesaid Coroner, we, the Jurors, have hereunto put our hands and seals, on the day and year, and at the place above mentioned.

Cornelius Asbury [SEAL.]
John Burke [SEAL.]
C. Shlegel [SEAL.]
Heber McDowell [SEAL.]
S. D. White [SEAL.]
R. H. Moorhead [SEAL.]
H. Davis Miller [SEAL.]

REMARKS:

(Houses of Mourning, continued)

brother, who would not permit the association to bear the expenses of the funeral.

FATHER WIDER'S SERMON.

Following the casket to the grave was the Rev. Dr. Raymond Wider [Wedder], the pastor of the Slav Catholic Church at Braddock. Clad in cassock and white surplice he walked down the hill to the grave. He stood on the further side and intoned a prayer for the dead. His voice was so musically soothing as he chanted that when he began to speak the heavy eyes opened in wonder.

Standing there in the glare of the sun, his foot touching the edge of the open grave, and the faces of the Slavs, heavy, broad, flat, and wrinkled, rising above him tier on tier on the steep hill, the priest poured forth such a torrent of eloquence with such fire and vigor that those who could not understand him were thrilled. What he said there, what made the heavy eyes light up and then melt into tears, the outside world would never know, because Father Wider speaks not one word of English, and those who did hear him and understand could translate but little of what he said.

They could tell only that he urged them to remain true and loyal to their society, the Church Society of St. Michael, and the Workingmen's Association, and that he had said that Peter Faris had died like a brave man in fighting for his home.

THOUGHTS NOW FOR THE LIVING.

The men of Homestead had cared for their dead. The living must care for themselves. Their families again flashed uppermost in their minds. Rumors were flying about like thistle-down. They must hurry back to the town and be prepared to meet any exigency that might arise.

The leaders marshalled their forces and hurried them down the steep hill. Not for moment must the men be away from the scene of possible activity. They must be where they could answer a call instantly. Quietly as they had come together the men melted away to their homes. . . .

———❖———

JULY 8, 1982 —Excerpted from the Pittsburgh Commercial Gazette.

OVER THE BIER.

Funerals of Three of the Dead Homestead Mill Men.

A CROWDED CHURCH.

The Sensational Sermon of a Methodist Pastor.

HE ATTACKS THE COMPANY.

Charging the Killing in Wednesday's Battle Upon Carnegie Officials—Affecting Scenes While He Eulogized the Dead—A Widow's Great Grief, Calling for Her Lost Husband in the Midst of the Throng of Mourners.

(facing page) Death certificates of Silas Wain and T. J. Connors.

(below) John Morris's gravestone in the Homestead Cemetery, paid for by the Odd Fellows. All of the other workers who died as a result of the battle were apparently buried in unmarked graves.

From a Staff Correspondent.

HOMESTEAD, PA., July 7. —Three victims of Wednesday's battle were interred this afternoon with much ceremony and the accompaniment of dirges from many bands. They were John E. Morris, a pitman; a Slavish laborer named Peter Farres, and Silas Waine [sic], an English laborer, who had been but two years in this country. All of these were employes of the firm. John E. Morris was 28 years old and an employee of the works for ten years. He was an Oddfellow and belonged to Munhall lodge of the Amalgamated Association. He was one of the fighters in the first engagement with the Pinkertons, and was shot through the head while standing on the bank.

Farres was shot in the mouth. He was a non-combatant and merely a spectator when death's messenger overtook him. Wain [sic] was killed, it is currently reported, by a wide shot from the 10-pounder operated from the Baltimore & Ohio side of the river. A missile struck him in the neck as he got on a pile of iron, talking to a friend. His death was immediate.

The ceremonies attending the funerals were the most impressive ever seen in Homestead. The route of the procession to the cemeteries was lined with sympathizing spectators, and a big crowd congregated at the church where funeral services over the remains of John E. Morris were held. It was a day long to be remembered by the Homestead people.

THE FUNERAL PROCESSION.

The local lodges of Oddfellows assembled at Morris' home at 2 o'clock and forming in line, headed by the Golden Eagle band, marched to the Fourth Avenue M.E. church, where services were to be held. The mother, widow and brothers and sisters of the dead man followed in carriages. When the line of Oddfellows reached the church they opened ranks and stood with uncovered heads as the hearse passed up to the church door. The casket was carried in and placed on a bier immediately in front of the pulpit. Several beautiful floral tributes accompanied the casket.

The mother and widow and the three sisters and two brothers of the deceased steelworker followed the remains into the church and occupied seats near the pulpit. The Oddfellows and a number of Amalgamated men next filed in, following them a number of ladies, and the church was soon filled. The pulpit was occupied by the Rev. J.J. McIlyar, pastor of the church; the choir and the representatives of the press. The choir of the voices sang a hymn as the audience took seats and then the pastor requested the

(Over the Bier, continued)

band to play a piece. By this time the little church, whose seating capacity is 450, was crowded, a number of people standing in the rear. The warm July sun glinted through the stained glass windows and a stray beam fell upon the casket, in contrast with its somber surroundings and the sorrowful occasion.

When the choir had sung another hymn Mr. McIlyar delivered the funeral oration. During the delivery Mrs. Morris, mother of the deceased, was so affected that she had to leave the church. As the pastor touched on the merits of the deceased the relatives and women present became affected.

EULOGY OF THE DEAD.

The reverend gentleman began his address by remarking that though he had officiated at many funeral services it had never before fallen to his lot to do so under such peculiar and unfortunate circumstances as the present. After rehearsing the matter at issue between the company and the men with which readers will be familiar, the preacher said the men sought a final interview and had been denied it.

"During all the time preceding the last day of June," he continued, "perfect peace reigned at Homestead, and it was hoped that things would be amicably settled. The men were at length locked out and the sheriff came upon the scene. He was offered as many men as he required, under bond, to maintain the peace, but he preferred to send his own men here. They came and had to return again. Even then hopes were strong that an amicable settlement could yet be made and thoughts of violence had not entered the minds of any man at Homestead.

"The Fourth of July broke as glorious a day as could be desired for the celebration of the national holiday. It was a day on which all nature rejoiced and peace prevailed everywhere. On this day two barges were floated down to a secluded place on the river and furnished with everything necessary. The men were acquainted with the preparations being made down the river; they knew what was going on in the mind of the president of the company. He had taken the matter

The Fourth Avenue Methodist Episcopal Church, where Rev. J.J. McIlyar preached the funeral oration for John Morris.

out of the hands of the sheriff and employed other means to effect his purpose. It will be told through the newspapers tomorrow from a source there can be no question about, that 150 left New York City for the express purpose of taking charge of the Homestead plant. Now the men having been notified of the movements of the boats and of their cargo, the Pinkertons, what would you have them do? This body of Pinkerton police that is not recognized by the United States government; that has no legal right to an existence as an organization; that has no legal right to act either in this or any other state; that travels from place to place as an armed force at the call of any man that needs their reprehensible services; that, in short, is a blot on civilization and a disgrace to the country—this body of men comes down here with rifles, and what would you have the Homestead men do? The millmen were organized in an association that enabled them to obtain just and adequate remuneration for

their services. The existence of this union of the men was threatened by this body of Pinkertons, employed by somebody for the purpose. . . .

"The firm ought to have been willing to arbitrate the issue. But instead of this an attack was made on the organization of the men. What do we gain by the dumping out of our old people and the bringing in of the wreckage of other shores? Why should men continue piling up millions and send Pinkertons to drive out men that are scarcely earning a living. There is no more intelligent body of workers in the world than the Homestead mill-men and one glance around this audience is sufficient to show that they are capable of maintaining that position.

A Town In Tears.

"This town is bathed in tears to-day, and it is all brought about by one man, who is the least respected by the laboring people of any man in the country. There is no more sense of excitement in that man [Frick] than there is in a toad.

"This brother," continued Mr. McIlyar, glancing at the casket at his feet, "has gone. How respected he was you can tell by the multitude of people here to-day. He belonged to the Oddfellows, an organization whose worth is familiar and which has 100,000 members in this state. That he belonged to this order says much for the purity and integrity of his life. The Oddfellows will take charge of the remains. Let us pray that the unyielding grasp of the miser's hand may be opened and that these men may have the just reward for labor performed. Of what use can combinations of capital and trusts be without the broad shoulders and horny hands of the toilers. These are the bone and sinew of the land; these are they that

makes [sic] its wealth and gives it its prosperity."

The preacher concluded by asking the prayers of his audience for the widow who bade her husband goodby [sic] when leaving for the mill, and in a few minutes afterwards had him brought back to her dead. The unfortunate woman was deeply affected as the minister proceeded, and sobbed audibly. Very many of the women present cried with her in sympathy, while the men cast tender glances of commiseration in the direction of the sorrowing relatives.

After the choir had sung another hymn the pastor announced that those who desired could come forward by one aisle and view the remains, then passing out.

The 300 or so men were not long in filing past, and following them came the women. As this ceremony was concluded the grief of the afflicted widow grew louder as she recognized that her husband's remains would shortly be borne on their last earthly journey. Many of the women held their handkerchiefs to their eyes. One of her brothers-in-law assisted the distracted widow to a place beside the casket.

The Widow's Grief.

"Oh! my poor old man," the poor old woman sobbed as she gazed for the last time on the face of him she held most dear. "My poor old man. Who will give him back to me. What can I do without him?"

The scene was affecting. The afflicted widow was helped to the porch and the deceased's sisters and brothers, as affected as the widow took a last look at John Morris and passed out.

While the services over the remains of Morris were being held in the church

(Over the Bier, continued)

preparations for the funeral of Peter Farres, the Slav, were being made from his house on Railroad street, between Dixon and Heisel streets. The hearse and two carriages composed the cortege and a body of Amalgamated men formed up in fours stood ready to act as an escort to the grave. This funeral was drawn up on Fourth avenue awaiting the termination of the services in the church.

At 3 o'clock the Morris funeral was ready to march. The Golden Eagle band struck up the "Decoration Day" dirge and the procession moved forward up Ann street in the following order: 225 members of the Independent Order of Oddfellows of Magdala lodge, No. 991, and of Homestead lodge 1040 and of Homestead lodge 479 of the Knights of Pythias; the L.W. Stoker band of Homestead; hearse containing remains of John E. Morris, and thirteen carriages. When Fifth avenue had been crossed the column of Amalgamated men, 300 strong, wheeled into Ann street, and headed by the Excelsior band, followed the funeral ahead. The hearse carrying the remains of the Slav and two carriages containing his brother, the Rev. Father Wedder [Wider], the Pastor of the Slavish congregation of Braddock, and other friends. The double funeral moved slowly to the burial place, passing at every corner groups of people who expressed sympathy with the deceased and their friends.

The Homestead cemetery is distant about half a mile from the center of the borough and is charmingly situated on gently rising ground. St. Mary's cemetery, the Catholic cemetery, is divided from it by the roadway. The surrounding country is gently undulating and from the top of the verdure clad mound which contains the general place of interment one affords views of much beauty. It was here that the last resting place of John E. Morris had been made. . . .

Three more of the men killed on Thursday will be buried tomorrow.

THE DEAD AND WOUNDED.

The Long List That Followed the Battle on Wednesday— Every Pinkerton Man Hurt.

The list of the dead and wounded of the battle is finally completed and embraces every one of the 305 Pinkerton men who were on the fatal barges. About midnight on Wednesday night Mike Connors, 40 years of age, a single man of Montgomery street, New York, died at the West Penn hospital. A shot in the arm severed the brachial artery at 5:30 on Wednesday morning, and all day long he lay without any attention. The wound itself was not dangerous, but lack of food for two days and attention after the shot was too much and he could not rally from the shock. Death was due to exhaustion. His death made the eighth in all. The completed list of dead and wounded is as follows:

THE DEAD.

JOHN [E.] MORRIS, Ninth avenue, married and leaves a wife.

SILAS WAINE [WAIN, WAYNE], Fifteenth avenue, unmarried.

THOMAS WELDON, shot accidentally while handling a gun after boarding barges. A resident of Second avenue; married, leaves a wife and family.

HENRY STRIEGEL [STRLEGLE], aged 19 years, son of Charles Striegel, a resident of Sixth avenue.

JOHN PARES [PETER FARRIS, FARES, FARIS], a Hungarian laborer.

J.W. KLINE, aged 25, Pinkerton detective, Chicago.

MIKE [T.J.] CONNORS, aged 40, Pinkerton detective, lived on Montgomery street, New York.

JOSEPH SOPPO [SAPPA], aged 33, millworker, shot in left knee and died from loss of blood and want of medical attention.

FATALLY INJURED.

PAT MCGOFF, 197 Ontario, Chicago, shot in the abdomen.

E.A. COVERT, 687 Herkimer street, Brooklyn, shot in the abdomen.

FRED PRIMER, 1315 Wheat street, Philadelphia, skull crushed and internal injuries.

WILLIAM FOY, Twelfth avenue, Homestead, mill worker.

GEORGE RETTER [W. RUTTER], Homestead, mill worker.

RICHARDSON DURHAM [RICHARD DURMAN], Homestead, mill worker.

THE OTHER INJURED.

ALFRED FAY, shot in hand. Claims he has been long employed by Pinkertons and carries several old wounds.

H.W. GREGORY, Philadelphia, shot in hand; also laceration of the scalp.

W.E. REGER, Philadelphia, contusion of the eye.

PATRICK MAGUIRE, Baltimore, shot in the arm.

CHRISTIAN LAMB, Philadelphia, struck with gun butt in the back.

E.R. SPEER, Chicago, gun-shot wound in calf of leg.

EDWARD MCSNEM [sic], shot in calf of leg.

CHARLES NORTHROP, Chicago, back injured from blow from club.

JOSEPH MALLEY, Chicago, shot in the thigh.

E.J. ZOELER, Philadelphia, kicked in the abdomen.

JOSEPH MURPHY, New York, face smashed.

FRED ASBERRY, Chicago, face badly cut.

GEORGE WAHL, Chicago, arm fractured.

GEORGE WRIGHT, Chicago, arm fractured.

ANTHONY COULTER, Chicago, wounded in the back.

JOHN LUTZ, New York, lacerated scalp.

LEWIS FLAGER, shot in the arm and scalp injuries.

WILL MCKINNON, New York, leg fractured.

FRED GERBERT, New York, scalp wounds and eye injured.

JAMES H. PUGH, Brooklyn, eye and arm injured.

ED WILSTED, Chicago, lip and nose mashed.

J.B. SCOFIELD, Chicago, head badly bruised.

W.H. JOHNSTON, Chicago, dislocated ankle.

JOHN CRIDLEON [sic], New York, injuries to eye and scalp.

CAPT. FRED W. HINDE [HEINDE, HINES] of the Pinkerton detectives, age 41 years, residence New York, shot in the leg.

MIKE GOUGH, Chicago, gunshot in the groin.

HENRY RUSISKI [ROSISKY], laborer, shot in shoulder, probably fatally wounded.

ANDY SUDIA, bullets in thigh and hand. Lives on Eighth avenue and has a family. Very badly hurt.

THOMAS KANE, burnt in leg. Lives on Fourth avenue, single.

CHARLES DAESKA [DOKSKA], laborer, hurt in thigh. At Homeopathic hospital. May die.

ANTONIO PALATKI [PALATKA], residing on Third avenue, shot in the leg.

JOHN HERSHI [HERSKI], resident of Third avenue, bullet in leg.

CHARLES MULANKIE [MULANKIS], shot in arm.

JOSEPH SODAK [SOTAK], shot through knee. At Homeopathic hospital.

In addition to these names might be added that of all the other detective guards, as not one escaped injury.

All the injured people at the Homeopathic hospital will recover. Many of them were much improved yesterday and some may be discharged to-day. No additional cases were brought in during the day.

Variant spelling from other sources included.

AT THE MORGUE.

Last evening the bodies of Edward Connors and J.W. Kline, both Pinkerton detectives, were shipped. Both men were identified by telegrams received from William A. Pinkerton of Chicago. Connors' body was sent to New York to his relatives and Kline's to Chicago, where he lived. . . .

Rawsthorne Engraving and Printing Co., the original publishers of Arthur G. Burgoyne's Homestead, *set aside 5 percent of the net profits from the sale of the book to purchase a monument in honor of the workers. The proposed monument, to be ordered from a catalogue, was never erected.*

JULY 7, 1892 —Excerpted from the Pittsburgh Catholic.

THE HOMESTEAD INCIDENT.

The present troubles at Homestead are an object lesson to be studied closely, and are not lightly passed over. So-called capital and organized labor have been brought face to face, the one breathing defiance, the other hurling back its threats with a spirit of rancor that forbodes ills in the future. The people are suffering under the abuse of high protection. Protectionism, which has established in its theory, the workmen could claim their share as a right, but which capital is receiving and the workmen are robbed of.

It has become the instrument of the capitalist, while masquerading as a philanthropist and proclaiming its mission to be the protection of the American workman and American industries.

The significance of the Homestead incident is not to be underestimated by any thoughtful person. The motives of the strikers are good, reasonable and substantial, while the application of their methods is undoubtedly wrong, and in defiance of legitimate authority, but it is a fact we must face and from which the country cannot escape. The organization we see there to-day, and the discipline and the determined purpose may become a united one, and the end cannot but be disastrous. . . .

If laws are to promote the healthy growth of our industries, and our industries must rely upon legislation to succeed, labor must have its full share of such legislation. Since capital demands such legislation, and has obtained it, it must share it with labor, must not use it to increase its millions and reduce to slavery labor which is the creator of capital, otherwise the darkest page in American history may yet have to be written.

JULY 8, 1892 —Excerpted from the **Pittsburgh Commercial Gazette.**

AN ARMED PEACE.

The Homestead Strikers Prepared to Resist New Workmen.

A Close Watch Kept for Detectives and Non-Union Workmen—a Rumor of an Approaching Barge Causes the Signal to Be Given.

From a Staff Correspondent.

HOMESTEAD, PA., July 7. —The streets are patrolled by an unusually vigilant force of special officers. The circulation of the inflammatory circulars by the six unknown men sent here from Pittsburgh has aroused the populace, and in all sides of the long, tortuous, and at night dangerous-to-tread streets, men, women, and children are to be seen sitting on stairs and in doorways. They dread the coming of another assault of armed men on the works. The anxiety of these people is something terrible. They have brothers, fathers, sons among the strikers and they momentarily fear the sounding of the alarm, the crack of Winchesters and the booming cannon that means the death or the wounding of their own loved ones or of neighbors, friends or shopmates of their own bread-winners.

An Awful Suspense.

War in all its forms furnishes no more horrible suspense than that endured by these people. The sign of slaughter yesterday, the three funerals to-day, two funerals before them to-morrow and half a dozen wounded lingering between life and death has served to terrorize the people, and they are ready to start at the slightest alarm. That such a situation as this exists in the republic that prides itself upon being the land of the free and the home of the brave must seem incredible to the calm reader of these lines, but that they exist is attested by the fact that at this moment the telegraph office is thronging with armed and excited men called out by the alarm sounded by the whistle at the electric-light power station.

A Sunday-like quiet has prevailed here all day and will continue until another attempt is made by the Carnegie company to land men on the mill property.

When that occurs again, if it ever does, a fiercer and far more bloody battle will be the result. The hope and prayer of all strikers and citizens here is that no occasion may arise to cause a repetition of the scenes of yesterday; but the slightest attempt to break through the guard line of the strikers around the mill property will precipitate a battle in comparison with which the conflict of Wednesday will be a mere skirmish.

With the addition of the 240 rifles and the boxes of ammunition taken from the surrendered Pinkerton men the strikers are prepared to make a deadly onslaught on any man or body of men who shall attempt to wrest the mill property from their control. Yesterday's success has pushed them to the full and they now have greater confidence in their power to hold Fort Frick against all comers than ever before.

The strikers are not seeking more bloodshed, but it was a common remark among them that if another body of Pinkertons and black-sheep were sent here no quarter would be shown them. It will be a war of extermination from now on, the strikers arguing that the fate of the imported men on the two ill-fated barges, whose hulls now rest on the bottom of the river at the end of Ann street, while the ashes of their decks have been blown to the four winds of heaven, should be sufficient warning to others to keep away from Homestead.

Under the Black Flag.

If they come they know what to expect. They must either march over the dead bodies of the strikers and gain possession of the iron mills or be killed themselves. The day for surrender and protection such as is given in war is past. "We have no mercy to expect at their hands after what occurred yesterday and they should expect none at ours." These were the words this morning of a score or more of excited strikers as they gathered on a street corner and discussed the events of Wednesday.

Chairman O'Donnell, David Lynch, George Saiver [sic, Sarver] and a committee of merchants went to Pittsburgh this afternoon and the rumor at once spread that they had been invited by H.C. Frick to a conference. Another and more plausible story was that the party was going to Harrisburg to make a personal appeal to Gov. Pattison to visit Homestead. The people here, of course, are delighted at the governor's refusal to send troops here in response to Sheriff McCleary's call, and although it is generally conceded that the governor was actuated principally by political motives the fact that he so far has kept the national guard away from Homestead has won him the adulation of the local populance [sic].

The quietude of to-day did not prevent the circulation of scores of startling remarks, the most ominous of which was that Agent Nordrum of the Pinkerton Company, who was among the prisoners here yesterday, was about to return here with about 150 trained Pinkerton men as soon as they could be shipped on from Chicago. Nordrum is ex-chief of the World's fair police and was before that a member of the Chicago front-office force. His name appears on the log book of the barges, secured by Chairman O'Donnell before the boats were burned. Nordrum has a record as a fearless and determined man, and this reported move of his would not be at all surprising.

The roll of names in the captured log book shows that only forty-one of the 248 men on the list were trained Pinkerton patrolmen and the rest were raw recruits. Had the entire list been old-time Pinkertons the chances are that the men in the barges would have made a more bitter battle and that the death list on both sides would have mounted into the hundreds. As it was the regular Pinkertons, with the addition of only a few of the recruits, used the Winchesters, while the other new men crouched and huddled in groups wherever the thought they could

be sheltered in the boats from the shots from shore.

Anarchistic Circulars.

At 8 o'clock this evening the town was thrown into a wild state of excitement by the circulation of a lot of Anarchistic circulars.

The circulars were distributed by six men who came here from Pittsburgh on the evening train and took advantage of the supper hour to get their work out. The men threw the circulars out by thousands, and when the strikers found out the import of them there was an immediate chase to discover who was circulating the inflammatory documents. Soon two men were landed in the little brick lockup, and four others, who had been handing out the offensive documents, were escorted to the 10:02 train for Pittsburgh and forced to board it and get out of town. This the men were glad to do. They had been employed to give out these circulars, and did so unwittingly, not knowing what they were doing. The strikers repudiate the authorship of these addresses and insist vehemently that they are not responsible for their utterance.

A Press Censorship.

The circulars are poorly printed and evidently designed by men who desire to cause further bloodshed. The honest workmen here do not want this, and are doing their utmost to preserve the peace. They want no man armed who is not [sic] antagonistic to their interests, and stand prepared to defend everybody who signifies a willingness to aid in the preservation of peace and good order.

The circulation of the Anarchistic order has led to press censorship in a modified form. While the strikers are willing to trust to the veracity of the accounts of the reporters . . . [they] object to being represented in the guise of outlaws, cutthroats, desperadoes and marauders, and insist that, truth to be told, their battle is one for fair play and a living.

———

PEACE AT HOMESTEAD.

—————

But It Is Only the Peace That Comes from Non-Interference.

HOMESTEAD, PA., July 7. —After the carnage of yesterday and last night the town of Homestead to-day was almost as quiet as a sleepy country village. The interment of three workmen killed in the battle was the chief evidence of the storm of yesterday. Up to 8 o'clock tonight nothing occurred to mar the peace, which is profound.

The strikers are masters of the situation to-day. The best evidence of their intention to protect property lies at the scene of last night's battle, where the immense plant of the firm of Carnegie, Phipps & Co. stands practically uninjured. The damage due to yesterday's preparation for warfare has been repaired. The fence around the works has been rebuilt, the yard cleared of all debris, and the hose used in throwing oil on the water restored to its place. The watchmen of the firm have been reinstated, McBloom having been granted permission to bring his men back. No property has been destroyed, no pillage except that attending the disgraceful scenes enacted after the surrender last night has been attempted, no disorder has occurred, and all those scenes familiar to later outbreaks in Europe are absent.

The darkest story of the whole affair is that of the running of the gauntlet after the surrender and the brutality inflicted upon the defenseless Pinkertons. Careful inquiry among eye witnesses shows that reports of it were not exaggerated. The women were the most virulent and savage after the surrender and it was due largely to their acts and to their goading of the men that the leaders were unable to restrain the mob. Tales in numbers are told of the scenes along the gauntlet. The Mme. Defarge of the movement was a woman who stood near headquarters and outdid all the men. That the more intelligent and conservative men realize that the mobbing of the defenseless men cannot but injure their cause is shown by their sensitiveness to publications on this

(Peace, continued)

subject. It must be said, however, that it is the non-combatants who should be charged with the work. While peace reigns to-day it is an armed peace. No reasonable man who is here doubts for a moment that fighting would be resumed at once if another attempt were made to introduce Pinkerton men into the town. Homestead, so far as the introduction of these men goes, is in a state of siege. The town is picketed and no man can enter without his presence being noted. A cordon of watchful and intensely suspicious workmen are around the entire city. Every road is guarded. Along the river, above and below, on this bank and on the opposite bank a ceaseless patrol is maintained. No boat, no party of men can come along without being followed, and if it is thought worth while, questioned. Railroads are watched as they have been from the first.

The men intend that the works shall not be taken by surprise. They are stronger now in numbers and death-dealing equipments. Besides this they are encouraged by the prestige of last night's success and the arrival of a number of fellow workmen from outside towns, bringing with them assurance of sympathy on the part of their co-laborers and of assistance, physically and financially if needed. Wheeling, W. Va., sent twenty mill men well supplied with money as an advance guard. They said that they were a delegation from 1,000 iron-workers who would lend financial aid and would come here to fight if their presence were desired. They pay their own expenses.

———❖———

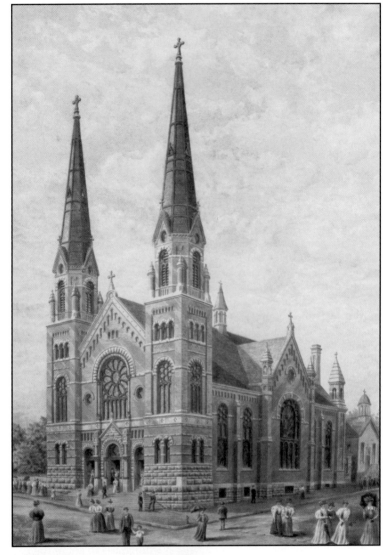

In this turn-of-the-century painting, St. Mary's Catholic Church in Homestead almost hides the small edifice at the far right which was the church in 1892 at the time of the funeral services.

(left) Rev. Father John J. Bullion

JULY 9, 1892 —*Reprinted from* The World, *New York.*

BURIAL OF THE DEAD.

Henry Striegel, Thomas Weldon and Joseph Sotak Laid in Their Graves.

[SPECIAL TO THE WORLD.]

HOMESTEAD, PA., July 8.—Six newly made graves in the village cemeteries are the silent evidences of Homestead's loss in the conflict with Pinkerton's forces Wednesday morning. They are strewn with flowers and evergreens, placed there not by friends alone, but by men and women who love the cause for which the men buried there gave up their lives. Before the grass has grown upon these six mounds, almost before the flowers strewn there have all withered, marble pillars erected by the citizens of Homestead will tell the history of the struggle in which the six men died.

Three of the men who were killed Wednesday were buried yesterday. The remaining three were buried to-day. The sturdy determination and lack of emotion which characterized yesterday's funerals were equally manifest at those which took place to-day.

Notwithstanding the fact that nearly every person in Homestead passed the night awake, expecting another struggle with the Pinkerton forces, hundreds of the locked out men, with their families, attended the funeral of Henry Striegel at 9 o'clock this morning. Striegel was a member of the Eintracht Saengerbund Society and the active Turners, the latter an athletic organization. A delegation of Turners from the south side of Pittsburg, accompanied by a brass band, arrived on the early morning train to attend the funeral.

After a brief service at the house the procession headed by the Homestead brass band and the Turners dressed in their athletic suits, marched to the German Catholic Church. The leader of the band carried an American flag, draped in mourning. Preceding the hearse a member of the Turners' society walked carrying a similarly draped flag.

SERVICES AT THE CHURCH.
The services at the church were brief, consisting of the customary mass. Then the bell in the church tower began tolling and the funeral carriages followed by a long line of workingmen went up the hall to the cemetery, a mile distant.

There was no priest at the grave. The rules of the Catholic Church forbade it, as Striegel had not attended mass or confession in a long time. It was only by a special dispensation from the Bishop at Pittsburg that the funeral was held in the Catholic church. But there was a sexton at the churchyard, a kindly faced, gray-haired workingman, and as the mourners and friends knelt around the open grave the sexton, with his shovel resting against his shoulders and his hands clasped, went through the solemn service.

AN OMINOUS SOUND.
Once during the prayer at the grave the deep whistle of a locomotive came from the direction of the village. It sounded much like the steam whistle of the electric-light works, which was blown at midnight last night to call the locked-out men to arms. The men kneeling at the graves instinctively turned their eyes towards the village and the look of tenderness on their faces gave way to an expression of determination. In a second the whistle stopped and the workmen again bowed their heads in prayer.

The second funeral was that of Thomas Weldon, which took place at 2 o'clock. Weldon was a member of several societies, including the Hibernian, and hundreds of workmen, neatly dressed and wearing white gloves, gathered at the house. Weldon was a roller in the mills and he was fatally hurt by the accidental discharge of a gun in the hands of one of the locked-out men after they had taken possession of the barges. He was taken home dying and the shock to his wife, who was in confinement, prostrated her. There are four small children and the family is left destitute.

FATHER BULLION'S SERMON.
The funeral procession, headed by a band, proceeded to the Catholic church. The customary funeral service was gone through, then Father Bullion delivered a short address. He spoke with deliberation and force, and as he referred in scornful tones to the murders of the Homestead workmen there was a decided sensation throughout the church. Once the mother of Weldon fainted and a glassful of water was brought to her, while others of the mourners fanned her back to consciousness. During his remarks Father Bullion said:

"It is sad for us to note that the usually quiet and peaceful town of Homestead should have been transformed into a battle-ground. When we inquire into the reason for this we are told that differences exist between capital and labor which have not been satisfactorily adjusted and that, on this account, we experienced the scenes we have witnessed during the past few days—differences that exist between the great corporation, the Carnegie Steel Company, and the honest workingmen of Homestead.

"It is sad that it should be necessary to have recourse to the use of firearms. It is strange to me that these differences could not be adjusted in some other way than by such violent means.

"It apparently becomes necessary in the eyes of the firm to send to this peaceful town men who are called Pinkerton detectives, but whom I would rather call Pinkerton rowdies in order to murder honest workingmen who have taken possession of the property to defend it, and to which property they have a certain right, as Senator Palmer has said. I agree with him to an extent that the workman has a certain right on account of the length of time he has been employed—not the deed

(Burial of the Dead, continued)

of the property but a certain claim—and that when he protects that property he is doing only what is right. As long as he does nothing wrong he has a right to expect permanent employment, and hence it is wrong for a mob to come here and deprive the workman of the right that is his.

"I hope the time will come when workingmen will have the right to permanent employment as long as they conduct themselves properly, and that laws will be promulgated so that there will not be occasion for such riots as have taken place during the past few days. I do not intend to speak here to-day in regard to the merits or demerits of the strike now going on, as I consider this neither the time nor the place."

EULOGY OF THE DEAD.

The kind-hearted priest spoke of the life and character of the man who lay in the coffin before him. He said he had been an honest hearted workman, a kind parent, and one who had proved himself worthy of the name of a true Christian. In concluding, Father Bullion said:

"Do not forget the man who has lost his life in endeavoring to protect his home and provide for his family. He merits our continued thoughts and prayers for the welfare of his soul and the temporal and spiritual welfare of the family he has left

alone in the struggle against poverty. Our duty is plain. Let us see that it is performed."

The tolling bell announced the beginning of the funeral march to the cemetery. As the long procession left the church another funeral procession appeared in an adjoining street. It was the Slavs bearing the body of their companion, Joseph Sotak, who died in the hospital from wounds received in the riot.

The funeral had been held in the Methodist Church. Rev. J. Cedochi, a Slavonian minister from Pittsburg, conducted the services in the Slavonian language. The subject which he used as a funeral text was, "All Reforms Are Brought About by Bloodshed." He spoke in a full, clear voice, and his words seemed to electrify the people who filled the church.

IN THE CEMETERIES.

The funeral processions, a few rods from each other, filed slowly up the hill to the cemeteries, the feet of the marchers keeping time to the funeral dirges played by the bands.

The services at the cemeteries were soon completed, and, with many a look backward to the cemetery where six of their number lay buried, the workmen returned to the village and quietly dispersed to their homes.

———❖———

JULY 9, 1892 —Excerpted from the **Pittsburgh Commercial Gazette.**

AFRAID OF SPIES.
Newspaper Men Subjected to Close Scrutiny By Strikers.

HOMESTEAD, PA., July 8. —The large number of newspaper men here are causing the workers much concern. This is not because they object to the fraternity, but because the excuse of "I am a newspaper man" is so easily made for one's presence that the workers are inclined to the belief that it is being used by some other than legitimate members of the craft.

Committees of the men commenced rigorous inquiries into the virtue of the correspondents' claims last evening. Some of the eastern men run the gauntlet of some close questioning, which they would not have been newspaper men if they did not take philosophically, and one writer from a northern city had a little difficulty in establishing his bona fides. The workers think that more than one detective is operating under the guise of a correspondent, and where there are so many men, most of whom are strangers to each other, this might have some semblance of truth about it.

———❖———

Reprinted from the **National Labor Tribune,** *December 8, 1892.*

A PARODY ON THE "BLUE BELLS OF SCOTLAND"

Oh, where, and oh, where is that Highland lairdie, man?
He has gone to merrie Scotland to hunt for some new plan
That will pull down the wages of all the working clan.

Oh, why, and oh, why should he pull down poor men's pay?
"To build another library that at some future day
Will be another monument," is what the people say.

Oh, where, and oh, where will he take his surplus hoard?
He'll take it to the Highlands to pay for bed and board,
And in buying Cluney castles in which to reign as lord.

Oh my, and oh my, can this philanthropist see
That his name will live forever to execrated be,
As an inconsistent teacher of true democracy?

Alfred Morton

JULY 10, 1892 —Excerpted from an article, "Sanctioned by Carnegie," in the St. Louis Post-Dispatch.

"FRICK'S COURSE MEETS THE BARON'S FULL APPROBATION."

KINLOCH RANOCH, PERTHSHIRE, SCOTLAND. July 9 —The Sunday Post-Dispatch correspondent today called at this magnificent [sic] shooting cottage occupied during the summer by Mr. Andrew Carnegie and requested an interview with that gentleman.

For three days Mr. Carnegie has been coaching from Edinburgh via Braemar and Pitlochry, coming to this place. He drove through here today behind four superb grays in the most elaborate coach that Scotland has ever seen upon its roads and which has figured in the guide books and the literature of this neighborhood.

This cottage for which Mr. Carnegie has found it desirable to reduce the wages of his workmen in order that he may pay $10,000 to occupy it for eight weeks, is situated ten miles from Kinloch and at the head of the Loch, a beautiful sheet of water, surrounded by broad grouse moor and dark green forests, both fat with game. It is a comfortable, rambling, two-story building of gray stone, fronting on the lake and surrounded by stone outbuildings with gardens and lawns running down to the edge of the water.

The correspondent drove this afternoon to the lodge where he was received by a dignified English servant in blue livery, white stripes on his trousers giving him in this uniform quite a military or even Pinkerton air.

In response to the correspondent's request to see Mr. Carnegie he was ushered into a bare, sportsmanlike reception room whose walls are covered with antlers, twenty-eight pairs in all, each bearing the card of the gentleman who had killed the buck, the absence of a card being presumed to indicate that Mr. Carnegie had been the victor himself. On a table in the center of the room were two newspapers open and articles in them marked, showing that Mr. Carnegie was perfectly au courant with the situation at Homestead. One of these papers was a London Times of Friday last containing the story of the riot and telling that six strikers had been killed outright and six fatally wounded and that nine Pinkerton men fell in the struggle. Around these figures Mr. Carnegie or someone else had drawn a ring with a lead pencil. The other paper was the Pall Mall Gazette and on its open page was the deadly parallel column, one showing Mr. Carnegie's philanthropic talk at the opening of the free library in Aberdeen, where the Earl and Countess of Aberdeen were flanking him, on the other side was the table of the reduction of wages at Homestead. In this room the correspondent sat for over an hour without any intimation being given that he was to be received. Finally, Mr. Carnegie came through the hall with a quick, energetic step and entered the room.

The correspondent asked him if he cared to say anything in regard to the troubles at his mills, and Mr. Carnegie in the most contemptuous and insulting manner replied: "I have nothing whatever to say. I have given up all active control of the business, and I do not care to interfere in any way with the present management's conduct of this affair."

"But do you not still exercise a supervision of the affairs of the company?" he was asked.

This cartoon from The Chicago Times, *July 10, 1892, mocks Carnegie's "Gospel of Wealth," which proclaimed that every millionaire must benefit society by investing his wealth in public institutions that help the average man.*

(Frick's Course, continued)

"I have nothing whatever to say on that point. The business management is in the hands of those who are fully competent to deal with any question that may arise."

"Have you heard from Homestead since the riot occurred?"

"I have received several cables and among them several asking my interference with the parties in control."

"But you must have some opinion in the matter that you are willing to express."

"No, sir. I am not willing to express any opinion. The men have chosen their course and I am powerless to change it. The handling of the case on the part of the company has my full approbation and sanction. Further than this I have no disposition to say anything."

When Mr. Carnegie had thus delivered himself he turned abruptly and left the room. All that had been said was said standing. The correspondent was neither invited to take a seat nor was there any hesitancy on the part of Mr. Carnegie to indicate that the visit was an intrusion upon his ducal magnificence, [sic] and it is not at all likely that had he known that it was a correspondent who awaited him that he would either have appeared at the end of an hour or spoken when he did appear.

As the correspondent stepped upon the stairs the dignified and uniformed servant who had so courteously borne off his card an hour or so earlier ascended the steps, and with a suavity that any ten of the ironworkers at Homestead would willing have sacrificed their entire wages to have seen, said: "Mr. Carnegie is in the garden. I have just found him, and he does not care to have anything to say to you."

"Thank you," your correspondent replied, "I found him myself five minutes ago."

It can only be said then that Mr. Carnegie is watching the fluctuations of the situation from an indifferent and untroubled district 2,000 miles away from the agitation and he has nothing to say.

————❖————

A MAN NAMED CARNEGIE

Sing ho, for a man named Carnegie,
    Who owns us, controls us, his cattle, at will.
Doff hats to himself and his lady;
    Let the sigh of the weary be stiller and still.
Drink, boys, to the health of Carnegie,
    Who gives his slaves freedom to live—if they can.
Bend knees, and cheer, chattels, cheer. He
    May still be a chattel who can't be a man.

But, oh, there was weeping last night at the Homestead!
    The river ran red on its way to the sea,
And curses were muttered and bullets whistling,
    And Riot was King of the land of the free.

Sing ho, for we know you, Carnegie;
    God help us and save us, we know you too well;
You're crushing our wives and you're starving our babies;
    In our homes you have driven the shadow of hell.
Then bow, bow down to Carnegie,
    Ye men who are slaves to his veriest whim;
If he lowers your wages cheer, vassals, then cheer. Ye
    Are nothing but chattels and slaves under him.

But, oh, did you hear it, that mad cry for vengeance,
    Which drowned with its pulses the cannon's loud roar?
For women were weeping last night at the Homestead,
    And the river ran red from shore unto shore.

Then woe to the man named Carnegie!
    His vassals are rising, his bondsmen awake,
And there's woe for the lord and there's grief for his lady
    If his slaves their manacles finally break.
Let him call his assassins; we've murder for murder.
    Let him arm them with rifles; we've cannon to greet.
We are guarding our wives and protecting our babies,
    And vengeance for bloodshed we sternly will mete.

And, oh, did you hear it, that wild cry for mercy
    The Pinkertons raised as they fell 'neath our fire?
They came armed with guns for shooting and killing,
    But they cowered like curs 'neath our death-dealing ire.

Sing ho, if the man named Carnegie
    Were under our guns, where the Pinkertons stood,
He would shrink like a dog and would cry like a baby;
    But his country he's left for his country's best good.
He rides in a carriage; his workmen "protected"
    Pray God for a chance that their dear ones may live;
For he's crushing our wives and he's starving our babies,
    And we would be hounds to forget or forgive.

But, oh, it was awful, that day at Homestead,
    When the river ran red on its way to the sea,
When brave men were falling and women were weeping.
    And Riot was King of the land of the free!

Anonymous, Stockton, California, July 7, 1892.

THE CHURCH SIDES WITH LABOR.

PASTORS TALK PLAINLY OF THE ODIOUSNESS OF PINKERTONISM.

[SPECIAL TO THE WORLD.]

BOSTON, July 10. —From the pulpit of the Church of the Carpenter this morning the Rev. W.D.P. Bliss, in speaking of the recent troubles at Homestead, Pa., said:

"Homestead has spoken to the country. It has thrilled the ranks of labor with new life, new courage, new manliness. Workmen have met and defeated the desperado hirelings of capital, and for their victory we need to thank God. Democratic papers might be accused of using the incident for political purposes, but Republican papers have almost unanimously declared the employment of the Pinkertons as needless and unjust. One Republican paper of this city has even said that we want a little less of music hall and library charity and a little more humanity from Andrew Carnegie.

"The prime issue at Homestead was whether Mr. Carnegie, skulking in ease in Scotland, shall win all the benefit of improved machinery and workmen get no better wages; and secondly, whether workingmen shall or shall not have the right to organize as capital is organized."

The Rev. Charles G. Ames, at the New South Church, held the attention of a large congregation for nearly three-quarter of an hour's talk on the Homestead troubles. He began with this:

"Close following the celebration of our national independence with its grand boast of liberty, equality and fraternity, there comes from Western Pennsylvania a tumult of angry workers, with the short crack of rifles and the groans of dying men—a bloody, horrible business. Yet it is only one incident to the mad struggle between capital and labor. The flash of those guns reveals a situation as wide as the continent."

Dr. Louis Albert Banks of the First M.E. Church, Temple street, pulled Carnegie over the coals with a vengeance. What the public wants of Carnegie, he said, is justice and not the kind of charity he has been dealing out of late. The sorest point in the whole trouble he thought was the refusal of the mill owners to meet them squarely and show a disposition to do what is right.

"A few years ago," said Mr. Banks, "Mr. Carnegie wrote a book entitled 'Triumphant Democracy,' which attracted wide attention. But this refusal on the part of himself and associates to recognize his employees as equals in the situation and worthy of being met in generous, brotherly conference, is a cruel stroke at the very root of democracy. It is a practical assertion of the divine right of the plutocracy. The whole affair would indicate that the Old World castle in which Mr. Carnegie is spending his summer has saturated himself and associates with Old World ideas as well."

PITTSBURG, PA. July 10. —A number of the Pittsburg preachers referred to the Homestead troubles during the course of their sermons.

The Rev. David McAllister of the Eighth Street Reformed Presbyterian Church said: "The Christian teaching bears on all problems springing from the relations between labor and capital. The problem at Homestead has lost its original cast. It has become a question of law and good government. Their natural sympathies with the workman have led many people and a few newspapers to express themselves in such a way as to make the problem infinitely hard. No matter what motives may have existed, their position has been to incite riot.

"Modern Communism will not solve this Homestead problem. Modern Communism is a perversion of the gospel. It lets a man share in property no matter if he has not helped to earn it. In the Gospel of Christ the personal claim is recognized. There can be no settlement at

Andrew Carnegie at Skibo Castle, 1914.

(Church Sides, continued)

Homestead as long as the law and Constitution are trampled under foot as they are at present. One breach of the law has led to another.

"When I read of the abuse of those Pinkerton men my blood boiled, and I felt ready to take up a musket and help restore order at Homestead. I hope every man in my congregation felt so. Believing in reforms as I do, it is necessary to say that, first of all, the law must be maintained at any cost. The treatment of those Pinkerton men after they had surrendered was shameful. The actions of the strikers would have disgraced savages. The treatment before their surrender, when the white flag was shot away three times, was an infinite disgrace.

"If we had the right kind of man at the head of the Government that riot would have been quelled in twenty-four hours. The situation is growing in seriousness hourly. Those men are now flushed with a so-called victory.

"I recognize the grievances of the workingmen and the justice of many of their claims, but property rights are sacred.

"The leading feature of it all is that the law has been scoffed. It is a burning shame that we should be taxed to uphold a military force and then be refused its help. A government that does not govern should step down and out for one that has the grit to meet an emergency like this, which is not local but national."

CHICAGO, ILL., July 10.—The Rev. Alfred Henry, a prominent west side pastor, preached a sermon on the Homestead trouble to-day. He defended and upheld the locked-out millmen, and claimed that all men situated as they were would have done as they did.

The company's statement struck him as a fine bit of burlesque writing. It showed that while the output of the mills was largely increased, and consequently the prosperity of the company increased, this was used as an argument to cut wages instead of allowing the men to share in the prosperity. He denounced the company and its methods.

———❖———

JULY 11, 1892 —*Excerpted from the* New York Herald.

SERMONS ON THE LOCKOUT.

————

Pastor Dixon Thinks If Pinkertons Were Hanged It Would Spoil Good Rope.

At Association Hall at the morning service yesterday the Rev. Thomas Dixon, Jr., spoke of "the terrible occurrences at Homestead," and sharply criticized Andrew Carnegie for his treatment of the steel workers. He also denounced the Pinkertons, and said that "if every man of them were taken out and hanged the only loss to the nation would be the wear and tear of rope." The congregation loudly applauded these remarks.

The Rev. Dr. W.W. Boyd, pastor of the First Baptist Peddie Memorial Church, of Newark, preached yesterday on the late happenings at Homestead, Pa.

"A mistake was made by the Carnegie company," he said, "in refusing to submit to arbitration the differences between itself and the workmen or to meet their representatives, for in these days of concentration of capital the organization of workers is necessary to the protection of their rights. The second mistake which was morally, if not legally, a crime, was in the employment of Pinkerton detectives, a body which entered armed in time of peace into a well organized State to usurp powers inherent only in the State or nation. The employment of these men was not an alternative but a deliberate choice, and seemingly premeditated, for Mr. Frick had not appealed to the Governor for protection nor had he notified the authorities of the county that they would be held responsible for any damage to his works, and the boats in which the detectives came were steel lined, provisioned and fitted with all the munitions of war. The manager of the Carnegie company is morally, if not legally, guilty of the bloodshed which has taken place.

"The working men made a mistake in coming and holding the property of the company, but let it be said to their credit that up to the present they have preserved it intact. But in declaring that the non-union men shall not be employed in the works and in attempting to ensure that results, they put themselves in a wholly indefensible position. The true course would be obedience to law and appeal to public sentiment."

———

IN HOMESTEAD'S CHURCHES.

Prayers for a Speedy and Peaceful Settlement of the Trouble.

. . . The Rev. Father John J. Bullion made no allusion to the fight in his sermon in the Catholic Church, but while making the parochial announcements for the week he spoke of the trouble and said:— "I hope that arbitrators will be appointed by the employers and by the workmen to look into this matter and agree upon a settlement. Things should never have come to this sad pass. The lives destroyed in this awful war cannot be replaced. Think of the families left fatherless, the children who will be left without guidance because of this cruel and unnecessary strife. I hope the law will soon appoint a way to settle these differences between capital and labor by arbitration, and, meanwhile, let employer and employed come together peacefully now. It is not too late."

Special prayers that there may be a peaceful and speedy settlement of the lockout were offered this evening in all the Homestead churches. The Rev. Father Bullion is an earnest, kindly man of middle age, with a warm hand grasp and mild gray eyes. He is a type of the big hearted, benevolent priest. He feels keenly that his parishioners have been killed without cause. I asked him why he had not spoken more at length in his sermon about the war.

"Oh, no," he replied, "it would never do. I could not trust myself. My head

(Sermons, continued)

whirls when I think of the murderous onslaught on the Homestead men by an army of hired men from outside of the State. No, I cannot speak of it."

In speaking about the matter afterward Father Bullion said:— "This is a peaceable community, but a fearless one. They will submit to the law, but they will not submit to what they deem illegal forces. If another attempt is made to force the Pinkertons into Homestead I fear the very worst end. There will be bloodshed. The quarrel cannot be settled that way, the firm and the men must arbitrate."

"But what if the firm refuses to arbitrate?"

"How can it in reason reject a reasonable solution of this most calamitous affair?"

"But if it did reject the solution?"

"Then I should doubt its honesty and would believe that it was cloaking its real purpose under a false and suspicious cover. Both sides must come together or we will have a most shocking and demoralizing sequel to the wild work of last week."

———❖———

JULY 11, 1892 —Excerpted from The World, *New York.*

FEARED A MOB IN CHICAGO.

—————

Wounded Pinkertons Return to That City Telling a Story of Horrors.

[By Associated Press.]

Chicago, Ill., July 10. —A number of the Pinkertons who were in the fight at Homestead returned to this city last evening. One of them said of their experience on the barges:

"It was a place of torment. Men were lying around wounded and bleeding and piteously begging for someone to give them a drink of water, but no one dared to get a drop, although water was all around us. We dared not move for fear of sharpshooters on shore. We were hungry, too, although there was plenty to eat on the barges, but the fear of being shot in going for it overcame the gnawings of hunger. And then the booming of cannon, the bursting of dynamite bombs, the burning oil on the river, and the yells and shouts on the shore made our position and tortures appalling. It is a wonder we did not all go crazy or commit suicide. Some of the men were greatly affected, and on our way here one man became crazy and kept shouting: 'Oh, don't kill me! For God's sake, don't kill me!' And when near Cleveland he jumped from the train and, it is said, was killed."

One of the crew of the train on which the men came said:

"Every one of them appeared to have been caught in the shuffle and hurt some way or other. I don't know how it was before our crew got hold of the men, but after we took them they could not have been more uneasy and frightened if the train had gone down through a bridge. This feeling increased as the train approached Chicago. Some of the men seemed to have got it into their heads that a mob was waiting here to receive them and give them another dose like they got down East.

"When the train got to South Chicago, one man, who saw the coast clear, got up and left and he was followed by a dozen others, the lot of them scampering off in different directions. This was repeated at all the stations as far as Twenty-second street, except when any unusual sized crowd happened to show up on the platform. Then our passengers crouched down in their seats. I tell you I felt sorry for them.

"I talked to a number of them and nearly all of them said they had been misled, seemingly having been given a misunderstanding of the work required of them, and you could not get them to go back for the whole of the steel works."

———❖———

Published in The Chicago Times, *July 8, 1892, this cartoon interpreted the Battle of Homestead as brought about by the pro-capital protectionist policies of the Republican administration.*

From the **National Labor Tribune, August 27, 1892.**

TYRANT FRICK

In days gone by before the war
    All freemen did agree
The best of plans to handle slaves
    Was to let them all go free;
But the slave-drivers then, like now,
    Contrived to make a kick
And keep the slaves in bondage tight,
    Just like our Tyrant Frick.

CHORUS:
    Of all slave-drivers, for spite and kick,
    No one so cruel as Tyrant Frick.

The brave Hungarians, sons of toil,
    When seeking which was right,
Were killed like dogs by tyrants' hands
    In the coke districts' fight.
Let labor heroes all be true—
    Avenge the *bloody trick*!
Be firm like steel, true to the cause,
    And conquer Tyrant Frick.

CHORUS:
    Of all slave-drivers, for spite and kick,
    No one so cruel as Tyrant Frick.

The traitorous Pinkerton low tribe,
    In murdering attack,
Tried hard to take our lives and homes,
    But heroes drove them back.
O! sons of toil, o'er all the land,
    Now hasten, and be quick
To aid us, in our efforts grand,
    To down this Tyrant Frick.

CHORUS:
    Of all slave-drivers, for spite and kick,
    No one so cruel as Tyrant Frick.

The battle of "Fort Frick" is stamped
    On page of history,
And marked with blood of freemen true,
    Against this tyranny!
The sons of toil, for ages to come,
    His curse will always bring;
The name of *Frick* will be well known—
    The Nigger driver King!

CHORUS:
    Of all slave-drivers, for spite and kick,
    No one so cruel as Tyrant Frick.

THE HOMESTEAD POETS RECALL THE CIVIL WAR
by Don Woodworth

*T*he bloodshed at the Homestead mill was news at once. The story moved by telegraph in time to make the evening papers on July 6, 1892, and headlines in the weeklies published on Thursday, Friday, and Saturday.

Across the country, poets responded by expressing their outrage at the attack on the Homestead workers. As these poems appeared in the press in the weeks and months that followed, emotion intensified, issues were defined and sympathizers linked the Homestead Strike to the American tradition of resisting tyranny.

It was slavery and the Civil War that provided the poets with the most compelling images for the struggle at Homestead. The Civil War remained fresh in America's consciousness. The press still carried accounts of battles; the Grand Army of the Republic met in annual encampments; veterans led town parades and were honored by school children; old soldiers were called to attend the funerals of their comrades at GAR posts. And veterans were everywhere in the workforce. From this intense and still recent shared experience, poets could call on a reservoir of feeling to define the Homestead struggle as a new chapter in the American quest for freedom. (See TYRANT FRICK, in adjacent column.)

The poets understood that the battle at the Homestead was about the right of the men in the mill to have a say about their wages and working conditions. If those rights were lost, all was lost.

A MAN NAMED CARNEGIE
Sing ho, for a man named Carnegie,
    Who owns us, controls us, his cattle, at will.
Doff hats to himself and his lady;
    Let the sigh of the weary be stiller and still.
Drink, boys, to the health of Carnegie,
    Who gives his slaves freedom to live—if they can.
Bend knees, and cheer, chattels, cheer. He
    May still be a chattel who can't be a man. (See page 116.)

The intention of the owner was made very clear. Robert A. Pinkerton was quoted July 8 on the front page of the Youngstown Evening Vindicator: "No further effort will be made to force the workers into order. It simply means a lockout forever as far as union men are concerned; I know what I am talking about when I say no union man will ever again set foot in the Homestead mill."

To rally all workingmen to the Homestead cause, the poets emphasized the mill owner's power. Whether they wrote as realists recounting the details of the battle or as moralists calling for defenders of Truth and Justice, the focus of their poems was Carnegie and Frick's attack

on the workers. Did the workers have the right to carry arms? Here again, the Civil War offered a powerful parallel to the battle at Homestead. This is evident in a poem by D. T. Morgan, published in the National Labor Tribune, October 8, 1892:

A SONG FOR A DAY
Ye noble sons of Vulcan,
      Yea, all ye sons of toil,
From you that plow the mighty main
      To the tillers of the soil,
And you men who work beneath the surface of the earth,
The same great God made you as gave the "lords" their birth.
Although they think they're made of some superior blood.
Look up, my fellow man, and put your trust in God,
Who of one blood hath made all nations of the earth.
He measures not by gold or bonds, but by our moral worth.
United with your fellow men in all that's just and right,
For the Fricks and Lovejoys will attempt to crush you in their might!
But a brighter day is dawning, men; but you must help it come,
When you must vote as you do pray, and free yourselves from rum.
This, this is labor's greatest foe, and you can put him down—
Needs no armed force to conquer and despoil him of his crown,
But march right up with heart and soul upon election day;
Let not the old parties' tools or tricks lead you men astray.
For five long years did battles rage, with cannon shot and shell,
And, O! the sacrifice it cost no tongue on earth can tell!
The money cost was very great, but naught to precious life
It cost this nation to redeem five millions in that strife.

In their use of the Civil War to rally support, the poets equated the heroism of soldiers and workers and affirmed the value of rights achieved.

"'Fort Frick's' Defenders," by Youngstown poet Michael J. McGovern, exemplifies the blend of moralism and Civil War evocation characteristic of many of the Homestead poems. (See adjacent column.)

The poems were widely read. Roger Evans, another retired steelworker, recalled that copies of McGovern's poems went from hand to hand until they were in tatters: "Many there were who memorized the poems and could repeat them as readily as the author himself." A hundred years after the Battle of Homestead, the words of the poets who memorialized that event convey the sense of outrage that inspired them. ❖

From the **National Labor Tribune**, *July 16, 1892.*

"FORT FRICK'S" DEFENDERS

Hurrah for the light of Truth and Right!
      Whose rays our cause illumine;
Which shows the way how toilers may
      Unite and all be true men;
Which wakes the slave to a sense of brave
      Pursuits, and truly renders
To timid men the power to win,
      Like "Fortress Frick's" Defenders.

Hurrah for the cause which to it draws
      Of Freedom's minds the purest!
Whose love of truth and right forsooth
      Affects its foes the surest;
Whose courage defied the thugs who tried
      To come as peace offenders,
With the "Little Bill," to Homestead mill—
      Hurrah for the bold Defenders!

Hurrah for the men who were ready, when
      Aroused through Frick's defiance,
To man the breach and nobly teach
      The grist of self-reliance!
That Vulcan's sons 'gainst Pinkertons
      Were steel compared to cinders;
Hurrah for such men, and hurrah again
      For "Fortress Frick's" Defenders!

Hurrah for the bright redeeming light
      Which guides the cause of Labor,
And union men who, with tongue and pen,
      Fear not the gun or sabre;
Who'll wage the fight till despot might,
      Like the Pinkertons, surrenders.
Hurrah! true Sumter heroes are
      Our brave "Fort Frick" Defenders!

      Michael J. McGovern

JULY 10—*Governor Robert E. Pattison orders the Pennsylvania militia—some 8,000 men—to Homestead at the request of Allegheny County Sheriff William H. McCleary.*

JULY 12—*The troops arrive in mid-morning. Commanded by Major General George R. Snowden, a contingent establishes a picket line at the mill site, then marches into town. Refusing to recognize the status of Amalgamated officers, Snowden declares, "I am absolutely in control."*

JULY 12-14—*The Judiciary Committee of the U.S. House of Representatives—already investigating the use of the Pinkerton Detective Agency by corporations engaged in interstate commerce—holds hearings in Homestead and Pittsburgh.*

mid-JULY—*Carnegie Steel brings charges of conspiracy and murder against half a dozen of Homestead's Amalgamated leaders, including McLuckie and O'Donnell. They are freed on bail. By mid-September the charge has been extended to 167 individuals.*

mid-JULY—*O'Donnell travels to New York to confer with Republican Party leaders who want the strike to be settled before the November election. Reached indirectly in Scotland, Carnegie refuses to change policy.*

mid-JULY—*Sympathy strikes are underway at Carnegie plants in Duquesne, Beaver Falls, and the Lawrenceville section of Pittsburgh. Declarations of support and contributions of money come from union groups and sympathizers throughout the land.*

mid-JULY—*The company begins to hire replacement workers and announces plans to build 100 houses on mill property to shelter them.*

Workers welcome the militia in this cartoon from The Chicago Times, *July 13, 1892.*

The Eighteenth Regiment of the Pennsylvania Guard was the first to enter Homestead. This illustration from Harper's Weekly, *July 23, 1892, shows townspeople greeting the guardsmen as they pass the office and works of the Carnegie Company, visible behind Frick's fence.*

JULY 11, 1892 —Reprinted from the **New York Herald.**

ADVISORY BOARD AGAIN.

———

The Old Committee Reorganizes and Assumes Charge of Affairs.

———

[BY TELEGRAPH TO THE HERALD.]

HOMESTEAD, PA., July 10, 1892. —The Advisory Committee that was formed to conduct the affairs of the locked out men and which dissolved and disavowed all responsibility for what might happen if the Sheriff sent deputies here was reorganized to-night. It formally disbanded and destroyed its books last Tuesday in the presence of the Sheriff, and nominally it has had no existence since, although its members have been in charge of affairs.

The meeting for reorganization was held in the headquarters building in the old room the committees occupied before. The reason for the reorganization was that a number of irresponsible men were assuming authority and strutting around town giving conflicting orders. It was thought best to have some head, and so the committee will resume charge of civil matters and take responsibility of preserving order. Governor Pattison told the deputation from Homestead that waited on him that he would have to call out the militia if any overt or illegal act were committed in the town.

It is a wonder that half the inhabitants of the town are not in hospitals. Wells for drinking water and cesspools seem to be interchangeable here, one overflowing into the other and vice versa, and much of the sewage running into the gutters, making the visitor wonder if there is a State Board of Health in Pennsylvania and how it is there are any survivors here for Frick to lock out of his mills.

The reorganization of the Advisory Committee is a fatal blow to the men who hid in flour barrels and cellars during the fighting and who have been posing as heroes on the street corners, lying about a battle they didn't see and molesting any one who looked a little sick, consumptive or dyspeptic. These sewer rat warriors will be taken care of by the committee.

One of the leaders said:—"It must not be understood that the committee's duty is to formulate signals and plans of defense or offense. Our work is merely to preserve order."

It may be stated that there is no necessity for the formulation of any signals, as they were all devised long ago. A weak demonstration in favor of Mr. Carnegie has been made by the fifty or sixty clerks employed in the mills, and who wear blazers and young ladies' straw hats. These young men, indignant at what they consider the representatives of a communistic press fraternizing with the strikers, tried to get up a movement to expel the reporters, circulating stories that they were all detectives in disguise, which some of the hot headed ones were ready to believe. A member of the committee went to the lair where the youths were sipping lemonade and trembling and told them that if they didn't keep quiet he would appoint a sub-committee on spanking to come out and discipline them. The poor fellows all began to weep and their apologies were accepted.

———

IN HOMESTEAD'S CHURCHES.

———

Prayers for a Speedy and Peaceful Settlement of the Trouble.

———

[BY TELEGRAPH TO THE HERALD.]

HOMESTEAD, PA., July 10, 1892. —"We shall have triumphant democracy when Christ, instead of Carnegie, is king. Then the lion of capital will lie down with the lamb of labor, and there will be no Pinkertons to destroy them."

These words aroused a murmur of approval in the Homestead Methodist Episcopal Church this morning. They were uttered by the Rev. Mr. Thompson, of Genessee, N.Y., who relieved Pastor McIlyar of the burden of preaching.

The church was crowded. Everybody expected some stirring reference to the war which has raged in this hitherto peaceful riverside borough through the week.

But Pastor McIlyar could not trust himself on such a theme. He feared that as he had already referred to the warfare in every one of his funeral sermons it might be charged against him that he was trying to stir up strife. The Rev. Mr. Thompson came here to visit his brother, who is a steel worker.

In the opening prayer Mr. McIlyar said:—"We pray that demagogues may take a back seat and that honest men may be brought to the front in the crisis through which we are living."

That was his only reference to the trouble between Carnegie and his men.

PLANS FOR A CAMPAIGN.

―――――

Suggestions by Mail and Telegraph to Fight by Fire, Dynamite, Law, etc.

―――――

[By Telegraph to the Herald.]

HOMESTEAD, PA., July 10, 1892. —Though one hundred telegrams a day expressing sympathy, approval and offers of financial aid are still pouring in, a more interesting stage of the epistolary features of the situation has been reached in the opening of the burdened mills.

Hugh O'Donnell, accompanied by Secretary Madden, of the national organization of the Amalgamated Association, and President David Harris, of the Cigarmakers's International Union, went to the newspaper headquarters, which have usurped the places of the ice cream eaters of Homestead in Harrigan's parlor today, and read some of the choicest of these missives. They were all suggestive in their character and run all the way from bills in equity to boiling oil as weapons for the steel workers' use in continuing their warfare against capital.

That proposing a bill in equity was from one Horace Stiles, now of Washington late of Company B, Seventy-seventh New York Volunteers.

Mr. Stiles says:—

I think we have put an end for all time to the Pinkertons, and I am tempted to say, notwithstanding your sorrow and mourning, that it is worth the cost. If you assume an attitude strictly legal you can be supported for years, and I think your Advisory Committee ought to get together again and consider the matter of incorporation and filing a bill in equity claiming a legal lien upon the company's property.

As you are in possession the company could not legally eject you as summarily as they seem disposed to do. Let your committee announce that your possession is under color of title and demand of the Sheriff that he serve legal warrant for your dispossession. Get the best legal talent from Pittsburg, Harrisburg, and Philadelphia and give them a battle royal. Institute criminal action against Mr. Frick for murder and treason. He was at Homestead with an armed force and without process and against the peace of the Commonwealth.

Attacks Pinkerton's Record.

Mr. Stiles then proceeds to lay the blame of the melancholy chapter of Homestead's war history on the elder Pinkerton. He says:—

As for Pinkerton, he was a marxist during the war, and was either disloyal or a very poor detective. During the peninsular campaign of General McClellan, in 1862, he kept that otherwise able general fully impressed with the idea that 310,000 rebel troops were constantly in his front, while subsequent events fully proved that at no time did they amount to a third of that number. The old soldiers will be with you to a man in any and every way in which they can make themselves felt. If Carnegie, from his home in the Scottish Highlands, or his employés here, or capital anywhere in the Republic, can direct and levy war, we have lost the essence of the republican form of government.

Next a letter from a general storekeeper in West Milton, Ohio, asking to be informed of the nature of the products of the Carnegie works in order that he might boycott them. As there is probably no greater demand in West Milton for steel armor plate it is not probable that the general storekeeper's request will be considered of sufficient urgency to merit a voluminous reply.

The Cleveland and Stevenson Campaign Club, of Aqquanock, N.Y., sent a congratulatory letter.

From the anarchistically inclined were two letters. One contained a diagram illustrating the use of dynamite. Wednesday's work and the preparations since for a repetition of it on a larger scale if necessary show no particular need in this quarter for instruction in the particular art of war and the diagram was not preserved for reference.

. . .

Thanks for O'Donnell

Then Mr. O'Donnell began reading a letter from the Pinkerton men whom he had personally guarded when he closed the rear of the procession from the works to the rink on Wednesday evening. It was dated from Pittsburg and ran in the diction of a man used to a polite, epistolary style:—

I wish to thank you for the courtesy which you professionally extended to me last evening. You must pardon my saying that while walking along by your side I was not only conversing with you but was observant as to my surroundings, and wish to say that I spent some years of my life (no matter how many) in the so-called lawless West and I'm a good judge of nerve, with a big N. I make no excuse.

Here Hugh O'Donnell stopped and blushed like a school girl.

"I can't go on with this boys," he said, showing his fine teeth in a nervous laugh. "It would sound too egotistical. All there is about it is that I warded a few blows from this man by raising my arm and breaking the force of them and he thanks me for it. . . ."

―――――❖―――――

TROOPS ORDERED TO HOMESTEAD BY GOVERNOR PATTISON.

Convinced That Sheriff McCleary Is Unable to Cope with the Locked Out Men, He Calls Out the Entire National Guard.

AN ARMY OF 8,500 MEN READY FOR ACTIVE SERVICE.

The Work of Mobilization Begun Last Night and the Whole Body to Move on the Stronghold of the Toilers as Soon as Possible.

EXPECTS THE BIG FORCE WILL OVERAWE THE STRIKERS.

Believing That There Might Be a Conflict if Only One Regiment Went to Homestead, the Governor Sends All the Militia of Pennsylvania.

HOMESTEAD RECEIVES THE NEWS.

Most of the People Asleep, but Those Who Received the Bulletin Are Sorrowful and Feel That Their Cause Is Lost– No Talk of Resistance.

[BY TELEGRAPH TO THE HERALD.]

HARRISBURG, PA., July 10, 1892.—Governor Pattison, being convinced that Sheriff McCleary is unable to restore order at Homestead, has ordered out the entire National Guard—8,500 men—all the available military force of the state, to Homestead for service.

It is understood that the Governor's purpose in calling out the entire National Guard is to make sure that there will be no demonstration on the part of the locked-out men. He thinks that the men will quietly submit before such an overwhelming force, while they might resist if one regiment was sent there.

The news was given out at the Executive Department at ten o'clock to-night that the Governor, having received a dispatch from Sheriff McCleary calling for troops, had given orders to Major General Snowden to proceed with the entire National Guard to Homestead.

The following correspondence has been made public:—

PITTSBURG, July 10—Midnight.
To Robert E. Pattison, Governor, Harrisburg, Pa.:—

The situation at Homestead has not improved. While all is quiet there, the strikers are in control and openly express to me and to the public their determination that the works shall not be operated unless by themselves. After making all efforts in my power I have failed to secure a posse respectable enough in numbers to accomplish anything, and I am satisfied that no posse raised by civil authority can do anything to change the condition of affairs and that any attempt by an inadequate force to restore the right of law will only result in further armed resistance and consequent loss of life. Only a large military force will enable me to control matters. I believe if such force is sent, the disorderly element will be overawed and order will be restored. I, therefore, call upon you to furnish me such assistance.

WILLIAM H. McCLEARY, Sheriff.

ORDERED OUT.

Governor Pattison, as Commander in Chief of the National Guard, at once issued the following order:—

GEORGE R. SNOWDEN, Major General Commanding National Guard of Pennsylvania:—

Put the division under arms and move at once, with ammunition, to the support of the Sheriff of Allegheny county at Homestead. Maintain the peace. Protect all persons in their rights under the constitution and laws of the State. Communicate with me.

ROBERT E. PATTISON, Governor.

(Troops Ordered, continued)

To Sheriff McCleary the following telegram was sent:—

WILLIAM H. McCLEARY, Sheriff of Allegheny county, Pittsburg:—

Have ordered Major General George R. Snowden, with the division of the National Guard of Pennsylvania, to your support. At once put yourself in communication with him. Communicate with me further particulars.

ROBERT E. PATTISON, Governor.

General Snowden, with the Adjutant General and Quartermaster General, at once proceeded to formulate the orders for the mobilization of the Guard. Some troops will be under way early in the morning.

GENERAL GREENLAND'S REPORT.

The tone of the Governor's talk since the labor eruption at Homestead had been pacific rather than warlike. He had uniformly declared against an appeal to arms in the settlement of the controversy between the Carnegie Steel Company and its employés unless he had conclusive evidence of the inability of the civil authorities to cope with the matter. He had hoped that peaceful arbitration would follow the bloody conflict precipitated by the effort of the armed Pinkerton men to capture the works.

Adjutant General Greenland's return to the capital and the news he conveyed to the Governor as to the real condition of things at Homestead effected a change in the mind of the Chief Executive.

The Adjutant General made a thorough inquiry into the situation, and it is understood that he told the Governor that a collision more sanguinary and appalling than that of Wednesday was sure to result if the militia were not sent to Homestead.

WHY HE CALLED OUT THE TROOPS.

In view of the inefficiency of Sheriff McCleary and the disinclination of the citizens of the county to do deputy duty he thought the Governor should act.

General Greenland told the Governor that while the Carnegie Company had control of its works, the locked-out workmen were in control on the outside, and, in his opinion, any attempt to put non-union men to work would result in another battle.

While the sentiment in Pittsburg was favorable to the stand the Governor had taken in not rushing troops to the scene of disturbance, the Adjutant General reported that the opinion prevailed among the people in the neighborhood that the trouble would culminate in an open conflict.

The Adjutant General had an interview with Manager Frick, of the Carnegie works, and reported him firm in his purpose not to have anything to do with members of the Amalgamated Association. The National Guard comprises about eight thousand five hundred officers and men, who are generally well disciplined.

WILL THEY OBEY ORDERS?

The Pittsburg Militia Composed Almost Entirely of Workingmen.

[BY TELEGRAPH TO THE HERALD.]

PITTSBURG, PA., July 10. 1892.—The news of the ordering out of the entire National Guard by Governor Pattison reached here to-night and has caused considerable excitement. Opinion is about evenly divided as to how the Pittsburg troops will behave in the matter. The two regiments here are composed almost exclusively of workingmen and it is feared that a large number of these may seek to evade the Governor's call.

The troops in this vicinity, comprising the Second brigade, will be under command of General Wylie, whose headquarters are at Franklin. This brigade comprises the Tenth, Fifteenth, Sixteenth, Fourteenth and Eighteenth regiments and Battery B, in all 2,500 men. The officers, however, are all good soldiers and men of nerve and executive ability, and in the event of any serious trouble at Homestead it is not thought that the Pittsburg militia will refuse, as they did in the riots of 1877, to obey the command of their officers to fire upon their own townsfolk.

Union Response to Governor's Ordering Out of Militia.

This afternoon on the call of the Burgess a public meeting was held in the Opera House, and 300 orators piled into the building pell-mell, and fell over one another in the expressions of high regard for the National Guard and the downtrodden reporters. The latter were put on the stage, and were eulogized and invited to make speeches, and they were made to realize that for the time, at least, they were sitting on velvet with the promised land spread out before them.

Chairman Hugh O'Donnell of the Advisory Committee called the meeting to order, and Burgess McLuckie presided. The latter addressed the audience as fellow-workmen and gentlemen. He declared that the troops were coming as friends and allies, and would be received as such. "If that unclean Pinkerton horde strikes our shores again," he said, "there must be death."

There were cries of "Death to the Pinkertons!" through the hall. The Chairman advised children not to hoot at the troops, and offered to help duck in the river any indiscreet and hooting citizen of any age and of either sex.

"I move," said a well-dressed mill hand in the gallery, rising and bringing into view a pair of long corkscrew mustaches, "that any man who insults the troops be ducked in the Monongahela."

"Good! duck 'em!" resounded in all quarters.

The proposition was put amid applause and was adopted by a large majority. "So ordered," shouted Burgess McLuckie, raising his clenched fist toward the ceiling.

———❖———

JULY 12, 1892 —Two excerpts from the St. Louis Post-Dispatch.

IN FORT FRICK

———

The Militia in Peaceful Possession of the Carnegie Mills

———

The Troops Greeted with Cheers by the People of Homestead.

———

NOT A SHOT FIRED OR AN INSULT UTTERED

———

A Strike of 20,000 Men May Follow the Introduction of Non-Unionists Into the Homestead Plant—Manager Frick Refuses to Disclose His Plans—Hunger Among the Hungarians.

HOMESTEAD, PA., July 12. —The night passed quietly and all Homestead was in holiday attire this morning in anticipation of the militia. Arrangements had been perfected for an elaborate reception to the blue coated representatives of the State, and it was even understood an address of welcome would be delivered by Burgess McLuckie if a suitable occasion should be offered. Everybody had expected that the troops would invade the city by day break, but when 7 o'clock, 8 o'clock and 9 o'clock passed without any news from the militia, the situation became somewhat ludicrous. The Homestead bands were all on hand waiting orders, and one of them relieved the high pressure of anxiety shown by marching up and down the streets and playing, "McGinty," "Annie Rooney," and various other familiar airs, calculated to arouse the spirits of the community. All this was well received, but when the band master launched into the classics and played "The Lost Chord," and "The Heart Bowed Down," the chill reception which followed their efforts deterred him from a plunge into Wagner, which was evidently next on the programme.

There was an air of disappointment at the strikers' headquarters as 9 o'clock passed without the slightest information from the militia. The people reflected that nearly two days had now passed since the militia had been ordered out and not a blue coat had yet shown up on the scene of hostilities.

PERFECT ORDER MAINTAINED.

"We could have blown up the mills and sacked Allegheny before those troops had got here, if we had not been peaceful and law-respecting," remarked a brawny striker and his remark caused approbation all around.

In the main, however, the most perfect gravity was maintained on all sides and a critical survey of the town failed to reveal a single intoxicated workman among the thousands of mill men who thronged the streets. Burgess McLuckie's proclamation had been religiously respected and it was stated that the saloons were preparing to close their doors promptly on his order. That order, it was announced, would be given an hour in advance of the arrival of the militia if sufficient notice of their coming were obtained.

The special police summoned from among the strikers by the Burgess were the best representatives of brawn and muscle which their industrial community could furnish and nobly performed their duty with commendable impartiality. All loud talkers, whether strikers or sympathizers, were promptly suppressed,

(In Fort Frick, continued)

and to give an insolent answer to these special guardians was to be unceremoniously hustled off to the lockup. Several of the fellow workmen of these impromptu police presumed upon past familiarity to the extent of mildly guying the tin-starred officers, but in every instance they had occasion bitterly to regret their temerity and one boisterous individual, who resisted arrest by force, was so hustled to the lockup that he arrived at his destination minus hat and one sleeve of his coat and with his short shirt front trailing from a fence picket, where he had unsuccessfully attempted to apply the brakes.

THE TROOPS ARRIVE.

At a few minutes past 9 o'clock the cry suddenly went up, "The troops are coming, the troops are coming," and instantly the greatest excitement prevailed. The militia came in by rail from above the town and at once surrounded the Carnegie Mills. They were received with a few cheers from the few surrounding bystanders as the train rolled in and most respectful consideration was accorded them in every respect. The first detachment of troops numbered at least 8,000 men and was in command of Gen. Snowden. They comprise the second and third brigades of the First Division. The Fourteenth and Eighteenth Regiments from Pittsburg are here and Battery D of the First Brigade has shown up with two Gatling guns and three field pieces. Portions of the Tenth and Fifteenth Regiments are on the field, and Companies A, C, E and H of the Eighteenth Regiment are also recognized among the bluecoats. The troops came from a point of rendezvous two miles this side of Greensburg, and it is stated that the First Brigade is now at Mount Gretna, where it will remain until further orders.

Immediately on the arrival of the trains there was great bustle and excitement, but the militia themselves preserved perfect order and responded silently and promptly to every order of their superiors. Rapidly descending from the train, the troops formed in a column at the switch yards just beyond Munhall Station. One company was at once detatched to act as pickets, and a line was immediately thrown out among the mill yards.

THROUGH THE STREETS.

Then the main body of the troops marched down the streets, headed by the Regiment Band and along what is known as "Scab Hill." This is an eminence overlooking the mills and the scene of last week's hostilities and the bluff was covered with spectators, mostly young men. There was not the slightest manifestation of hostility and although the troops had arrived so suddenly that all the leaders were absent, it did not require their presence to maintain proper respect from the rank and file. Once or twice there was some hand-clapping from the younger element as the jaunty militiamen hove in sight and the band was of much interest.

WHAT WILL IT COST.

Pittsburg, Pa., July 12. —The Homestead expedition of the militia is an expensive undertaking and will cost the State a good round sum of money. The National Guard of Pennsylvania has 8,470 members, of which fully 8,000 have responded to the Governor's call. It will cost the state about $22,000 per day until the troops are recalled. This estimate is based on the cost of the annual encampment of the State militia.

CAMP OF THE GUARDS.

The camp of the National Guard is on a plateau of the high hill directly south of the Carnegie mill property and the city farm mills, and overlooks not only the Carnegie plant but the borough of Homestead and many miles of surrounding country. The camp is about 300 yards distant from the celebrated high fence which incloses the mills and the city farm. Guards are stationed along Eighth avenue.

The troops suffered considerably from the heat as they marched from the railroad up the steep hill to their camp. When the different regiments had taken their positions, the men threw themselves upon the ground, and stretching their rubber blankets from the bayonets of four muskets formed a screen from the rays of the sun.

The camp ground is a meadow, from which the grass had not been cut, and it made a very comfortable resting place for the men, most of whom were tired out after their all night's experience on the cars. It took several hours to unload the men and move them to their stations on the hill. That the troops did not come to Homestead on any idle errand is shown by the fact that each man has ten rounds of ammunition, and is equipped for active service. . . .

JULY 12, 1892 —Excerpted from **The New-York Times.**

THE STRIKERS AND THE MILITIA.

It will be a mistake for Mr. Frick and the company to hold obstinately to the position that they will not treat with these men, and that they will replace them with others who are not connected with the Amalgamated Association. There are matters to be considered in this case besides the cold-blooded principles of supply and demand. It may be that the company can hire other men on more satisfactory terms, economically considered, and they have the right to control their own business with reference to the labor factor, but there are human considerations in this business. These people belong in Homestead, and their labor as well as the company's capital has built up its great industry. They have a right to organize, and organization is necessary to enforce their just claims. They should be treated as a party to a contract in furnishing their labor and not as a soulless factor in processes of manufacture, like capital or raw material. The company derives an advantage to which it is not entitled from the Government in the suppression of foreign competition. Shall it turn it all to profit for capital and crowd wages down under the doctrine of supply and demand? It is surely possible to settle this matter equitably with the men who have been locked out of the Carnegie mills, and if they surrender the position they have taken in opposition to legal rights and public authority, the company should give up the policy of arbitrary assertion of power and come to reasonable terms. The opportunity is likely to come in the next few days, and it will not be good policy for this corporation, which has been deriving wealth from the people of the country, to let it pass.

———❖———

(facing page) Another scene at the train station in Swissvale, a hilltop community across the Monongahela River from Homestead.

(left) The label on this 1892 stereograph reads "Strikers on the lookout."

JULY 12 and 13, 1892 —Reprinted from **The New-York Times.**

TO PROSECUTE THE LEADERS.

————

CONSPIRACY AND MURDER TO BE CHARGED AGAINST THEM.

PITTSBURG, July 11. —It is announced on what is considered to be good authority that the Carnegie Steel Company is about to begin prosecution against the leaders of the Homestead riot for conspiracy and murder.

The company is said to have retained several of the best criminal lawyers of Western Pennsylvania, and instructed them to institute proceedings at once. A flash-light camera is alleged to have been used from the tower of the Carnegie mill during the riot, and the pictures of the men thus obtained are to be used as evidence.

The arrests are expected to be made as soon as the National Guards go on duty at Homestead.

———❖———

LEADERS TO BE ARRESTED.

————

SHERIFF M'CLEARY WILL BEGIN THIS PART OF HIS WORK TO-DAY.

PITTSBURG, PENN., July 12. —Sheriff McCleary has sworn in a number of special deputies who will issue bench warrants on the leaders of the strike.

It is said that such a step will have a greater effect at Homestead than even the troops. The fact that those arrested will be put in jail and cannot be released under bail, being accused of murder, will take many of the leaders away, and their counsel will be missed. On the other hand, it is claimed that this step may cause the more hot headed to break out as soon as the cooler leaders are removed.

Nothing will be done before to-morrow by the Sheriff, and by that time he will be fully supported by the militia. How the men will take the wholesale arrests is a question, but they will scarcely resist.

———❖———

*JULY 12 and 15, 1892
—Reprinted from the*
St. Louis Post-Dispatch

Hungry Hungarians.

ONE RESULT OF THE LOCK-OUT AT THE HOMESTEAD MILLS.

HOMESTEAD, PA. July 12. —Many men, women and children are hungry in Homestead as a result of the lock-out. All of them are Hungarians. Not so thrifty as their fellow workmen of other nationalities they paid little attention to the warnings of the coming rainy day and basked in the sunshine of procrastination until too late. The wages paid Hungarians are not princely; their weekly stipends were eaten away in the purchase of the necessaries of life. When the lock-out began the great majority of them found themselves without means of subsistence. Most of the Hungarians have habitations in houses built by the Carnegie company near the idle mills. They are well-housed but food is not to be had. The refusal of the leaders to accept outside contributions of money to carry on the fight practically makes the condition of the Huns hopeless, and realizing this many of them have left town to seek work elsewhere. A large number of the Hungarians here were workers in the coke regions during the great strike there, and they know what it is to look into the barrels of rifles held in the hands of the State Militia. The fear that trouble would ensue with the arrival of the National Guard was a greater inducement to some to leave Homestead than empty stomachs were. Conservative men among the strikers when asked if they believe the Carnegie company will attempt to place non-union men in the works under cover of the militia, shake their heads dubiously and do not care to discuss the matter. Opinion seems to be general that Mr. Frick will not let his mills remain idle if he can possibly help it. If he places non-union men in charge after the militia arrive, no one can foretell the result with accuracy; but it is probable that the sight of thousands of blue coated soldiers will be sufficient inducement to the men to let the non-union men alone. But the workers know that the state troops can not remain in charge of the mills for any great length of time. When they are withdrawn trouble will surely ensue if non-union men remain, and that trouble will be of a serious character. It has been openly declared that non-union men shall not run the works; the leaders have sanctioned this idea. There is no doubt the trouble in Homestead has not neared a settlement.

———❖———

FILLING HUNGRY MOUTHS.

July 15, 1892. —The question of relief, especially among the locked-out Hungarian workmen, is assuming serious proportions. Many of them are said to be without the necessaries of life, and the mass-meeting of the locked-out steel workers, called at the Rink this morning, was called to provide for these people. The treasury of the Amalgamated Association is full of money, not a dollar having been up to the present time spent on the strike, and the members of the association say that none of their members will need help for a month to come. The trouble is among workmen who are not members of the association, the day laborers among the mills who have lost their employment in the shut down. Just what measures will be taken for their subsistence is not known as yet, but it is believed that the Amalgamated Association will charge itself with their support. The meeting, which is now in progress, is a secret one, but the strike leaders openly express their opinion that the Hungarians must be taken care of.

———❖———

JULY 13, 1892 —Reprinted from **The New-York Times.**

GEN. SNOWDEN MEANS BUSINESS.

THE STRIKERS GIVEN TO UNDERSTAND THAT THEIR REIGN IS OVER.

HOMESTEAD, PENN., July 12. —Gen. Snowden, commander of the division, was standing at his headquarters that morning surrounded by his staff and conversing with Sheriff McCleary and Gen. Gobin, commander of the Third Brigade, when a committee of the strikers was seen toiling up the hill, headed by Hugh O'Donnell, Chairman of the Homestead Advisory Board. With him were ex-Captain of Militia Ollie Coon, Frederic Schuckman, and others of the Amalgamated leaders. As the committee reached the military group Coon looked hard at the division commander.

"Gen. Snowden, I believe?" he said.

The General made no reply. O'Donnell espied Sheriff McCleary and asked for an introduction to Gen. Snowden. The Sheriff bowed with dignity, but said nothing. Then Coon made a speech.

"We have come," he said, "to speak for the citizens and for the locked-out men of the Amalgamated Association of Iron and Steel Workers."

"I neither know nor care anything about them," said Gen. Snowden sharply. "I have no opinion to express on this subject one way or the other. I am not here to look after the strike or the Amalgamated Association or to pay any attention to either. I do not accept and do not need at your hands the freedom of Homestead. I have that now in my possession, and I propose to keep the peace. I want no strikers to come near the troops as strikers, and I want it distinctly understood that I am in absolute control of the situation."

Then up spoke O'Donnell in haste to modify the impression obviously made by Coon's address. "General," he said, " I think that Capt. Coon's reference to the Amalgamated Association and the strikers was accidental and unintentional. We came as representing the citizens of Homestead as well as the Amalgamated strikers. I will amend Capt. Coon's speech, and withdraw his reference to the Amalgamated Association. We are citizens of Homestead and of Allegheny county."

Gen. Snowden bowed again. "I am always glad," he said, " to meet the citizens, the good citizens, of any community."

"We have been peaceful and law-abiding citizens," said O'Donnell.

"No, you have not," interrupted Gen.

Snowden, speaking sternly and emphatically; "you have not been peaceful and law-abiding citizens, Sir; you have defied and insulted the Sheriff, and I want to say to you and to the strikers that the Governor has instructed me to announce to you that we are here to aid the Sheriff. You have refused to deal with him, but it is he with whom you will have to deal now. If you insist on it, Sir, I can go further into the conduct of you and your men. You had better not insist. I want to assure you, however, once more that we care nothing about your association or your strike. The peace will be preserved at any cost."

The committee stood silent for a moment with flushed and downcast faces. Finally, O'Donnell plucked up courage.

"General," he said, "we've got four brass bands, and we would like to have them and a parade of our friends pass in review before the camp."

"I don't want any brass-band business while I'm here," said Gen. Snowden, quickly. "I want you to distinctly understand that I am master of this situation."

The strikers' committee stood still, looking at one another in dismay. Then they beat a retreat. As they hurried down the hill, they were heard swearing at the troops.

"We'll show him before we get through," said one of the committee, "that he doesn't run the town."

There was no parade, and nothing has been heard of the four brass bands since Coon came down the hill.

———❖———

This National Guard unit posed in front of a City Poor Farm sign. The Homestead Works had acquired this site in 1890.

JULY 13, 1892 —Excerpted from **The Pittsburg Leader.**

SAY IT'S A BLUFF.

***

The Locked-Out Men Take No Stock in the Story That Their Men Are to be Prosecuted.

HOMESTEAD, July 13. —"I consider it a gigantic bluff and simply intended to create a scare among the workmen in order that they might return to work," was the reply of one of the advisory committee this morning when interrogated by a *Leader* man on the statement alleged to have been made by Sheriff McCleary, that the ringleaders of Wednesday's battle would be arrested and charged with murder and inciting riot. The speaker continued: "Mr. Frick may think this bluff will go, but in that he will find himself badly fooled. Of the 200 or more men who remained at the front on Wednesday, I am positive that not one of their names is known by the county authorities or company officials, and what's more, I feel sure their identity will never be disclosed." Not a little consideration should be given this man's talk, as it bears out articles previously published in the *Leader* that all who participated in the bloody scrimmage are oath-bound not to divulge anything. As for arresting Hugh O'Donnell and others who have occupied prominent positions, it may be that they will find themselves in the hand of the law, but the workmen say, "What of it? Nothing can be trumped up against O'Donnell. Witnesses are ready to prove that at the beginning of the battle O'Donnell with Captain Kuhn [Coon] was the first in appeal to the men. His course from the first day has been one of advocating peaceful measures." Criminal action against the leaders will bring about a great legal battle the final ending of which will not be reached before one of the most sensational trials on record has taken place. Should the county authorities or Carnegie company officials carry out the proposed plan of arrest, the legal complications which will necessarily arise will cause much trouble. ❖

JULY 13, 1892 —Excerpted from **The New-York Times.**

BAYONET RULE IN FORCE

***

The Reign of the Strikers Ended in Homestead.

***

GEN. SNOWDEN AND THE STATE TROOPS TAKE POSSESSION OF THE TOWN—NO RESISTANCE OFFERED TO THE NATIONAL GUARD—THE CARNEGIE WORKS TURNED OVER TO THE OWNERS—GEN. SNOWDEN ANNOUNCES THAT THE LAW MUST BE RESPECTED—THE STRIKERS ALMOST ABJECT IN THEIR SUBMISSION.

HOMESTEAD, Penn., July 12. —Mob rule in Homestead has come to an inglorious end. The town has been wrested without bloodshed or struggle from the rioting locked-out Amalgamated workmen, who have ruled with absolute and despotic sway for two weeks, and has been taken under the protecting care of the National Guard.

The five-million-dollar mills of the Carnegie Steel Company (Limited) have been formally turned over in writing to their owners by the Sheriff of Allegheny County, to do with them as they please, and 7,000 soldiers of the Keystone state, under Gen. George P. Snowden, are encamped on either bank of the Monongahela, armed with Gatling guns and Springfield rifles.

Five thousand of the troops have pitched their tents and stacked their guns on the brow of the steep hill on the south side of the river, in sight of the historic spot where Gen. Braddock fell in the French and Indian war. Far below them are the town and the deserted mills. The rest of the troops are established on the opposite side of the river. The mills are occupied and surrounded by a strong picket guard. There is a picket line clear around the town and far up and down the river, while sharpshooters and artillerymen occupy every point commanding the river and the approaches to the village.

The notes of the cavalry bugle resound through the valley today for the first time since the civil war, and the reverberations of the sunset gun awoke echoes that had not been waked since the engagement in which George Washington acquired his reputation for a charmed life.

———❖———

Important locations of the battle and occupation in this view of Homestead are, left to right: the Pinkerton landing site, General Snowden's headquarters, the encampment of Battery B, the Pemickey Bridge, and "Little Bill."

JULY 14, 1892 —Excerpted from
The Iron Trade Review.

The Homestead Situation.

The matter uppermost in connection with the Homestead trouble, the past week, has been, not the points of difference as to wages, between the Carnegie Steel Co. and its employes, but whether that town should be singular among all the municipalities of the country in having the law of the land suspended by the rule of a self-constituted committee of citizens. We have been told, from day to day, since the single day of rioting and carnage, that all was quiet at Homestead and that peace prevailed, rendering unnecessary the sending of militia or of sheriff's deputies. It was the same sort of peace that any man may have with the law-breaker who seizes his property. If the wronged man makes no outcry and no resistance, the proceeding is exceedingly peaceful! With the Homestead workmen in complete possession of the mills, and no opposition to their lawless conduct by sheriff or governor, the situation certainly presented an ideal picture of peace and harmony.

That the introduction of the Pinkerton detectives by the company was a mistake, is admitted—how great a mistake, the awful record of Wednesday made plain.

Politicians have had their day, in the general flood of comment, and partisan newspapers have let no day pass without attempting to obscure the real question of present moment at Homestead, with irrelevant and often demagogic descantings upon the country's industrial policy. As if, forsooth, there had never been, outside of a country that adopted a protective tariff to encourage industry, any such thing as strikes, lockouts, or fatal labor riots.

The Carnegie Steel Co. has given out, through its chairman, Mr. Frick, that it will not again have anything to do with the Amalgamated Association in any conference over the wages it shall establish. Members of that association have for more than two weeks had the company's works in their hands; they took an active part in the riot of last week, and the company does not wish to have further dealings with them. It is one of the most unfortunate features of the contest, that an organization, generally so wisely man-

aged, and with so much in its record that is good, should have put itself in such an attitude toward the law. To say that Mr. Frick had in mind from the beginning, a war upon the association, that should wipe it out in Homestead, does not gainsay the fact that the Amalgamated leaders in Homestead have given him occasion for just the stand he wanted to take, granting that this statement concerning his intention be true.

Now that the militia have taken possession of Homestead and the Carnegie Steel Co. has again been permitted access to its works, the situation is just what it was on the day of the lock-out. There can be no permanent peace in Homestead, on any basis that is not agreed upon between the company and its old employes, hundreds of whom own their homes and had counted on life residence in the town the great mills have made. The chances of such an agreement, in view of the declarations of the company's officers, are very slight. If the employes in the other Carnegie mills should go out, as seemed probable on Wednesday, a contest will ensue that promises to be one of the bitterest and most determined the iron and steel trade have ever seen. Every resource of the Amalgamated Association would be employed, because with it, such a struggle would be a matter of life and death.

(facing page) The Swissvale camp site on the bluff across the river from Homestead was called Camp Cowell.

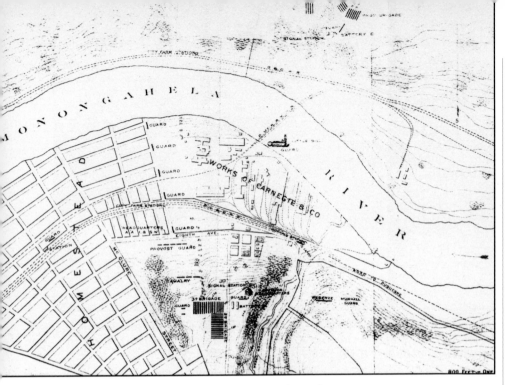

Disposition of the militia in Homestead as shown in a report dated November 30, 1892.

JULY 15, 1892 —Reprinted from **The Pittsburg Press.**

WATCHING THE FOUR HUNDRED.

─────

Some Mysterious Movements on the Part of the Troops.

HOMESTEAD, July 14 –[Special]–Last evening there was every indication that the mill authorities are intending to take some decided steps in the matter of putting workmen into the deserted plant, and the same conditions of affairs exist this morning. I was in Camp Black until a late hour last night, and when I reached the town it was to find that the military patrol had been fully doubled and that every guard was more than usually on the alert.

At the P.,V.&C. depot I found a lieutenant in charge of a detail of about 20 men. The soldiers were concealed in the deep shadows cast by the electric lights, and the officer claimed to be as much in the dark as to what was expected as were the privates. All along Fifth, Sixth, Seventh and Eighth avenues I found guards standing at almost every street corner, and some of the workmen who were talked to seemed quite positive that an attempt was to be made to put the much-talked-of 400 non-union men into the works before daylight.

About 3 o'clock this morning I met Hugh O'Donnell on the street near his house. He denied that the strikers were preparing to resist any new move on the part of the company, and said that the more cool-headed ones would not attempt to resist by force the introduction of non-union men into the mill. He admitted, however, that the disorderly element were likely to fight for what they considered their rights in case of an attempt to introduce non-union labor.

The two camps were in communication up to a late hour last night, the flashes of light from the apparatus used by the signal corps conveying the messages of one camp to the other. The Western Union branch line was got into working late last evening, and the steady clicking of the sounder added to the air of mystery which hangs over the headquarters.

I remained on the streets in the vicinity of the mills until daybreak, but up to that hour the contingent which is now known as Carnegie's 400 had not put in an appearance.

The foreign element here is completely mystified by the movements of the signal corps, which has taken its stand on the brow on the hill immediately in front of Gen. Snowden's headquarters. The location is extremely conspicuous, and as soon as the machine-like waving of flags commences little knots of men gather along Eighth avenue and watch with awed expressions the mysterious movements.

Last evening I discovered a party of them standing on one of the street corners watching in almost unbroken silence the steady flashing of the light in use by the signal corps. It was apparent from their actions that this performance was even more mysterious than the moving of flags.

GLADDEN.

─────

SMOKE FROM THE STACKS.

─────

Steam Issuing From the Pipes at the Armor Mill.

HOMESTEAD, July 15. –[Special]– The armor plate mill of the Carnegie works is apparently in partial operation this morning. Smoke is seen issuing from one of the tall smoke stacks of the mill, and the two steam exhaust pipes are spouting forth steam at a rapid rate, indicating that the machinery is in motion. The Carnegie guard at the main gate was questioned about the matter, but declined to give any information or to admit the reporter. Many of the strikers are curiously viewing the armor plate mill from a distance, but tell nothing about it. Evidently they are uneasy about it.

Provost Marshal Green was asked about the matter, but knew nothing save that the mills were not being operated by any of the national guard. A rumor to this effect was current about the time the smoke and steam were first observed....

───── ❖ ─────

Governor Pattison reviewed the State Guard five days after the call-up. This sketch appeared in Frank Leslie's Illustrated Weekly, *July 28, 1892.*

JULY 16, 1892 —Reprinted from **The New-York Times.**

Those Captured Rifles.

————

Attorney General Hensel Refuses to Advise O'Donnell.

HARRISBURG, PENN., July 15. —Yesterday Hugh O'Donnell, one of the leaders of the strikers at Homestead, sent a telegram of inquiry to Attorney General Hensel asking what disposition should be made of the firearms captured from the Pinkertons after the battle of the 6th inst. at the Carnegie Mills. As both the Attorney General and his Deputy left the city before the reception of the telegram became known, it was impossible to learn the tenor of Mr. Hensel's reply. To-day it was learned that he had telegraphed O'Donnell as follows:

Harrisburg, Penn., July 15.
Mr. Hugh O'Donnell, Homestead, Penn.:
I do not think it is within the scope of my official duties to advise you upon the subject of your telegraphic inquiry. If you have in your possession private property

as to the ownership of which you are not informed, you should be guided by private counsel as to how to dispose of it. If you have any reason to believe that it will be needed in any legal inquiry or for the purpose of evidence in prosecution to be brought, lay the facts before the District Attorney of your county and consult with him. Very truly yours,

W. A. HENSEL, Attorney General.

The inspection of the First Brigade (Gen. Decherts) at Mount Gretna was finished to-day, and the Governor and staff returned to this city this evening well pleased with the showing made by the troops. It is said that some of the volunteers at Mount Gretna are becoming restive and long to go home, but hesitate to do so through fear that the brigade will be ordered to Homestead, and they are not willing to take the risk of being absent from camp in such an emergency.

Rumors have been current here that the First Brigade would eventually be sent to Homestead to join the troops there. Adjut. Gen. Greenland said to-night that as a matter of course the brigade would be sent West promptly if occasion arose, but as the situation is at present he sees not the remotest possibility of such a contingency. It is probable that the Governor and staff will start on Monday night for Pittsburg and Homestead to inspect the troops there.

————

MR. FRICK IS DECIDED.

PITTSBURG, PENN., July 15.—H.C. Frick sent the following telegram to Superintendent Wrigley of the Beaver Falls Mills this afternoon:

I am just in receipt of the following telegram from Beaver Falls:
We, the Amalgamated Association of Beaver Falls, the roll mill, wire mill, and nail mill, have come to the conclusion that we will refuse to work until such time as H.C. Frick, Chairman of the Carnegie Steel Company, (Limited.) is willing to confer with the Amalgamated Association in order to settle the Homestead affair.

ARTHUR THORNTON,
Chairman of Committee

You will please say to Mr. Thornton, Chairman of the committee, and ask him to so notify the men, that if they, composing the Amalgamated Association at Beaver Falls and who signed an agreement with us for one year, do not go to work on Monday next, or when you are ready to start, we will consider their failure to do so as a cancellation of the agreement existing between us, and when these works do resume it will be as non-union, and former employes satisfactory to us who desire to work there will have to apply as individuals. You can say that under no circumstances will we confer with the men at Homestead as members of the Amalgamated Association.

THE CARNEGIE STEEL COMPANY (Limited.)
By H.C. FRICK, Chairman.

————

FOREIGN LABOR'S SYMPATHIES.

————

NO WORDS IN FAVOR OF CARNEGIE— THE WORKINGMEN UPHELD.

LONDON, July 15. —The labor struggle at Homestead is watched with excited interest here, especially among the working classes. The ardent sympathies of the trades unionists are with the strikers. Last evening's meeting of the London Trades Council voted urgency for a resolution, which was unanimously passed, protesting against Mr. Carnegie's employing "a gang of irresponsible armed bullies to coerce men struggling against a reduction of wages," and satisfaction was expressed that the men had been able to defeat the tactics of their employers.

One prominent member suggested that if Mr. Carnegie was still a member of the National Liberal Club, he ought to be kicked out immediately. The leading workmen's organ deplores the action of the Aberdeen Corporation in conferring the freedom of the city upon Mr. Carnegie, and expresses regret that American capitalists have power "to use a gang of ruffians to shoot down workmen."

————❖————

JULY 11, 1892 —*Reprinted from*
the New York Herald.

THEY WILL STRIKE, TOO.

—————

Employees in Other Mills Threaten Trouble Unless Frick Backs Down.

—————

[BY TELEGRAPH TO THE HERALD.]

PITTSBURG, PA., July 10, 1892. —The employés of the Carnegie mill at Beaver Falls have joined with those of the Twenty-ninth and Thirty-third street mills in Pittsburg in deciding to strike if Chairman Frick insists in refusing to recognize the Amalgamated Association at Homestead. A joint meeting of representatives of the workmen in the three mills was held to-day.

It was secret, but after the adjournment it was stated that a committee had been appointed to see Chairman Frick to-morrow, and that the workmen were ready for any action that might be found necessary. It is announced to-night that the scale has been signed for the Moorehead-McClean Company's mill. This is a large concern, and is being operated by a trustee in the interest of the creditors. The latter think they can afford to pay the wages demanded by the workmen.

———❖———

JULY 14, 1892 —*Excerpted from*
The Pittsburg Leader.

CARNEGIE'S PITTSBURG WORKMEN.

—————

Will Injure the Cause of the Homesteaders by Going Out on Strike. Something Startling Promised Before the Week is Over.

—————

HOMESTEAD, PA., July 14. —Homestead's locked-out workmen do not want the employes of Carnegie's Thirty-third and Twenty-ninth street mills to cease work on account of the trouble in this place. This statement is official. Your correspondent got it from those high in authority in the Homestead Amalgamated association lodges. One of these gentlemen said: "We do not want Carnegie's employes in other places to come out on our account. Such a step at this time would be very unwise. It cannot but hurt us. While we appreciate the spirit prompting such proposed action on the part of our brethren in other places we are sorry they have decided upon such a course. 'Tis true, as Mr. Frick testified before the congressional committee yesterday afternoon, that the Amalgamated association has never broken a contract or a pledge. The men now working in the Carnegie upper and lower mills are par-

ties to contracts with the company and we do not want them to break them. Such a step would be just to Mr. Frick's liking. It would give him and other enemies of organized labor a hold they do not at present possess and our association cannot afford anything of the kind. Should the employees of the other mills strike now it would give Frick the opportunity he has long been looking for to make those mills non-union. For the men to come out would also result in increasing the present trouble. Frick would not fight the men in the Pittsburg mills. He will pay no attention to them but will redouble his efforts to defeat us here. There is no need of Amalgamated men in other places sacrificing good positions and causing their families to suffer simply to aid us. I do not think the Homestead company will attempt to start its works. Mr. Frick will pursue an entirely different policy. He will try to starve the men into submission. Hunger, you know, will make a man do almost anything, and no one knows this better than Mr. Frick. I am reliably informed that all the superintendents and bosses have declared that under no circumstances will they go to work if non-unionmen are brought in. But, laying aside all else, we, the employees of the Carnegie steel works, earnestly request the men in the employ of Carnegie in his Pittsburg mills to remain at their posts. We do not want them to make any such sacrifice as they at present contemplate."

———❖———

JULY 15, 1892 —*Reprinted from*
The Pittsburg Leader.

BRADDOCK MEN WON'T STRIKE.

——

Out of Sympathy for the Homestead Workmen— Feeling at the Edgar Thomson Works.

BRADDOCK, July 15. —So much has recently been said about the prospect of the Braddock workmen in the Edgar Thomson works showing their sympathy for the Homestead strikers by quitting work that a *Leader* reporter has taken the trouble to make an exhaustive investigation, with the result that he can state positively that no such action is even contemplated. "Why," said one man spoken to, "should we attempt to assist Homestead? For years past no name in their vocabulary has been too vile to hurl at the workmen of this place." "Do you think us a lot of fools?" said another, "to deliberately quit

our work for a mere sentiment that could not possibly help any person while it would put us in the position of violating our agreement with the firm." Many similar expressions were heard and it is quite sage to assert that whatever the result at Homestead, Braddock men will not come out to assist them. Indeed beyond the sympathy for labor in general, but little appears to be entertained for the Homestead workers. This is probably attributable to the illy disguised ill feeling that has existed between the two places for some years.

———❖———

JULY 15, 1892 —*Excerpted from the* St. Louis Post-Dispatch.

ON OLD LINES.

————

The Homestead Men Will Battle Against Carnegie.

————

Physical Force Will Be Supplanted by the Boycott.

————

ONLY AGAINST PINKERTONS WILL WINCHESTERS BE USED.

Homestead, Pa., July 15. —In discussing the situation to-day Hugh O'Donnell said: "We will fight this strike out on legitimate lines. The Pinkerton incident has put a false complexion on affairs and changed the channel of public estimation of our rights and wrongs. Many people think we intend endeavoring to maintain our position by lawless means. Such never was our intention. The workman's only effective weapon, the boycott, will be employed, and we will endeavor to strike a blow at Carnegie's every industry.

"It is stated that he intends starving us into submission. We have not as much money as he, but we are willing to meet him on his own grounds. Such assistance as the strike of the Lawrenceville mills and action of the carpenters in refusing to work in buildings where Carnegie beams or materials are used; that we want. Help us that way and we will win.

"I'll guarantee there will be no harm offered non-union men coming here, but I can not offer the same protection guarantee to Pinkertons, for every man, woman and child in Homestead goes wild at the mention of one."

Mr. O'Donnell was asked what chance the Carnegies have to start the mill with deserters from the Amalgamated ranks. "None in the world," he said. "There is not a man who will desert the association— not a single man. There has probably never been such a unanimity of opinion in a strike in this country and we will present an unbroken front to the end. Mr. Carnegie may be able to get non-union laborers, helpers, blacksmiths, mechanics, carpenters and painters, but all of these have to depend on the skilled men who make the steel.

"Without rollers, heaters, shearers, cutters and other skilled workmen the mills cannot start, and it is this class of men who will hold out to the last."

The entire force of assistants to the civil engineers in the employ of the Carnegie Steel Co. struck this morning out of sympathy for the locked-out men. They had no grievances of their own. This will stop all outside work until a new force can be secured. . . .

————❖————

JULY 15, 1892 —*Excerpted from* The Pittsburgh Post.

A STRIKE OF SYMPATHY.

— — — —

Lawrenceville Mill Men Do as They Said They Would.

— — — —

ABOUT 2,000 ARE NOW OUT OF A JOB.

— — — —

They Won't Do Work That Should Be Done at Homestead.

Yesterday shortly after dinner hour the Amalgamated Association members employed in the Carnegie Upper and Lower Union Mills quit work and went out on strike in support of the locked-out workmen of the Homestead steel mill. This action was the result of a meeting of the Amalgamated men at which the situation was discussed, and it was decided that the members of the association should stop work and uphold the Homestead men. They believed that they were performing work in the Union mills which had been transferred from the Homestead mill, and in that way balking their fellow-workmen who were engaged in the fight up the Monongahela.

At the Lower Union mill it was impossible to learn the exact number of men who stopped work. Some of the men placed the number at 250, but at the company's office it was stated that only the rolling department quit work and that there were 148 men all told employed in this department. At any rate the Amalgamated men all went out, and this was a sufficient number to stop operations at the mill. The other departments can work for a limited time, or until the material is used up, and then the works will be idle. The men finished up the day turn and some of them did not get through until after 3 o'clock, but as they concluded their work they took their dinner buckets and walked home, not knowing when they would return. During the afternoon the following notice was posted in different places outside the mill. "All persons not employed at these works are positively prohibited from entering. Call at the office."

Knots of men gathered about reading these signs and commenting upon them. There were no threats made nor any excitement over the strike, but the men simply walked out, declaring that they would not return until the Amalgamated Association had been recognized.

WHY THEY QUIT WORK.

In conversation with a *Post* reporter one of the strikers said: "We are quitting work to-day with a view of winning the fight which the Carnegie people have made upon the Amalgamated Association, and we will win it. We have got to win this fight, for if we lose it the backbone of our association will be broken. We have been doing work which was brought from the Homestead mill and in this way we have been working against the men there. We don't propose to do this any longer. In 24 hours there will not be any work going on in this mill, and we can hold out a long time if it is necessary. We will have the support of the iron and steel workers all over the country. This Homestead affair is an attempt to kill our organization, but we are determined it shan't be killed. If it comes to bloodshed again it will take more than the State militia to whip us, for there will be more men on the scene than they have counted on."

The men in the blacksmith shop are not in the Amalgamated Association and will not strike, but they may be forced to quit work by lack of material. One of them said to a *Post* reporter yesterday: "Why should we strike? We could not do anything for the Homestead workmen by leaving our jobs. We are not in the association, and are well paid and satisfied, so I see no reason why we should go out. I have worked here for 22 years, and during the big strike in 1883 I was the last man in our shop to go to work. We were in the Amalgamated Association then, but they went back on us. Nobody is in greater sympathy with labor than I am, for I have been a workingman all my life, but there is absolutely nothing we could do for the Homestead men by going out with the Amalgamated men. I will not be affected by the strike, for I work in scrap iron and my supply of material will not shut off.

. . .

DON'T WANT THE GIFT.

"There is one thing, however, that is being agitated in Lawrenceville just now, and that is the proposition to return Mr. Carnegie's $1,000,000 for the free library. This is being talked of among the businessmen of the Seventeenth ward, and they are really serious in the matter. I would not be surprised if they should hold a mass meeting and ask councils to return the money to Mr. Carnegie. There is a great feeling out here in that direction, and to me the gift of the free library is like borrowing so much money and taxing the workmen in the Carnegie mills to repay it."

At the Upper Union mill most of the men stopped working at noon. The number is estimated at 600. Yesterday afternoon when a *Post* reporter visited the works the men were leaving in twos and threes, and Thirty-third street was lined with groups of workmen discussing the situation. At the office no information could be obtained other than that the men had stopped work. It is claimed by the strikers that the mill can run only a short time until the supply of material is exhausted, and then the whole plant will be idle. The Amalgamated Association includes the puddlers and the rollers, and upon their product the rest of the mill depends. It is estimated that about 2,000 men are employed at the two mills, including all classes of workmen. Not more than half, or possibly 10 per cent, of these are members of the Amalgamated Association.

The strikers do not seem to be afraid of any immediate attempt to put non-union men in their places. In the first place they do not think the company could obtain men who would go into the mills as black sheep, and furthermore they do not intend to permit such a thing if they can prevent it.

. . .

POSITION OF THE COMPANY.

————

Their Reasons For Not Recognizing the Amalgamated Association at the Homestead Mills.

There is a feeling that the employes of the Carnegie Steel Company at the Upper and Lower Union mills have made a mistake in their present strike. The criticism is made that the men have not only cut themselves off from their base of supplies and added thousands of new mouths to be fed from the common treasury, but that they have broken a contract giving them all that they asked for. Not only this but

in addition they have precipitated a fight against the Amalgamated Association in mills where there was no attack upon it. To a *Post* reporter an official of the Carnegie Steel Company made this statement last evening:

"The assertion that the company had intended to make the Upper and Lower Union mills and our mills at Beaver Falls non-union next year is false. We have no especial objection to the Amalgamated Association in these mills for the reason that the product for the main part is merchant iron and steel, in the manufacture of which we compete with similar union mills all over the country. The basis of the scale in these mills is the same that is in the mills of our competitors and is satisfactory to us, or we would not have signed it. At Homestead it is different. The scale that is applicable to Jones & Laughlin's mills, for example, is not applicable to Homestead, for the reason that the mills are altogether different. It is impossible to find a basis from which to figure a scale just and equitable to all parties at Homestead. It should be understood that there are no mills in the world like the Homestead mills, and in no mills in the world are steel workers so anxious to secure positions. We are willing to pay the highest market price for labor, but the Amalgamated Association insists that conditions not applicable to these mills shall be made the basis upon which this shall be determined. Beyond this we will candidly admit that there is a great deal of satisfaction in running your own business. Nearly all of this trouble comes from the best paid men in our mills—men who receive from $4 to $10 a day. The poorer paid men, whom these men are anxious shall not learn to fill the better paid positions, are always made to suffer. In this strike they have nothing at stake. Without a pretense even of bettering their own wages, they are asked to fight for still better wages for the best paid men. One of these men who was at my office to-day referred to the beneficiaries of the Amalgamated Association who draw from $4 to $10 a day as the aristocracy of labor, and he declared that he was tired fighting for them without improving his own condition. The company is receiving letters by the bundle every day from iron and steel workers making application for positions in the Homestead mill.

"So far as the Upper and Lower mills are concerned it is now probable they will also be made non-union. The Amalgamated Association has voluntarily broken the contract with us and we are forced to ignore them in making new contracts."

———❖———

(facing page) **Illustrated American, July 30, 1892. Headquarters of the Ninth Pennsylvania Guards in Camp Sam Black. The headquarters of the Amalgamated Association were located in the Bost Building, seen in the background.**

(below) From the same issue of **Illustrated American,** *a view of Camp Sam Black taken from the windows of the Amalgamated Association headquarters.*

RECRUITS FROM CINCINNATI.

―――――

Three Hundred Non-Union Men for Fort Frick.

―――――

ALSO AN ANARCHIST CHEMIST.

―――――

Who Says, If He Wants to, He Will Blow the Homestead Steel Works Into Atoms. The Workmen Are Able-Bodied, but Not Skilled.

―――――

CINCINNATI, O., July 15.—[Special]—There has been notable decrease during the last few days in the number of loafers in and about the saloons on Vine and Walnut streets. Observing persons, too, have missed many familiar faces that were wont to be seen along Fountain square and the court house esplanade. Since Sunday there have been collected in this city by a well known detective agency 270 or 280 men.

They were gathered, one by one, from among other habitues of various downtown saloons and street corners by agents, who held out to them the flattering proposal of $3, $4, and $5 per day should they consent to go to Homestead.

The gang thus collected has been sent on to the Carnegie mills in sections. So quietly has the work been carried on that scarcely an intimation of the proceeding has come to the surface. The men are now all on the way toward their destination, the last section having been sent Wednesday night. The men were shipped to take the places of the strikers in the mills.

But little attention was paid to the qualifications of the men collected as regards the particular work they are expected to perform.

No one, however, was accepted who was not physically well proportioned and in the best of health. The whole story has leaked out through the indiscretion of one of the men thus enlisted.

Tuesday last, John Gerke, a former employe of A. Staat, the shoemaker, at the southeast corner of Sixth and Vine, accosted the latter with, "Well, I'm going to leave." "Where are you going?" was asked. "To Homestead," was the answer, after some hesitancy. "Oh, you oughtn't to do that." "Well, I'm going to, anyhow. There are about 280 men already collected and we are promised $3 a day up. I haven't anything to do here, and might as well take up the offer."

Further questioning by Mr. Staat elicited the fact that they were going as workmen, and not as guards or watchmen.

For several months there has resided in this city a quiet foreigner. He lived in retired apartments and devoted his entire time to chemical experiments.

He spoke English indifferently and made few acquaintances. He admitted being an anarchist, and his manner impressed those who met him with the idea that he was a man of great learning and former wealth. The police soon came to know him as a chemist of the greatest skill, with a penchant for explosions. Recently he claimed to a policeman he had discovered an explosive ten times more powerful than dynamite, safe to handle, and occupying scarcely one-twentieth of the bulk. He gave experiments which seemed to prove his claim. A piece of the new agent as large as a lima bean would tear a hole several feet deep in the solid ground, and hurl stones 100 feet. Last Tuesday night this man left for Pittsburg, saying that if desired he would blow Homestead mills to atoms.

―――――❖―――――

Excerpted from House of Representatives, Report No. 2447,
"Labor Troubles at Homestead, Pa. Employment
of Pinkerton Detectives" (1893)

INVESTIGATION OF THE EMPLOYMENT OF PINKERTON DETECTIVES IN CONNECTION WITH THE LABOR TROUBLES AT HOMESTEAD, PA.

PITTSBURG, Pa., *July 12, 1892.*

In the House of Representatives on May 12, 1892, Mr. Oates, from the Committee on the Judiciary, submitted the following report, which was adopted:

The House of Representatives having ordered this committee to report back the resolution proposing an investigation of the Pinkerton Detective Agency, the Committee on the Judiciary, having had the same under consideration, report therefor the following substitute and recommend its adoption:

"Whereas it has been alleged that a certain organization known as the Pinkerton detectives has been employed unlawfully and to the detriment of the public by railroad corporations engaged in the transportation of the United States mails and interstate commerce: Therefore, be it:

"*Resolved*, That the Committee on the Judiciary be, and it is hereby, directed to investigate the said Pinkerton detectives, to wit: The character of their employment by corporations engaged in the transportation of interstate commerce or the United States mails, the numbers so employed, and whether such employment has provoked breaches of the peace or caused the destruction of property, and all the material facts connected with their alleged employment, and to report the same to this House by bill or otherwise at any time."

. . .

Also on July 6, 1892, in the House of Representatives, Mr. Williams, of Massachusetts, submitted the following—

"Whereas the Pinkerton detective or private police force, to the number of several hundred, is now engaged in an armed conflict at Homestead, Pa., with the late employés of the Carnegie Iron Works at said place, and a great loss of human life and destruction of property are likely to result from same; and

"Whereas the Judiciary Committee has been directed by a resolution of the House to investigate the nature and character of the employment of Pinkerton detectives by corporations engaged in interstate commerce; therefore, be it

"*Resolved*, That said committee shall investigate and report on the character of the employment of said forces in the present instance, and the causes and conditions of the sanguinary conflict now going on at Homestead, Pa."

Which was referred to the Committee on the Judiciary and was reported back favorably on July 7, 1892. ❖

The subcommittee of the Committee on the Judiciary under the Chairmanship of William C. Oates held hearings in Pittsburgh from July 12 to July 14, 1892.

JULY 16, 1892 — Reprinted from
The Pittsburg Leader.

OATES COMMITTEE.

————

Investigating the Homestead Affair Returns to Washington.

————

The Chairman Says They Got to the Bottom of the Trouble and the Report Will Be Ready Soon—"Frick A Remarkably Cunning Fellow"—A Prediction of More Bloodshed When the Troops Are Withdrawn.

————

WASHINGTON, July 15.—The Homestead investigating committee returned to Washington this morning. When they reached the capitol they were surrounded by eagerly inquiring colleagues, anxious to get an opinion as to the situation at Homestead. "I think," said Chairman Oates, "we got all the information possible. We got down to the bottom of the trouble. It will not take long to prepare the report. The chief delay will be caused by the fact of the stenographer's notes being so voluminous. There was an immense amount of testimony. We examined Mr. Frick, his superintendent and a number of the workmen as you have seen. Mr. Frick is a remarkably cunning fellow and a great manager. He has one of the brightest lawyers I ever met to advise him. The leaders of the workmen are of intelligence and capacity. The workmen as a body are very able and shrewd, certainly the most intelligent lot of manual workers I have ever seen." Mr. Oates then referred to the excellent condition of the Homestead men and their families. He spoke of the wages as ranging for skilled men from $65 to $275 a month, while laborers, he said, receive $1 to $1.50 a day. Mr. Oates also referred to Mr. Frick's refusal to tell the committee the cost of making a ton of steel billets.

(Oates Committee, continued)

He regarded Mr. Frick's refusal as significant. When asked how he thought the trouble would end he hesitated. Law and order, he said, must be vindicated in the long run even if the statutes and equities conflict. "Do you think there will be further trouble?" "Yes, yes, I do, more trouble and bloodshed, and a great deal of it. The workmen are not acting on impulse. They are pursuing a course dictated by their calm judgment. Legally they do not claim to be right, but morally they think they are. The non-union workmen will soon be introduced into the works under military protection. They will probably be armed. On the withdrawal of the troops the trouble will be renewed." The committee will probably make the report that the Homestead case is beyond the reach of federal legislation.

———❖———

This image of guard duty around "Fort Frick" at City Farm Lane is part of a series of stereoscopic photos on the occupation by Underwood & Underwood.

JULY 16, 1892 —Reprinted from **The Pittsburg Leader.**

MEN AT WORK.

————

A "Leader" Man Goes Through the Carnegie Plant

————

And finds About 25 Men at Work, Some of Them Non-Unionists—Members of the Office Force Hard at Work—Provisions for a Whole Army of Workmen Brought Up by the "Little Bill"—More Men Are Expected Soon.

————

HOMESTEAD, PA., July 16. —The statement was made this morning, that not less than 100 non-union men are at work in the Carnegie steel works. In order to get at the exact status of affairs, your correspondent with considerable difficulty succeeded in getting within the enclosure. This done, there was nothing to prevent a tour through every department of the immense plant. As a result of the tour of investigation the *Leader* is able to state that all told fifteen or twenty men are at work today. Some of these are men belonging to the company's clerical force. They have donned blouse and overalls and are in charge of the few non-union laboring men. In the pressing mill no work of any consequence has been done, while in the armor plate mill nothing has been accomplished further than the lighting of fires in one or two furnaces. In the pressing mill there are eighteen or twenty cots, while in the engine room at the pump station were found a dozen more. These cots are not the regulation canvas affairs. They are supplied with comfortable looking mattresses and are really substantial couches. The men took dinner in a rough restaurant fixed up in the pressing mill. A range has been put in and the culinary department is in charge of a cook from Pittsburg.

On all sides were to be seen boxes, barrels and bags of provisions. The dinner was spread on a long table well supplied with new dishes, knives, forks, etc. Much of the provender is stored in the office building, just above the railroad trestle, but when your correspondent left the place, two men, evidently laborers, were engaged in transferring the supplies to the pressing mill. A few minutes after 12 o'clock the steamer Little Bill came across the river and dumped a cargo consisting of numerous sacks of ground coffee, three barrels of sugar, six sacks of flour, three firkins of butter, two or three baskets of bread, etc. One of the men, when questioned, said that provisions sufficient to feed several hundred men for a month had already been laid in, but that every time Little Bill pulled up at the mill landing she unloaded additions to the supply. "We are being well fed and are having an easy time of it," said one of the men. "It will be many weeks before the company gets everything going nicely. No, there are not over 20 or 25 men in the entire mill, but I understand more are expected soon."

At this juncture one of the dudish looking bosses was seen approaching, and the interview came to a sudden and very unsatisfactory close. Once or twice the *Leader* correspondent, who was accompanied by a Baltimore *News* man, was stopped by watchmen and bosses, but the passports produced were satisfactory, and the newsgathers were not interfered with to any extent, though their every movement was closely watched by the workmen. It was the first time newspaper men had succeeded in entering the works and the suspicions of the little handful of non-unionists were aroused.

———❖———

COTS FOR NON-UNIONISTS.

————

Four Hundred Beds Said to Have Been Received at Homestead

————

And Placed in Carnegie's Plant for the Accommodation of New Workingmen.

————

HOMESTEAD, PA., July 16. —It has been learned that the Carnegie company has placed cots for nearly 400 men within the works with rations enough to furnish subsistance for several days. Stoves, cooking utensils, etc., are there. In fact, a complete outfit for housing and supporting a large body of men had been provided, having been brought by boat from Pittsburg Thursday. It is stated this has been done not for the accommodation of Pinkertons, but for non-union workmen, who are expected to arrive Monday night. This may possibly substantiate the rumor that over 200 workmen are coming from Cincinnati.

It has been said in certain quarters that the men in a company of the Eighteenth regiment have declared they would turn over their arms to the locked-out workmen if a conflict should take place. The rumor, however, is undoubtedly untrue. While members of both Pittsburg regiments have relatives and intimate friends living here, their devotion to duty has never been questioned.

Last night the big search light flashed its way out over the river from the tower of the converting mill. It was turned in all directions to give a commanding view of all avenues of approach. During the night previous a search light was used to examine every skiff that passed up or down the Monongahela.

————

Yesterday afternoon when smoke was seen issuing from one or two of the cupolas of the great Carnegie steel plant the idle workmen were for the time being excited. When the locked-out men caught the first glimpse of the dark smoke curling from the cupolas they could do naught but stand and gaze with open eyes and open mouths. They were as men transfixed. Suddenly some one in the little group assembled on the Pemicky [sic] tracks, near the entrance to the works, suggested the propriety of investigating. Instantly the men, oblivious of the fact that the entire steel plant was under a strong military guard, started on a run down the tracks. But they didn't go far. "Halt!" came from the stern-visaged pickets, and the excited workmen found it impossible to proceed further. "You wouldn't stand between union workmen and their rights, would you?" asked one of the excited individuals. "All I know is that you cannot sagely advance another step," quietly replied the guard, who faced the men with his gun at a charge. Then the men, who feared non-union men had gone to work in the mill, slowly retraced their steps. They knew it would be useless to attempt to pass through the lines.

Speaking of the relighting of the fires. In some of the furnaces, a member of the Amalgamated association said to your correspondent last night: "The fact that smoke has been issuing from some of the cupola stacks should not make the men feel uneasy. The company has rekindled the fires to prevent the destruction of the dolomite in the furnaces. The character of the material is such that should it be exposed to the air it would crumble like so much stacked lime. We do not blame the company for trying to save their material, but you may rest assured that the mere relighting of these fires has but very little significance."

In yesterday's *Leader* appeared an account of the arrest of High Constable Stewart, of Homestead, by the guard on duty at the corner of Eighth avenue and Amity street, Thursday night. This fact recalls a little incident that transpired the day previous. During a storm lightning killed a cow that was grazing in front of the provost marshal's headquarters. When Constable Stewart learned of this he repaired at once to the camp ground, hunted up Colonel Green, the provost marshal, and said: "In the name of the commonwealth of the state of Pennsylvania, I command you to remove the carcass of yonder dead cow."

"And pray who might you be?" asked Colonel Green.

"My name is Stewart," was the reply. "I am high constable of the borough of Homestead, and if you do not haul that dead cow away and bury her I will place you under arrest."

"If you want that cow removed from this field you had better do it yourself," responded Colonel Green. "And I might add that if you do not get out of this camp at once I will place you under arrest. Go."

Very much crestfallen the high constable of this little municipality very wisely lost no time in getting out. The unfortunate cow was buried at the expense of the borough.

————

TO HOUSE NON-UNION MEN.

————

The Carnegie Steel Company Advertise for Proposals to Build 100 New Houses at Munhall.

————

The Carnegie steel company this morning advertises for proposals to build 100 houses on the City Farm plan of lots, at Munhall station, half a mile north of Homestead. The contract will be given out at noon on July 23.

This indicates that the company intend providing living places for the non-union men who are to be brought on to operate the Homestead works. It is certain houses for non-union men could not be gotten in Homestead and there are none inside the works.

————❖————

JULY 15, 1892 —Excerpted from the St. Louis Post-Dispatch.

"A NOVEL BOYCOTT"

One of the curious incidents is the boycott which the servant girls at the Club house have put upon Gen. Snowden and the officers of the militia. The club house, also called the Frick Hotel, is just opposite the main gate of the mill property and contains the best restaurant in Homestead. It has been doing a land office business since the militia arrived, but this morning the cooks and the female help declined to minister to the wants of the military and the camp commissary had to be called upon to provide food at headquarters. Orders were issued this morning that no officer may leave camp unless on detailed duty or with the special permission of the General commanding. The order has excited some comment as heretofore the officers were free to go and come as they pleased and the rumor mongers at once went to work and distilled the information that this meant that General Snowden believed that the troops would be needed today.

. . .

JULY 16

Negro waiters have taken the place of the waitresses at the Carnegie Clubhouse, or Frick Hotel, who struck yesterday because of the presence of Gen. Snowden and his officers there. It has been learned that the local waitresses were also induced to take their action by the presence of so many un-uniformed strangers at the house. They thought some of these might be non-union men, and to be on the safe side of popular opinion in Homestead, they refused to serve at the hotel during the prevalence of the rumors that non-union men were in town. It can be stated as a fact based on personal observation that Gen. Snowden and his officers are not starving as a result of the strike at the hotel.

———❖———

JULY 16, 1892 —Reprinted from The Pittsburg Press.

And the National Guard Uniforms Don't Attract Homestead Maids.

HOMESTEAD, PA., July 16. —[Special]— One of the peculiar features of the encampment of the national guard at this point is the apparent indifference shown on the part of the ladies of Homestead for the soldiers. It is popularly supposed that blue coats and brass buttons have an irresistible charm for the fair sex, and an encampment is usually visited by girls and women by the score. Such is not the case at Homestead. There have been very few visitors of the gentler sex at Camp Black, and a walk about the borough this evening failed to reveal a single case of "mash" in which a member of the P.N.G. figured.

A citizen, commenting upon this feature, attributed the lack of enthusiasm on the part of the ladies to the manner of the soldiers coming and to the reason for them being here. Said he: "The girls of Homestead are union men, and they don't like to see any one coming here who is opposed to the cause in which they have enlisted their sympathies. Then, too, many of the people, regardless of sex, feel a little angered over the manner in which Gen. Snowden received the overtures of the representatives of the Amalgamated association, and this feeling keeps them as far from the soldiers as possible. The instincts of the sex will conquer, and tomorrow our ladies will visit the camps and admire the brass buttons to their full capacity. As to individual flirtations there will not be much. For our girls are not as a rule given to that sort of thing and I don't believe even the attractive uniforms of the militia will turn their heads."

FENTON.

JULY 17, 1892 —Reprinted from the St. Louis Post-Dispatch.

WOMEN OF HOMESTEAD.

THEY RULE THE TOWN BUT ARE MODEST AND WOMANLY.

HOMESTEAD, PA., July 16.—The story of the women of Homestead is the story of home. Since the famous fight of Wednesday there have been smuggled into the stories which have gone forth from here many references to the women of Homestead, but they have given no idea of what sort of human beings they are.

To be sure there was much printed in connection with the beating they gave the captured Pinkertons when the Hessians were compelled to run the gauntlet. There is not the slightest doubt that the Hessians had a very uncomfortable time of it at the hands of the women. When the people away from here heard the story they promptly jumped at the conclusion that the women were fierce amazons, prepared to take the whole world by the ears and do as they please.

An impression seems to have been spread abroad that by merely twisting their faces, that they can assume an expression so frightful that they will terrify all manner of people. Of course, this is very wrong and nonsensical.

It is true that the women of Homestead are different from those found in most cities, but the difference lies in the fact that they are the kind that make good men remember their mothers, and think that good women are yet born on earth. The fiercely intellectual women who talk about their down-trodden sex and the slavery of woman to dishes and scrub brushes would weep bitter tears should they come to proselyte among the wives and mothers of Homestead. Here they seem to never have heard of woman's rights or to have learned that they have been emancipated. In truth they want no rights they have not already, and they do not want to be emancipated because they live in their homes with their husbands and they are happy.

There is something great and old fashioned about them. They show that gentle dignity and wholesomeness of women who believe in their honest worth and who are respected for it rather than for the gowns they wear and the smallness of their waists. Not that the women are not well dressed. They are feminine if they do live in Homestead, and their gowns are as simple and as attractive as their nature.

The women of Homestead can be generally divided into two classes—those who speak English and those who do not. Of the latter there are some six or seven hundred, so they form a small part.

The first thing that impresses a visitor at Homestead is the fact that few women are to be seen. After the first two or three days he concludes that there are few women in town. And those who are seen quietly going in and out of the houses are dressed so quietly and carry themselves so modestly that one sees only glimpses of them. They never seem to promenade through the streets, and when they go out for a walk their husbands seem always to be with them. When the women of Homestead are known—which is no easy matter, for they are shy of strangers—the marvel of them grows. They seem to be of another race than those of the cities. And when they are studied, the secret of Homestead quietness is easily understood.

To the man who knows the women the reason why it is the model town of all manufacturing places is no longer a secret. It is because the women rule the town through their husbands and the women are good.

It is a remarkable thing in these days of Long Island marital difficulties and Dakota divorces to go into a town where the women are honestly good, not because they have to be, but because they want to be; where they are faithful and loving and true, because they are so happy in it that it never occurs to them to think of anything else. Of course, you will not believe that it is really true that the better educated a woman or husband is the prouder she is of her home and husband. To some women the thought of marrying a mechanic makes her tilt her nose in an unmistakable way, she would rather marry a rich man, but as between a mechanic who makes good wages and a $10-a-week clerk she prefers the clerk. The girls in Homestead think differently.

Perhaps you think the workmen of Homestead are not well educated. It is almost impossible to find one who was not graduated from the public schools. Scores of them have been graduated from the Normal schools and academies which are scattered about. In this part of the country they do not permit their women to work in factories. They think it is the place for the men. It is the man's duty to earn the living, the duty of the woman is to make the home pleasant. They live up to this philosophy. The girls go through the schools, train their minds and absorb as much of books as they can. Not that they may go out into the world and be independent, but because they expect to become the wives of good men and want to help them as much as they can, for in this country there are fewer men than women and good husbands are always wanting. The women are far better educated than the men, that is, in the way of schooling. This thing of women carefully preparing themselves to make good wives of hard working mechanics by securing the best schooling they can makes the man who comes from the large city rub his eyes and wonder if he has dropped into another world. It seems altogether too good to be real.

———❖———

SALOONS

Members of the National Guard have ceased their liberal patronage of the saloons. About 5 o'clock yesterday evening the streets were patrolled and every man in uniform who could not produce a written leave of absence from camp was placed under arrest. The patrol visited all the saloons and captured several bibulous "sojer boys" and conducted them back to camp. As a result of this very commendable move few blue coats were seen on the streets last night and the scenes of Monday and Tuesday evenings were not repeated. Several amusing incidents characterized the movements of the patrol. When the officers in charge entered the ballroom of the Amity hotel several guardsman started for the rear door. In their haste they fell over each other and over chairs. Finally they reached the door leading to a side street. They jerked it open and were congratulating themselves on their success, when, to their surprise and dismay, they found further progress impossible on account of four sharp-pointed and glistening bayonets. One of the boys ran up against one of the pieces of steel before he fully grasped the situation. Then, in evident alarm, he blurted out: "What do you mean, I might have been hurt." By this time the officer had laid his hands on the shoulders of the indiscreet individuals, and, very much crestfallen, they were led back to headquarters.

———❖———

JULY 18, 1892 —Excerpted from
The New-York Times.

WHOLESALE ARRESTS DEMANDED.

———

WORKINGMEN CHARGE FRICK AND THE PINKERTONS WITH MURDER.

CHICAGO, July 17. —If the sentiments expressed by the Trades and Labor Assembly at its meeting to-day were carried out, the Pinkertons—William and Robert—together with Manager Frick of the Carnegie works, would be placed under arrest on the charges of murder, treason, inciting riot, and insurrection. By far the most radical declarations yet made by any labor organization in the United States, respecting the Homestead troubles were adopted at the meeting of the assembly.

As soon as the meeting was called to order, "Tommy" Morgan arose and moved to suspend the rules and receive a report from the Executive Board on the "Homestead affair." The motion was quickly carried, and Mr. Quinton of the Tin and Sheet Iron Workers, read a long preamble and resolutions. They recite the existence of the Pinkerton agency and its "habit of sending armed assassins into different States and territories to shoot American citizens and workingmen," [and] state that Mr. Frick conspired with the Pinkertons to send "armed assassins, called watchmen, to Homestead, where, by Frick's instructions, the armed hirelings attacked, killed, and maimed citizens and workingmen, creating riot and imperiling the welfare of the United States. Such acts are anarchistic and against the spirit of our liberties." They continue:

Resolved, That we demand of the Governor of Illinois the arrest of William Pinkerton of Chicago on the charge that he incited riot and insurrection; that we call upon Gov. Flower of New-York to cause the arrest of Robert Pinkerton of New-York City on a similar charge, and we call upon the Governor of Pennsylvania that he cause the arrest of Manager Henry Frick of Homestead, Penn., on the charge of treason, murder, inciting riot, insurrection, and rebellion; and at this moment trying to deprive American citizens of their homes and of the right to earn their living at their homes and at the mills which their labor has built up and created.

The radical spirit of the resolutions was received with cheers which were given again and again. A committee of five was appointed to draw up charges of murder against the Pinkertons and Mr. Frick. . . .

———❖———

Illustrated American, *July 30, 1892.*
The Provost Guard stationed at Camp
Sam Black patrols the town.

JULY 19, 1892 —Excerpted from **The New-York Times.**

THE LEADERS HAD FLOWN

———

HOMESTEAD STRIKERS DID NOT RELISH ARREST.

———

O'DONNELL AND SIX OTHERS EVADED THE SERVICE OF WARRANTS—CONCEALED BY THEIR FRIENDS FROM THE CONSTABLES — NOT ONE OF THEM RETURNED TO THE MILLS.

HOMESTEAD, PENN., July 18. —The past twenty-four hours have been fraught with interest and excitement to the people of Homestead.

Three incidents of more than passing moment have occurred—a midnight scare which led to the reinforcement of the guard; the opening of the mills this morning and the refusal of the old men to return, and the attempt of three Pittsburg constables to serve warrants, under the protection of the military, upon the leaders on the charge of murder. The latter was the most exciting episode of the day. The attempt had been tried and failed before it was generally known that it had been made.

Yesterday afternoon a tall, well-built man stepped off a train and asked the way to Hugh O'Donnell's house. He was piloted there. For half an hour he was under lock and key with the leader of the strike. Within an hour O'Donnell informed a committee of workmen from the Duquesne Works that he was compelled to break the engagement he had made to speak at their meeting that afternoon, because he had been suddenly called out of town. O'Donnell boarded the 6:30 o'clock train for Pittsburg at the City Farm station and took a seat furthest from the window. Arriving in Pittsburg at the Union Station, his railway, and sleeping car tickets were handed to him, having been previously secured. Who the stranger was is not known. Where he came from is a matter of conjecture.

At noon to-day a dozen of the other leaders left Homestead. Various explanations are given for their departure.

About the same time three constables—Joseph Weber, W.J. Morris, and W.J. Price—from Pittsburg appeared before Sheriff McCleary at division headquarters and demanded protection in serving seven warrants which had been issued by Squire McMasters against seven leaders of the strike on the charge of murder, and which they had in their possession. The document which the constables presented read this way:

Commonwealth of Pennsylvania vs. John McLuckie, Hugh O'Donnell, Sylvester Critchelow, Anthony Flaherty, Samuel Burkett, James Flanagan, and Hugh Ross.

State of Pennsylvania, County of Allegheny,:

Before the subscriber, James V. McMasters, Alderman in and for the City of Pittsburg and ex officio a Justice of the Peace of said county, personally came F.T.F. Lovejoy, who, upon oath administered according to law, deposeth and saith that in Mifflin Township, in the County of Allegheny and State of Pennsylvania, on the 6th day of July, 1892. John McLuckie, Hugh O'Donnell, Sylvester Critchelow, Anthony Flaherty, Samuel Burkett, James Flanagan, and Hugh Ross did of malice aforethought feloniously and notoriously and with force and arms and deadly weapons kill and murder one Silas Wayne, then and there being in the peace of the Commonwealth of Pennsylvania. This is made upon information received and believed to be true by the deponent.

Complainant therefore prays and desires that a warrant may issue, and that the aforesaid defendants may be arrested and held to answer the charge of murder, and further deponent saith not.

Mr. Lovejoy, who makes the complaint, is the Secretary of the Carnegie Company. Wayne, who was killed, was one of the strikers and was shot by a glancing shot from the guns in the hands of his own friends.

As soon as the constables made their request, the Sheriff laid the matter before Gen. Snowden, who promptly offered all the protection necessary. Two companies of the Twelfth Regiment—B, Capt. Sweeny, of Williamsport, and E., Capt. Clements, of Sunbury—were detailed for the risky work. The whole was under command of Major Brooks. The troops loaded their pieces and carried twenty rounds of ammunition. Major Campbell of Gen. Snowden's staff accompanied them. As a precautionary measure, the entire Fourth Regiment, Col. Case, and Twelfth, Col. Coryell, detailed for provost guard duty, were ordered to be prepared to move at a moment's notice. The three troops of cavalry were mounted, and Capt. Hunt's battery was harnessed up and took position on the Munhall Road, to be ready for any emergency.

The two companies started out, and Gen. Snowden, from the topmost window of headquarters, watched its progress through the town with field glasses. The Constables proceeded to the residences of the seven accused strikers, but at each succeeding house found the windows closed, the shades drawn, and the doors locked. Their expedition was a failure. No arrests were made. The troops returned to camp and the Constables to Pittsburg.

What connection the mysterious man who arrived here at noon yesterday had with the failure is purely a matter of conjecture. That the accused strikers were given an intimation of the plans of the day is only too apparent, and that Gen. Snowden will support with troops every legal demand made upon him by the civil authorities was again fully demonstrated.

When the strikers learned what had been done, a ripple of excitement ran through their ranks. They have been informed that the Carnegie Company had taken during the fight with the Pinkertons fifty or more photographs, and that the faces of a number were captured by the camera. Some of the photographs represent strikers in the act of firing muskets at the unfortunate Pinkertons; others show the men who dragged the brass cannon through the yard.

The disappearance of the leaders, coupled with the knowledge that the law is reaching out its powerful hand and that the military force of the State stands ready to enforce its mandates, can produce only demoralization among the strikers. . . .

———❖———

MCLUCKIE STILL IN JAIL.

————

REPUBLICAN POLITICIANS TAKE A HAND IN THE GAME.

PITTSBURG, July 19. —The ponderous iron door of the Allegheny County Jail yawned wide to-day, but none of the Homestead rioters passed within its gloomy portals. Back in the cavernous recesses of the prison lingered Burgess McLuckie, much against his will, denied the companionship and comfort which misery loves.

The Burgess made a virtue of necessity and surrendered himself in a burst of drunken bravado last night. He did not expect to be clapped into jail, or at most hoped for only one night behind the bars, but owing to the technicalities which hedge the law, he will not have a hearing until to-morrow. It will then be decided whether he can be admitted to bail.

McLuckie's case is to be made a test one, and both the Carnegie Company and the strikers are putting forward extraordinary efforts. Constable Joseph Weber went to Homestead to-day and subpoenaed forty persons, mostly mill hands and merchants, who are expected to testify to McLuckie's whereabouts and conduct on the morning of the riot.

Alderman McMasters's constables have been unable to find the six other rioters for whom warrants were issued. "I guess we won't find 'em to-day," quoth the Alderman this afternoon. "They are going to lay low till they see what becomes of McLuckie." The constables think likewise, and if the six men are captured before McLuckie's case is decided, it will be an agreeable surprise to Alderman McMasters and his three able-bodied constables.

W. J. Brennen, attorney for the Amalgamated Association, said to-night that no information would be lodged against the Carnegie officials before to-morrow, if then.

BURGESS M'LUCKIE AT LARGE.

————

DRIVEN IN TRIUMPH THROUGH THE STREETS OF HOMESTEAD.

PITTSBURG, PENN., July 20. —Burgess John McLuckie of Homestead, no longer drunk and full of braggadocio, as when he surrendered on a charge of murder and rioting, but meek and sober, and looking as pious as a Baptist Elder, was brought from his cell in the Allegheny County Jail this morning and taken before Quarter Sessions, Judge Magee, in one of the lofty chambers of the new Court House.

Long before the doors of the court were opened at 9:30 A.M. a crowd of Home-steaders was collected around the building discussing the Burgess's prospects for getting bail. When the oaken doors of the courtroom were unlocked by the bailiffs they rushed inside and formed a compact body of deeply-interested spectators, standing ten deep in the rear of the chamber. When the constable brought McLuckie in his fellow-rioters trod on one another's toes in their anxiety to grasp his hand and offer him comfort, and they created a mild uproar, which was stopped in a moment by the sharp rapping of Judge Magee's gavel.

McLuckie walked to the prisoner's box with soft, catlike step, his head bent forward on his breast. He wore spectacles and his manner was profoundly subdued. Once in the box, he gazed gravely through his gold-rimmed spectacles at the Judge and the lawyers, and was the picture of solemnity. His semblance to a back county circuit rider was heightened by a new black Prince Albert coat, tightly buttoned across his breast.

At 9:45 o'clock Judge Porter stepped briskly to the bench, and Judge Magee told District Attorney Burleigh he was ready to proceed. Two lawyers were on hand for McLuckie and three for the Carnegie Steel Company, Limited.

"Your Honor," said Mr. Burleigh, "I have gone into the law of this case pretty thoroughly, and have looked up some of the evidence, and I am satisfied that this is a bailable offense and that the prisoner cannot be convicted of a higher crime than murder in the second degree. I am willing to accept bail, but I ask that it be fixed at a figure commensurate with the serious nature of the riot."

Burgess McLuckie smiled sedately at the crowd of grinning Homesteaders in the rear of the court and readjusted his glasses.

"I am led to coincide with the District Attorney, and I am glad that the lawyers on both sides have agreed," said Judge Magee. "I have myself gone carefully over the law, and I am satisfied that some of those who participated in that riot at Homestead are guilty of murder, unless they have a good defense. The law makes every man guilty of rioting who stands

(continued from facing page)
Secretary Lovejoy of the Carnegie Steel Company (Limited) swore out four more warrants to-day against leaders of the riot, and a different gang of constables is hunting for the men.

McLuckie spent a lonely day in jail. His friends sent him tidbits for breakfast, dinner, and supper, and his lawyer called and gave him comfort. None of his friends were allowed to see him. The Burgess case was the first to be disposed of this morning in Judge Magee's part of the Criminal Court. There were few persons on hand as spectators. McLuckie was represented by W.J. Brennen, attorney for the Amalgamated Association. District Attorney Burleigh was present for the Commonwealth, and John S. Robb appeared for the Carnegie Steel company, (Limited.) McLuckie was not brought forth. Lawyer Brennen presented a petition from McLuckie asking for a hearing, denying his guilt, declaring that the prosecution was not made in good faith, and praying for admission to bail.

By consent of counsel McLuckie waived a hearing before Alderman McMasters, and his hearing before Judge Magee was set down for to-morrow morning at 9:30 o'clock. If he does not succeed in getting bail he will stay in jail until court meets in September.

There will be another scale conference to-morrow between the committee of the Iron and Steel Manufacturers and the committee of the Amalgamated Association. Yesterday's conference ended unsatisfactorily, as did the dozen that preceded it , and the feeling is spreading among the manufacturers in favor of a general lock-out of Amalgamated men. The plan and reasons for the lock-out have been outlined in *The Times* by one of the largest manufacturers in Pittsburg.

. . .

Secretary Lovejoy was asked if he had received protesting telegrams from Republican leaders urging a speedy and satisfactory settlement of the Homestead trouble. He declined to answer, and when pressed for a declaration, said:

"I refuse either to affirm or deny. Business first and politics next. We have tried to keep politics out of this mess. After it has settled, then let politics come in. . . .

"Everything depends on the outcome of the fight at Homestead. We do not look for any trouble resuming work at Homestead. There is a considerable force of men already in the mills, and we are tolerably well assured that there will be a break in the Amalgamated ranks inside of a week. There is no doubt of the existence of a large conservative element among the locked-out men, and it is a question of but a short time when some of them will apply for their former good positions. When one moves, others will follow like sheep. I know that the men of the mechanical department are anxious to return."

———❖———

(continued from facing page)
idly by without any effort to suppress the disorder. If the mob designs and commits murder, each man in it is guilty of murder.

"Such a man is responsible for all the consequences of the disorder and rioting, either whether such rioting results in the loss of property or the loss of life. No matter what the result, every such man is equally guilty for such degree of crime as the facts and results warrant. This may be murder in the first or second degree. I feel that in the case of Mr. McLuckie his crime, if any, does not reach that of murder in the first degree, and am therefore glad there was no objection made to his release on bail.

"As I have said, every man in the vicinity of a riotous gathering must do all in his power to suppress the riot, and he is responsible for every act of every man in such an assemblage, and he must show that he is not guilty or that he did all he could to suppress the riot. I will fix bail at $10,000. I may modify the amount if it is shown that the prisoner cannot furnish

that amount of security. I do not want to make the bail prohibitive, but I intend to make it plain that I have no sympathy with riots."

These words created a stir among the Homesteaders. Lawyer John F. Cox asked the court to make the same disposition of the cases of the six fugitive rioters for whom warrants were issued at the same time the warrant was issued against McLuckie. District Attorney Burleigh objected to wholesale bail before the surrender. J. Brennen announced that it was uncertain when the informations would be lodged. Lawyer Brennen further announced that O'Donnell, Burkett, Critchlow, and Ross would come to Pittsburg to-morrow and surrender themselves. O'Donnell was reported to have been in the city to-day, but he could not be found.

Flaherty and Flannagan, two of those for whom warrants were issued Monday, are said to have fled the State owing to the character of the evidence against them.

———

HUGH O'DONNELL RETURNS.

THREATS OF A GENERAL STRIKE THROUGHOUT THE COUNTRY.

Homestead, Penn., July 20. —Hugh O'Donnell returned to Homestead at midnight. With him was Master Workman Dempsey of the Knights of Labor organization, District No. 3, of Pittsburg.

O'Donnell says he has been in New-York and that his mission was successful. He says he will go to Pittsburg in the morning and give himself up to the authorities on the charge brought against him by Secretary Lovejoy.

It is the impression here that his mission was solely political. The strikers who saw him predict that, unless the Carnegie Company come to their terms, a great strike will be started which will embrace all the Knights of Labor organizations in the country.

———❖———

The strikebreakers who came during the occupation were housed in Potterville (named after Superintendent Potter), the compound constructed by the company on its property.

THE WEEK AT HOMESTEAD.

...

A LAST INVITATION

On Saturday the Carnegie company posted this notice:

"Individual applications for employment at the Homestead Steel works will be received by the General Superintendent, either in person or by letter, until 6 P.M., Thursday, July 21, 1892. It is our desire to retain in our service all of our old employes whose past record is satisfactory, and who did not take part in the attempts which have been made to interfere with our right to manage our business. Such of our old employes as do not apply by the time above named will be considered as having no desire to re-enter our employment, and the positions which they have held will be given to other men, and those first applying will have the choice of unfilled positions for which they are suitable."

THE CARNEGIE STEEL CO., (Limited.)
H.C. FRICK, Chairman.

Like notifications were sent through the mail to all but 40 of the Homestead strikers, but none of them have responded thus far. The company took a quantity of bedding and large numbers of cots into the inclosure of the works on Saturday, and it became noised about Homestead that non-union men were being introduced. Very few such have been secured, however, if any. There were fires in the cupolas on Saturday and a few furnaces were fired to save them from dampness, but beyond this there was no work done. The company gave out that it would have men at all its mills to make a start, on Monday, July 18, but none appeared. The report was current at Homestead, Monday, that a party of non-union men, engaged in Cleveland, were on the way. It is known that agents of the Carnegie Co. are hiring men in various cities. There are rumors that foreign steel workers are to be brought over, but this would be prevented by the application of the anti-contract labor law.

ARREST OF STRIKERS.

Action that had been threatened for several days, was taken on Monday, July 18, when Secretary Lovejoy, of the Carnegie Co. filed informations for murder against Hugh O'Donnell, the strikers' leader; John McLuckie, Burgess of Homestead; Sylvester Critchlow, Anthony Flaherty, Samuel Burkett, James Flannagan and Hugh Ross. They are charged with the murder of J. T. Connors and Silas Wain, on the 6th day of July. Constables, accompanied by military, hunted Homestead through on Monday afternoon, but found none of the accused men. Burgess McLuckie went to Pittsburgh and was lodged in Jail. The others were arrested on Tuesday, with the exception of O'Donnell, who left for the East on Sunday night on a secret errand. The strikers' advisory committee met Monday night, and decided to make information for murder against Frick, Carnegie, Lovejoy, Potter and the two Pinkertons. The company got out 15 more informations against strikers on Tuesday and says that yet more arrests will follow.

Secretary Lovejoy said on Tuesday that arrests of strikers would be made daily for several weeks. Up to Wednesday morning, the strikers had made no retaliatory move, pending further advice from their counsel. It is said that Gen. Benj. F. Butler and ex-Governor Hoadly have been engaged by the workmen, and that O'Donnell's trip to the East was for the purpose of conferring with Gen. Butler.

A tour of the Homestead plant made by an Associated Press representative on Tuesday showed that about 150 men are at work. Four furnaces in the armor plate department were charged on Tuesday and the melting department has been fired up. The open-hearth departments, Nos. 1 and 2, the mechanical department and the armor plate department were being worked in a desultory way. Secretary Lovejoy said, Tuesday, that men were being introduced into the enclosure each day and that the company had more men ready to work by Thursday than was generally supposed. The mechanics, who had been relied upon to make repairs in the works, have given notice that they will remain neutral in the struggle, and that for the present they will not return to work. The start will therefore have to be made without repairs.

———❖———

A WORKING-CLASS IMAGE OF THE BATTLE
by Rina Youngner

*B*oth in title and imagery the "Great Battle of Homestead" proclaims partisanship. Unlike other representations of the Homestead Strike, this broadside originated among factory workers: it expresses the spirit with which they entered the strike and celebrates one moment of success.

The artist, Edwin Rowe, lived at the corner of Tenth Street and West in Homestead. He was a 57-year-old English carpet weaver who had come to America 22 years earlier. Two of his sons worked in the mill: Edwin Jr., almost 30 years old and married with children, was a self-employed carpenter who also appears in the 1892 rolls of the Homestead Works as a laborer at Open Hearth #2. Twenty-year-old Charles was still a bachelor in 1892. He remained in the mill as a machinist; in 1900 he was a plate driller.

Six years after the strike, in 1898, Edwin Rowe combined carpet weaving with picture selling. The town directory of that year lists him as having a "Picture Store." In later years, the directories call his establishment a carpet-weaving shop and picture store. Perhaps the "Great Battle of Homestead" represents Rowe's first success in making money from pictures. In any case, his design was copyrighted in Washington, D.C., on October 11, 1892. It was lithographed by Kurz and Allison Art Studio in Chicago. Copies of this broadside decorated the walls of Homestead homes and bars for many years. The one reproduced here hung in the Homestead union hall.

In a direct and naive style, this black and white broadside—22 by 28 inches—reflects the assumptions of the workers. The large central vignette is a view of the Homestead Steel Works from the Pittsburgh side of the Monongahela River. Dominating the composition, the railroad bridge of the Pittsburgh, McKeesport and Youghiogheny line, called the Pemickey Bridge by the workers, emphasizes how the plant fronted the river as if it were a moat. The tug "Little Bill" floats in the river; the General Office Building of the factory, John Munhall's home, the School House which became General Snowden's headquarters, as well as the plant's layout are clearly indicated. The town itself is beyond the right margin of the composition. Clearly, the "Homestead" of the title refers to the plant, not the town. While we may note the irony of calling a factory "homestead," the broadside embodies the assumption that the workers defended the mill as if it were a homestead to which their labor gave them claim. Indeed, a declaration of the Workers' Advisory Committee stated that the general public and the employees of the Homestead Steel Works shared with its owners "equitable rights and interests in the . . . mill."

The two vignettes in the top corners of the broadside, "Workmen Cannonading the Barges" and "Workmen Attacking the Barges"—in spite of the specific details of the cannon in one and a barge labeled "Tennessee River Navigation Co." in the other—recall popular images of Americans defending their homesteads against the claims of others. The men in the vignettes are calm, kneeling in a line to fire their rifles; some wear ammunition pouches that look like army issue. Perhaps Rowe looked at Civil War images for inspiration. In any case, these images of discipline do not correspond to the descriptions of the impetuous, improvised way the workers fought the Pinkertons. In fact, these vignettes do not document the actual event; instead, they serve the idea that the workers steadfastly defended the plant from the Pinkerton invaders. The pictorial formulas Rowe chose convey a specific message.

The two bottom vignettes, "Surrender of the Pinkerton Men," and "Pinkerton's [sic] Captives on their way to Prison," celebrate the defeat and capture of the Pinkertons. The latter vignette represents "The Gauntlet," the incident in which the townspeople and workers threatened, beat, and wounded the defeated, hatless Pinkertons. Again pictorial conventions convey an interpretation of the event. Three women—one with the crowd, two above it on a hillock—dominate the composition; two other women are lost in the crowd. Curiously, the three conspicuous women wear dresses and hats and carry parasols; their silhouettes are fashionable and properly middle class. Instead of the bareheaded women wearing aprons and blouses who appear in the news pictures of Harper's Weekly and Frank Leslie's Illustrated Weekly, these women are groomed and carefully dressed. For an 1892 audience, their presence mitigated the brutality of the Gauntlet and their anger justified it, since the figure of the middle-class lady was the universally accepted symbol of moral rectitude. Whereas an image of belligerent uncorseted women could be easily read as an image of license and riot, these lady-like figures introduced propriety and principle into the scene.

Only the top central vignette

WORKMEN CANNONADING THE BARGES.

SOLDIERS IN CAMP.

WORKMEN ATTACKING THE BARGES.

GREAT BATTLE OF HOMESTEAD.
Defeat and Capture of the
PINKERTON INVADERS
July 6th 1892.

PROP. E.D. WALTERS.

SURRENDER OF THE PINKERTON MEN.

PINKERTON'S CAPTIVES ON THEIR WAY TO PRISON.

A copy of Rowe's broadside, reproduced here, hung in the hall of the United Steelworkers Local 1397, Homestead.

does not illustrate the broadside's title. It is the only image not concerned with the workers and their fight with the Pinkertons. Instead, "Soldiers in Camp" shows one of the State Militia encampments. When the militia entered town on July 12, the workers welcomed the soldiers as allies. The militia's mission, however, was to protect company property and its presence ensured the defeat of the strikers. How can one explain this image in a broadside celebrating the workers' victory? Perhaps Rowe finished designing this poster just when the troops entered Homestead. Perhaps he still believed that the militia would uphold the workers' cause when he asked Munn and Co., a

New York agency, to begin the paper work involved in getting a copyright. If this guess is correct, Rowe dispatched his drawing very soon after July 12. On the other hand, perhaps the drawing was done later. Then the image of the militia foreshadows the defeat of the union. By September or October, Rowe may have felt that the workers had won the battle against the Pinkertons but had lost the war against management. Soon after Rowe received his copyright, the Amalgamated Association of Iron and Steel Workers called off the strike on November 21.

By using conventional battle images which recalled the nation's wars, Rowe gave visual embodi-

ment to the assumption that the workers, not Frick and Carnegie, represented the American ethos. The well-dressed ladies also communicated the rightness of the workers' action. The inclusion of the militia camp, however, contradicts the title of the broadside; whatever Rowe's intentions, that vignette indicates the failure of the strike. The rhetoric of the strikers of 1892 referred to the Constitution, to citizenship, to rights, to American national values. This broadside expresses the belief that the strikers acted in the American tradition. However, in the years after 1892, it became an ironic reminder of dashed hopes. ❖

DATELINE HOMESTEAD
by Russell W. Gibbons

*F*or fully half of 1892, Homestead, Pennsylvania, was transformed from an obscure steel town to the focus of worldwide attention. Anticipating the coming clash between capital and labor, newspapermen, artists, and telegraphers converged on Pittsburgh and its satellite steel town during June; the last of them would depart with the collapse of the strike in November.

On arrival, correspondents rushed to take positions in the town and make contact with the Advisory Committee of the Amalgamated Association, which had set up headquarters in the new Bost Building on Eighth Avenue, not far from the mill's main entrance. The Advisory Committee was on the third floor and soon a pool of journalists and telegraphers had transformed the first floor into headquarters for the press.

Even before the June 29 lockout by the Carnegie Steel Company, at least 50 journalists and sketch artists had gathered in Homestead. B.L.H. Dabbs, a well-known Pittsburgh photographer who would take many pictures of events at Homestead in subsequent months, assembled most of them sometime in June for the group photo below.

The press contingent in Homestead prior to the arrival of the state militia was a sampling of the major newspapers of the day including: the Times, the Herald, the Tribune, and the World from New York; the Post-Dispatch from St. Louis; the Inquirer from Philadelphia; the Sun from Baltimore; and the Tribune from Chicago. The nation's opinion press—Harper's Weekly, Frank Leslie's Illustrated Weekly, and the North American Review— assigned special correspondents.

To this army was added "a large staff of Associated and United Press reporters, which furnished regular accounts to every newspaper of any consequence in the country." Also on hand were overseas correspondents from the London Times.

For Pittsburgh's newspapers, it was a field day for journalistic competition. Four morning papers—the Commercial Gazette, the Times, the Dispatch, and the Post each had a stable of correspondents and artists in Homestead. All were Republican except the Post, the city's only English-language Democratic paper. Four German language dailies and a morning paper in Allegheny (the North Side, a separate city until 1907) also were in the field. Present as well were the evening Press, the Chronicle-Telegraph, the Leader, and many other weeklies and semi-weeklies.

The Pittsburg Press, ahead of the local pack, published three editions and seven "extras" the day of the battle, with messengers on horseback reportedly backing up the clogged telegraph wires to the downtown typesetters. The Post had an exclusive interview with Frick on July 7, in which he declared "that under no circumstances will I have any further dealings with the Amalgamated. This is final."

The Leader editorialized that Carnegie's previous writings about the rights of the workingman were "extinct as a dodo." And the Chicago Globe decried the Pinkertons as no better than hired assassins who were "not entitled to the privileges of civilized warfare."

The Local News of Homestead, which seems to have appeared three times a week including Saturday,

Reporters from many places posed for this picture in June 1892. Until the late 1980s, this photo hung in the now disbanded Pittsburgh Press Club.

provided some of the most detailed reporting. Its arrangement to share news with the New York World *helps explain the density of that paper's coverage of events at Homestead. Commenting on the activities of the out-of-town journalists, the* Local News *of July 23 noted that "they were eye witnesses of the first and second battles. They were present all day during the siege, saw the capitulation, the burning of the barges and interviewed the Pinkertons in the Opera Hall." The* World *reporter alone had sent out "4,300 words of copy by telegraph" after the July 6 battle.*

The term "rioters" was used interchangeably with "strikers" by The New-York Times *and other publications that tended to favor property owners. The* Times *ran a lengthy article about alleged "intimidation" of the "penny Pittsburg Press," whose correspondents, it said, were being bullied by the Advisory Committee if their dispatches "did not conform" to the Committee's version of events.*

After the confrontation, when the number of correspondents swelled to more than a 100, the strikers' Advisory Committee began to court the media with a sophisticated press relations program. Hugh O'Donnell, the Committee's chairman, issued large white badges to the press, taking note "of the badge number, name of reporter, and the paper represented."

Reported the Local News, *"during the lockout, 110 press badges have been given out and there were probably 25 or more that came in after the arrival of the militia and did not obtain badges." The correct inference is that after July 12, the 8,000 militia men replaced the Advisory Committee as the significant force in town.*

Following the military occupation, the press dug in to see if the "new men" brought in by Carnegie and Frick would restart the mill,

This drawing appeared in Harper's Weekly, July 23, 1892. **The flag marks the headquarters of the Amalgamated Association. The pole and wires leading to the first floor office were installed for the telegraph office from which the reporters sent their dispatches.**

and journalistic enterprise took over. The Pittsburgh Post *reported on July 20 that "a* Post *reporter today succeeded in obtaining entrance to the works and spent an hour looking about the millyards," having secured a "pass from General Snowden and transportation obtained on the Little Bill."*

Within days the press rushed to the telegraph office to spread the news of Alexander Berkman's attempt on Frick's life, and devoted columns of print to him and suspected associates. In subsequent months, legal proceedings against the strikers, the restarting of the mill, and increased hardship for the strikers and their families were reported, as was the continuing national debate on the moral issues of the confrontation of July 6 and the assassination attempt. With the national election looming, the tariff issue became more prominent.

On November 30, the Local News *complained, "For six long months the big dailies have had a continual pull on Homestead and worked the ground until now it is a barren field, and yet they won't*

quit." But by then the strike was over, and the Homestead plant was in full operation with its complement of "new" workers. Many of the strikers, blacklisted in the industry, would never work at their trade again. The power of the Amalgamated had been broken.

In the end, nobody emerged unscathed. The names of H.C. Frick and the Pinkertons would be forever linked with the violence of July 6, and Carnegie's attempt to distance himself failed. After the collapse of the strike, the St. Louis Post-Dispatch *commented, "Say what you will of Frick, he is a brave man. Say what you will of Carnegie, he is a coward. And gods and men hate cowards." The steelmaster also took his lumps from the foreign press. The* London Times *declared, "Here we have this Scotch-Yankee plutocrat meandering through Scotland in a four-in-hand opening public libraries, while the wretched workmen who supply him with ways and means for his self-glorification are starving in Pittsburgh."* ❖

PHOTOGRAPHERS AT HOMESTEAD IN 1892
by Randolph Harris

*O*f the many people making photographs in and around Homestead during the summer of 1892, two photographers—one well known in the Pittsburgh area—provided vivid, on-the-spot documentation of significant incidents during the lockout, strike, battle, and military occupation taking place between July and November 1892.

Benjamin L. H. Dabbs of Pittsburgh and Captain Fred E. Windsor of Warren, Pennsylvania, captured scenes of the momentous events from different perspectives. Their work, however, was decidedly supportive of the Carnegie interests and the goals of the occupying forces of the Pennsylvania militia.

B. L. H. Dabbs, born in London in 1839, established an "art photography" studio at various locations in Pittsburgh in the latter decades of the 19th century. Newspaper writer Arthur Burgoyne's 1892 book Pittsburghers of All Sorts features both a short biography and caricature of Dabbs. He was known as the photographer of choice of Pittsburgh's social elite, but on July 6, 1892, he (and probably many of his assistants) devoted their energies to covering the dramatic scenes of the battle at Homestead.

Dabbs's photos were sold to publications ranging from Harper's Weekly to Scientific American. Since the mass-production printing techniques of the period did not permit quick use of photographs in time to meet deadlines, artists employed by the various publications set to work, producing sketches based on the photographs.

A particularly compelling Dabbs photograph of the Pinkerton surrender, transformed into a draw-

ing that hit home across America, was the July 16, 1892, cover of Harper's Weekly, (see page 90) the first issue of the magazine containing accounts of the battle. This is probably the most widely recognized image of the battle, since Harper's was a popular magazine with national readership.

Dabbs and his crew were also stationed across the Monongahela River in Swissvale, capturing another famous scene that graced the pages of Harper's Weekly and other publications: the conflagration of the Pinkerton barges with the expanse of the mill shown in the background. (See pages 96 and 97.)

So well known was Dabbs's work and so extensive were the number of images made by him and his crew on July 6, that some of the photos may have been bought by the Carnegie Steel Co. and later used as evidence in the Commonwealth's

case against Sylvester Critchlow, the first steelworker to be tried for murder in the deaths of one of the Pinkerton guards.

According to Burgoyne's Homestead, published in 1893, the Commonwealth closed its case by entering into the record "photographs of burning barges, the barricades and the mill yard taken by order of the Carnegie Steel Co." Originals of these exhibits have not been found to date. Around 1894, Carnegie Steel gave Dabbs the major photographic assignment of documenting the steel production facilities at Homestead in large format, sepia-toned prints. A looseleaf folio of 27 prints at the Carnegie Library of Homestead highlights the major technological advances in use at the Homestead Works in armor plate forging, heat treating, and in the expansive system of electric overhead cranes employed to move the massive forgings.

Unlike Dabbs, Captain Windsor (1859-1936) was neither a well-known nor a published photographer. He was simply a prominent military man—and later oil producer—from the Warren area who took his semi-professional box camera along on all of his campaigns. During the occupation of Homestead, he was the commanding officer of Company "I" of the 16th Infantry Regiment of the National Guard of Pennsylvania, based in Warren.

The Warren County Historical Society holds his collection of hundreds of mostly small (3 $\frac{1}{2}$ x 2 $\frac{1}{2}$ -inch black and white prints) meticulously labeled—and at times oddly cropped—photos of his military service at Homestead, in Puerto

Rico, and in the Philippines.

Windsor and many of his contemporaries in the state militia have been described as "soldier boys," the name generally given to a generation of young men enamored with veterans' tales of the "glory" of Civil War battle, but too young to have joined the Union cause in the early 1860s.

Captain Windsor's Company I was made up of about 60 militiamen who arrived by train at Munhall Station, just east of the Borough of Homestead, on the morning of July 12, 1892. Windsor and his men were first stationed at Camp Sam Black, the strategic hillside overlooking the steel works in Munhall, where Carnegie would build his public library in 1898. Within a few weeks, Company I's troops were moved and positioned at Camp Cowell, a bluff overlooking the Homestead Works across the Monongahela river within the City of Pittsburgh limits. From this position, the troops could sound the alert and fire upon any river craft that might attempt to retake the works.

Like the rest of the soldiers, Windsor and his boys had little to do all summer except drill, drink, and try to capture the interest of the young women. Windsor's photos show feats of acrobatics by the guardsmen, military bands playing, and groups of men generally passing time in their tents in the sweltering heat or avoiding some of the many downpours which hit the town in the early days of the occupation.

Windsor and his men were among the last troops to leave the area as it became more and more apparent that no attempt was likely to be made to engage the militia. In late October, Company I broke camp and its members left for home, back to their farms and businesses

While Dabbs and Windsor are known, many of the other photographers whose work is represented in this book remain anonymous. One such unknown photographer captured scenes of the militia in the Swissvale area, beginning with troops getting off trains at Swissvale Station. Other views show cavalry and infantry soldiers drilling and setting up camp. These photographs came into the possession of the Swissvale Historical Society through Melvin Wach, a long-time Swissvale resident. A Swissvale Borough councilman gave the pho-

tographs to Mr. Wach more than 50 years ago.

Still other views are available today from many of the professional photographers assigned to Homestead by producers of stereographs. Companies such as Keystone Stereograph, Atlas, "Perfec" Stereographs, and Underwood & Underwood produced the double image photography that gave home users three dimensional views from around the world. The curved cards—upon which two identical photographs are mounted—were placed in a holder / viewer and held in front of a light source. Such high quality stereographic images of Homestead in 1892 are available at the Library of Congress and other archives, but it is important to know that the photographers who took them arrived on the scene days after the battle. None of these stereographs embodies the historic immediacy of the work of Dabbs, Windsor, and unknown local shutterbugs whose prints may still exist in Homestead attics. ❖

National Guard troops drill in front of the union headquarters in the Bost Building, the three-story structure at right. This stereograph from Underwood & Underwood drew on the drama of thousands of heavily armed soldiers occupying an American town.

Alexander Berkman in 1892, at age 21. Jailed immediately after the July 23 assassination attempt on Frick, Berkman was found guilty of attempted manslaughter and served 14 years in Pennsylvania's Western Penitentiary (a few miles down the Ohio River from Pittsburgh).

Emma Goldman in the 1890s. Then in her mid-20s, she was already a major figure in the international anarchist movement. Though New York's Lower East Side remained her home base, Goldman established in the '90s her lifelong commitment to arguing her views through extended lecture tours.

E V E N T S

First week of JULY 1892—In Worcester, Massachusetts, where they had opened a small lunchroom Alexander Berkman and Emma Goldman follow events at Homestead in the newspapers. Lovers and political comrades—anarchists—both of them had emigrated recently from Russia, she in 1885, he in 1888. In July 1892, Berkman is 21, Goldman 23.

Second week of JULY 1892—Back in New York—they have sold their business in order to take action in the Homestead affair—Berkman has decided that Frick must be assassinated in an act of terrorist propaganda on behalf of working people. Failing in attempts to make a dynamite bomb, Berkman leaves for Pittsburgh, determined to buy a pistol there when he and Goldman have enough money.

2 pm, Saturday, JULY 23, 1892—Berkman attacks Frick in his downtown Pittsburgh office and is immediately apprehended and jailed. Frick finishes his day's work and tells the press: "The company will pursue the same policy and it will win."

H.C. Frick

JULY 23, 1892—At the militia's bivouac in Homestead, guardsman W.L. Iams is arrested, hung by the thumbs, and drummed out of the corps for shouting, "Three cheers for the man who shot Frick."

ASSASSINATION ATTEMPT

"Jack, it was for you, for your people . . ." —A. Berkman

7

Excerpted from Living My Life, *Vol. 1, Chapter VIII, by Emma Goldman, originally published by Alfred Knopf, New York, 1931.*

SASHA LEAVES FOR PITTSBURGH

One afternoon a customer came in for an ice-cream, while I was alone in the store. As I set the dish down before him, I caught the large headlines of his paper: "LATEST DEVELOPMENTS IN HOMESTEAD—FAMILIES OF STRIKERS EVICTED FROM THE COMPANY HOUSES—WOMAN IN CONFINEMENT CARRIED OUT INTO STREET BY SHERIFFS." I read over the man's shoulder Frick's dictum to the workers: he would rather see them dead than concede to their demands, and he threatened to import Pinkerton detectives. The brutal bluntness of the account, the inhumanity of Frick towards the evicted mother, inflamed my mind. Indignation swept my whole being. I heard the man at the table ask: "Are you sick, young lady? Can I do anything for you?" "Yes, you can let me have your paper," I blurted out. "You won't have to pay me for the ice-cream. But I must ask you to leave. I must close the store." The man looked at me as if I had gone crazy.

I locked up the store and ran full speed the three blocks to our little flat. It was Homestead, not Russia; I knew it now. We belonged in Homestead. The boys, resting for the evening shift, sat up as I rushed into the room, newspaper clutched in my hand. "What has happened, Emma? You look terrrible!" I could not speak. I handed them the paper.

Sasha [Alexander Berkman] was the first on his feet. "Homestead!" he exclaimed. "I must go to Homestead!" I flung my arms around him, crying out his name. I, too, would go. "We must go tonight," he said; "the great moment has come at last!". . .

We left on an early morning train [to New York]. . . .

A few days after our return to New York the news was flashed across the country of the slaughter of steel-workers by Pinkertons. Frick had fortified the Homestead mills, built a high fence around them. Then, in the dead of night, a barge packed with strike-breakers, under protection of heavily armed Pinkerton thugs, quietly stole up the Monongahela River. The steel-men had learned of Frick's move.

They stationed themselves along the shore, determined to drive back Frick's hirelings. When the barge got within range, the Pinkertons had opened fire, without warning, killing a number of Homestead men on the shore, among them a little boy, and wounding scores of others.

The wanton murders aroused even the daily papers. Several came out in strong editorials, severely criticizing Frick. He had gone too far; he had added fuel to the fire in the labour ranks and would have himself to blame for any desperate acts that might come.

We were stunned. We saw at once that the time for our manifesto had passed. Words had lost their meaning in the face of the innocent blood spilled on the banks of the Monongahela. Intuitively each felt what was surging in the heart of the others. Sasha broke the silence. "Frick is the responsible factor in this crime," he said; "he must be made to stand the consequences." It was the psychological moment for an *Attentat* [an act of political assassination]; the whole country was aroused, everybody was considering Frick the perpetrator of a cold-blooded murder. A blow aimed at Frick would re-echo in the poorest hovel, would call the attention of the whole world to the real cause behind the Homestead struggle.

(Living My Life, continued)

It would also strike terror in the enemy's ranks and make them realize that the proletariat of America had its avengers.

Sasha had never made bombs before, but [anarchist Johann] Most's *Science of Revolutionary Warfare* was a good text-book. He would procure dynamite from a comrade he knew on Staten Island. He had waited for this sublime moment to serve the Cause, to give his life for the people. He would go to Pittsburgh.

"We will go with you!" Fedya and I cried together. But Sasha would not listen to it. He insisted that it was unnecessary and criminal to waste three lives on one man.

We sat down, Sasha between us, holding our hands. In a quiet and even tone he began to unfold to us his plan. He would perfect a time regulator for the bomb that would enable him to kill Frick, yet save himself. Not because he wanted to escape. No; he wanted to live long enough to justify his act in court, so that the American people might know that he was not a criminal, but an idealist. "I will kill Frick," Sasha said, "and of course I shall be condemned to death. I will die proudly in the assurance that I gave my life for the people. But I will die by my own hand, like Lingg [Chicago Haymarket Affair]. Never will I permit our enemies to kill me. . . ." Sasha . . . went to Staten Island to test the bomb. When he returned, I could tell by his expression . . . the bomb had not gone off.

• • •

Our whole fortune consisted of fifteen dollars. That would take Sasha to Pittsburgh, buy some necessaries, and still leave him a dollar for the first day's food and lodging. Our Allegheny comrades Nold and Bauer, whom Sasha meant to look up, would give him hospitality for a few days until I could raise more money. Sasha had decided not to confide his mission to them; there was no need for it, he felt, and it was never advisable for too many people to be taken into conspiratorial plans. He would require at least another twenty dollars for a gun and a suit of clothes. He might be able to buy the weapon cheap at some pawnshop. I had no idea where I could get the money, but I knew that I would find it somehow.

Those with whom we were staying were told that Sasha would leave that evening, but the motive for his departure was not revealed. There was a simple farewell supper, everyone joked and laughed, and I joined in the gaiety. I strove to be jolly to cheer Sasha, but it was laughter that masked suppressed sobs. Later we accompanied Sasha to the Baltimore and Ohio Station. Our friends kept in the distance, while Sasha and I paced the platform, our hearts too full for speech.

The conductor drawled out: "All aboard!" I clung to Sasha. He was on the train, while I stood on the lower step. His face bent low to mine, his hand holding me, he whispered: "My sailor girl" (his pet name for me), "comrade, you will be with me to the last. You will proclaim that I gave what was dearest to me for an ideal, for the great suffering people."

The train moved. Sasha loosened my hold, gently helping me to jump off the step. I ran after the vanishing train, waving and calling to him: "Sasha, Sashenka!" The steaming monster disappeared round the bend and I stood glued, straining after it, my arms outstretched for the precious life that was being snatched away from me. ❖

(right) This composite image, one of several depicting anarchists in Harper's Weekly, *August 20, 1892, shows Justus Schwab, a well known revolutionary and proprietor of a famous saloon on New York's Lower East Side; John Most, a leading anarchist and editor of* Die Freiheit; *and "the High Priestess of Anarchy," Emma Goldman. She broke violently with Most when he failed to support Berkman's action against Frick.*

Excerpted from Prison Memoirs of an Anarchist *by Alexander Berkman, originally published by Mother Earth Publishing Association, New York, 1912.*

From Chapter I, THE CALL OF HOMESTEAD

"Ticket, please!" A heavy hand is on my shoulder. . . . I have difficulty in keeping myself from falling back into reverie. I must form a definite plan of action. My purpose is quite clear to me. A tremendous struggle is taking place at Homestead: the People are manifesting the right spirit in resisting tyranny and invasion. My heart exults. This is, at last, what I have always hoped for from the American workingman: once aroused, he will brook no interference; he will fight all obstacles, and conquer even more than his original demands. It is the spirit of the heroic past reincarnated in the steelworkers of Homestead, Pennsylvania. What supreme joy to aid in this work! That is my natural mission. I feel the strength of a great undertaking. No shadow of doubt crosses my mind. The People—the toilers of the world, the producers—comprise, to me, the universe. They alone count. The rest are parasites, who have no right to exist. But to the People belongs the earth—by right, if not in fact. To make it so in fact, all means are justifiable; nay, advisable, even to the point of taking life. The question of moral right in such matters often agitated the revolutionary circles I used to frequent. I had always taken the extreme view. The more radical the treatment, I held, the quicker the cure. Society is a patient; sick constitutionally and functionally. Surgical treatment is often imperative. The removal of a tyrant is not merely justifiable; it is the highest duty of every true revolutionist. Human life is, indeed, sacred and inviolate. But the killing of a tyrant, of an enemy of the People, is in no way to be considered as the taking of a life. A revolutionist would rather perish a thousand times than be guilty of what is ordinarily called murder. In truth, murder and Attentat are to me opposite terms. To remove a tyrant is an act of liberation, the giving of life and opportunity to an oppressed people. True, the Cause often calls upon the revolutionist to commit an unpleasant act; but it is the test of a true revolutionist—nay, more, his pride—to sacrifice all merely human feeling at the call of the People's Cause. If the latter demand his life, so much the better.

. . .

"Pitt-s-burgh! Pitt-s-burgh!"

The harsh cry of the conductor startles me with the violence of a shock. Impatient as I am of the long journey, the realization that I have reached my destination comes unexpectedly, overwhelming me with the dread of unpreparedness. In a flurry I gather up my things, but, noticing that the other passengers keep their places, I precipitately resume my seat, fearful lest my agitation be noticed. To hide my confusion, I turn to the open window. Thick clouds of smoke overcast the sky, shrouding the morning with sombre gray. The air is heavy with soot and cinders; the smell is nauseating. In the distance, giant furnaces vomit pillars of fire, the lurid flashes accentuating a line of frame structures, dilapidated, and miserable. They are the homes of the workers who have created the industrial glory of Pittsburgh, reared its millionaires, its Carnegies and Fricks.

The sight fills me with hatred of the perverse social justice that turns the needs of mankind into an Inferno of brutalizing toil. It robs man of his soul, drives the sunshine from his life, degrades him lower than the beasts, and between the millstones of divine bliss and hellish torture grinds flesh and blood into iron and steel, transmutes human lives into gold, gold, countless gold.

From Chapter III, THE SPIRIT OF PITTSBURGH

The spirit of the Iron City characterizes the negotiations carried on between the Carnegie Company and the Homestead men. Henry Clay Frick, in absolute control of the firm, incarnates the spirit of the furnace, is the living emblem of his trade. The olive branch held out by the workers after their victory over the

Pinkertons has been refused. The ultimatum issued by Frick is the last word of Caesar: the union of the steelworkers is to be crushed, completely and absolutely, even at the cost of shedding the blood of the last man in Homestead; the Company will deal only with individual workers, who must accept the terms offered, without question or discussion; he, Frick, will operate the mills with non-union labor, even if it should require the combined military power of the State and the Union to carry the plan into execution. Millmen disobeying the order to return to work under the new schedule of reduced wages are to be discharged forthwith, and evicted from the Company houses.

. . .

From Chapter IV, THE ATTENTAT

The door of Frick's private office, to the left of the reception-room, swings open as the colored attendant emerges, and I catch a flitting glimpse of a black-bearded, well-knit figure at a table in the back of the room.

"Mistah Frick is engaged. He can't see you now, sah," the negro says, handing back my card.

I take the pasteboard, return it to my case, and walk slowly out of the reception-room. But quickly retracing my steps, I pass through the gate separating the clerks from the visitors, and, brushing the astounded attendant aside, I step into the office on the left, and find myself facing Frick.

For an instant the sunlight, streaming through the windows, dazzles me. I discern two men at the further end of the long table.

"Fr—," I begin. The look of terror on his face strikes me speechless. It is the dread of the conscious presence of death. "He understands," it flashes through my mind. With a quick motion I draw the revolver. As I raise the weapon, I see Frick clutch with both hands the arm of the chair, and attempt to rise. I aim at his head. "Perhaps he wears armor," I reflect. With a look of horror he quickly averts his face, as I pull the trigger. There is a flash, and the high-ceilinged room reverberates as with the booming of cannon. I hear a sharp, piercing cry, and see Frick on his knees, his head against the arm of the chair. I feel calm and possessed, intent upon every movement of the man. He is lying head and shoulders under the large armchair, without sound or motion. "Dead?" I wonder. I must make sure. About twenty-five feet separate us. I take a few steps toward him, when suddenly the other man, whose presence I had quite forgotten, leaps upon me. I struggle to loosen his hold. He looks slender and small. I would not hurt him: I have no business with him. Suddenly I hear the cry, "Murder! Help!" My heart stands still as I realize that it is Frick shouting. "Alive?" I wonder. I hurl the stranger aside and fire at the crawling figure of Frick. The man struck my hand,—I have missed! He grapples with me, and we wrestle across the room. I try to throw him, but spying an opening between his arm and body, I thrust the revolver against his side and aim at Frick, cowering behind the chair. I pull the trigger. There is a click—but no explosion! By the throat I catch the stranger, still clinging to me, when suddenly something heavy strikes me on the back of the head. Sharp pains shoot through my eyes. I sink to the floor, vaguely conscious of the weapon slipping from my hands.

"Where is the hammer? Hit him, carpenter!" Confused voices ring in my ears. Painfully I strive to rise. The weight of many bodies is pressing on me. Now— it's Frick's voice! Not dead ? . . . I crawl in the direction of the sound, dragging the struggling men with me. I must get the dagger from my pocket—I have it! Repeatedly I strike with it at the legs of the man near the window. I hear Frick cry out in pain—there is much shouting and stamping—my arms are pulled and twisted, and I am lifted bodily from the floor.

Police, clerks, workmen in overalls, surround me. An officer pulls my head back by the hair, and my eyes meet Frick's. He stands in front of me, supported by several men. His face is ashen gray; the black beard is streaked with red, and

In this image from Harper's Weekly, *August 6, 1892, Berkman aims at Frick's head. He apparently acted alone in Pittsburgh. Although two local anarchists were convicted as accomplices, they seem to have had no knowledge of his plan to assassinate Frick (see page 176).*

blood is oozing from his neck. For an instant a strange feeling, as of shame, comes over me; but the next moment I am filled with anger at the sentiment, so unworthy of a revolutionist. With defiant hatred I look him full in the face.

"Mr. Frick, do you identify this man as your assailant?"

Frick nods weakly.

The street is lined with a dense, excited crowd. A young man in civilian dress, who is accompanying the police, inquires, not unkindly:

"Are you hurt? You're bleeding."

I pass my hand over my face. I feel no pain, but there is a peculiar sensation about my eyes.

"I've lost my glasses," I remark, involuntarily.

"You'll be damn lucky if you don't lose your head," an officer retorts. ❖

JULY 24, 1892 —Reprinted from
The New-York Times.

BERKMANN AN ANARCHIST.

───────

TOO RADICAL IN HIS VIEWS TO GET
ALONG WITH HIS FELLOWS HERE.

Berkmann, or as the Pittsburg police call him, Bachman, the Russian Jew, who shot Mr. Frick, is an Anarchist, and several years ago worked at his trade in this city on the *Freiheit*, the organ of the Anarchists, edited by John Most. As such, he was a member of German Typographical Union No. 7, now known as International Typographical Union No. 427. Many of the members of this union are radical Socialists or out-and-out Anarchists, and Berkmann was one of the most rabid and uncompromising of the lot.

Berkmann believed in murdering capitalists who should refuse to give up their property. He was reported to have said that if a capitalistic employer should refuse to yield to the demands of his employes, and if he, Berkmann, had anything to say in the matter, he would go straight to the employer and shoot him down.

Berkmann's fanaticism, it was said, alarmed even his associates on the *Freiheit*, and even John Most himself. They feared he might get them all into trouble by some act of violence. They got him to resign his position, and he went to New-Haven, where he worked as a printer.

After leaving New-Haven Bachman went to Elizabeth, where he worked in the Singer sewing machine factory. While there he joined what is known as the Penkert group of Anarchists, who are distinguished from the [John] Most type of anarchists in that they believe in every individual member looking after himself and settling his own quarrels and letting every one else go to the dogs.

From Elizabeth, Bachman returned to New-York, but did not succeed in getting work, and again left. He has not been seen by his friends here since that time. The Anarchists in this city were disinclined to talk about him yesterday.

────❖────

This composite of "Apostles of Anarchy and Hops" in Frank Leslie's Illustrated Weekly, *August 11, 1892, accompanies a text that gives an anti-Semitic description of anarchism: "Here is the typical Jew, as generally understood, with his long nose and beard and his repulsive cast of face . . ."*

Excerpted from **The Inside History of the Carnegie Steel Company,** *Chapter 15, by James Howard Bridge, originally published by The Aldine Book Company, New York, 1903.*

ATTEMPTED ASSASSINATION OF MR. FRICK

Before the country had recovered from the thrill of horror which succeeded the Homestead battle, an attempt was made to murder Mr. Frick; and the bloody details of the assault were cabled to the ends of the earth, bringing fresh disgrace upon the unhappy town of Homestead. On Saturday, July 23d, a Russian anarchist shot and stabbed Mr. Frick while he was seated in conversation with his associate, Mr. Leishman. This man had made several previous visits to the Carnegie offices, where he represented himself as the agent of a New York employment bureau. Once he had a brief interview with Mr. Frick, who told him he thought there would be no need for the services of any agency, as the managers were making arrangements by which they hoped to get their old employees back.

On the day mentioned this man called again and sent in his card to Mr. Frick, who had just returned from lunch and had dropped into a chair at the end of the flat-topped desk at which he usually worked. It was not his usual seat; and he had moved into it to be nearer Mr. Leishman, who sat diagonally opposite. Mr. Frick had swung round in his chair so that his side was turned to the door through which the boy brought the card. Before the boy could regain the front office with Mr. Frick's message, the man stepped through the swinging door and glanced quickly around. Mr. Frick looked up in surprise at the sudden entry of a stranger, and saw the man make a quick movement towards his hip pocket. Realizing the meaning of the movement, Mr. Frick sprang to his feet. At the same moment the fellow had drawn and fired a revolver with lightning rapidity, and the bullet, after passing through the lobe of the left ear, struck Mr. Frick in the neck. The shock sent him to the floor; and as he lay on the carpet the assassin fired a second time, and again the bullet struck Mr. Frick in the neck.

While this was happening Mr. Leishman had jumped from his seat and was running round the long desk to get at the fellow. He reached him just as he fired a third time, and either seized or knocked up his hand, so that the shot went wild, the bullet striking the wall near the ceiling. Mr. Leishman courageously grappled with the fellow, and while he was wrestling with him for the revolver, Mr. Frick struggled to his feet and grasped his assailant from behind. In this way the three men swayed violently to and fro for a few thrilling moments, and then all three fell with a crash against the low wall just under the window overlooking Fifth Avenue, the Russian underneath. A crowd, attracted by the shots, stood on the opposite side of the street; and seeing Mr. Frick struggling near the window, thought he was trying to raise it to give an alarm, or to escape from some enemy invisible from the sidewalk. This occasioned one of the many erroneous reports sent out to the newspapers.

The fall had loosened Mr. Frick's grasp of the fellow's left arm; and while Mr. Leishman still held on to the right hand and the revolver, the Russian drew a dagger made from an old file and plunged it again and again into Mr. Frick, who, bending over him and weak from his exertions and wounds, was unable to avoid the blows. First the dagger was thrust into his hip, just behind the head of the femur; then it struck him in the right side and glanced along one of the ribs; and a third blow tore open the left leg just below the knee. Despite his terrible injuries Mr. Frick again threw himself on the ruffian, and finally pinioned his arm to the floor. Then the clerks, who had watched the struggle from the door as if spellbound, rushed in and secured the anarchist. The revolver and dagger were torn from his grasp and he was dragged to his feet. Covered with the blood that had flowed from Mr. Frick's wounds, he was a sorry looking object; and Mr. Leishman looked almost as bad. The latter, who had so bravely seized the smoking revolver a few moments before, and heard the trigger snap even a fourth time, now collapsed utterly, and had to be carried from the room. Mr. Frick, the only calm person present, leaned against the desk and watched the last ineffectual struggles of the wretch who had tried to kill him.

(The Inside Story, continued)

Thrown at last into a chair and held there, the Russian appeared to be mumbling something, and all but Mr. Frick were too excited to notice it. At this moment a deputy sheriff rushed in with a drawn revolver and made as if he would shoot the man. Mr. Frick interposed. "No, don't kill him," he said; "raise his head and let me see his face." As they did so it was seen that the man's apparent mumbling was caused by his chewing something; and on his mouth being forced open, a cap containing fulminite of mercury, such as anarchists had previously used to commit suicide, was found between the desperate fellow's teeth. Even when overcome by numbers, he still sought to carry out his devilish purpose by an explosion which would involve Mr. Frick and a dozen innocent men in his own destruction.

By this time the office was filled with an excited crowd. A German carpenter, who had been at work in the building, broke through the throng and aimed a blow at the Russian's head with his hammer. It missed him. Then arose cries of "Shoot him!" "Lynch him!" and amid all the excitement no one seemed to give a thought to Mr. Frick, who still stood leaning against the desk, with the blood streaming from his many wounds. A number of policemen who had been attracted by the noise quickly surrounded the assassin to protect him, and led him from the room. Then the others turned to Mr. Frick. A score of hands hastened to his support; and he was gently placed on a lounge in an inner room, while hurried calls were sent for physicians.

While the blood-sodden clothes were being removed, and before the physicians arrived, Mr. Frick talked calmly about the assault, and commented with a smile on the assassin's amazing muscular power; nor did his courage fail him when the surgeons began probing for the bullets. At first the doctors said there was little hope of recovery. The first bullet had entered the side of the neck, cutting the lobe of the ear, and had ranged backwards and downwards until it almost reached the shoulder. The second bullet had followed a similar course, but from right to left.

While the doctor was probing in the wounds Mr. Frick calmly directed him as to the place where the bullet would be found, and then as the instrument reached it, he remarked: "There! that feels like it, doctor." And while the probing, cutting, and sewing up of the wounds were going on, he dictated a cablegram to Mr. Carnegie, telling him that he was not mortally injured, and he signed several letters which he had previously dictated. He also completed the arrangements which he had begun earlier in the day for a loan; and signed all the necessary papers. The doctors said that it was the most magnificent exhibition of courage they had ever seen.

Most touching of all, and even more characteristic of the man, was his manner of greeting Mrs. Frick on his arrival home a few hours later in the ambulance. Mrs. Frick had been critically ill; and the excitement of the Homestead battle had rendered her condition precarious. Mr. Frick's first thought after the attack was of his wife; and he gave very emphatic orders that no alarming reports be permitted to reach her. Then he sent two of her relatives who had hastened to the office on hearing of the assault, to break the news to her gently, and to let her understand that his injuries were trifling. So well did they succeed that, as Mr. Frick was carried past her bedroom door, she was in no way alarmed. Telling

This illustration of an ambulance drawn up to take the wounded Frick home appeared in Frank Leslie's Illustrated Weekly, *August 4, 1892.*

the stretcher bearers to turn his head around so that he could speak to his wife, Mr. Frick addressed her by name, and called out a cheery inquiry after the youngest child. Then he assured her that he was not seriously hurt and would be in to see her before very long.

The fanatic who made this ferocious attempt on Mr. Frick's life had nothing to do with the strikers. He was of the usual type of European anarchist; and he had been only a few years in the country. He went from New York to Pittsburg specially to kill Mr. Frick. When asked why he selected Mr. Frick in particular, he exclaimed in astonishment: "Why, what would the company do without Mr. Frick? Carnegie is thousands of miles away, and he would not dare to oppose the men as Frick has done." So here again was an echo of Carnegie idealism. As for the undiscriminating criminal himself, he was sentenced to twenty-one years in the penitentiary for the assault, and one year in the workhouse for carrying concealed weapons.

The news of the attempted assassination created intense excitement at Homestead, where it was bulletined a few minutes after the occurrence. Crowds gathered at every street corner and in front of the telegraph stations and newspaper offices; and whenever a man received a message hundreds crowded around him to hear the latest news. The strikers heard of the attempt with mixed feelings. The more ignorant workmen rejoiced openly. "Frick's dead by this time and we've won the strike," shouted one. "Carnegie Company don't amount to shucks without Frick," commented another, as he joyfully predicted the early collapse of the firm's resistance. But at the headquarters of the labor-union the news was received with dismay. While the leaders believed the strikers blameless of this particular horror, there already had been so much to set the public against them that they feared the discredit of this fresh act of violence would fall on them. And their alarm was justified. From one end of the country to the other, and across the oceans from distant lands, swept a wave of fierce indignation against the strikers and denunciation of their methods. Innocent of this particular crime, the strikers had to bear the disgrace of it.

On Mr. Frick himself the incident seemed to have no effect except for the pain and inconvenience it occasioned. His sorely wounded body suffered; but while nurses and attendants were prostrate under the intense heat of July, the patient made no complaint. From the first day he insisted on being kept informed of the progress of events. Newspapers, letters, and telegrams were read to him; and he dictated answers to many of the latter. His grasp on the strike situation was never relaxed for a moment. No move was made by the men that was not instantly telephoned to him; and nothing was done by the managers that did not emanate from him, or that was not previously submitted for his approval. Except that the contest was now conducted from Mr. Frick's Homewood residence instead of from his Fifth Avenue office, no difference was to be seen in the situation. . . . ❖

Frick's office on Fifth Avenue in downtown Pittsburgh, as illustrated in Harper's Weekly, *August 6, 1892.*

Reprinted from **Henry Clay Frick:
The Man,** *Chapter X, by George
Harvey, originally published by
Charles Scribner's Sons,
New York, 1928.*

ATTEMPTED ASSASSINATION

While the wounds inflicted by the nihilist's jagged dagger were being staunched Mr. Frick arranged for notification of his sick wife in such a way as to cause a minimum of anxiety and dictated the following telegram to his aged mother, who had been prostrated since the outbreak of violence:

Was shot twice but not dangerously.   H. C. FRICK.

A similar message was cabled to Mr. Carnegie with these words added:

There is no necessity for you to come home. I am still in shape to fight the battle out.

Meanwhile the physicians, preparatory to probing, were providing an anaesthetic, which Mr. Frick resolutely refused to have administered, saying that it was quite unnecessary and was inadvisable because he might help in locating the bullets. This surmise proved correct from the moment the surgeon inserted the instrument and pushed it forward gently and tentatively in pursuance of the patient's directions until in each of the two searches he heard "There, that feels like it, Doctor," and extracted both balls with unerring precision.

Mr. Frick, propped up in a chair at his desk after a brief rest, then proceeded to finish his day's work, specifying the final terms of an essential loan which he had been negotiating, signing several official documents and many letters which he had dictated in the forenoon and finally, just before submitting to be carried to an ambulance, he made the following statement to be given to the press:

This incident will not change the attitude of the Carnegie Steel Company toward the Amalgamated Association. I do not think I shall die but whether I do or not the Company will pursue the same policy and it will win.

. . .

Although not permitted to leave his bed that evening or for several days following, Mr. Frick summoned his secretary as soon as the doctors had left the next morning and dictated and signed this notice to the new employes, then numbering about five hundred:

CARNEGIE STEEL COMPANY, (LIMITED):

NOTICE:—*To all men who entered our employ after, July 1st, 1892.*

In no case and under no circumstances will a single one of you be discharged to make room for another man. You will keep your respective positions so long as you attend to your duties. Positive orders to this effect have been given to the general superintendent.

By order of the board of managers,

The Carnegie Steel Company, (Limited)

H.C. Frick, Chairman.

Homestead Steel Works, July 24th, 1892.

During the succeeding ten days, propped up in bed and swathed with bandages, with a telephone installed within reach and secretaries in constant attendance in defiance of the doctors' orders, ignoring pain and scoffing at the sweltering heat, Mr. Frick not only kept fully informed but personally dictated every move in the continuing contest and attended to all other details of the Company's business with customary thoroughness.

On Wednesday, August 3rd, he was summoned to behold the passing of the spirit of his little son and namesake, born less than four weeks previously, on the day of the battle at Homestead, and on Thursday afternoon his eyes rested upon the tiny coffin during a brief funeral service. The long evening, passed at the bedside of the stricken mother, finally wore away and he slept for a few hours.

*Frick's home, "Clayton," on Penn
Avenue in Pittsburgh's East End
as depicted in* Frank Leslie's Illustrated Weekly, *August 4, 1892.*

Rising and breakfasting promptly on the following morning, thirteen days after he had been attacked, he walked alone across the lawn, stepped upon an open street-car, entered his office on the stroke of eight and rang for the morning's mail. . . .

There was no bodyguard. Mr. Frick does not like bodyguards . . . . "If an honest American," he remarked to the *Times* reporter, "cannot live in his own home without being surrounded by a bodyguard, it is time to quit." ❖

JULY 28, 1892 —Reprinted from the **Pittsburgh Catholic.**

A WARNING.

The attempted assassination of H.C. Frick has evoked a storm of condemnation against the Anarchist and his methods. As is usually the case, this is after the act is done. We are so carried away in this country by the cry of a free press and free speech, that men may come and go, using the most violent and seditious language, but until some overt act is committed we lull ourselves into a false security. We rely too much upon a spirit of self pride and conscious superiority of nationality, as to lead us to believe the murderous methods of continental conspirators against the law and order can never be successfully inaugurated here. The attempt on Mr. Frick's life is an eye opener. We are no better, no safer, no securer, than the people residing in France, or Germany, or Russia. Our lax laws have given these Anarchists a foothold here. It is very true when we look into the terrible atrocities practiced upon the down trodden races of Europe, especially the barbarities of the Russian Government, it is no wonder a class springs up, that in the secret plottings of the midnight conclave seeks with the pistol and the dagger to find a remedy, at least, a vengeance on their oppressions. From the minds of these men God is blotted out, life is a dream that ends with its extinction. Before their diseased imaginations are the absorbing thoughts, revenge, murder, a saturnalia of licentiousness, the uprooting of all legitimate forms of government, the utter subversion of law.

We pride ourself upon being a religious people. We invoke our superior civilization, when we read of the tragic doings whose foul and murderous blots dim every page of European history, and we thank God in free and enlightened America such things cannot be. But are we not finding ourselves mistaken? Is not our boasted freedom of speech which allows these men to detail their alleged grievances, and to gloat over their proposed remedies, bearing fruit. Take Herr Most, here, in this city, have we not seen large halls packed from pit to gallery, while this notorious Anarchist defied God and society, blasphemed, raved and ranted to the vociferous plaudits of many. Sowing the seeds which germinate, and bear the fruit, whose blossoms were blood red. Law. How have we observed the law? Do we not see it daily defied? Is capital less innocent than labor? No need to partionlarize [sic]. The burthen of violated laws rests as heavily on capital as on labor.

———❖———

JULY 28, 1892 —Excerpted from **The Nation.**

WEEK'S NEWS

The attempt to assassinate Mr. Frick is a natural result of the attitude taken by the Homestead strikers. His assailant appears to be one of those "cranks" whose mental weakness makes them the easy prey of the preachers of anarchy, and whose love of notoriety is quite as strong as any desire to help the cause of "Labor." There seems no ground for supposing that the Homestead men had any direct connection with his crime, but the leaders who organized the attack upon the Pinkertons three weeks ago, and who have never expressed any regret for the act, are morally responsible for Berkman's performance. The leaders of the strike attacked the watchmen sent by the manager of the mills, and killed as many of them as they could; he simply tried to kill the manager who sent the watchmen. If it was right to murder the Pinkertons— and nobody among the strikers, from O'Donnell down, has ever admitted that it was wrong—it was right and logical to try to kill the employer of the Pinkertons.

———❖———

According to **Frank Leslie's Weekly,** *August 4, 1892, this was "a cheap coffee-house" . . . where "social reformers of every grade meet."*

JULY 25, 1892 —*Excerpted from the* Pittsburgh Commercial Gazette.

"A GUARDSMAN'S TREASON"

National guardsmen of Pennsylvania will never forget the scenes that transpired in the provisional brigade camp beginning Saturday at 2 o'clock and ending this morning at 8 in the ignominious expulsion of a private from the camp. A counterpart is not known in the guard's history. W. L. Iams was yesterday a member of Company I of Waynesburg Tenth regiment. He lolled with twenty soldiers under the single tree in the camp that stands at a knoll directly in front of Lieut.-Col. Streator's quarters. With the news of the shooting of Mr. Frick, Iams jumped to his feet, waved his cap and shouted:

"Three cheers for the man who shot Frick!"

The privates were surprised into being still at the utterance. Iams gave the cheers himself. Lieut.-Col. Streator heard the exclamation and shouts in his tent. He came out and, without explanation, ordered the regiment to fall in line. Then, facing his men, he said:

"Who spoke those words about Frick?"

"I did," Iams answered, stepping forward promptly with an [air] of bravado.

"Do you know their meaning? They were in violation of your oath to support the laws of this state. You are guilty of treason, sir. Will you apologize to your superior and your regiment?"

"I refuse," Iams now spoke sullenly.

Col. Streator ordered his arrest and confinement in the guard-house. Gen. Snowden was notified of the treasonable talk. He at once ordered a court martial, which, consisting of the commissioned officers of the regiment, sat at once. Little time was consumed in arriving at a verdict of guilty.

Col. Streator ordered the punishment. Iams was first sentenced to be strung up by the thumbs, leaving the tips of his toes barely touching the ground, and to remain suspended for thirty minutes. The culprit went through the ordeal under the direction of Surgeon Neff. He was suspended in a position of such awful misery that in twenty minutes he was unconscious and ordered cut down. This was inflicted Saturday afternoon. He was allowed to rest until this morning when the marks of treason were put on him and he suffered banishment from the camp.

"Marked for His Crime."

When Iams rose at daybreak he was taken in charge by a detail. His hair on the right side of his head was shaven off close. The line of shame extended over his face and the right half of his moustache was sacrificed. Then his suit of blue was taken from his back and with all the arms he formerly bore confiscated to the state. A civilian suit in tatters and a hat, faded and old, were then given to him.

After these preparations Col. Hawkins ordered the entire provisional brigade, in addition to Battery C, in line. Iams was placed in position in front of the troops. He marched with his head thrown defiantly in the air, and at the camp limits Adjt. Hayes read the charges, verdict and punishment. Iams listened without a show of emotions. At the order of Col. Streator the Eighteenth regimental band played "The Rogues March," and Iams marched out of sight to the music of disgrace. Then a detail conducted him to Swissvale and turned their backs on him.

This punishment carried with it a dishonorable discharge from the guard, a prohibition from ever after enlisting in the United States Militia in Pennsylvania. Iams is said by Col. Streator to have always been an unruly soldier.

———❖———

Private W.L. Iams was hung by the thumbs for shouting "Three cheers for the man who shot Frick." Frank Leslie's Illustrated Weekly, *August 4, 1892, published this sketch.*

JULY 27, 1892 —Excerpted from The Pittsburg Leader.

TO EXPEL COL. STREATOR.

MEMBERS OF THE RANDALL CLUB SAY THEY WILL PREFER CHARGES.

————

Against the Guardsman—The Attorneys' Consultation To-day—Colonel Freer, a Friend of General Grant and a Prominent Criminal Lawyer, to be One of Iams' Counsel—Sympathetic Letters from Various Parts of the Country.

A sensational feature in the Private Iams case was brought out this morning when members of the Randall club announced they would take steps to have Lieutenant Colonel Streator expelled from the Randall club of this city. Colonel Streator takes an active interest in the Democracy in Washington county, but, as stated, is a member of the Democratic organization referred to that has its headquarters in this city [Pittsburg].

Attorneys C. C. Dickey, Frank P. Iams, S. W. Trent and J. D. Watson held a long consultation in Mr. Iams' office this morning in regard to the proposed civil and criminal actions to be entered against Col. Streator. Attorney Iams said after the meeting: "We have just wired Colonel Freer, of the West Virginia National Guard, to help us in this matter. Colonel Freer is an uncle of Private Iams and is one of the prominent criminal lawyers of the state of West Virginia. He served with honor during the war, having been an aide-de-camp and close personal friend of General Grant during the campaign of the Army of the Potomac. We expect to receive a reply by telegraph and we shall at once arrange a conference.

"We have spent two hours in examining the Pennsylvania laws this morning, and it is shown clearly that Streator had no authority for his actions by either civil or military law. We do not propose to take any steps against Colonel Streator's military position. If the officers of the National Guard will serve with him, and Governor Pattison and General Snowden take no action and keep him for a subordinate then we have nothing to say. We shall prosecute Colonel Streator for damages and for aggravated assault and battery.

"To-day several members of the Randall club called upon us and said they would bring charges against Streator and have him expelled from the club."

Mr. Iams has received many letters and papers from all over the country.

R.W. Ledwith, a former Pittsburger and now one of the editors of the *Chicago Herald,* writes: "I will mail you to-day a marked copy of our paper containing editorial reference to the shocking brutality visited upon Private Iams. I do this as a former Greene county man and I beg to express the hope that you and the friends of Private Iams will not rest until the outrage is properly and completely resented [sic] and annulled. I do not think the good people of Western Pennsylvania will quietly submit to this species of czarism; on the contrary, I believe their sense of justice will unite them in an effort to effectually curtail the presumption of a 'colonel,' whose military laurels, I assume, were gathered at a time when the shock of battle and the tread of armies were unknown in the land."

————❖————

In a summary court martial, Iams was discharged and drummed out of the regiment. He, in turn, brought a legal action against the regiment's officers. However, they were ultimately acquitted by a Pittsburgh jury.

JULY 27, 1892 —Excerpted from
The Pittsburgh Post.

ANOTHER SUSPECT.

————

He Is Bagged by the Police After Many Hours of Weary Waiting.

————

HIS NAME IS HENRY BAUER.

————

He Is the Admitted Leader of the Anarchists in Allegheny.

————

SUCCESSOR OF OLD JOE FRICKE.

————

Sensational Discoveries Made in His Dwelling House.

. . .

Henry Bauer, who appears to be the leader among Northside Anarchists, was arrested by the police yesterday morning at his home, 73 Spring Garden avenue. His apprehension is considered very important, and the police believe they have now proofs of a big, carefully laid conspiracy against the life of Chairman Frick. Bauer supplied all the anarchists of this city and vicinity with inflammatory literature. In fact he made his living by it. A wagon load of literature on a par with that found at the house of Carl Nold was taken from Bauer's house and brought over to the Central police station. Weapons were also found and several plans for making infernal machines.

The arrest was made at ten o'clock in the morning by Detectives McTighe and Shore of this city and Detective Steele of Allegheny. Bauer was then at his home. He submitted quietly when the police stated their mission. He was first taken to the Allegheny lockup, and later brought over to this city. He is now in the Central police station, but his cell is not near that of Nold, so there is no possibility of their communicating with each other. After the arrest the detectives again visited Bauer's house and searched it. They found, in addition to the bloodthirsty literature, a lot of ammunition that makes things look bad for the prisoner. There was an ugly American bulldog revolver of 50-caliber, and a box of cartridges to fit it. There were a lot of other cartridges of a smaller caliber. There was a good rifle in the house, and one of the villainous looking daggers sometimes found on Italians. It was short, strong, and sharp as a razor. It was evidently made from a file. It had a small hook on the end that would help greatly in the maiming of any one. There was another in the shape of a knife with a blade fully four inches long, and which was also curved at the point. All this stuff was confiscated and brought to the Central police station, where it was put in Inspector McKelvey's room, and last night thoroughly examined.

WHY BAUER WAS SUSPECTED.

The clue to Bauer was obtained through the fact that his name was spread over the papers found at Nold's house. Then the police say they have kept close tab on the movements of the Northside anarchists, and know where all of them reside. They know that Bauer has succeeded to the mantle of the late Joseph Fricke, the anarchist who was the admitted leader until his death about a year ago.

The police had a long wait for Bauer, though. For four mortal hours Monday night Detective McTighe watched his little home on Spring Garden avenue and waited to nab him. But he did not appear that night, and it was believed he was hiding. Detectives McTighe, Shore and Steele, were after him bright and early yesterday morning, and after waiting awhile got him. No. 73 Spring Garden avenue is a two-story frame. Bauer and a cobbler named Maxwell Albrecht had the first floor. It was divided into three compartments, in which the two men did all their business. On one side was Albrecht's shoeshop; on the other was Bauer's bookstore with hundreds of German and English books ranged along the shelves. At the rear was stretched a curtain, behind which was the sleeping apartment of the two. It was all much crowded, and the detectives wondered how the men could exist there during this awful hot weather. The upstairs is occupied by a respectable German family, whom the detectives think had nothing to do with the anarchists. . . .

Yesterday Bauer told McTighe he had not gotten home until after 1 o'clock that morning. He had been out, he said, but on what mission or where he did not disclose. He was not averse to going with the officers. Bauer is a fine looking fellow, six feet tall, weighs 200 pounds and has black hair and a black mustache.

At the Central station he was questioned by Inspector McKelvey as to what he knew of Bergmann [sic]. He said that he had met the assassin at Nold's house one day last week. He was introduced by Nold, and was told by Bergmann that he had come here seeking employment. Bauer told Bergmann this was a bad place to come for work now on account of the strike.

"I asked Bergmann if he had a card from some typographical union," said Bauer, "and was told he had not. I then said it would be very hard for him to get a job around the city without a card."

"When did you see him last?" was asked.

"I understood he went away on Friday," replied Bauer.

SUSPICIOUS LOITERING.

This statement was disproved later, when Bauer was identified by W. Tustin as a man seen loitering around the Carnegie offices on Saturday morning. He was seen on the avenue a short time previous to the shooting by Mr. Tustin. There was talk about a man handing a package to Bergmann as he entered the Hussey building, where the Carnegie offices are located. If this man was Bauer it has not yet been stated, but there is a very strong suspicion that he is the one who handed the package.

"I don't know anything about the shooting of Mr. Frick," protested the prisoner when he was asked about that. "There was no plot that I know of."

The police learned that Bauer had been at Nold's home on Monday night, and seeing that Nold had been arrested concluded to avoid his own home for a while. It is known that the anarchists meet at his house frequently, and that he is the recognized head and leader of the band that infests this city and vicinity. The fact that he succeeded to the work of the late Anarchist Fricke is demonstrated by the fact that he is in possession of many letters and papers of the deceased. His dealing in anarchist literature is regarded as another proof that he is the leader of the red-handed tribe. There were found letters to him concerning anarchistic matters: also an envelope, with a special delivery stamp, addressed to John Most, care Henry Bauer, 73 Spring Garden avenue, Allegheny. The date of this is not discernable, but the police know to a certainty that Herr Most was in Allegheny about one month ago. Part of that time he stopped at the house of Nold, and there it is claimed made all arrangements for the arrival of Bergmann. It is noted with striking emphasis that among all the letters and papers found at Bauer's house there is none bearing a date within the past two months, so that if there was any correspondence relative to the attempt on Mr. Frick's life it has been destroyed or hidden where the police have not yet found it.

Superintendent O'Mara, one of the detectives said last night, has been keeping tab on the meetings of the anarchists right along and knows to a certainty what they have been doing, so that he is enabled to act speedily and promptly in the

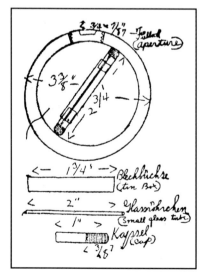

Diagram for a bomb found in the home of Pittsburgh anarchist Henry Bauer.

JULY 30, 1892 —Excerpted from the **National Labor Tribune.**

AS TO ANARCHY

Murder that partakes of the elements of assassination, that is to say, murder not done in the heat of passion, is particularly detestable. When the motive of the act is other than personal and the crime is committed in a republic such as the United States, it becomes more especially one to be repudiated promptly and emphatically. Of this latter class was the attempt upon the life of Chairman Frick of the Carnegie Steel Company on Saturday last. The prisoner Berkman is held on a charge of felonious shooting. In case there be no fatal result he can be punished on the charges, felonious assault upon Mr. Frick and upon Mr. Leishman. Whatever the term of imprisonment may be it will be inadequate to fit this crime— a crime that is against both capital and workman. Wholesome minded men, whether workmen or employers, will regret that the law does not take cognizance of the intention of a criminal and punish in accord with that intention.

As to the *status* of the assassin. It seems he is an Anarchist of the extreme type, which is designated among that violent class as an Autonomist or Individualist, which we take to mean those who hold that they are called to take action as individuals, in accord with the individual theory, for the regeneration of society. The other sort of Anarchists pursue their theories in organized bodies.

This man who made the desperate attempt upon the life of Chairman Frick, it is inferred, came to the conclusion that he individually was charged with the removal of that gentleman. Why he became thus instigated can only be inferred. Possibly his inspiration was that the chairman had been guilty of a great moral sin in having employed the Pinkertons, and was thus the primary cause of the shedding of blood on July 6, and that he, the Anarchist, should take the vindication of the moral law into his own hands. To act thus was to forestall the judgement of the Almighty, in whose authority such vindication rests. The personal conceit which led to this step could exist only in an Anarchist of the individualistic type, and of so insane characteristics as to fancy that Anarchy has any legitimate reason to plant itself in the American Republic. This assassination episode is in the direction of general Anarchy in this country, a stride in advance of the Pinkerton episode at Homestead. Both of these notable events are in the line of that bloody revolution which nineteenth century civilization should use its best brains to avoid by peaceful reform. Thoughtful people should not hide from themselves the fact that both these events are a part of such revolution, hence that it is incumbent now upon statesmanship, upon every person having thinking powers, to address themselves to this greatest problem of the age, the relations of capital and labor.

———❖———

(Suspect, continued from column 1) present crisis. Bauer took his arrest coolly, and the detectives thought he seemed to look upon it as a matter of course. . . .

DIAGRAM OF A BOMB.
The most important thing discovered in the whole lot of anarchistic stuff was the diagram of a dynamite bomb. There were several sketches of it in lead pencil on a plain white piece of paper. . . .

The bomb could be carried in perfect safety by any person who took care to avoid a collision. It is similar to those used in France and Germany by the anarchists. . . .

There were no bombs found at Bauer's house, however. The police think they have been hidden, if there are any in possession of the Pittsburgh anarchists at present.

———❖———

Excerpted from Emma Goldman in America, *Chapter 5, by Alice Wexler, Beacon Press, Boston, 1984.*

THE ANARCHIST TRADITION

Berkman's decision to assassinate Henry Clay Frick placed him squarely within the anarchist tradition of individual acts of terror that had developed in Europe during the 1870s and 1880s in the aftermath of the Paris Commune of 1871 and the assassination of the Russian czar in 1881. At this time, the severe political repression in most European countries had persuaded some revolutionists, including even Kropotkin [leading Russian anarchist], of the futility of striving for legal political reform, and had encouraged tactics of "illegalism" and violence. In the United States, too, the harsh suppression of strikes had encouraged support for armed retaliation by workers, a position strongly advocated by Johann Most. In France, particularly, a series of sporadic explosions and assaults in the 1880s intensified between 1892 and 1894 with a wave of dramatic terrorist attacks, including the assassination of French President Sadi Carnot in 1894. After a series of murders and bombings beginning in March of 1892, one of the most celebrated of the anarchist terrorists, Ravachol, was executed on July 11, 1892—a little over a week before Berkman's attempted *attentat*.

Aware of the precedents for his act within European anarchist tradition and of anarchist belief in the apocalyptic value of an act of self-immolation and assassination, Berkman drew his primary inspiration from the Russian revolutionary ethic of sacrifice for the cause. He identified with the Nihilist heroes of his adolescence. "Inexpressibly near and soul-kin I feel to those men and women, the adored, mysterious ones of my youth, who had left wealthy homes and high station to 'go to the People,' to become one with them, though despised by all whom they held dear, persecuted and ridiculed even by the benighted objects of their great sacrifice." [Berkman *Prison Memoirs.*]

...[Berkman's] trial took place September 19, with Berkman acting as his own counsel, despite his limited English. His failure to use any of his rights to challenge the jurors or make objections later severely limited his rights of appeal. Despite his youthful bravado in court—he announced contemptuously that he expected no justice and grandly identified himself with "those who were murdered at Chicago"[executed for the Haymarket bombing]—he was nevertheless devastated by his twenty-two-year prison sentence (which exceeded by fifteen years the usual maximum sentence of seven years for attempted manslaughter). [*The New-York Times*, September 20, 1892.] Carl Nold and Henry Bauer were both convicted as accomplices and sentenced to five years in prison for having sheltered Berkman prior to the assassination attempt—of which they had known nothing. Far from inspiring the workers at Homestead or anywhere else, as Berkman had hoped, his act was almost universally condemned, even by many anarchists. It did not break the strike, as has sometimes been claimed; instead it blurred the important issues that had been dramatized by the battle of July 6 and deepened the association between anarchism and terrorism. ❖

Excerpted from Prison Memoirs of an Anarchist, *by Alexander Berkman, originally published by Mother Earth Publishing Association, New York, 1912.*

From Chapter VI, THE JAIL

[D]uring exercise hour, I watch with beating heart for an opportunity to converse with the Homestead steel-worker [a fellow prisoner]. I shall explain to him the motives and purpose of my attempt on Frick. He will understand me; he will himself enlighten his fellow-strikers. It is very important *they* should comprehend my act quite clearly, and he is the very man to do this great service to humanity. He is the rebel-worker; his heroism during the struggle bears witness. I hope the People will not allow the enemy to hang him. He defended the rights of the Homestead workers, the cause of the whole working class. No, the People will never allow such a sacrifice. How well he carries himself! Erect, head high, the look of conscious dignity and strength—

"Cell num-b-ber fi-i-ve!"

The prisoner with the smoked glasses leaves the line, and advances in response to the guard's call. Quickly I pass along the gallery, and fall into the vacant place, alongside of the steel-worker.

"A happy chance," I address him. "I should like to speak to you about something important. You are one of the Homestead strikers, are you not?"

"Jack Tinford," he introduces himself. "What's your name?"

He is visibly startled by my answer. "The man who shot Frick?" he asks.

An expression of deep anxiety crosses his face. His eye wanders to the gate. Through the wire network I observe visitors approaching from the Warden's office.

"They'd better not see us together," he says, impatiently. "Fall in back of me. Then we'll talk."

Pained at his manner, yet not fully realizing its significance, I slowly fall back. His tall, broad figure completely hides me from view. He speaks to me in monosyllables, unwillingly. At the mention of Homestead he grows more communicative, talking in an undertone, as if conversing with his neighbor, the Sicilian, who does not understand a syllable of English. I strain my ear to catch his words. The steel-workers merely defended themselves against armed invaders, I hear him say. They are not on strike: they've been locked out by Frick, because he wants to non-unionize the works. That's why he broke the contract with the Amalgamated, and hired the damned Pinkertons two months before, when all was peace. They shot many workers from the barges before the millmen "got after them." They deserved roasting alive for their unprovoked murders. Well, the men "fixed them all right." Some were killed, others committed suicide on the burning barges, and the rest were forced to surrender like whipped curs. A grand victory all right, if that coward of a sheriff hadn't got the Governor to send the militia to Homestead. But it was a victory, you bet, for the boys to get the best of three hundred armed Pinkertons. He himself, though, had nothing to do with the fight. He was sick at the time. They're trying to get the Pinkertons to swear his life away. One of the hounds has already made an affidavit that he saw him, Jack Tinford, throw dynamite at the barges, before the Pinkertons landed. But never mind, he is not afraid. No Pittsburgh jury will believe those lying murderers. He was in his sweetheart's house, sick abed. The girl and her mother will prove an alibi for him. And the Advisory Committee of the Amalgamated, too. They know he wasn't on the shore. They'll swear to it in court, anyhow—

Abruptly he ceases, a look of fear on his face. For a moment he is lost in thought. Then he gives me a searching look, and smiles at me. As we turn the corner of the walk, he whispers: "Too bad you didn't kill him. Some business misunderstanding, eh?" he adds, aloud.

Could he be serious, I wonder. Does he only pretend? He faces straight ahead, and I am unable to see his expression. I begin the careful explanation I had prepared:

"Jack, it was for you, for your people that I—"

Impatiently, angrily he interrupts me. I'd better be careful not to talk that way in court, he warns me. If Frick should die, I'd hang myself with such "gab." And it would only harm the steel-workers. They don't believe in killing; they respect the law. Of course, they had a right to defend their homes and families against unlawful invaders. But they welcomed the militia to Homestead. They showed their respect for authority. To be sure, Frick deserves to die. He is a murderer. But the mill-workers will have nothing to do with Anarchists. What did I want to kill him for, anyhow? I did not belong to the Homestead men. It was none of my business. I had better not say anything about it in court, or—

The gong tolls.

"All in!" ❖

Portrait of Alexander Berkman from Harper's Weekly, *August 6, 1892. After he was released from prison in 1907, Berkman returned to New York, where he became editor of Emma Goldman's magazine,* Mother Earth. *In 1919, he and Goldman were among the most prominent of several hundred radicals deported as subversives by the U.S. government.*

The trials of the Homestead strikers took place in the massive Allegheny County Court-house and Jail building designed by Henry Hobson Richardson and finished in 1888.

E V E N T S

Late JULY—*The Advisory Committee rejects Hugh O'Donnell's attempts to improvise settlements with the company.*

Early AUGUST—*Roughly a thousand replacement workers are in the mill.*

AUGUST 4—*The Amalgamated brings countersuits for murder against Carnegie Steel officials. Frick and the others each post $10,000 bonds.*

SEPTEMBER 30—*Chief Justice Edward H. Paxson of the State Supreme Court issues a warrant charging 33 members of the Amalgamated from Homestead with treason against the state.*

NOVEMBER 8—*Democrat Grover Cleveland is elected president. The press attributes his victory to a rejection of the Republicans' "protective tariff" in the wake of the Homestead troubles. For the first time, Homestead votes Democratic in a presidential election.*

NOVEMBER 18—*The mechanics and laborers, some 2,000 men, are released by the Amalgamated from their pledge to support the union. They return to work.*

NOVEMBER 21—*In a final meeting, Homestead's Amalgamated members vote 101 to 91 to give up the strike.*

NOVEMBER 23, 24—*A U.S. Senate committee, investigating the Pinkertons visits Homestead and takes testimony. In reports released in February 1893, neither the House nor the Senate investigating committee recommends federal legislation.*

NOVEMBER 18-24—*Sylvester Critchlow is acquitted of murder in a jury trial in the Allegheny County Courthouse in Pittsburgh. When McLuckie, O'Donnell, and other union leaders are acquitted in February 1893, the company and union agree to drop all charges on both sides.*

DECEMBER—*The food situation in Homestead grows desperate for those who have been without regular wages. Various union and community relief funds—in the region and across the country—send aid for "women and children who want for bread."*

JANUARY, FEBRUARY 1893—*Hugh Dempsey, a member of the Knights of Labor, and several co-defendants, are found guilty of administering a diar-rhetic powder to the food of Carnegie Steel's replacement workers.*

JULY 27, 1892 —Excerpted from **The Pittsburgh Post.**

IS HE WEAKENING?

―――――

Chairman O'Donnell Said to Be About to Resign His Position.

―――――

ASKED MR. POTTER FOR TERMS.

―――――

Two Newspaper Men Acted as the Mediators.

―――――

ACTION OF THE ADVISORY BOARD.

―――――

FROM STAFF CORRESPONDENT.
HOMESTEAD, PA., July 26. —It is quite likely Hugh O'Donnell will resign the chairmanship of the advisory committee if he has not already done so, and the indications are that the committee is now casting about to secure another leader. The breakup was caused by the refusal of the committee to approve of O'Donnell's sentiments looking toward an "almost unconditional surrender" in the fight at hand. He expressed himself as being anxious to see a settlement even if he had to be sacrificed, and vowed that if the advisory committee did not agree with him he would resign the chairmanship.

He authorized F.D. Madeira of the New York *Recorder* and J. Hampton Moore of the Philadelphia *Public Ledger* to see Mr. Potter and ascertain his terms for a settlement. When they had executed their commission Mr. O'Donnell wanted to bring them before the committee, but the committee would not admit them. This rebuff has undoubtedly caused Mr. O'Donnell's resignation, according to his statement that he would resign if his colleagues did not indorse his sentiments. To-day he had little to give out to reporters, and it is evident a new leader will be chosen by the committee. The effort on the part of the two newspaper men to open a way for a settlement proved futile.

Himself a Sacrifice
After his return from Pittsburgh Mr. O'Donnell said he was anxious to see the Homestead trouble settled, and would even sacrifice himself in the interest of the idle men who are walking the streets. He said he was in earnest in this and would recommend an almost unconditional surrender of the men. He said he would report his sentiments to the advisory committee and if they didn't agree with him he would resign as chairman. Messrs. Madeira and Moore saw him later and suggested that they were willing to see Superintendent Potter and find out on what terms the men could return to work. He said their idea was a good one and he would like to hear from them as soon as possible.

They called on Sheriff McCleary and Colonel Gray, the sheriff's special deputy, and the latter took them to Mr. Potter's office, where they were introduced to the secretary, Mr. Childs, assistant to the chairman and Assistant Superintendent Woods. They told these gentlemen they had reason to believe they were able to open the way for a return to work and wanted to know upon what terms the company would accept their old employes. Treasurer Curry and Superintendent Potter answered their questions kindly and candidly. They said there was no vindictiveness in their dealings with the men, but they would not take back certain objectionable strife makers under any circumstances. The officials did not name any, but said those against whom official charges were produced were among them. Even they might not be rejected if the informations against them proved to be incorrect.

No Questions Asked.
They further stated they would not ask the men who applied for work anything about their membership in organizations

(Is He Weakening, continued)

or otherwise, but would require them to sign agreements as individuals fixing the scale on wages, which scale is based upon a $23 billet rate. The officials assured the mediators that under no circumstances would they agree to conferences or have dealings with associations or committees, except as provided in the agreement, and pointed out that the agreement provided for a conference every quarter between six employes chosen by the workmen and three officers of the steel company, whose duty it would be to fix the price of billets. It was also granted by the officials that if there was any delicacy on the part of the men about applying singly they could come in groups and be accepted or rejected as the case might be. On no condition would men who have already been employed be discharged if their work was satisfactory.

...

The Agreement.

The following is a copy of the agreement above referred to:

"Entered into by and between the limited partnership association of the Carnegie Steel Company, limited, and the workmen employed by it at the Homestead steel works, Munhall, Pa.

"(1) The agreement shall go into effect July 1, 1892, and shall remain in force for the remainder of this year and during the year 1893 and thereafter until notice is given as provided in the following:

"(2) This association or its employes can give notice not later than October 1, 1893, of a desire to terminate this agreement, in which event it shall cease on December 31, 1893. If such notice is not given by either party by October 1, 1893 or by October 1 in any later year, then this agreement shall remain in force for the following years, until such notice is given.

"(3) Wages will be paid upon a quarterly sliding scale, based upon the average net market price for 4x4-inch Bessemer steel billets, delivered on cars at the works during the preceding quarter.

"(4) The market price of billets shall be established quarterly at a conference to take place not later than the 25th day of the last month of each quarter, between a committee of six employes to be chosen by the workmen: one from the Bessemer department, one from the plate mill, one from the slabbing mill, one from the 23-inch mill, or the 33-inch mill, and one from the 40-inch mill or the 35-inch mill, and a committee of three of the executive officers of the Carnegie Steel Company, limited. The price of billets for each quarter shall be the average between the highest and the lowest cash quotation, given by the *American Manufacturer* each week during the said quarter.

"(5) We, the undersigned, having read the above and examined the scale of wages hereto annexed and made a part hereof, hereby apply for employment under their conditions, and for the valuable consideration of employment given by the association we each one for himself hereby pledge ourselves as men and citizens to adhere faithfully thereto, and to take such position at said steel works as may be assigned to us; to accept as full payment for our service wages at the rates set forth in the scale referred to, and that we will abide by and obey the rules and regulations publicly posted at said steel works, a copy of which is hereto attached."

———❖———

JULY 27, 1892 —Reprinted from
The New-York Times.

THE MILLS RAPIDLY FILLING UP.

O'Donnell Will Try To Reach Carnegie
Through Platt and Blaine.

HOMESTEAD, PENN., JULY 26.—The great Homestead strike or lock-out has had its back broken. Hugh O'Donnell has been practically deposed as leader, and the Advisory Committee will hereafter conduct affairs in its own way.

To-day 600 men are at work in the mills, the steel produced has been approved by the experts stationed here and the managers of the mill declares [sic] that the skilled non-union men employed are superior in ability to the old men. Gen. Snowden is so confident that the worst is over that to-day he ordered home the Eighth Regiment and the City Troop of Philadelphia; to-morrow the Fourteenth Regiment of Pittsburg returns, on Thursday the Ninth and Fifteenth Regiments will be relieved from duty, and by Saturday it is possible that the Third Brigade will be ordered to return home.

Superintendent Potter is confident that over 1,000 men will be employed by Saturday, as over 200 are expected by to-morrow in addition to those already engaged. The open hearth furnace was fired up for the first time to-day. The company has formally announced that no member of the Advisory Committee will be re-

This sketch from **Frank Leslie's Illustrated Weekly,** *July 28, 1892, shows the Carnegie Schoolhouse, headquarters for General Snowden. The last contingent of the militia left on October 13, 1892.*

employed, nor any man who is accused of having participated in the killing of the Pinkertons.

To-night Hugh O'Donnell left for New York, ostensibly on a visit, as a matter of fact to enter into a political dicker with Thomas C. Platt. The strikers understand that Mr. Platt and James G. Blaine are intimate friends, and that through Platt and Blaine pressure might be brought upon Mr. Carnegie to put an end to the strike. O'Donnell, ever since his arrest, has been advocating a settlement of the strike. He has seen that the locked-out men were losing ground every day, and that so long as the militia remained here non-union men would continue to come and the troops would protect them. If the matter were left solely to O'Donnell a settlement would be effected at once, but unfortunately the Advisory Committee, which is dominated by four or five men, have come to the conclusion that the only possible way for them to secure their old positions is by fighting to the end, have repudiated O'Donnell, and have set up shop for themselves. They expect to hold their ignorant and foreign followers by deception, by underestimating the number of men actually employed in the mills, by spreading reports that workmen are detained in the mills against their will, and by other tricks and devices equally absurd and untenable.

As to the manner in which false reports are spread by the strikers the following is a good instance: This afternoon word was brought to the newspaper men that 140 non-union men were detained in the mills by the company, and had been refused permission to leave. It was further declared that three of these unfortunate men had managed to escape, and desired to inform the newspaper men what terrible experiences they had endured. When the newspaper men offered to conduct a committee to Col. Green, ex-Provost Marshal General, and ask for the release of the 140 alleged prisoners in the mills, they were informed that the Mechanical Union was not only neutral, but that furthermore the 140 men aforesaid were not detained in the mill against their own consent, but were afraid to go outside of the works so long as the strike lasted.

————❖————

AUGUST 4, 1892 —Excerpted from an article, "Work for the Militia," in **The New-York Times.**

COUNTER SUIT.

PITTSBURG, PENN., AUG. 3. —The threatened action against the Carnegie officials and the Pinkertons, charging them with murder, was begun this morning, and warrants issued for the arrest of the defendants. At 11 o'clock Messrs. Brennen and Cox and Hugh Ross, the prosecuting witness, went to Alderman King's office on the south side and made the information, and the warrants were issued.

The information is as follows:

"Commonwealth of Pennsylvania vs. H. C. Frick, T. F. Lovejoy, Robert Pinkerton, William Pinkerton, J. A. Potter, C. A. Corey, J. G. A. Leishmann, L. M. Curry, C. W. Bedell, Fred Primer, W. H. Burt, John Cooper, and Fred H[e]inde.

"Before me, the subscriber, Festus M. King, an Alderman in and for said City of Pittsburg, personally came Hugh Ross, who upon oath disposes and says that in Mifflin Township, Allegheny County, and State of Pennsylvania, on the 6th day of July, 1892, said defendants did of their malice aforethought, feloniously and riotously with force and arms and deadly weapons kill and murder, and did cause feloniously to be killed and murdered Joseph Sotax [sic, Sotak], John E. Morris, George W. Rutter, and Silas Wain, then and there being in the peace [sic] and Commonwealth of Pennsylvania.

"This information is made on information received and believed to be true. Complainant therefore prays that a warrant may issue and the aforesaid defendants may be arrested and held to answer this charge of murder, and further deponent saith not."

This afternoon Secretary Lovejoy, Vice President Leishmann, and Treasurer Curry of the Carnegie Company appeared before Judge Ewing in the Criminal Court, and said they had decided to surrender themselves. Judge Ewing refused to hear an application for bail until the accused had surrendered to Alderman King. The magistrate was sent for, and after he had presented his docket the hearing was

(Counter Suit, continued)

held. Messrs. Leishmann, Curry, and Lovejoy waived a hearing, as did H.C. Frick, Nevin McConnell, James S. Dovey, and Superintendent Potter, who were absent, but represented by W.F. Patterson, their attorney.

Messrs. Frick, Lovejoy, Leishmann, and Curry were released on $10,000 bail each. The hearings on the application of the others were postponed until to-morrow morning.

Judge Ewing said: "This information is made by a man who himself is charged with murder, and is now on bail. It would have been better had it been made by some other person. I think, if the story in the newspapers is true, none of the men charged in the information can be held for murder and certainly not in the first degree. The men on shore were there illegally and unless you can show me there was a malicious and deliberate killing there is no use wasting any more time. The men on the barges were there legally and the others were there illegally."

Superintendent Potter has not yet been arrested, and it is not at all probable that he will surrender himself until to-morrow. H.C. Frick's young son, born a few weeks ago, died to-day. It is not probable that the warrant for Mr. Frick's arrest will be issued until after the funeral, and not then unless he is able to be again at his office.

Bauer, one of the Anarchists charged with being an accessory to the shooting of Frick, was released on $5,000 bail to-day. Judge Ewing refused to accept bail in the case of Anarchist Knold [sic], as he said there was evidence that Knold had shown Bergmann [sic] the Carnegie offices.

President Weihe of the Amalgamated Association stated to-day that he did not know when O'Donnell would return. It is understood that he will attend a gathering at Ridgewood Park, Brooklyn, on Friday. The nature of O'Donnell's mission East, he said, would probably not be revealed until he got back.

OCTOBER 1, 1892 —Excerpted from an article "Treason to the State," in **The New-York Times.**

A SURPRISE FOR THE HOMESTEAD STRIKERS.

—————

The Carnegie Company Causes the Arrest of the Advisory Board on a Sensational Charge—"They May Persecute Us, but They Can't Make Us Work."

—————

PITTSBURG, SEPT. 30.—Chairman Frick went through the Homestead mills to-day and on his return declared everything running nicely, and that the strike or lock-out was certainly a thing of the past.

This evening, in direct contradiction of the statement, a warrant was issued by Chief Justice Paxson of the State Supreme bench for the arrest of the entire Advisory Board of the locked-out mill men, as follows:

David H. Shannon, John McLuckie, David Lynch, Thomas J. Crawford, Hugh O'Donnell, Harry Bayne, Elmer E. Bail, Isaac Byers, Henry Isaac Critchlow, Miller Colgan, John Coyle, Jack Clifford, Dennis McCush, William McConegly, Michael Cummings, William Combs, John Dierken, Patrick Fagan, Matthew Harris, Reid Kennedy, John Miller, E. Searight, John Murray, W.H. Thompson, Martin Murray, Hugh Ross, William T. Roberts, George Rylands, and George W. Server [sic, Sarver].

The charge is treason.

. . .

Five of the defendants were arrested to-night. Two are in jail. At least two are out of the State, and the others, it is expected, will be arrested to-morrow.

The maximum penalty for the crime named is twelve years, and the Carnegie officials couldn't have adopted a better means of letting the public know that the strike is not broken than by striving to get the leaders of the men out of their way. ❖

OCTOBER 2, 1892 —Excerpted from an article, "Homestead Men Scared," in **The New-York Times.**

THE ARRESTS FOR TREASON FRIGHTEN THEM.

—————

The State Means Business, and Bail Is Fixed at $10,000—The Strikers Had Been Previously Advised to Have the Carnegie People Arrested for Treason.

—————

HOMESTEAD, PENN., OCT. 1.—The borough has not yet recovered from the shock of last night's bombshell. To-day business has been practically suspended, and anxious groups stood at every corner discussing this latest coup. "What does it mean?" That is the query on every tongue. The thought of the State of Pennsylvania interfering in the struggle is frightening the sturdy workers. They would accept with derision murder, riot, or conspiracy suits brought by the Carnegie Steel Company, but to be arrested by the State, and on a charge of treason, is different.

———❖———

Thomas J. Crawford

MANY WANTED BY THE STATE ARE IN HIDING.

─────

PITTSBURG, OCT. 3. —Four of the Homestead strikers charged with treason furnished the required $10,000 bail each this morning and were released. The men released are John Dierken, George Rylands, Daniel Lynch, and W. H. Gaches.

David Lynch, another of the strikers, who has been diligently sought for a month on charges of murder, riot, conspiracy, and treason, was arrested this morning and lodged in jail. He will be given a hearing to-morrow.

The search for the remaining twenty-eight Homesteaders who are accused of treason continues, and the police are inclined to think they have left this part of the country. Friends of the accused, however, say they will surrender when their lawyers advise and proffers of bail are said to be plentiful from Pittsburg merchants.

The excitement over the treason charges is abating, though there is still much discussion of the subject and great interest manifested in the coming trials before the Supreme Justice of the Commonwealth.

The Supreme Court opened this morning at 10 o'clock, and probably three weeks will be spent in disposing of cases from the other counties of the Western district before Allegheny County is touched. This, however, will not necessarily interfere with Justice Paxson hearing the treason cases, and the attorneys on both sides say they are ready for the fray.

Mr. Brennan, counsel for the defense, says he expects the cases to come up within two weeks, and the attorney for the prosecution says that there is no reason why the matter should not come up early in the term.

Jury Commissioner Mullen, who was formerly a member of the Amalgamated Association, says the national organization has now recognized the Homestead strike in a much more determined way than formerly. "The lodge," says Mr. Mullen, "now realizes that the loss of the Homestead strike means the death of the organization. They will now levy an assessment upon the members to sustain it. At Youngstown, Ohio, yesterday all of the men willingly consented to contribute from one to two days' wages a month for the benefit of the Homestead men.

Even the rollers, who earn as high as $16 a day, have agreed to contribute two days' wages a month; and the heaters did the same. I am informed that $80,000 has been raised in this way, and that hereafter the income will be steady. During the strike not one cent of the surplus of the national lodge, which amounted to $268,000 at the time of the last convention, has been touched, but it has now been determined to use every cent of it, if necessary, to win."

A non-union man named Smith, employed at Carnegie's Thirty-third Street mill, was attacked by strikers while on his way home Saturday night and so badly beaten that it was feared he would die. When found he was unconscious, and has been lying ever since in a stupor.

His assailants are known and are being shadowed by detectives to prevent their escape. Andrew Volskie, another non-union worker, was assaulted on the same day. He was approached from behind and felled with an iron bar. His injuries are not serious. The suits against H. C. Frick, Secretary Lovejoy, Messrs. Leishman, Curry, Potter, and others of the Carnegie Company and the Pinkerton detectives go before the Grand Jury to-morrow. The charges embrace murder, conspiracy, and riot. Burgess John McLuckie and Hugh Ross are the prosecutors.

────────

PHILADELPHIA, OCT. 3. —Major Gen. Snowden, commanding officer of the National Guard, declared this evening that he was responsible for the arrest of the Homestead Advisory Board for treason.

────────❖────────

JUDGE PAXSON DEFINES TREASON AGAINST THE STATE.

─────

PITTSBURG, OCT. 10. —Chief Justice Paxson charged the Grand Jury to-day as to what constituted treason against the State in the cases against the Homestead strikers' Advisory Committee. Judge Paxson said:

"The mutual right of the parties to contract in regard to wages, and the character of the employment, whether by the piece or by the day, whether for ten hours or less, is fixed as any other right which we enjoy under the Constitution and laws of this State. It is a right which belongs to every citizen, laborer or capitalist, and it is the plain duty of the State to protect them in the enjoyment of it."

Coming up to the formation of the Advisory Committee, and the part taken by it in the strike, he said:

"It is alleged that the Advisory Committee did more than to induce others not to accept employment from the company; that it allowed no persons to enter the mill of the Carnegie Steel Company, and even permitted no strangers to enter the town of Homestead without its consent; that it arranged an organization of a military character, consisting of three divisions, with commanders and Captains, the Captains to report to the division commanders, and the latter to report to the Advisory Committee."

He detailed how the authority of the Sheriff had been defied, the arrival of the Pinkertons, the riot following, and finally the mobilization of the State troops, adding:

"We can have some sympathy with a mob driven to desperation by hunger, as in the days of the French Revolution, but we can have none for men receiving exceptionally high wages in resisting the law and resorting to violence and blood-

(Judge Paxson, continued)

shed in the assertion of imaginary rights, and entailing such a vast expense upon the taxpayers of the Commonwealth. It was not a cry for bread to feed their famishing lips, resulting in a sudden outrage, with good provocation; it is a deliberate attempt by men, without authority, to control others in the enjoyment of their rights.

"The men had a right to refuse to work, and persuade others to join them, but the moment they attempted to control the works and resorted to violence they placed themselves outside the pale of the law.

"If we were to concede the doctrine that the employe may dictate to his employer the terms of his employment, and upon the refusal of the latter to accede to them to take possession of his property and drive others away who were willing to work, we would have anarchy. No business could be conducted upon such a basis; that doctrine, when once counte-nanced, would be extended to every industry."

The Justice then defined as treason the organization of a large number of men in a common purpose to defy the law, resist its officers, and to deprive any portion of their fellow-citizens of their rights under the Constitution and laws. Said he:

"It is a state of war when a business plant has to be surrounded by the army of the State to protect it from unlawful violence at the hands of former employes.

"Every member of such asserted Government, whether it be an Advisory Committee, or by whatever name it is called, who has participated in such usurpation, who has joined in a common purpose of resistance to the law, and a denial of the rights to other citizens, has committed treason against the State.

"With the definition of this offense is the designing or overturning of the Government of the State. Such intention need not extend to every portion of its territory. It is sufficient if it be an overturning of it in a particular locality, and such intent may be inferred from the acts committed. If you find from the evidence that the defendants have, or any of them has committed, participated, and aided in any of the acts which I have defined to you as constituting the offense of treason, it will be your sworn duty to find a true bill against the party or parties so offending.

"We have reached the point in the history of the State where there are but two roads for us to pursue; the one leads to order and good government, the other leads to anarchy. The one great question which concerns the people of this country is the enforcement of the law and the preservation of order."

———— ❖ ————

OCTOBER 12, 1892 —Excerpted from an article, "Bills in All the Cases," in **The New-York Times.**

Jack Clifford

BOTH SIDES AT HOMESTEAD INDICTED.

————

Thirty-One Strikers Held For Treason Against the State–The Carnegie Officers Held for Murder and Conspiracy–Text of the Indictments Presented.

————

PITTSBURG, OCT. 11. —The Grand Jury, sitting in the treason cases against the Homestead strikers and the murder and conspiracy charges against H. C. Frick, various other officials of the Carnegie Steel Company, and the Pinkerton detectives, at 3:10 this afternoon brought in true bills in all the cases.

. . .

The true bill in the treason charges, after reciting the names of the defendants, reads:

"The Grand Jury of the Commonwealth of Pennsylvania, now inquiring in and for the body of the County of Allegheny, upon their oaths and affirmations respectively, do present that the defendants then and there being inhabitants and residents within the said Commonwealth of Pennsylvania, and under the protection of the laws of said Commonwealth, and owing allegiance and fidelity to the said Commonwealth of Pennsylvania, not weighing or regarding the duty of their said allegiance, but wickedly devising, disturbing the peace and tranquility of the said Commonwealth of Pennsylvania, devising to disturb and destroy, and to stir up, move, and incite insurrection, rebellion, and war against the said Commonwealth of Pennsylvania, on the 1st day of June in the year of our Lord 1892, at the borough of Homestead in the said county, and in the township of Mifflin, and elsewhere within the said Commonwealth of Pennsylvania, and beyond the borders of the State unlawfully, feloniously, falsely, maliciously, and traitorously compassed, imagined, and intended to raise and levy war, insurrection, and rebellion against the said Commonwealth of Pennsylvania.

"And in order to fulfill and to bring into effect the said traitorous compassings, imaginings, and intentions of them, the said defendants, on the 5th day of September, 1892, and on divers other days and times between the said first day of June and on the 5th day of September, at the said borough of Homestead, with other persons whose names are to the said inquest unknown to the number of 1,000 and upward, armed and arrayed in a warlike manner—that is to say, with guns, revolvers, cannon, swords, knives, clubs, dynamite bombs, and other warlike and deadly weapons, offensive and defensive—being then and there feloniously, unlawfully, maliciously, and traitorously assembled and gathered together, did feloniously and traitorously join and assemble themselves together and then and there did dispose themselves against the said Commonwealth of Pennsylvania, and did obtain, prepare, and levy war against the said Commonwealth of Pennsylvania, to the end that its Constitution, laws, and authority might be and were defied, resisted, and subverted by the said defendants and their armed allies, to wit: The said persons whose names are to the said inquest unknown, contrary to the duty of allegiance and fidelity of the said defendants, to the evil example of all others in like cases offending contrary to the form of the act of General Assembly in such case made and provided against the peace and dignity of the Commonwealth of Pennsylvania."

The witnesses whose names are given by the Grand Jury as having testified before them are Henry Beltzhoover, county detective; Samuel Cluley, Deputy Sheriff; E. C. Bishop, telegraph operator at Homestead; Henry Lewis, Robert Herbert, C. W. Danziger, E. C. Christie, newspaper correspondents, and Joseph H. Gray, special Deputy Sheriff.

The indictment against the Carnegie officials for murder reads as follows in the case of Silas Wain:

"The grand inquest of the Commonwealth of Pennsylvania do present: That said defendants on the 6th day of July, 1892, with force and arms, then and there being, did make an assault on Silas Wain and feloniously, maliciously, and of their malice and aforethought did kill and murder, contrary to the form of Assembly and against the peace and dignity of the Commonwealth of Pennsylvania."

The prosecutor in the murder cases is Hugh Ross, against whom there are charges of murder, treason, conspiracy, and riot. The witnesses for the prosecution were Capt. Kuhn [sic, Coon], F. G. Miller, Dr. Barton, Dr. Fogelson, C. E. Marcey, W. B. Rodgers, J. H. Gray, Dr. Osborn, William Taylor, Dr. Purman, Dr. McCoslin, J. H. Gilleam, Emma Neester, and Charles Mansfield.

The indictments against Mr. Frick and his associates for conspiracy sets forth, among other things, that:

"Said defendants did unlawfully, falsely, and maliciously conspire, combine, federate, and agree together to depress, lower, lessen, and diminish the wages, price and compensation of labor of divers persons employed by the Carnegie Steel Company, Limited, to then and there close up the steel manufacturing, and to cease work and operations, and caused to be sent 200 men and upward armed with guns, to overwhelm, intimidate, and frighten divers persons in the said township of Mifflin who were employed by the said Carnegie Steel Company to invade the said township of Mifflin, and to attack and to shoot off and discharge the said deadly weapons against said persons lately employed by said Carnegie Steel Company, Limited."

In regard to the fight on the morning of July 6 the bill says the defendants "did counsel and advise the shooting." Among the conspiracy witnesses is John McLuckie, Burgess of Homestead. The indictment in the riot cases against Frick officials differs little from that in the conspiracy charge.

The Grand Jury's action did not cause much excitement among the people, and the defendants themselves took it quite coolly. The Carnegie officials declined to be interviewed on the subject of the charges. It is not known yet what terms of the criminal court the cases will be assigned to.

———❖———

NOVEMBER 21, 1892 —Reprinted from
The Pittsburg Leader.

EDITOR LEADER:—In reply to your request for an expression of opinion concerning the action of the men at Homestead in declaring the strike off, I can say but little at the present time. Owing to the fact that certain of my acts in that most memorable struggle are *sub judice*, I am not in a position to criticize the acts of my late associates. Great battles are rarely, if ever, fought as planned. The world has never witnessed before so much suffering and sacrifice for a cause. The action of the three thousand laborers and mechanics who came out with our men on pure principle alone is unexampled in the history of labor struggles.

But to the men in the Lawrenceville and Beaver Falls mills too much praise cannot be given. Their loyalty and steadfastness to the principles for which they were contending should never be forgotten. Out of consideration for them I regret that the Homestead struggle should have terminated in the manner in which it did.

HUGH O'DONNELL.

"Allegheny county jail, November 21."

Excerpted from **Homestead,** *by Arthur G. Burgoyne, originally published by Rawsthorne Engraving and Printing Company, Pittsburgh, 1893.*

From Chapter XVI, THE FIRST BREAK

The usual Saturday afternoon meeting [of the strikers] on November 13 was marked by symptoms indicating only too plainly that the end was near at hand. William T. Roberts, fresh from a campaigning tour in the East, made an address substantially conceding that the cause of unionism at Homestead was on its last legs. He spoke of the desertion of the finishers from the ranks of the Amalgamated Association as an assault on the integrity of organized labor inspired by the Carnegie people for the purpose of defeating the Homestead men and added, "In view of the confidence you have placed in me, I don't propose to come here and tell you that everything is rosy when it is not. If you think with this combined opposition in your own ranks you can fight it out to the end, I am with you." The men, being asked what they wished to do, shouted with one voice, "Fight it out to the end!" There were few among them, however, that did not comprehend the intent of Mr. Roberts' words. The first doubt of ability to go on with the strike had been openly expressed by one of their own leaders and listened to without protest. This was the beginning of the end. . . .

At Homestead, the mechanics and laborers were the first to weaken. These men, to the number of about 2000, met on the morning of Thursday, November 18, and appointed a committee to wait upon the Amalgamated men and submit the proposition that the strike be declared off and the mechanics and laborers be released from further obligations. The Amalgamated men met in the evening, with President Weihe in the chair.

The proposition of the mechanics and laborers was rejected by a vote of 106 to 75.

A ballot was then taken on the advisability of continuing the strike and resulted in an affirmative decision by a vote of 224 to 129.

A committee was appointed to notify the mechanics and laborers that they could act as they liked, but that the Amalgamated Association would not be responsible for their actions.

Next morning the mechanics and laborers re-convened, received the report of the committee of the Amalgamated Association, and agreed unanimously to return to work, but under no circumstances to accept tonnage jobs, as by so doing they would trespass on the rights of the Amalgamated men.

The meeting adjourned quickly, and the men proceeded at once to the mill and put in their applications for reinstatement. More than half of the mechanics were turned away, as the number of vacancies was limited, but the laborers were all put to work or assured of employment in a few days. So great was the rush of returning prodigals that two clerks were required to make out passes for the applicants. Chairman Frick was on hand to supervise the re-employment of the old men and enjoyed, in his undemonstrative way, the successful culmination of his plans to break up unionism in Homestead.

From Chapter XVII, CAPITULATION

It was a mournful little band that assembled in the rink on Sunday morning [November 21]. In that memorable meeting-place which had again and again re-sounded with triumphant oratory and with the plaudits of sanguine multitudes, less than 300 dispirited men now came together to register the confirmation of their defeat. There were some who argued passionately against capitulation. To yield, they said, would be to hasten the disintegration of the Almagamated Association. Better go naked and starve than sacrifice the principles on the vindication of which the men of Homestead had staked everything. But this reasoning was of no avail. A standing vote was taken on the question of declaring the mill open and the proposition was carried by 101 to 91. ❖

NOVEMBER 23, 1892 —Reprinted from **The New-York Times** *after the vote ending the strike.*

CARNEGIE REDUCES WAGES.

─────

Having Conquered the Strikers, He Profits Thereby.

─────

HOMESTEAD, NOV. 22. —The closing act in the famous strike was performed last night. The Advisory Board, which has been the Gordian knot of the strike, was severed, and the last official gathering is at an end. The board, which has directed the destinies of the locked-out men throughout the entire struggle, met for the last time in its hall on Eighth Avenue, and, after disposing of the unfinished business, was dissolved.

Ex-President Weihe of the Amalgamated Association was quoted as saying in connection with the strike: "No other strike was so broad in its influence, and men were never so persecuted in any other strike. On an estimate of $1.40 a day for laborers and $3 for skilled workmen, the 7,300 strikers in the Homestead, Lawrenceville, and Beaver Falls mills lost $22,000 daily, or $2,000,000 during the entire strike."

The strikers still continue to keep up the rush for their old positions at the steel works, and although many are turned away, others are more fortunate and are told to report for work next Monday. The new men are leaving the works in groups of five and six. Some few are discharged, but the greater number are leaving of their own accord.

Every train leaving Munhall carries away more than a dozen of the new men, who have become dissatisfied and will seek employment elsewhere.

Improvements to the amount of $175,000 have been contracted for by the company, this sum to be expended in putting extensions to the several mills.

The Council of this borough held its regular session last evening, and from the report made by the Treasurer of the town it was found that its finances were in an embarrassed condition. Action was taken to relieve the borough of its stringency. Failure to collect taxes is the cause of the condition of affairs.

─────

PITTSBURG, NOV. 22. —In the future the Carnegie Company intends to treat with its employes as individuals. Each man employed is required to sign an agreement, in which he pledges himself to refrain from belonging to any labor organization and to be governed entirely by the rules and regulations of the company.

Each department Superintendent is provided with these blanks, and no one can be employed unless he signs the agreement.

─────

BEAVER FALLS, PENN., NOV. 22. —Many of those who have regained their old positions at the Carnegie mills here are feeling much depressed over the notification given that their wages would be reduced.

The boiler men, who formerly received $2.25 per day, must now work for $1.89. The wages of the others are cut in proportion.

The assistant boss roller on one of the turns refused to go to work yesterday. His wages before the strike were $9 a day, but yesterday he was notified that they would be reduced to $4.

The reduction has created considerable excitement, but appearances do not indicate that it will further complicate the situation.

───────❖───────

From **The Saturday Globe,** *Utica, New York, July 9, 1892, a pro-union weekly. One of the nation's first illustrated papers, it had a national circulation of 150,000 which doubled with events like the Homestead Strike.*

FORTY-MILLIONAIRE CARNEGIE IN HIS GREAT DOUBLE ROLE.
AS THE TIGHT-FISTED EMPLOYER HE REDUCES WAGES THAT HE MAY PLAY PHILANTHROPIST AND GIVE AWAY LIBRARIES, ETC.

CRITCHLOW'S DEFENSE.

_____

IT IS TO PROVE THAT HE WAS NOT PRESENT DURING THE SHOOTING.

PITTSBURG, NOV. 22. —The Critchlow trial was continued to-day, the first witness being John Malley. He said he saw the defendant several times on July 6 with a gun in his hands.

A number of photographs were offered in evidence and also the bullets dug out of the barges by Capt. Cooper. Here the Commonwealth rested. George W. Argo of Sioux City opened for the defense.

"To me," said he, "is assigned the important duty of opening the defense in this most extraordinary case. I ought to explain the presence of Mr. Erwin and myself here. We were sent here by the laboring men of the Northwest to aid, so far as we can, this defendant."

Mr. Argo then told the story of the sending of the Pinkertons to Homestead, and continued: "We say this was an invasion by a foreign armed force; an assault on the county; an assault on the Commonwealth; an assault on the soil, and an assault on you and all the people of this county and State.

"This armed body of men who invaded this State were not employed as laborers. They were men who could not have been made Deputy Sheriffs. They were emissaries for what purpose? When they reached Homestead they made an attack on the people of this county and this State. So far as has been shown they were not there to protect property; there is no evidence to show what they were doing there. They were met by the good citizens of Homestead, and when they attempted to land they were met with resistance.

"We say all persons on the banks of the river when this armed body attempted to land had a right there; that each had a right to defend himself and all others present; that all had a right to use deadly weapons as their people on shore were attacked; they had a right to defend themselves and each other; that Critchlow had nothing to do with death of Connors.

"The evidence, so far as Critchlow is concerned, will be that about 9:30 A.M. July 6 he passed up the Munhall Road, crossed the ferry, went to Braddock, and remained there till noon and returned home; that he was not in the mill, was not present during the trouble; but that it was another Critchlow, not the defendant, whom witnesses say they saw behind the breastworks; that he did not fire a gun from behind such breastworks, and that he did not go on the barge, as has been testified to.

"That he passed along by the office gate on the morning of July 6, and that he had a gun is true; but he did not use it. He had no ammunition. We expect to prove by a witness that the shot which killed Connors came from the Braddock side."

Mr. Erwin then addressed the jury. He said in part: "The theory of the prosecution is that there was a riot. That is a doubly damned fiction. If there was a riot, Critchlow is on one side guilty, and those on the other side equally guilty. This is a fictitious attempt to shut out the truth from the jury. The wish to hide the cowardly, tyrannical, and unscrupulous conduct of Carnegie and Frick, and they expect this court to act as Pontius Pilate.

"Never since the days of Herod has there been such a hard-hearted, cold-blooded man as this man Frick. It is a most disgraceful thing to note that while this yeoman, this skilled worker, is here on trial for murder, this man Frick, who caused all the trouble, is hobnobbing with the heads of our Government. This man Frick, this brutal tyrant, dared to commit treason by bringing into the boarders of this State an armed body of men for his own private purpose."

When the case was resumed this afternoon, Mrs. Critchlow took a seat beside her husband and the two talked for some time.

. . .

The defense will probably close to-morrow morning, and the case may go to the jury in the evening. It is the opinion of Attorneys who have heard the evidence that Critchlow has proved a good alibi and that conviction is not probable.

———❖———

Sylvester Critchlow

THE CRITCHLOW TRIAL.

————

HIS DEFENSE WAS SIMPLY AN ALIBI.

————

SUMMING-UP SPEECHES WELL STOCKED WITH "FLAPDOODLE"—FRICK AND THE PINKERTONS COME IN FOR A GENERAL ROASTING BY THE DEFENSE.

PITTSBURG, NOV. 22. —The Critchlow trial was concluded to-day.

. . .

At 1 P. M. Attorney John S. Robb began his address to the jury. He said in part:

. . .

"It makes little difference in this case who fired the first shot, but there is no doubt in my mind that the first shooting came from the shore, and I am certain you believe me. The murder of J. T. Connor took place long after this first assault, and his murder was premeditated, deliberate, and willful.

"If the defendant was there that day, aiding and abetting, armed with a gun, and shooting, he is guilty of the crime with which he is charged. Six witnesses swear Critchlow was there and all swear he had a gun in his hands, and one witness swears he saw Critchlow behind the breastworks firing his gun through the portholes in the breastworks.

"Who says he was not there? He goes on the stand and picks out certain hours when he says he was not on the mill premises. He does not pretend to say he was not there at any time; he does not say where he was; he does not even corroborate his own witness who tries to prove an alibi; he does not say he did not have a gun; he does not say he did not fire at the barges; he does not say he did not fire the shot that killed Connor; he denies nothing but that at certain hours fixed by himself he was not in the mill yard."

William M. Erwin of Sioux Falls, S. D., for the defense said the jury could not presume that there was any strike at Homestead; it was not in evidence; there was no proof that there was any dissension. There was no evidence that Frick, who sends armed invaders to the shore of Homestead, had any property there. There was no evidence that the men, women, and children were there for unlawful purposes, but the Commonwealth said they must infer.

"Infer! A way to wink when logic could not speak! All the jury knew was that there were armed foreign invaders there. There was no evidence that those men were hired as watchmen. The absence of proof gives rise to the presumption that the people's territory had been invaded by armed foreign men—armed by Quartermaster Frick. Why he did not know, but presumed the purpose was so damnable that Frick would not dare to tell it before the open forum of the court.

"Was the battle at Homestead a riot or an invasion? If the latter, that's the end of it, for the people never delegated away their right to repel invasion. Unless the right of the Pinkertons to be there was made plain the people should have shot them down, should have shot them after leaving the barges, should have followed them to their hearthstones and shot them down there, should have shot them at God's own altar, and, if possible, should have followed them across the great boundary—should have followed them across the grave and shot them down as they lay on the bosom of the Prince of Hell.

"But in case you do not agree with me that the force was an illegal armed invasion, was there any organized resistance to the landing? Not a bit of evidence was introduced to show that. There was a cry of 'Scabs, you can't land.' There were no scabs there. No resistance to legally-authorized watchmen. The people were there; not for riot.

"The testimony is given by detectives, by that human hyena, the hunter of men, who will not do God's work—earn his bread by the sweat of his brow. These detectives are indicted, and so measure how far they will stretch the truth to prevent your jury from stretching their necks.

"The first shot came from the boat—aimed at what? Strikers? No; men, women, and children. God in heaven! Do you deny the right of those on shore to defend themselves? No! Hasten the defense. Fire, oil, and dynamite should be used upon these who fire on the people."

Mr. Erwin reviewed the evidence given by the witnesses for the prosecution, and argued to show much of it unworthy of belief. In conclusion, he said:

"I leave my client in your hands, and you in the higher hands of the Almighty."

———◆———

CRITCHLOW ACQUITTED.

————

OF THE MURDER OF CONNOR DURING THE HOMESTEAD RIOT.

————

PITTSBURG, NOV. 23. —The trial of Sylvester Critchlow, charged with murder in connection with the Homestead riot, was brought to a close this evening by the jury bringing in a verdict of acquittal. . . .

In his charge to the jury Judge Kennedy said: "A riot is the tumultuous assemblage of three or more persons for an unlawful purpose, and all persons who are present and not attempting to suppress it are prima facie participants and principals, and any one who joins the rioters after they are assembled is equally guilty. . . .

"If the jury is satisfied that the defendant took part in the riot of July 6, which resulted in the death of T. J. Connor, and that it was the common intent of such rioters to resist the landing of these men on the barges to the extent of taking life, then he is guilty of murder in the first degree, as are all who took part in such a riot.

"If you believe that there was no malice, that the killing was done in the heat of combat, then you can convict him of manslaughter. If you believe these rioters met for a common purpose to resist this landing, but not to the extent of taking life, then a verdict of murder in the second degree could be rendered."

He closed at 3:25 and the jury brought in the verdict at 6.

———◆———

THE LAW TAKES SIDES
by Robert S. Barker

In 1892, the law provided little protection for workers in their dealings with management. Labor relations were purely contractual in nature, and the law placed great stress on "liberty of contract"; that is, the freedom of employers and employees to agree on wages, hours, and working conditions, without government interference. The concept was regarded as so important that the United States Supreme Court found it to be part of the "due process of law" guaranteed by the Constitution, and courts routinely invalidated state and federal wages-and-hours laws, industrial health and safety laws, and laws prohibiting yellow-dog contracts, as unconstitutionally impairing "liberty of contract."

The ability of the federal government to protect workers was further limited by the Supreme Court's narrow interpretation (at least in labor matters) of the power of Congress to regulate interstate commerce, and by its broad interpretation of the Tenth Amendment's reservation of rights to the states. This approach led the courts to the conclusion that working conditions in manufacturing were purely local matters, beyond the authority of the national government.

In the early decades of the 19th century, attempts by workers in Pennsylvania to deal collectively with their employers were regarded as criminal conspiracies, and were often punished as such. Although a series of mid-century statutes decriminalized union activity, concerted action by workers could still result in the imposition of civil liability, and strikes were often bro-

ken by federal and state-court injunctions.

Despite this unfavorable setting, the Homestead lodges of the Amalgamated Association of Iron and Steel Workers, preparing in the spring of 1892 for negotiations with the Carnegie Steel Company, had no reason to suspect that the law would be a major factor in the matter. They believed that the wage scale—the only significant item in dispute—would be settled by direct, good-faith negotiations between the union and the company. In labor's view, the legal system would be a remote and neutral observer.

Management saw the situation differently. The Carnegie officials did not plan to engage in good-faith bargaining, and wages were of only secondary importance. The company's plan was to create the appearance of bargaining, force the talks to fail, lock-out the workers, raise its own private army, clothe the troops with public authority, occupy the Homestead works, import nonunion workers under cover of law, destroy the Amalgamated, and dictate terms to the workers. The first steps proceeded as planned: negotiations collapsed on June 24 because the company refused to talk further. When the old contract expired on June 30, the company locked-out the workers. Its mercenaries, the Pinkertons, began to move toward Homestead, but as private police, not deputy sheriffs. (Unfortunately, it was the sheriff's weakness and indecision, rather than any principled opposition to the misuse of public power, that left the Pinkertons undeputized when their barges arrived at Homestead.)

After the bloody confrontation of July 6, the company prevailed on government to carry out the remainder of its plan. The governor dispatched the entire Pennsylvania National Guard to Homestead. The announced purpose was to maintain the peace, but the Guard's real assignment was to provide cover for the introduction of nonunion workers into Homestead. National Guard officers conferred regularly with Carnegie managers and lawyers, but refused to meet with representatives of the union or to work with the burgess and council of Homestead.

Other public officials acted with the same partiality as the National Guard. Although it was by no means clear who fired the first shot at Homestead, when Carnegie officials filed murder, riot, and conspiracy charges against 167 steelworkers, the district attorney, the sheriff, and the judges moved vigorously against the accused. All were forced to spend time in jail, some were denied bail, and the grand jury was promptly summoned to indict all of them. In contrast, when the steelworkers filed similar and no-less-plausible charges against company officials, the officials were shown great courtesy, promptly admitted to bail, and permitted to go on their way. The cases against the company's men were not moved forward.

Perhaps the greatest abuses of public power concerned the treason charges. Major General George R. Snowden, commander of the National Guard troops at Homestead, suggested to company lawyers that the strikers be charged with treason

Sylvester Critchlow is escorted out of the court room while the jury confers. The trials of the Homestead labor leaders drew large audiences.

against the Commonwealth. The company prevailed upon the Chief Justice of Pennsylvania to take the unusual steps of assuming the powers of a judge of the Court of Oyer and Terminer of Allegheny County and, in the presence of his Supreme Court colleagues, summoning a county detective to file charges of treason against 33 strikers. Having thus intervened, the chief justice remained in charge, hearing all bail petitions and personally instructing the grand jury. The Pennsylvania Constitution expressly provided that the members of the Supreme Court were ex officio judges of the courts of oyer and terminer in each of the counties of the state. But that provision was intended to enable the highest court to act when the local courts could not. In Allegheny County in 1892 there was no reason to believe that the local judges could not handle whatever business might come before them. The intervention of the chief justice and his associates, gratuitously and in connection with highly improbable charges, was meant to send the message that the entire judicial system was arrayed against the workers.

The chief justice instructed the grand jury that the company had the right to lock-out its employees and to protect its property by the use of whatever armed force it considered appropriate. As to the workers, the chief justice said:

". . . [W]hen a large number of men arm and organize themselves by divisions and companies, appoint officers and engage in a common purpose to defy the law, to resist its officers, and to deprive any portion of their fellow-citizens of the rights to which they are entitled under the Constitution and laws, it is a levying of war against the state, and the offense is treason. [Commonwealth V. O'Donnell]"

This expansive and imaginative definition went well beyond the accepted juridical meaning of treason. Be that as it may, a less partisan jurist, applying the same rationale, might have concluded that the list of "traitors" should be expanded. The company had violated its common-law duty to deal in good faith with the other party to the contract, the Amalgamated, thereby depriving the workers of their rights under traditional con-

tract law. The company organized an armed force and sent it in opposition to the wishes of the duly-constituted authorities of the Borough of Homestead.

In fact and in law, there were no traitors at Homestead; but the charges against the workers were taken seriously by some of the highest authorities of the Commonwealth. At the same time, and in spite of the facts, it seems not to have occurred to those same officials that there might have been wrongdoing on the company's side as well.

While the treason charges were pending, the murder cases against the workers moved forward. The grand jury returned indictments, and on November 18 the district attorney, aided by Carnegie Company lawyers, proceeded to trial against Sylvester Critchlow, a steelworker, for allegedly shooting and killing one of the Pinkertons. After a lengthy trial, it took the jury but one hour to find the defendant not guilty. On February 2, 1893, another Homestead steelworker, Jack Clifford, went on trial. He too was acquitted. Undaunted, the district

(The Law, continued)
attorney proceeded against the leader of the union's advisory committee, Hugh O'Donnell. Again the verdict was, "not guilty." Faced with three successive acquittals, the Carnegie Company abandoned its litigation, and, with the agreement of all concerned, all criminal prosecutions ceased.

The Homestead saga demonstrates that the law is always in danger of being subverted. The most obvious danger is posed by those of power and influence who would make public officials mere agents of private interests, and by public officials who would abdicate their responsibilities out of fear or in expectation of gain. A more subtle, and perhaps greater threat comes not from the corrupt, but from the righteous. Most of the judges and scholars who read "liberty of contract" into the Constitution, and who imposed unique limits on the commerce power where labor was concerned, were honorable people who believed that their theories would benefit society; but they burdened the Constitution with rules that had more to do with personal and partisan politics than with anything in the Constitution itself.

The legal system was vindicated, in the aftermath of Homestead, not by those of learning and power who moved every day through the halls of justice, but by the jurors who acquitted Critchlow, Clifford, and O'Donnell. Those three dozen citizens, picked at random for temporary service, reminded all who would listen that the heart of the law is common sense fairness. It was that sense of fairness that gave the law, and those who loved and respected it, the strength to survive the events of 1892 and to move forward to happier days. ❖

NOVEMBER 24, 1892 —Reprinted from the **Pittsburgh Catholic.**

THE STRUGGLE ENDED.

————

The long struggle at Homestead is at an end. It was a hard fought struggle that lasted twenty weeks, and cost a score of lives and millions in money. The local Amalgamated lodges have decided by a close vote to open the mills and all the old employes may apply for work. While the company is giving the men requesting work a hearing, Manager Schwab finds that he will have to disappoint the majority of them. The old positions of renumeration are gone, and many in their necessity will be compelled to make the best terms they can. Very many unfortunately, will not be taken back. The step taken this week should have been done three months ago. But, buoyed up by hopes of assistance from the outside, which did not materialize, judgment was lacking, and prudence overlooked. It was a noble set of the 3,000 men, the laborers and mechanics, who went out in sympathy with the Amalgamated men, and sacrificed so much for the men who were directly affected by the strike. But sympathy, however noble, becomes the rashest of virtues when not judiciously exercised.

There is now no need to go into the merits or demerits of this strike. It only remains to build up and make good the losses incurred. From a business standpoint the loss is bad. Here we see a once thriving town reduced almost to beggary, its houses tenantless, its business men bankrupt, and what is worse the taint of misrule and lawless violence over all. This is the mournful part. It has hurt honest labor, weakened its cause, and given it a blow it will take a long time to recover from. But if a lesson is learned which will be heeded in the future, that only through peaceful methods can the right be maintained in this country, then the lesson of Homestead and its unfortunate history will not be in vain. The recuperative power of these workmen will yet restore them their prosperity now, apparently, but not hopelessly lost. ❖

DECEMBER 9, 1892 —*Reprinted from* **The Pittsburg Press.**

IN HUMANITY'S NAME.

_____

The Press Appeals for Aid for Suffering Homestead.

_____

EXTREME DESTITUTION IN THE UNFORTUNATE BOROUGH

_____

What the Investigation of a Press Reporter Revealed.

_____

WOMEN AND CHILDREN WHO WANT FOR BREAD.

_____

The Work of Relief Far Greater Than the Local Committee Can Undertake.

_____

PRIDE SEALS THE LIPS OF STARVING MEN AND WOMEN.

_____

The Press Starts the Relief Fund With a Contribution of One Hundred Dollars.

_____

SOLOMON & RUBEN ADD ONE HUNDRED DOLLARS MORE.

_____

Unconditional surrender!
—*From the Chicago Times.*

Reprinted from **The Inside History of the Carnegie Steel Company,** *by James Howard Bridge.*

"The strike is over," familiar heading this to those who read of Homestead. Yes, it is over but the train of evil and misfortune which must follow in its wake has just begun.

What of those who took part in the disastrous effort to secure what they deemed their rights? Some—a comparative few—are back in their old positions, thankful they were not turned away with the cold answer "There is no work for you," but in Homestead there are to-day 1,800 men, most of them with families for whom no employment can be found. For many of them the Christmas prospect is an empty cupboard and a cheerless hearth. For many of them there is even now an empty cupboard.

But it is not of the men of Homestead, unfortunate though they be, that the *Press* would speak. It is of their suffering families; the wives and children who sit in once prosperous homes, lamenting, starving—the words are not too strong; they are not strong enough, for those who have seen and heard.

Along the river banks, where the big mills are located, there is a scene of activity; the wheels are turning; the rolls are revolving, and above all the buildings and machinery can be seen the steam clouds, the smoke clouds. It is down in those yards, a lost paradise to the hungry men who stand outside and watch what they so well know is a positive reality—a successful resumption of work in the great steel plant which for months they tried to hold silent.

They see in the effort a failure. Whose failure was it that it was not otherwise, the *Press* is not disposed to examine into now. Employer or employed—it is not the question. Graver is the situation that confronts the people of Homestead—Want.

The wolf is at the door; innocent children, hard-working mothers, fathers who in the majority of cases simply obeyed higher authorities—all are suffering in the land of plenty.

Around us in this prosperous city the heralds of a great anniversary are announcing "peace on earth, good will to men"; eight miles away, mothers sit wringing their hands in a grief the sight of which effects you all the more because it is the grief of the proud, the grief that will not ask for alms, yet needing them.

For these unhappy ones, with the Christmastide bringing humanity closer together, there should be sympathy, practical sympathy. It will not do to say,

(In Humanity's Name, continued)

"I am sorry for the poor creatures." Sorrow don't clothe children, don't feed the hungry.

And the *Press* wants to say that, unless there is something done, 100—yes, 200—families in Homestead and at Munhall, within one month, will be as badly off for the necessaries of life as were the Russian peasants, who in the famine, so lately appealed, and not in vain, to American sympathy for aid. Personal investigation is sufficient to establish this as a fact, not a possible condition of affairs.

A member of the *Press* staff who was sent to Homestead the other day to investigate the condition of those who, after the long and weary fight was over, found themselves out in the cold, rents due and not paid; grocers, butchers and other tradesmen who had been advancing the necessaries of life willingly, hoping that all would come out all right in the end, also unpaid. These people were only low-priced laborers; but as is always the case with the poor, they are blessed with large families, and the end came too quickly. Poor or rich, no man wants to ask for charity.

. . .

But the winter is approaching and 1,800 men, with families, out of work—what is the outlook? The question is repeated.

You would like to read the narrative of a day spent in Homestead? You shall read it. If you, who are wealthy, sleep soundly upon the reading; if you look forward to a happy Christmas, not having put forth a helping hand, your turkey ought to choke you.

The *Press* reporter was met at the headquarters of the Homestead and Union mills' relief and aid committee, on Sixth avenue, by several of the members. Among them were President David Lynch, Secretary George Hadfield and a number of others who were interested in the work of relieving those who were unfortunate.

. . .

"We need everything," said Mr. Hadfield. "We need clothing and coal; we need flour, potatoes, everything in fact. Money is needed. Many are sick and unable to obtain medicines because they have no money. I want you to visit some of the houses of the suffering people and see for yourself what is needed. The time is now, not a month later."

A committee, consisting of three men, William Johnson, Edward Kauts and William Bakewell, went with the writer. "Look for yourself, ask for yourself," said Mr. Kunts, as we started out. Half way up Eighth avenue we met a man, and Mr. Johnson said to the writer: "I will ask him some questions. Listen."

"How are you doing this morning, Mr.—?"

"Can't complain, William; can't complain."

"But speak out, man; are you in want?"

The man's lips twitched; his face grew white, and he said in reply: "William, I haven't anything in my house to eat. Now, that's the God's truth. You can go and see for yourself."

"How much of a family have you?" asked the writer.

"Six children and a wife, sir."

An hour later a visit was made to the house. A woman with an intelligent face, a room that was tidy and neat, several children sitting about the room—that was what was seen.

Mr. Johnson is a kind-hearted man, but he came to the point at once and asked how they were faring. "Speak the truth, woman," and she did. Without looking up she said that there wasn't a scrap of anything in the house for the dinner. Everything was gone. It didn't take long to see that she was telling the truth. The hopeful eyes of the children, who guessed that help was coming, showed it, Mr. Bakewell made a few entries in his book, and said that food would be sent before noon, and it was.

"We will go up this valley," said Mr. Johnson. "There are dozens of such places as we have just now left. I'll ask this man coming there," and he pointed ahead to a stout-looking, middle-aged man, "how he is fixed."

"Well, men, it is no use keeping it back. I have enough to eat to-day, but to-morrow will find my family without a bite in the house."

He was promised help, and then a house was visited in which a man lay ill with the typhoid fever. He had a wife and two children. His story was a sad one. He had not applied for help, but when pressed, told his story. "I had saved up considerable money, and last spring thought I would visit England. I came back and was only here a short time till the strike came. I stayed out like the others. Then my two children took sick and I had a doctor to pay. In September I took the fever and all my money soon went and now I owe a doctor bill of $98. I have had a hard time and so has my wife. We have no money and my wife is ashamed to go to the store for more goods on credit. The doctor says I need beef tea and something to build me up. How can I get it? We need something to eat and I am sorry to say it, if we don't get it there will be dreadful times in our family."

He was a handsome young man and his wife was a model of neatness; convalescent, but without food. It was hard for him to accept a situation that he could not avoid. The committee promised to see that he got something stronger than the plain white bread that was the only article of food in the house.

. . .

The *Press* will receive, acknowledge and superintend the disbursement of any contributions for the relief of the Homestead sufferers which may be sent to its main office, No. 79 Fifth avenue. It heads the subscription list with a contribution of $100. Let every friend of humanity join hands with it and help to swell the fund.

———❖———

DECEMBER 12, 1892 —Reprinted from **The New-York Times.**

POISONED AT HOMESTEAD.

－－－－

Strikers Charged With A Terrible Conspiracy.

－－－－

A COOK IN THE CARNEGIE WORKS CONFESSES TO HAVING POISONED THE FOOD OF NON-UNION MEN–SIX DEATHS BELIEVED TO BE DUE TO HIS WORKS– ARRESTS TO BE MADE.

PITTSBURG, DEC. 11. —A Sunday paper published a startling story to-day of a conspiracy to poison, by wholesale, the non-union men at the Carnegie steel plant in Homestead. The developments may, it is said, implicate members of the Advisory Committee, members of the Amalgamated Association, and officers of some of the labor organizations sympathizing with the locked-out men at Homestead.

As a result of this conspiracy, it is alleged that several persons have lost their lives, while scores of others are still suffering at their homes and in hospitals from the effects of poisonous drugs administered to them with criminal intent. To-day nine or more persons, more or less identified with the strike, are under arrest, ostensibly on less serious charges, but really for the purpose of averting suspicion until all who are claimed to be in the conspiracy have been secured. The only name given of those charged with administering poison is Robert Beatty, who was arrested at Louisville last night.

Several others, however, are under heavy bail on other charges, and the new charge will probably be made, as all are under surveillance and can be taken at any moment.

It will be remembered that soon after the arrival of the State militia at Homestead and the non-union men had commenced to work in the mills, complaints became prevalent about the unwholesome water supplied to the men, especially to those who lived within the fence surrounding the plant.

Many cases of sickness were reported, but they were all attributed to the impurity of the water. So firmly impressed were the physicians and the officials of the company that the water was causing the sickness that a supply from other sources was secured, and notices were posted conspicuously about the mill warning the employes to refrain from drinking the water.

Despite this precaution the sickness continued, and soon it became current at Homestead that an epidemic was prevailing among the men within the inclosure. A number of the sick were taken to the hospitals for treatment, and nearly all recovered, although many of them are still ill. There being rumors that typhoid and other diseases were epidemic in the mill, a representative of the State Board of Health made an official investigation. He found the sanitary arrangements good and attributed the sickness to the water.

The first intimation that the officers had that the diagnosis of the physicians was incorrect, and that the men were the victims of a conspiracy to poison that was being persistently and successfully executed, was obtained more than two month's ago. It came in such a manner, however, that it was impossible to make arrests immediately, and it was not until yesterday that the evidence was deemed to be sufficiently strong to warrant the apprehension of at least one of those who are alleged to have been implicated in the conspiracy to get rid of the hated non union men either by death or by creating such a panic among them that they would flee from the fated place in a body. The price to be paid when the mills were closed down was $5,000.

The plot, according to the information obtained by the reporter from a man who was in the conspiracy, was substantially as follows:

The informant said that one of the chief cooks at the Homestead works with whom he was intimately acquainted met him in the city one day and asked if he did not want a job at Homestead. He said he wanted at least two assistants, and said the informant and his friend could make big money if they would help him. He told them he was not only employed by the Carnegie Company, but was also in the pay of the labor associations and members of the strikers' committees, and was just coining money. As he grew more confidential, and, prompted by the questions about the pay from the associations, he told of a plan to poison the food of the men employed in the mill so as to make them sick and render them unable to work. He detailed the plan he had been pursuing, and asserted that nearly if not all the sickness among the men, of which reports had been current, was caused by the poisons he had placed in the food. He said he was to get $5,000 if he succeeded in closing the mill.

. . .

They said that the death of some of the men had unnerved him, and they believed he would make a clean breast of the whole plot if he was summoned to the office and placed under arrest.

This was done, and when confronted with the facts as stated above, the cook broke down and made a full confession, in which he gave the names of those who had employed him, the amount of money he had received, and the manner in which he had carried out his part of the crime. He stated also that he frequently visited the camps of the militia and dosed the food prepared in the cookhouse. His visits were always followed by increased sickness among the members of the National Guard. This confession was taken by a stenographer in the presence of several witnesses. He also exhibited vouchers for the money due him.

. . .

Charles Glosser died two weeks after going to Homestead. It is said that since the confession made by the cook the body has been exhumed and the stomach submitted to a chemist for analysis. The result of the analysis is not known, but it is said the chemist's report will be submitted in evidence when the case comes up for trial. . . .

E. I. Beck, Esq., counsel for the Carnegie Steel Company, Limited, was seen to-night and confirmed the story of the poisoning. He says his information is that at least six deaths resulted from poisoning. A Homestead druggist and physician are implicated. The powder was given to a dog and it died in a few minutes. A number of arrests will probably be made in a few days.

－－－－❖－－－－

JANUARY 31, 1893 —Excerpted from The Local News, *Homestead.*

WILL VISIT HOMESTEAD.

———

Andrew Carnegie Arrives Here This Morning.

———

Accompanied by Company Stockholders—The Mills May Be Inspected—A Statement Made in Pittsburg—What He Has to Say of the Strike—No Power to Interfere in the Management of the Works.

———

Andrew Carnegie is expected to visit the Homestead steel mills this morning. He will be accompanied by H. C. Frick, chairman of the company, Henry Phipps, Jr., and George Lauder, stockholders.

On Saturday Messrs. Phipps and Lauder came up from the city and went immediately to the main office. A conference, which lasted about an hour was held with Superintendent C. M. Schwab in his private office. The two gentlemen then returned to Pittsburg. It is probable that arrangements were then made for the trip of the stockholders to-day. The party will arrive here about 9 o'clock and will make an inspection of the mills. How long they will remain or whether there is any special business on hand could not be learned.

The following statement was given out by Andrew Carnegie in Pittsburg on Sunday afternoon:

I did not come to Pittsburg to rake up, but to try to bury the past, of which I knew nothing. That is beyond recall, it should be banished as a horrid dream and only the lessons that it teaches laid to heart for the future. For 26 years our concerns have run with only one labor stoppage at one of the numerous works, and I trust and believe that even this record will be fully equalled in the 25 years to come. When employer and employed become antagonistic, each considering the other its enemy, it is a contest between twin brothers. There is no genuine victory possible for either but defeat for both capital and labor.

. . .

When I could not bring my associates in business to my views by reason, I have never wished to do so by force. As for instructing or compelling them, under the law, to do one thing or another, that is simply absurd. I could not do it if I would, and I would not do it if I could.

A STOCKHOLDER, BUT NOT ACTIVE.

I am still a holder of a majority of the shares of the Carnegie Steel Company Limited, never having changed my policy of concentration. I made my first dollar in Pittsburg, and I expect to make my last one here, and as long as my young partners are willing or desire my capital to remain in the business, it shall so remain, and they shall always have my best advice when asked, gratis. . . .

I have hoarded nothing, and shall never accumulate money. I shall not die rich apart from my interest in the business which may still be had at my death. Much has been said about my fortune. I have plenty only if the works in Pittsburg are prosperous; unless they are, I have nothing, and that is how I elect to stand. All my eggs are in one basket, right here in Western Pennsylvania. I take my chances with my partners. And I have the satisfaction of knowing that the first charge upon every dollar of my capital is still the payment of the highest earnings paid to labor in any part of the world for similar services. Upon that record I am proud to stand.

SPEAKS OF FRICK.

And now, one word about Mr. Frick, whom I recommended to the Carnegie Steel Company, Limited, as its chairman, and my successor, four years ago. I am not mistaken in the man, as the future will show. Of his ability, firmness and pluck no one has now the slightest question. His four years management stamps him as one of the foremost managers in the world—I would not exchange him for any manager I know. People generally are still to learn of those virtues which his partners and friends know well. If his health be spared, I predict that no man who ever lived in Pittsburg and managed business there will be better liked or more admired by his employes than my friend and partner, Henry Clay Frick, nor do I believe any man will be more valuable for the city. His are the qualities that wear; he never disappoints; what he promises he more than fulfills. Good workmen or able men, who wish to do what is fair and right, will learn to appreciate Mr. Frick. Inefficient officials or bad, unreasonable, violent workmen he does not like, and these will not thrive with him.

CAN'T INTERFERE.

I hope after this statement that the public will understand that the officials of the Carnegie Steel Company Limited, with Mr. Frick as their head, are not dependent upon me, or upon any one, in any way, for their positions, and that I have neither power nor disposition to interfere with them in the management of the business. And further, that I have the most implicit faith in them. I hope also that I shall be thought a very wise man in having retired from the care of business before old age set in, and that the public will agree that a record of 40 years of hard work entitles one to devote his remaining years to less exacting and more congenial pursuits. We know, however, upon the best authority, that where the treasure is, there will the heart be also. Well, all my treasure is here, in and around Pittsburg, and my heart, wherever I go, can never be very far off, and this I can most truthfully say, that one of the chief thoughts of my life must always be, how I can best repay the inextinguishable debt I owe to the once again smoky, but still dear old Pittsburg.

———❖———

Orson Lowell's drawing, "Corner of Library and of Dining-Room in one of the Company's Boarding Houses," 1894.

THE FATE OF THE PRINCIPAL CHARACTERS

by Steffi Domike and Nicole Fauteux

"Here the atmosphere was at times heavy with disappointment and hopelessness. Some of the men seemed afraid to talk. . . . The absence of freedom resembled that of the small mining villages in the eastern part of the State. . . . If all that I saw while with the managers of the Carnegie works might be described under the title of 'Triumphant Democracy,' nearly all that I saw while with the men might be described under the title of 'Feudalism Restored.'"

—Charles B. Spahr, America's Working People, 1900.

Charles Spahr's impressions of Homestead were recorded in 1899, only seven years after the strike. His portraits of the people of Homestead as fearful and dominated by the company stand in marked contrast to the fiercely independent community depicted by observers in 1892.

The new regime had taken its toll. Leaders of the 1892 strike had been blacklisted by the Carnegie Company and excluded from steel mills across the country. One of these leaders, Tom Crawford, was able to secure work at the Uniontown Steel Company before the strike was called off in November 1892, but many leaders of the Amalgamated were forced to leave the steel industry and their homes. Several were still idle when journalist Arthur Burgoyne completed his account in 1893.

When interviewed in 1899 by Charles Spahr, Crawford was working as a roller in a small shop and had returned to live in Homestead. Because he had already been blacklisted, he was free, unlike most citizens, to criticize conditions in the town and the mills, and went so far as to question Carnegie's largesse in donating the Homestead Carnegie Library. "I have always hoped to educate myself, but after my day's work, I haven't been able to do much studying . . . After working twelve hours, how can a man go to a library?"

Burgess John McLuckie did not run for re-election in Homestead, but remained active in politics. In November 1893 he campaigned for the Democrats. His subsequent involvement with the Free-Silver campaign brought him into contact with Emma Goldman. In Living My Life, Goldman recounts how he tried to recruit her as a spokesperson for the cause. She refused the offer, but the meeting brought other satisfactions. McLuckie gained an understanding of Berkman's motives in his attack on Frick and Goldman learned firsthand why her lover's deed was so poorly received in Homestead.

McLuckie's political endeavors did not bring in a steady income and, as he was barred from working in the steel industry, he soon joined the ranks of the poor. Following the death of his wife, he moved to Mexico where he remarried. In the spring of 1900 he was living in Guayamas, driving wells for the Sonora Railway. There he was discovered by an acquaintance of Carnegie who subsequently offered

(The Fate, continued)

him money. McLuckie refused to accept it. In his autobiography, Carnegie reported the following exchange:

"No, no," said the modest McLuckie. "I don't want assistance. I'm very much obliged to you, professor, but I'm making good and can continue to do so, if the Lord gives me health."

"Why, the offer comes from Mr. Carnegie," answered Prof.VanDyke.

"Well, that was damned white of Andy!" exclaimed McLuckie.

To Carnegie, McLuckie's words implied that he had been kind to one of his workmen. He declared that they should be inscribed on his tombstone. "I would rather risk that verdict of McLuckie's as a passport to Paradise than all the theological dogmas invented by man."

William Weihe resigned as president of the Amalgamated Association of Iron & Steel Workers after the strike in 1892. In 1897 he was working as an organizer for the United Mine Workers in western Pennsylvania. Two years later he was a member of the arbitration committee that settled a strike with Carnegie, Phipps & Company. He ended his career as an immigration inspector at Ellis Island. Weihe died in Pittsburgh in 1908.

There are sparse accounts of the fate of other unionists. Little is known of the controversial Hugh O'Donnell. Unable to find work in any steel mill in the country, he left Homestead to manage a concert company, then moved to Chicago to write for a weekly journal. Later he moved back East and much of the time made his living as a reporter. Another Amalgamated member, George DeBolt (frequently misspelled as Diebold), who had been indicted in the deaths of striker Silas Wain and Pinkerton guard T. J. Connors, remained in Homestead. Unable to find steady

work, he founded his own transportation company in 1897. A century later the family business is still intact, and DeBolt's grandson is a leader in the local business community.

The Carnegie Company offered most of the remaining strikers jobs in the mill. The general superintendent of the Homestead Works, John A. Potter, was appointed chief mechanical engineer of the Carnegie Co. in November 1892 and replaced by Charles M. Schwab, the former superintendent of the Edgar Thomson Works. As manager of the Homestead Works, Schwab refused to honor his predecessor's guarantees of permanent employment to the nonunion replacements. By early 1893 he had discharged them and rehired many of the experienced workers who lost their jobs at the time of the strike.

After the Homestead Strike of 1892, the business lives of Andrew Carnegie and Henry C. Frick became overtly acrimonious. Even before the final fracture in 1900 that led the two down different paths, Frick and Carnegie had little in common. Although Frick's hard line against organized labor in the coking fields was well known and was one of the reasons Carnegie had asked him to manage the 1892 negotiations with the Homestead workers, Carnegie privately blamed Frick for the bloodshed. Frick was more than a little annoyed when, at the dedication of the Carnegie Library of Homestead in 1898, Carnegie asserted that if he had been present, the tragic events of July 6th would never have occurred.

The differences between the two entrepreneurs went well beyond Homestead. Frick opposed Carnegie's constant war with the railroads. Against Carnegie's express commands, Frick supported partner Henry Oliver's brilliant proposals to acquire the Mesaba iron ore mines.

Their final split came over the substance that had originally brought them together—coke. In October 1899, Frick and Carnegie had agreed on a price at which this essential ingredient of steelmaking would be sold by the Frick Coke Company to the Carnegie Steel Company. Carnegie then sought assurances that if the market price should drop, so would the price that the steel giant would have to pay. Frick refused to sign the amended agreement and charged Carnegie the ever-rising market price for coke. Infuriated, Carnegie then invoked what was known as the "iron-clad agreement" signed with all Carnegie partners since his early days with the Kloman brothers. Under the terms of the agreement, any partner's shares could be bought out at book price with agreement from three fourths of the board. With the partnership grossly undercapitalized, Frick stood to lose millions of dollars.

The widely publicized legal battle that ensued was eventually settled; the two companies were merged and recapitalized at $320,000,000. Frick remained a stockholder but was barred from ever holding an official position with the corporation. From this moment forward Frick and Carnegie never saw each other again. In the spring of 1901, shortly after Frick's departure, the Carnegie Steel Corporation was sold to railroad millionaire J.P. Morgan for $400,000,000.

Frick moved to New York, fearing that his valuable art collection at Clayton would be damaged by the foul air of Pittsburgh, and built a mansion on Fifth Avenue to house it. In 1901 he served as a senior advisor to J.P. Morgan in the formation of United States Steel, Carnegie Steel's successor, and later sat on that corporation's board of directors. With his old friend Andrew Mellon, he built the much smaller, but viable Union Steel Company, which was purchased by U.S. Steel in 1902.

Although involved in the steel business until 1901, Andrew Carnegie devoted most of his life after 1892 to his writing and to philanthropic and political activities. He revised and republished his first collection, Triumphant Democracy, in 1893 and continued writing and collecting his other previously published essays for republication. The volume that incorporates his most widely read work, The Gospel of Wealth *(whose lead essay was originally published in 1889)* outlines Carnegie's perceived mission in life: to properly administer his wealth for the good of society. Consistent with his intent, Carnegie continued to build free libraries and music halls. He gave the Carnegie Institute to Pittsburgh in 1896, founded the Carnegie Trade Schools in 1900, and the Carnegie Institution in Washington in 1902. Throughout his life Carnegie, who was an accomplished public speaker, used the podium to fervently defend capitalism as well as to promote the gold standard or more progressive issues such as the rights of Blacks and world peace. Before his death in Lenox, Massachusetts, on August 11, 1919, Andrew Carnegie had given away over $350 million, almost 90 percent of his fortune. In a curious twist of fate, one of America's greatest capitalists is buried in Sleepy Hollow Cemetery, Tarrytown, New York, next to Samuel Gompers, first president of the American Federation of Labor.

And what of Alexander Berkman and his cause? Berkman was released from prison on May 18, 1906. As leading proponents of anarchism in the United States, he and Emma Goldman continued to promote their controversial brand of politics through publications and speaking tours. Although anarchism never developed a serious following in this country, it sowed the seeds of many other movements. The impact of anarchists on U.S. politics can be measured by the important role they continued to play in supporting free speech for radical dissidents, opposing the draft during World War I and promoting workers' rights through organizations like the International Workers of the World.

In 1917 Berkman was arrested a second time, charged with conspiracy for his opposition to the draft, and sentenced to two years in prison. While he was still serving this sentence, immigration officials moved to deport him. On December 2, 1919, a judge ordered that Berkman, Goldman, and 247 other immigrant radicals be deported together to Russia. By a strange coincidence, Frick passed away earlier that day. When news of his death reached Berkman, the anarchist is said to have remarked, "Well anyhow he left the country before I did." ❖

Alexander Berkman and a friend at a demonstration held by the International Workers of the World [IWW] in Tarrytown, New York, June 6, 1914.

—A lady writes: "It remains to be seen however, what judgement will be meted out by the unbiased chronicler of the future, to the little town on the Monongahela, that has had the temerity to rise up and assert its rights— rights if not legal, why certainly moral—in the presence of mighty capital. The difference between a good deed and a bad deed, like individuals, is often dependent upon surrounding circumstances, the result nevertheless, is what makes or adds glory or dishonor to the deed. How will it be with Homestead?"

JULY 16, 1892 —**The Local News,** *Homestead, editorial page.*

Pay line at the Homestead Works around 1908.

Excerpted from **Homestead,** *Chapter XVII, by Arthur G. Burgoyne, originally published by Rawsthorne Engraving and Printing Company, Pittsburgh, 1893.*

KEARN'S ACT, MAY 1893.

The Pennsylvania legislature, which assembled in January, 1893, was obliged to meet the Pinkerton question squarely. All the members of the lower branch of that body—the House of Representatives—and one-half of the members of the senate came fresh from the people, having been chosen in the November elections, and a large proportion of them stood pledged to their constituents to aid in the passage of an anti-Pinkerton bill. Many measures of this character were introduced, but that upon which support was centered, by common consent, was a bill introduced by Representative John Kearns, of Pittsburgh, a gentleman in close touch with organized labor. The Kearns bill was entitled "An Act relative to the appointing of special deputies, marshals, detectives or policemen by sheriffs, mayors or other persons authorized by law to make such appointments, and by individuals, associations or corporations incorporated under the laws of this State or any other State of the United States, and making it a misdemeanor for persons to exercise the functions of an officer without authority."

SECTION 1. Be it enacted by the Senate and House of Representatives of the Commonwealth of Pennsylvania in General Assembly met, and it is hereby enacted by the authority of the same, That no sheriff of a county, mayor of a city, or other person authorized by law to appoint special deputies, marshals or policemen in this Commonwealth to preserve the public peace and prevent or quell public disturbances, and no individuals, association, company or corporation incorporated under the laws of this State or of any other State of the United States and doing business in this State, shall hereafter appoint or employ any person who shall not be a citizen of this Commonwealth.

SECTION 2. That any person who shall in this Commonwealth without due authority pretend or hold himself out to any one as a deputy sheriff, marshal, policeman, constable or peace officer, shall be declared guilty of misdemeanor.

SECTION 3. Any person or persons, company, association, or any person in the employ of such a company or association violating any of the provisions of this act shall be guilty of a misdemeanor and upon conviction shall be sentenced to pay a fine not exceeding five hundred dollars, or undergo an imprisonment not exceeding one year, or both or either at the discretion of the court.

Provided, That if any company or association is convicted under this act it shall be sentenced to pay a fine not exceeding five thousand dollars.

Provided further, That the provisions of this act shall not be construed as applying to policemen, constables or specials appointed by municipalities for municipal purposes. ❖

JUNE 1894 —Excerpted from an article by Hamlin Garland in
McClure's Magazine, **Vol. 3, No. 1.**

HOMESTEAD AND ITS PERILOUS TRADES

IMPRESSIONS OF A VISIT.

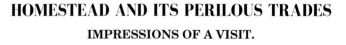

The streets of the town were horrible; the buildings were poor; the sidewalks were sunken, swaying, and full of holes, and the crossings were sharp-edged stones set like rocks in a river bed. Everywhere the yellow mud of the street lay kneaded into a sticky mass, through which groups of pale, lean men slouched in faded garments, grimy with the soot and grease of the mills.

The town was as squalid and unlovely as could well be imagined, and the people were mainly of the discouraged and sullen type to be found everywhere labor passes into the brutalizing stage of severity. It had the disorganized and incoherent effect of a town which has feeble public spirit. Big industries at differing eras have produced squads of squalid tenement-houses far from the central portion of the town, each plant bringing its gangs of foreign laborers in raw masses to camp down like an army around its shops.

Such towns are sown thickly over the hill-lands of Pennsylvania, but this was my first descent into one of them. They are American only in the sense in which they represent the American idea of business.

· · ·

Up at the pits again I stood to watch the "heaters" at their task. The crane and the travellers handled these huge pieces of iron deftly and surely, and moulded them into shape, as a girl might handle a cake of dough. Machinery has certainly come in here to lessen the horrors of the iron-worker's life, to diminish the number of deaths by exploding metal or by the leap of curling or breaking beams.

I watched the men as they stirred the deeps beneath. I could not help admiring the swift and splendid action of their bodies. They had the silence and certainty one admires in the tiger's action. I dared not move for fear of flying metal, the swift swing of a crane, or the sudden lurch of a great carrier. The men could not look out for me. They worked with a sort of desperate attention and alertness.

"That looks like hard work," I said to one of them to whom my companion introduced me. He was breathing hard from his work.

"Hard! I guess it's hard. I lost forty pounds the first three months I came into this business. It sweats the life out of a man. I often drink two buckets of water during twelve hours; the sweat drips through my sleeves, and runs down my legs and fills my shoes."

"But that isn't the worst of it," said my guide; "it's a dog's life." Now, those men work twelve hours, and sleep and eat out ten more. You can see a man don't have much time for anything else. You can't see your friends, or do anything but work. That's why I got out of it. I used to come home so exhausted, staggering like a man with a 'jag.' It ain't any place for a sick man—is it Joe?"

· · ·

Everywhere were grimy men with sallow and lean faces. The work was of the inhuman sort that hardens and coarsens.

"How long do you work?" I asked of a young man who stood at the furnace near me.

"Twelve hours," he replied. "The night set go on at six at night and come off at six in the morning. I go on at six and off at six."

"For how much pay?"

"Two dollars and a quarter."

"How much do those men get shoveling there in the rain?"

"One dollar and forty cents." (A cut has since taken place.)

"What portion of the men get that pay?"

Orson Lowell illustrated Hamlin Garland's article in the June 1894 issue of McClure's Magazine *with a series of drawings of life in Homestead. The one above was captioned "Up the Street from the Ferry Landing."*

"Two-thirds of the whole plant, nearly two thousand. There are thirty-five hundred men in the mills. They get all prices, of course, from a dollar forty cents up to the tonnage men, who get five and ten dollars per day when the mills run smooth."

"I suppose not many men make ten dollars per day."

"Well, hardly." He smiled. "Of course the 'rollers' and the 'heaters' get the most, but there are only two 'rollers' to each mill, and three 'heaters,' and they are responsible for their product. The most of the men get under two dollars per day."

"And it is twelve hours' work without stop?"

"You bet! And then again you see we only get this pay part of the time. The mills are liable to be shut down part of the year. They shut down part of the night sometimes, and of course we're docked."

. . .

As night fell the scene became still more grandiose and frightful. I hardly dared move without direction. The rosy ingots, looking like stumps of trees reduced to coals of living fire rose from their pits of flame and dropped upon the tables, and galloped head on against the rollers, sending off flakes of rosy scale. As they went through, the giant engine thundered on, reversing with a sound like a near-by cannon; and everywhere the jarring clang of great beams fell upon the ear. Wherever the saw was set at work, great wheels of fire rose out of the obscure murk of lower shadow.

"I'm glad I don't have to work here for a living," said the young man of the village, who stood near me looking on.

"Oh, this is nothing," said my guide. "You should see it when they're running full in summer. Then it gets hot here. Then you should see 'em when they reline the furnaces and converting vessels. Imagine getting into that Bessemer pot in July, *hot* enough to pop corn; when you had to work like the devil and then jump out to breathe."

"I wouldn't do it," said the young villager; "I'd break into jail first." He had an outside job. He could afford to talk that way.

"Oh no you wouldn't; you'd do it. We all submit to such things, out of habit, I guess. There are lots of other jobs as bad. A man could stand work like this six hours a day. That's all a man ought to do at such work. They could do it, too; they wouldn't make so much, but the hands would live longer."

"They probably don't care whether the hands live or die," I said, "provided they do every ounce they can while they do live."

"I guess that's right," said the other young fellow with a wink. "Mill-owners don't run their mills for the benefit of the men."

"How do you stand on the late strike?" I asked another man.

"It's all foolishness; you can't do anything that way. The tonnage men brought it on; they could afford to strike, but we couldn't. The men working for less than two dollars can't afford to strike."

"While capital wastes, labor starves," I ventured to quote.

"That's the idea; we can't hurt Carnegie by six months' starving. It's *our* ribs that'll show through our shirts."

. . .

"The worst part of the whole business is this," said one of them, as I was about saying good-by. "It brutalizes a man. You can't help it. You start in to be a man, but you become more and more a machine, and pleasures are few and far between. It's like any severe labor. It drags you down mentally and morally, just as it does physically. I wouldn't mind it so much if it weren't for the long hours. Many a trade would be all right if the hours could be shortened. Twelve hours is too long." ❖

(top) Lowell's "The Mills as seen from the backyard of a boarding house." (bottom) His image of the converter in blast, "By the light reflected from it one can read a paper a mile away."

NOVEMBER 5, 1898 —*Excerpted
from an account in the Library
File, The Carnegie Library of
Homestead, describing the dedi-
cation of that institution by
Andrew Carnegie.*

THE DEDICATION

"Take you, sir, this building, a gift of one workingman to thousands of others," said Andrew Carnegie last evening as finishing his peroration, the millionaire stood hand in hand with one of his blacksmiths and made the formal transfer of the beautiful library building to the workingmen and citizens of Homestead. It was a dramatic moment in the conduct of the exercises, and when the large audience realized the true significance of the situation both millionaire and mechanic were made recipients of an extended ovation.

The exercises began with the parade in the afternoon. The special train carrying Mr. Carnegie and his friends arrived at the Homestead station at 2:20 over the Pittsburgh, Virginia and Charleston railroad and the party was immediately driven to the Library. The latter took their places on the reviewing stand in front of the new building, staying there for nearly an hour, or until the procession had entirely passed.

Shortly before the party's arrival, rain began to fall quite heavily. This considerably marred the exercises of the afternoon. The downpour kept up with slight intermission during the passing of the procession. There were present with Mr. and Mrs. Carnegie on the stand, Mr. and Mrs. Henry Phipps, H.C. Frick, President C.M. Schwab and a number of the Carnegie Steel Company limited.

Mr. Carnegie never looked happier in his life. Around him at one time stood 1,500 school children singing the familiar strains of "Annie Laurie" for the delectation of the Star Spangled Scotchman. This they followed with "America," while the Pennsylvania Concert Band played a pretty accompaniment.

In stately file there passed before him, each bearing a miniature "Old Glory," the children of the public and parochial schools and the C. M. Schwab training school. Then followed thousands of the iron and steel workers of Homestead and her brave fine laddies. It is estimated that 6,000 were in line.

. . .

Over 1,500 invitations had been issued for the dedication and the assemblage soon filled the pretty music hall. It was a typical industrial audience, the majority of which was made up of the families of steelworkers, with a sprinkling of tradesmen and professional men.

After the Curtain rose, large bunches of beautiful red, white and yellow chrysanthemums were presented to Mr. and Mrs. Carnegie, Messrs. Schwab and Frick and Mr. and Mrs. Corey by the workers of the various departments of the Homestead Mills. Music was rendered by the Haydn Glee Club and the Ladies' Choir of Homestead and a concert by the band closed the ceremonies in the Music Hall. The prayer was offered by Rev. W. Q. Rosselle.

. . .

A storm of applause greeted the donor [Mr. Carnegie], and when quiet was restored, he said: "Few events in my life have filled me with such pleasure as I have in appearing before you to hand over this building, with its library rightly in the center, the hall upon the right, and the Workingmen's Club upon the left—three fountains from which healing waters are to flow for the instruction, entertainment and happiness of the people, the great mass of whom find useful and I am happy to say, well paid employment in these works which have become famous throughout the world.

. . .

"This is an occasion to which I have long looked forward. It has seldom or never been so long between my promise and its fulfillment as the period which has elapsed since I first promised a deputation from Homestead, who begged me to erect a library for it similar to that which I had given Braddock, that the first returns which I received from the Homestead Works should sacredly be devoted to the work.

. . .

"The recreation of the workingman has as important a bearing upon his character and development as his hours of work. How a man spends his time at work may be taken for granted—these are necessarily spent upon safe lines—but how he spends his hours of recreation is really the key of his progress in all the virtues. Our experience enables me to assure you to-night that the influence of the Workingmen's Club at Edgar Thomson Works has been as potent as it has been beneficial and surprising. I trust the Club will be so managed as to make admission to it an object of honorable ambition upon the part of the workingmen at Homestead, and that intercourse with each other in the halls of this Club will produce such improvement upon the manners and tastes of its members that the foreigners visiting Homestead, as many foreigners do, will be more surprised than ever at the gentlemanly deportment of the American workingman.

"I have been told by distinguished visitors from many lands to our works in Pittsburgh that this feature struck them forcibly. They found the American Workingman so much of a gentleman. I can corroborate that by comparing them with what I have seen in other parts of the world, but it does not seem strange to me, as it does to my foreign friends, knowing intimately, as I have done, the lives, thoughts and ambitions of the workingman—he is a man here, and the laws of his country proclaim him the equal of any other man; his voice counts for the same in the State; there is no privilege of another which is not his right, and in all the fundamental points of manhood he stands the equal of any.

"More than this, under our social and political system labor is noble; whether it is performed by hand or head matters nothing; labor of itself, the doing of something useful, makes the American Workingman a full man, at ease in the presence of other men, showing no sense of inferiority, because he does not feel any, nor has any reason to. The club will do more than improve manners; it will insensibly tend to establish a higher code of conduct, a stricter regard for the proprieties of life, and to produce the class of men incapable of anything disgraceful, a sober, self-respecting, industrious, educated, saving workman.

The Carnegie Library of Homestead c. 1900.

· · ·

"I can never cease to have among my fondest wishes this wish, that the workmen of Homestead will know no end to their present abounding prosperity, nor to the cordial and friendly relations which happily exist between the firm and its many thousands of skillful, intelligent, self-respecting workmen in all its works. The best of all unions is such a happy union as prevails everywhere between the firm and its men, the two contracting parties representing kind, friendly capital and self-respecting labor.

· · ·

"For the first time, my friends, I stand before a Homestead audience with peculiar feelings. Mrs. Carnegie felt she must be with me at Homestead. Why this occasion impresses us both today, as nothing else could, will be readily understood. The one great pain of our united lives, arising from business and which has haunted us for years, came from the deplorable event here, which startled us when far away, and which even yet has not lost its power at intervals to sadden our lives.

"The memories which Homestead has called up to this time have sometimes saddened us, and we hoped that this occasion might fill our minds with such a beautiful picture as to enable us to banish the cruel memories of the past forever. Imagine our happiness now, when this happy meeting, the cordial and joyous welcome accorded us and the thousands of children's happy smiling faces, stamp a new picture of Homestead upon our minds, which will gladden our hearts as it flashes before us wherever we may roam.

"By this meeting, by your welcome, by these smiling faces, all the regretful thoughts, all the unpleasant memories, are henceforth and forever in the deep bosom of the ocean buried. Henceforth, we are to think of Homestead as we see it today. This building, which I now dedicate, may it indeed be between capital and labor, an emblem of peace, reconciliation, mental confidence, harmony and union. Today, Mrs. Carnegie and I carry away with us enshrined in our hearts the happy faces of 10,000 friends." ❖

THE POPULIST PROTEST
AND REPUBLICAN DOMINATION
by Irwin Marcus

*I*mmediately after the defeat at Homestead, the workers turned to public protest and politics. At the local level, they could take some consolation in the acquittal of the strike leaders tried in the deaths of seven Pinkertons and in the election of five steelworkers to the nine-member Homestead Borough Council in 1892. In the national election, they deserted the Republicans and supported the Democrats in the presidential race.

A contingent of 600 strikers joined a massive Democratic parade in Pittsburgh early in October. The marchers cheered their strike leader and vented their anger against Carnegie with a chorus of groans.

Homestead hosted a major parade in honor of Grover Cleveland, the Democratic nominee, on October 23. In the November election, Cleveland carried Homestead decisively as workers perceived the Republican party, supported by Carnegie, as under the influence of mill owners and directly opposed to the interests of working men and women.

In 1894, the residents of Homestead welcomed Coxey's Army and other "industrial armies" protesting unemployment and calling for government intervention to cushion some of the effects of the severe economic dislocation wrought by the depression of 1893. The Homestead Populist party, part of a national farmer-worker alliance for democratic change, held meetings and participated in the nomination of candidates for the 1894 election. A vigorous Populist Club, an outgrowth of the earlier Coxey Club, held parades and well-attended meetings as the early November election neared.

Election results brought the expected Republican victory, but local Populists outpolled the Democrats and ran well ahead of their own party on the state and national levels. In 1892, Populist candidate James Weaver had received 8.5 percent of the national vote for the presidency, while Jerome T. Ailman carried less than 3 percent of the state vote in his campaign for governor of Pennsylvania in 1894. In Homestead, Ailman won 15 percent of the vote and other Populist candidates did even better. Congressional and legislative candidates polled 28 percent of the vote. The Populist candidate for Congress won more than 25 percent of the vote in the town of Munhall, the actual site of the original Pinkerton battle.

In the 1896 election the Republican party won decisive victories locally and nationally, and the Carnegie Company added political control over the town to its dominance in the plants. Although this hegemony lasted for decades, workers on occasion challenged the company's control. The steel strike of 1919 provided the most dramatic display of worker unrest but semi-skilled immigrant workers also challenged the company domination of local politics. In 1912, Eugene Debs polled 22 percent of the local vote in his bid for the presidency on the Socialist party ticket. He emphasized the importance of establishing a society based on political and economic democracy. These sentiments found a channel for partial fulfillment in the 1930s as the Committee for Industrial Organization (CIO) became a presence in Homestead and Franklin D. Roosevelt and the Democratic party won a decisive victory in the election of 1936. ❖

Grover Cleveland, president of the United States in 1885-89 and 1893-97. Labor, which helped elect him in 1892, felt betrayed when federal troops were sent to suppress the Pullman Strike two years later. **Illustrated American** *July 9, 1892.*

(facing page) Photo, 1913, from the Pittsburgh and Lake Erie Railroad Survey. In industrial towns children created their playgrounds amid factories and railroads.

Excerpted from **Homestead: The Households of a Mill Town,**
by Margaret F. Byington, originally published by
The Russell Sage Foundation, New York, 1910.

THE SLAVS

From the cinder path beside one of the railroads that crosses the level part of Homestead, you enter an alley, bordered on one side by stables and on the other by a row of shabby two-story frame houses. The doors of the houses are closed, but dishpans and old clothes decorating their exterior mark them as inhabited. Turning from the alley through a narrow passageway you find yourself in a small court, on three sides of which are smoke-grimed houses, and on the fourth, low stables. The open space teems with life and movement. Children, dogs and hens make it lively under foot; overhead long lines of flapping clothes must be dodged. A group of women stand gossiping in one corner, awaiting their turn at the pump,— which is one of the two sources of water supply for the 20 families who live here. Another woman dumps the contents of her washtubs upon the paved ground, and the greasy, soapy water runs into an open drain a few feet from the pump. In the center a circular wooden building with ten compartments opening into one vault, flushed only by this waste water, constitutes the toilet accommodations for over one hundred people. Twenty-seven children find in this crowded brick-paved space their only playground; for the 63 rooms in the houses about the court shelter a group of 20 families, Polish, Slavic and Hungarian, Jewish and Negro. The men are unskilled workers in the mills.

This court is one of many such in Homestead; one of hundreds of similar courts in the mill towns of the Ohio valley. The conditions produced by the incoming of these alien workers form one of the unsolved problems of the steel district.

Two elements in the old country feed the population of these crowded sections: the ambitious young men, with no ties, unless to aged parents; and the men with wives, sometimes with children, who come over here to make a better home for them. They are all stimulated by the successes of their friends, who perhaps have returned with savings that seem fortunes. Often these people mortgage their all for the passage money and if they fail here no place is left to which they can go back. From quiet villages they come to this smoky town; from labor in the open fields to heavy work in the yards and thundering sheds of the mill.

As employment is steady and the workman's needs are simple, the wages seem large. The newcomer if a single man finds groups of his fellow workers living in close quarters—three or four in a room—who are enjoying life and saving money at the same time. So he too begins to save, and presently, if he has a family at home, sends for them to join him. If he is single, he sends for his sweetheart or marries some girl of his race, whom he meets in the mill-town courts of an evening or at church or at one of the lodge dances. If she has been at service here, she too will likely have a small account in the bank. Then, as the family grows and expenses increase, they resort to the old expedient and begin themselves to take boarders. Children come and grow up. The man's wage does not increase; as he is a "Hunkie" the chances are that he will remain a laborer. Most of these men come intending some day to go back with a thousand dollars—men of property. But even if they return once to the old country, they often turn

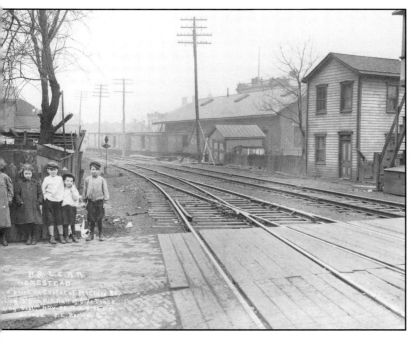

This 1908 drawing of a Croatian workingman, like all of artist Joseph Stella's portraits of Homestead steelworkers, recognizes the ethnicity, experience, and individuality of his subject.

(The Slavs, continued)

again to America; growing attached to the new world, they become permanent residents.

An occasional family, when the man gets into tonnage work or when the children reach earning age and add their wages to the common fund, achieves a long desired happiness; they move to a separate house in the suburbs, perhaps even to one of their own. But to many the crowded court with its isolation from the rest of the community continues to be America.

While there were no definite figures available as to the number of these foreigners in Homestead in 1907-8, two Slavs intimately acquainted with the foreign colony estimated that there were between 6000 and 7000. When the mills were running full in October, 1907, 3603 Slavic men were at work there, forming 53.2 per cent of the total number of employes. As 1092 of these were single men, the estimate as to the total Slavic population is probably fairly accurate.

. . .

Their labor is the heaviest and roughest in the mill,—handling steel billets and bars, loading trains, working in cinder pits; labor that demands mostly strength but demands that in large measure. They work usually under the direction of English-speaking foremen whose orders they often fail to understand. Accidents are frequent, promotions rare. In 202 families in the courts studied, 88 per cent of the men belonged to the unskilled group, a proportion roughly true for the mill as a whole. Only 2.2 per cent of the Slavs in the mill are skilled. Some of the men about the furnaces thus work up by slow degrees to be skilled or at least semi-skilled, but in the main, the Slavs have as yet small prospect of advancement. Of the 21 budget families whose men were earning laborer's wages, five had been here from five to nine years, two from ten to fourteen years, and four had been here fifteen years or over. If the rank and file are to satisfy their ambitions they must do it on less than $2.00 a day, or leave Homestead. ❖

Excerpted from The Steel Workers, *by John Fitch, originally published by* The Russell Sage Foundation, New York, 1910.

From Chapter XIII, THE WORKING DAY AND THE WORKING WEEK

The Amalgamated Association of Iron and Steel Workers was opposed to Sunday work and waged effective warfare against it. In the convention of 1882 they adopted a resolution opposing Sunday work and calling for a cessation of work in steel mills from Saturday evening until Monday morning. A similar resolution was passed in 1883. As a result of their determination they were able to report in 1887 that in no mill under the jurisdiction of the Amalgamated Association did the men begin to roll iron or steel on Sunday afternoon.

In the years immediately preceding the strike of 1892, then, a majority of the iron and steel workers, exclusive of blast furnace men, had their Sundays free in Allegheny County. No work was done in the union mills from Saturday night until Monday morning, except repairs and other work that was unavoidable. The week-day schedule of hours was, on the other hand, far from uniform. While the twelve-hour day was most nearly general, ten-hour positions were numerous and a very considerable number of positions were operated on an eight-hour schedule.

Beginning with 1892 a new order prevailed. The strike years were the pivotal years in the policies of the steel companies. The Carnegie Company thereafter began to introduce the twelve-hour day wherever possible. In 1892 the blooming mill, the converting department, and the 119-inch mill at Homestead were operated on the eight-hour basis. After the strike all the rolling mills were put on twelve-hour shifts. The substitutions in other mills were made more slowly, but the eight-hour day is now practically gone in the Pittsburgh steel mills. . .

From Chapter XVI, REPRESSION

I doubt whether you could find a more suspicious body of men than the employes of the United States Steel Corporation. They are suspicious of one another, of their neighbors, and of their friends. I was repeatedly suspected of being an agent of the Corporation, sent out to sound the men with regard to their attitude toward the Corporation and toward unionism. The fact is, the steel workers do not dare openly express their convictions. They do not dare assemble and talk over affairs pertaining to their welfare as mill men. They feel that they are living always in the presence of a hostile critic. They are a generous, open-hearted set of men, upon the whole; the skilled men are intelligent and are able and glad to talk upon a variety of subjects. But let the conversation be shifted to the steel works, and they immediately become reticent. It is safe to talk with a stranger about local option, the price of groceries, or the prospect of war with Japan, but it is not regarded as safe to talk about conditions in the steel industry. Concerning the most patent and generally known facts, intelligent men display the most marvelous ignorance.

Everywhere, even among the comparatively unintelligent, there is the same suspicion. One evening as I was walking on one of the streets of Munhall, the borough in which the Homestead steel works are located, I overtook a workman, dinner-pail in hand, on his way to the mill. I inquired of him the location of the street I was seeking, and as it lay further down the hill, I walked with him. We exchanged a few commonplace remarks, and as there had just been announced a reduction in wages affecting a large number of men, I spoke of that to see whether he would talk about it. His attitude immediately changed from cordiality to suspicion. "I don't know anything about it," he answered, shortly. "I haven't heard of any cut." Yet the reduction was being discussed in every steel worker's home in Homestead and Munhall. On another occasion I was walking through the Homestead steel works. Passing through the yard, I encountered a water-carrier, a man of little mental alertness apparently, so I thought I would see whether he would exercise the same discretion that I observed among the skilled workmen. I walked with him a short distance and asked him about the dangers of mill work. He never had heard of any dangers. When I asked him if accidents did not occasionally take place, he looked at me suspiciously and said, "I have never seen anybody hurt."

When I met the men in their homes, too, there was suspicion to be broken down. Sometimes I could not get an opportunity to see the man whom I was seeking. Business engagements would suddenly be remembered which prevented an interview. Several men refused to talk about mill work. A highly paid employe of the Corporation refused even to see me. I had been at his house, and finding that he was out, I left word that I would return at a specified hour. Returning at the time named, my ring brought the housewife to the door, who told me that her husband was at home, but that he would not see me or talk to me because the company had forbidden its employes to talk with strangers about mill work. Repeatedly I interviewed men who answered my questions guardedly, evidently in great perturbation of spirit, as if they feared that my visit boded them no good. Sometimes when meeting a workingman, and explaining to him my desire to talk over industrial conditions, he would say protestingly, "But I haven't anything to say against the company," although I had not once mentioned the company. On several occasions, at the close of an interview in which only the most careful statements had been made, my canny

Youths like the ones depicted in this 1908 stereograph titled "Water Boys," were the only source of drinking water for the 8,000 workers subjected to the intense heat within the plant.

Police on horseback patrolled the streets of Homestead during the 1919 Steel Strike.

(Repression, continued)

informant chuckled in evident relief, "There—I haven't told you anything against the company, have I?"

· · ·

In 1895 it was reported in the Amalgamated Association Convention that the Homestead steel workers had received "another reduction, ranging from 48 per cent to 60 per cent." A meeting with a thousand men in attendance had been held January 16 to protest, and officers of the Amalgamated Association had addressed the meeting. The next day the Carnegie Steel Company "discharged men by fives and tens for daring to attend a public meeting." Secret meetings were then held, and 25 men employed in the 119-inch mill were organized into a lodge of the Amalgamated Association. It was not long before the officers of this lodge were discharged, and the president of the lodge was told that it was for organizing. In concluding his report, Vice President Carney of the Amalgamated Association stated that the company was spending large sums of money in order to maintain a system of espionage. One man in each ten was thought to be a spy. Other similar occurrences have taken place at Homestead. On April 29, 1899, "T. J. Shaffer Lodge, No. 13," was organized there. When the convention of the Amalgamated Association met in May, it was reported that some of the members of this lodge had been discharged and the men were on strike for the right to organize.

· · ·

The officials of the steel companies make no secret of their hostility to unionism, and I have been told by two leading employers that they would not tolerate it. Any movement toward organization, they assured me, would mean discharge. That this was no idle boast is evident from the record of all attempts at organization since 1892. ❖

OCTOBER 1919 —Excerpted from **The Bridgemen's Magazine,** *the national journal of the iron-workers' union.*

A STRIKE VOTE

[T]he committee canvassed the strike vote ordered at the meeting in Pittsburgh, July 20th, [1919] and which the various organizations had been busily engaged in taking up ever since. The vote for a strike, in case all other means fail, was 98%. Many districts reported an absolutely 100% vote. In Homestead, Braddock, Rankin, McKeesport, Duquesne and other points along the Monongahela River, where the Steel Trust has ruled supreme for a quarter of a century, thousands of votes were cast, not one of which was negative. In Donora, where the unions have several thousand members, one negative vote was found during the count. This has created a scandal in the town. The union men are investigating. They feel that their movement has been insulted. Across the river, in Monessen, where the unions have organized the army of steel workers, the record is clear. Not one man voted "No."

This splendid display of militant solidarity comes as a result of the great campaign carried on in the steel industry for the past year by the American Federation of Labor and the twenty-four principal unions involved. Not alone is it manifesting itself by a unanimous vote to back up the committee, but, what is even better, it is resulting in bringing thousands of members into the organizations. It is questionable if ever there has existed a stronger movement for organization than is now raging in the steel mills in this country. Should it come to a strike, which can only happen after all other means have failed, the steel workers will bring every mill in the country to a standstill.

· · ·

The issue raised by this action of the National Committee is one of the most tremendous in the history of the labor movement. For many years the United States Steel Corporation has ruled supreme in its domain, giving no heed to the demands of its workers. But now these workers, feeling the great urge for industrial democracy now sweeping the world, have finally drawn themselves together into a compact organization and served notice that their claims must be heard. The next few weeks will produce great events in the steel industry.

Among the tyrannical boroughs along the Monongahela River, where the overlords in the steel industry reign supreme, Homestead has established itself firmly at the head of the list as the most despotic principality of them all.

Organizers working with the National Committee for Organizing Iron and Steel Workers have been jailed in practically all the great steel suburbs of Pittsburgh, but it remained for the small calibre, $4.50 per day police officials of Homestead to drag gray-haired, 89-year-old Mother Jones to their filthy jail for daring to speak in behalf of the enslaved steel workers. . . . ❖

Excerpted from The Autobiography of Mother Jones, *Chapter XXIV, edited by May Field Parton, originally published by Charles H. Kerr & Company, Chicago, 1925.*

THE STEEL STRIKE IN 1919

When the steel strike was being organized I was in Seattle with Jay G. Brown, President of the Shingle Workers of America.

"We ought to go East and help organize those slaves," I said to Brown.

"They'll throw us in jail, Mother!" he said. "Well, they're our own jails, aren't they? Our class builds them."

I came East. So did Jay G. Brown—a devoted worker for the cause of the steel slaves.

The strike in the steel industry was called in September, 1919. Gary [Judge Elbert H. Gary, Chairman of U.S. Steel] as spokesman for the industry refused to consider any sort of appointment with his workers. What did it matter to him that thousands upon thousands of workers in Bethlehem, Pennsylvania, worked in front of scorching furnaces twelve long hours, through the day, through the night, while he visited the Holy Land where Our Lord was born in a manger!

I traveled up and down the Monongahela River. Most of the places where the steel workers were on strike meetings were forbidden. If I were to stop to talk to a woman on the street about her child, a cossack would come charging down upon us and we would have to run for our lives. If I were to talk to a man in the streets of Braddock, we would be arrested for unlawful assembly.

· · ·

I was speaking in Homestead. A group of organizers were with me in an automobile. As soon as a word was said, the speaker was immediately arrested by the steel bosses' sheriffs. I rose to speak. An officer grabbed me.

"Under arrest !" he said.

We were taken to jail. A great mob of people collected outside the prison. There was angry talk. The jailer got scared. He thought there might be lynching and he guessed who would be lynched. The mayor was in the jail, too, conferring with the jailer. He was scared. He looked out of the office windows and he saw hundreds of workers milling around and heard them muttering.

The jailer came to Mr. Brown and asked him what he had better do.

"Why don't you let Mother Jones go out and speak to them," he said. "They'll do anything she says."

So the jailer came to me and asked me speak to the boys outside and ask them to go home.

Mother Jones's lifelong career as a labor crusader began in Chicago in the 1870s. She died at age 100 in 1930. In the foreword to her autobiography, Clarence Darrow described her as "a woman of action fired by a fine zeal. She defied calumny. She was not awed by guns or jails."

(The Steel Strike, continued)

I went outside the jail and told the boys I was going to be released shortly on bond, and that they should go home now and not give a trouble. I got them in a good humor and pretty soon they went away. Meanwhile while I was speaking, the mayor had sneaked out the back way.

We were ordered to appear in the Pittsburgh court the next morning. A cranky old judge asked me if I had had a permit to speak on the streets.

"Yes, sir," said I. "I had a permit."

"Who issued it?" he growled.

"Patrick Henry; Thomas Jefferson; John Adams!" said I.

The mention of those patriots who gave our charter of liberties made the old steel judge sore. He fined us all heavily.

During the strike I was frequently arrested. So were all the leaders. We expected that. I never knew whether I would find John Fitzpatrick and William Foster at headquarters when I went up to Pittsburgh. Hundreds of threatening letters came to them. Gunmen followed them. Their lives were in constant danger. Citizens Alliances—the little shopkeepers dependent upon the smile of the companies threatened to drive them out. Never had a strike been led by more devoted, able, unselfish men. Never a thought for themselves. Only for the men on strike, men striking to bring back America to America.

In Foster's office no chairs were permitted by the authorities. That would have been construed as "a meeting." Here men gathered in silent groups, in whispering groups, to get what word they could of the strike.

How was it going in Ohio?

How was it going in Pennsylvania?

How in the Mesaba country?

The workers were divided from one another. Spies working among the Ohio workers told of the break in the strike in Pennsylvania. In Pennsylvania, they told of the break in Ohio. With meetings forbidden, with mails censored, with no means of communication allowed, the strikers could not know of the progress of their strike. Then fear would clutch their throats.

One day two men came into Headquarters. One of them showed his wrists. They told in broken English of being seized by officers, taken to a hotel room. One of them was handcuffed for a day to a bed. His wrists swelled. He begged the officers to release him. He writhed in pain. They laughed and asked him if he would go to work. Though mad with pain he said no. At night they let him go . . . without a word, without redress. ❖

Excerpted from* The Speeches and Writings of Mother Jones, *edited by Edward M. Steel, University of Pittsburgh Press, 1988.

In Homestead [in 1919] the labor men were allowed to speak for the first time in 28 years. We were arrested the first day. When I got up to speak I was taken. Eight or ten thousand labor men followed me to the jail. They all marched there. When we went into the jail they remained outside. One fellow began to cry and said: "What for you take Mudder Jones?" and they took him by the neck and shoved him behind the bars. That is all he did or said. We put up a bond of $15 each. We were to come for trial the next day, but the burgess didn't appear. They postponed the trial on account of the mob that appeared outside. When they got me in jail the police themselves got scared to death. One of our men said: "Mother can handle those men." He was told, "No, nobody can handle them." "Yes, she can; let her get out." I went out and said: "Boys, we live in America. Let us give three cheers for Uncle Sam and go home and let the companies go to hell." And they did. Everybody went home, but they went down the street cheering. There was no trouble, nobody was hurt— they were law-abiding. They blew off steam and went home. ❖

Excerpted from **Madam Secretary, Frances Perkins,** *Chapter 24,*
by George Martin, Houghton Mifflin, Boston, 1976.

FRANCES PERKINS AT HOMESTEAD

At Homestead, after touring the mill, on the invitation of the town's burgess (the chief executive officer) she spoke and answered questions in the town hall. The workers were not very articulate. The discussion turned mostly on whether the maximum hours should be forty-four a week and the minimum wage $.40 an hour. Most of the mills were operating at less than half their capacity and employing men on eight-hour shifts on a share-the-work plan. For some men the problem was long hours, but for most it was a low wage, caused primarily by the irregularity of work.

At the end of the meeting as she was thanking the burgess for the use of the hall, sounds of a disturbance came up the stair. A reporter whispered to her that a number of workers had been excluded and were gathered outside the building. Turning to the burgess she asked if she could have the hall for a few minutes more.

"No, no," he said, his face darkening, "you've had enough. These men are no good. They're undesirable Reds. I know them well. They just want to make trouble."

Perhaps so, she thought, but as a public official she had a duty to hear all citizens. After bidding the burgess good-bye she went downstairs and discovered several hundred angry people in the street. Then, as she described it later, standing on the building's steps, she said:

"My friends, I am so sorry that you were not able to get into the hall. It was very crowded, but perhaps we can hear what you have to say right here."

By this time the burgess, two secretaries, and the police appeared, shouting, "You can't talk here! You are not permitted to make a speech here—there is a rule against making a speech here."

The men on the sidewalk were tense with interest, wondering what I would do next. There was a park across the way. "All right—I am sorry. We will go over to the public park. . ."

I protested, "This is just a hearing, not a meeting; it won't be long, only a few minutes."

The burgess kept reiterating that they were "undesirable Reds," although they looked like everybody else to me.

As I hesitated, my eye caught sight of the American flag flying over a building on the opposite side of the square. Ah, I thought, that must be the post office, and I remembered that federal buildings in any locality are under the jurisdiction of the federal government. I did not know the politics of the postmaster, but I was an officer of the federal government and I must have some rights there.

To the crowd I said, "We will go to the post office. There is an American flag."

It was almost closing time. I have never forgotten the postmaster and his assistance. I had only a moment to explain matters to him. Nothing very dramatic happened. The people filed in, and the employees hung around to enjoy the meeting. We stood in the long corridor lined with postal cages. Somebody got me a chair, and I stood on it and made a brief speech about the steel code. I asked if anybody wanted to speak. Twenty or thirty men did. They said they were greatly pleased with the idea. They said they wished the government would free them from the domination of the steel trust. One man spoke about philosophic and economic principles. A few denounced the community. I invited the most vocal and obstreperous of the speakers to come to Washington and promised that he would have an opportunity to appear at the public hearing. We ended the meeting with handshaking and expressions of rejoicing that the New Deal wasn't afraid of the steel trust."

This story was picked up by the papers, and though the bad judgment was entirely the burgess's own, the steel companies bore its burden. ❖

In 1933 the New Deal Administration of President Franklin D. Roosevelt initiated the National Recovery Act (NRA) which provided for collective bargaining but also called for a floor on wages and consultation with workers, even though they might not have a union to represent them. Since the Amalgamated had been reduced to a token representation in foundries and small shops in the steel industry of the 1930s, Frances L. Perkins, Secretary of Labor, set out to ensure that the NRA code was introduced to the steel industry. Her biographer, George Martin, recalled that she "wanted the workers to feel consulted," so in 1933 she made personal visits to several plants, including the Homestead Works of U.S. Steel.

Frances Perkins, Secretary of Labor 1933-45.

SWOC AND THE HOMESTEAD LEGACY

by Russell W. Gibbons

It was already hot on that Sunday morning on July 5, 1936, when Pat Cush arrived with half a dozen small American flags at the Franklin Cemetery on the Munhall hillside overlooking the Homestead Works. He had obtained the flags the previous day, when Independence Day ceremonies were held at the gazebo below the Carnegie Library.

Cush had been a steelworker since the age of eleven and had two brothers who were in the battle. A one time Amalgamated lodge president, he knew many men who had gone back after the crushing defeat of 1892. They did not like to talk about it, he told others. When the subject came up their eyes would move both ways, looking to see if a foreman or "super" or just an informant in the ranks was within earshot.

That was their legacy. Today something new was about to take place. An unusual sense of apprehension mixed with anticipation hovered over the town. Two Sundays ago the first open union meeting in a generation had taken place in McKeesport.

Another such meeting was about to take place in Homestead that very afternoon, though people still whispered that "the company" would never let it happen. Cush was convinced that it would. He was there to honor the 44th anniversary of the Homestead Strike and the seven workers who had died. Moreover, he was determined to locate and mark the long-ignored graves of the Homestead martyrs.

By 3 p.m., a crowd began to gather, coming from a nearby baseball field where the newly formed Steel Workers Organizing Committee had called a meeting. The Committee, dubbed SWOC, had brought the state's second highest elected official to that field. Lieutenant Governor Thomas Kennedy—who was serving as secretary of the United Mine Workers when he was elected to office along with Governor George Earle, Jr.—proclaimed, "we are going to see that the workers are granted their rights under the Constitution."

The 4,000 steelworkers and miners assembled cheered Kennedy; not so a well-dressed man at the fringe of the crowd. He was William S. Unger, the assistant general superintendent of the Homestead Works. For what must have been the first time in his life, reported SWOC organizer Patrick Fagan, workers looked Unger straight in the eye, "not downward," as if he were "somehow their better."

Fagan had succeeded Philip Murray as Director of the Miners District 5 and was part of the initial SWOC group that John L. Lewis had formed in June. He was chosen to give the eulogy at the cemetery, a link between the Homestead legacy and the new drive to organize steel:

"We have come to renew the struggle for which you gave your lives. We pledge all our efforts to bring a better life to the steel workers . . . let the seed of those labor pioneers who were massacred here be the seed of this new organization in 1936."

Later, veterans of the steel organizing drive would take pride in their attendance at the McKeesport and Homestead meetings—the opening guns of the campaign of the insurgent Committee for Industrial Organization to gain a presence

in the huge industries that the conservative American Federation of Labor had avoided. Lewis, the flamboyant president of the Miners, pledged the resources and organizing prowess of his 600,000-member union, confident that the National Labor Relations Act, which had become law the previous year would protect workers' efforts to organize.

President William Green of the American Federation of Labor ordered the Committee for Industrial Organization (CIO) to disband, but Lewis and his allies persisted in their efforts to organize the country's basic industries: steel, auto, shipbuilding, rubber, electrical, and other jurisdictions. Workers by the thousands flocked to join the CIO.

SWOC announced that 150 organizers were in the field and that it had a budget of $500,000, provided by the Miners (the American Iron and Steel Institute would spend that much for full-page ads denouncing the drive that same month). In Homestead SWOC opened an office at 410 East Eighth Avenue. Within the first month of its existence 30 offices were opened in steel communities under the three regional directors. In late 1936 the first lodge of the Amalgamated to be chartered since it had been disbanded in Homestead in 1892 was called to order at the SWOC hall.

It would take only eight months before the giant of the steel industry would recognize and deal with the union. On March 2, 1937, Lewis and Murray signed an agreement with U.S. Steel. After more than four decades, the Homestead Works was union once again. ❖

JULY 6, 1936 —Excerpted from **The Pittsburgh Press.**

STATE GUARDS STEEL LABOR'S CIVIL RIGHTS

————

Use of National Guard and Relief Bans Improbable In Case of Trouble

————

HUGE RALLY HELD

————

Homestead Meeting Urged To Avoid Clanking Of Sword

————

Leaders of the Steel Workers Organizing Committee to-day intensified their drive to unionize the nation's steel workers, with these developments:

The convention of the Amalgamated Association of Iron, Steel & Tin Workers in Canonsburg, Pennsylvania, April 1936.

PITTSBURGH—Workers held assurance that "they would get their constitutional rights" in event of trouble, the promise being given by Lieut-Gov. Thomas Kennedy at a rally in Homestead.

. . .

Steel workers of the Pittsburgh district were virtually assured yesterday that neither the National Guard nor relief bans would be used against them if trouble develops in the campaign to unionize the local mills.

Lieutenant Governor Thomas Kennedy, who is secretary-treasurer of the United Mine Workers of America, told several thousand workers at an open air meeting in Homestead that "Governor Earle, as commander-in-chief of the military and police organizations of the state, will see that workers get their constitutional rights."

On the relief matter, the Lieutenant Governor declared: "No strikes are looked for, but if the steel magnates throw people out in the streets as a result of organization activities. . .they will be entitled to relief."

The speaker declared that "The captains of steel can't get away with the stuff they got away with before. The government of the United States is now in Washington, and the government of Pennsylvania is now in Harrisburg—not in Pittsburgh or New York."

"You owe it to your wives and children, and to those who will come after you to bare your breasts to the enemy . . . to build in this country a new nation," he declared.

. . .

The meeting that he addressed was both a memorial for those who died in the Homestead riot of July 6, 1892—when the Amalgamated Association of Iron, Steel & Tin Workers was making its vain effort to unionize the Homestead plants—and a rally in the furtherance of the new unionization campaign.

The audience stood in the hot sun at the Seventeenth St. Playgrounds three hours, listening to addresses, then went to a nearby cemetery to place wreaths on the graves of four of the victims of the riot.

The meeting paused for a minute with heads bowed in prayer for the martyred strikers. The Morgan Miners' Band played "Nearer My God to Thee."

. . .

Assail 'Lords of Steel'

At the end of the meeting a "declaration of independence" was read to the assembled workers by Charles Scharbo, a pipe-fitter from the Homestead mills and a member of the Amalgamated.

The "declaration" read, in part:

"Through their control over the hours we work, the wages we receive, and the conditions of our labor, and through their denial of our right to organize freely and bargain collectively, the lords of steel try to rule us as did the royalists against whom our fathers rebelled.

"They have interfered in every way with our right to organize in independent unions, discharging many who have joined them.

"They have set up company unions, forcing employes to vote in their so-called elections.

"They have sent among us swarms of stoolpigeons, who have spied upon us in the mills in our meetings, and even in our homes.

"They have kept among us armies of company gunmen, with stores of machine guns, gas bombs and other weapons of warfare.

"We steel workers do today solemnly publish and declare our independence. We say to the world: We are free Americans. We shall exercise our inalienable rights to organize into a great industrial union, banded together with all our fellow steel workers."

————❖————

Homestead in Diego Rivera's "Labor Fights During the '90s"

*I*n 1933, Mexican artist Diego Rivera painted a series of 21 fresco panels, *Portrait of America*, offering an ideological interpretation of American history from the Colonial era to his own time. He created the murals for—and donated them to—the New Workers School at 51 West Fourteenth Street, New York. The director of the school, his friend Bertram D. Wolfe, belonged to a group of dissidents who had broken with the Stalinist Communist Party.

Thirteen of the panels were moved to Unity House in Forest Park, Pennsylvania (a summer resort owned by the International Ladies Garment Workers) in 1941. These panels, including "Labor Fights During the '90s" (shown above) were destroyed in a fire in 1969. The other eight panels had been donated to the International Rescue Committee and sold to raise money.

The above panel uses images from the two great strikes of the era—the Homestead Strike and the Pullman Strike of 1894

in Chicago. The upper portion of the mural depicts events at Homestead—the battle at the river, the disarming of the Pinkertons, and the militia. The mounting of the cannon is as romanticized as in Rowe's "Great Battle of Homestead" (page 157) and there is a hint of the Carrie Furnaces which were not yet in operation. But the overall tone is reminiscent of 19th-century images of the confrontation at Homestead.

The foreground is dominated by three major figures of the American labor movement: Daniel De Leon, a founder of the Socialist Labor and Trade Alliance; Eugene V. Debs, organizer of railroad workers and four-time candidate for the presidency of the United States on the Socialist ticket; and "Big Bill" Haywood, organizer of the Western Miners. Behind them are the banners of the American Railway Union, the Western Federation of Miners, and the Industrial Workers of the World.   *Russell W. Gibbons*

LIEUTENANT GOVERNOR KENNEDY

Urging the 2,000 steel workers present to join the rejuvenated Amalgamated Union under the Lewis "one big union" plan, Lieutenant-Governor Thomas Kennedy, himself a United Mine Workers official, spoke at Homestead yesterday.

Lewis Drive Lauded At Homestead Rally

————

2,000 Mill Workers, Miners Applaud Program.

————

Bonuses to top industrial executives were denounced, labor "spies" were excoriated and industrial unionism praised as the workers only path to economic security by speakers yesterday at a mass meeting of more than 2,000 steel workers and coal miners on the Seventh street playground, Homestead.

The rally, serving also as a memorial service for steel workers slain 44 years ago during a strike in Homestead mills, marked another step in the drive of the committee for industrial organization headed by John L. Lewis, president of the United Mine Workers of America, to enroll 500,000 steel workers in the Amalgamated Association of Iron, Steel & Tin Workers, one of the oldest international unions in the American Federation of Labor.

Stand With Bowed Heads.

The assemblage stood silent for a moment, with bowed heads, commemorating what Chairman P.T. Fagan, districts president of the United Mine Workers, referred to as the "Homestead Massacre."

"Let the blood of those labor pioneers who were massacred here be the seed of this new organization in 1936," Fagan said. "And may the souls of the martyrs rest in peace. Amen."

Lieutenant Governor Thomas Kennedy, who also is international secretary-treasurer of the United Mine Workers, backed previous speakers in reaffirming the peaceful intentions of the CIO and its 12 international unions backing the present organization drive. But he and the others also declared that whatever force is needed to win and form an effectively functioning organization must be injected into the campaign to organize the steel industry "from top to bottom."

A resolution, closely following the form of the original American Declaration of Independence, was adopted, pledging those assembled to "exercise our inalienable rights to organize into a great industrial union, banded together with all our fellow steel workers."

"Through this union, we shall win higher wages, shorter hours and a better standard of living," the resolution concluded. "We shall win leisure for ourselves and opportunity for our children. Together with our union brothers in other industries, we shall abolish industrial despotism. We shall make real the dreams of the pioneers who pictured America as a land where all might live in comfort and happiness.

"In support of this declaration, we mutually pledge to each other our steadfast purpose as union men, our honor and our very lives."

Corporations Are Accused.

In a lengthy preamble of the document it was asserted that "in the steel and other like industries a new despotism has come into being." Steel corporations were accused of having "sent among us swarms of stool pigeons, who have spied upon us in the mills, in our meetings and even in our homes." The same concerns were charged also with having set up "company unions, forcing employes to vote in their so-called elections," and with having employed gunmen with stores of machine guns, gas bombs and other weapons of warfare and with having discharged many workers who sought to join independent unions.

Lieutenant Governor Kennedy gave a pledge to provide relief for any who might lose their jobs through their industrial union activity.

"This is a peaceful, organized drive and we do not seek any strikes or trouble," said Kennedy, "but if the steel magnates throw you out you are entitled to and will receive state relief."

Hitting at "Company unions" as "illegitimate sons—kept organizations—of the steel trust," Kennedy told his audience the "economic royalists of the basic industries" had forced long hours and wages upon the workers because they were unorganized.

Conditions Declared Same.

Louis Leonard, secretary-treasurer of the Amalgamated union, and other speakers referred to the "Battle of the Barge," in which steel strikers were shot in 1892, and which brought about state intervention and the first defeat in the three major attempts so far made to unionize the industry. The second "big push," they said, met defeat in 1919.

Conditions in the steel industry are the same today as those of the anthracite coal industry from 1897 to 1901, when the United Mine Workers was organizing it, Kennedy said.

"We all stood together then, regardless of race or nationality," he said, "and there is not one nonunion man working in that great industry now.

"All we need to bring about such a state in the steel industry is inspired leadership and a determination to win. You have the inspired leadership here before you now in the person of that great leader of the workingman, John L. Lewis."

Leonard told the steel workers "if you accept this opportunity, the greatest you have ever had, you will put a stop to these $250,000 salaries and these million

(Lewis Drive, continued)
dollar bonuses, given to Eugene Grace and his ilk annually while you and your families were on the breadline or forced onto WPA or direct relief."

"The steel trust has spent millions in trying to destroy the Amalgamated union but has failed to do so," Leonard said.

Chairman Fagan said any spies or stool-pigeons that might be in the audience were "in the words of the late Tom Robertson, 'as welcome as a skunk at a lawn fete.'"

Regards Crowd "Very Good."

Clinton S. Golden, regional director of the steel workers' organization committee, declared the crowd, variously estimated at 2,000 to 4,000, "very good, in view of the general fear of spies and of the fact that the mills were kept operating today for the first time on a Sunday in seven years."

Judge M.A. Musmanno of common pleas court said there "is no necessity, and certainly no wisdom in capital being suspicious of labor." He asserted the present drive "should usher in an era of good feeling in the steel industry, rather than one of animosities."

Union organizers announced last week they anticipated 25,000 at yesterday's meeting.

Other speakers were Thomas Shane and Powers Hapgood, organizers for the steel workers' organizing committee.

After the speaking the crowd trooped to Homestead cemetery, five blocks away, to lay wreaths of flowers on the graves of men who died in the 1892 fracas.

———— ❖ ————

The unveiling in 1941 of the monument commemorating the steelworkers who were killed July 6, 1892. A year later, the Steel Workers Organizing Committee (SWOC) became the United Steelworkers of America.

SEPTEMBER 2, 1941 —Reprinted from **The Daily Messenger,** *Homestead.*

Parade, Speeches Feature Labor Day

Few Steelworkers Participate As Mills Work; Speech By Murray Is Read By David J. McDonald

Congress of Industrial Organizations unionists of Western Pennsylvania observed Labor Day here with all the trimmings, including parades and speeches, but steel workers were relatively scarce in yesterday's holiday proceedings because district steel mills kept their wheels turning and the stacks full of smoke to avoid a dangerous slackening of defense efforts.

The CIO gathering, sponsored by the Steel Workers Organizing Committee, Homestead No. 1397, sounded the keynote of yesterday's mass celebration here with speeches in the morning and afternoon in which the worker's part in the government's gigantic defense program was forcibly expressed.

Before the afternoon activities got under way, several hundred unionists gathered at the Homestead end of the High-Level Bridge at 10:30 a.m. to listen to CIO Regional Director James J. Thomas dedicate a four-ton granite shaft in memory of the workers killed in the bloody Homestead strike of 1892.

Frank Bell Speaks

Thomas, in an impressive ceremony, said that the monument was being dedicated "to the men who laid down their lives for the right to work for a living wage." B. Frank Bell, one of the men who participated in that now historic strike, was in attendance and made a few remarks.

Music was furnished by the Homestead High band and the Munhall No. 5 Drum and Bugle Corps. Rev. Father David Shanahan of St. Mary Magdalene church opened the exercises with an invocation while Rev. William B. Clancy of St. John's Lutheran church said benediction at the close of the speeches.

Several hours later at West Field the contrast between the violence of 1892 and the collective bargaining system of 1941 was emphasized in a message by Philip Murray, ill CIO president, which was read by David J. McDonald, secretary-treasurer of the SWOC.

"For Two Things"

"For nearly 50 years the name of Homestead has stood for two things—a great steel center, and the home of non-unionism" the message said. "The nation, and for that matter the world, thought of Homestead in terms of the steel strike of 1892. The cause of that strike has been lost in the screaming headlines of tragedy.

"Theirs is the right of free men, won for themselves, by themselves, through the Steel Workers Organizing Committee—their union.

"The building of this powerful organization in the steel industry, the building of the great Congress of Industrial Organization in which most of you at this celebration have had a part—this work will erase the tragedy of 1892: and from now on Homestead will symbolize—not the home of non-unionism, but the citadel of true unionism.

"The benefits brought to the steel workers through the SWOC are countless. Wages have been increased 30 cents an hour—approximately $600 a year added to the pay envelopes of a half-million steel workers. Hundreds of thousands of grievances have, as those men of 1892 put it, been found unjust and made right. Vacations with pay are now the right of steel workers rather than a gift. Because of the 40-hour week, workmen can now enjoy a normal family life. The men of the mills have job security, and seniority rights. In brief, the steel workers of the nation today have the things which only a strong union can bring them."

The program at West Field in which Dr. Port Eckles, superintendent of Homestead public schools, Thomas, and William Coombs, president of the Homestead SWOC, spoke and which was attended by Dr. John J. McLean, Albert Williams and Dr. John C. Sullivan, respective burgesses of Homestead, Munhall and West Homestead, followed a big parade through the streets of Munhall and Homestead.

Over 16 divisions participated in the processions which featured bands and drum and bugle corps from high schools of industrial communities scattered throughout Western Pennsylvania. Union delegates represented SWOC lodges, the United Mine Workers and the United Electrical, Radio and Machine Workers Union.

The delegation from SWOC Local 1074, Johnstown, travelled the longest distance for the affair. Steel workers were small in number at yesterday's celebration due to the steel mills' decision to keep operating through the holiday for the sake of defense.

The monument today.

Pete Seeger sang "A Fight for Home and Honor" when he performed at the New Leona Theater in Homestead in 1977.

THE HOMESTEAD BALLAD
by Archie Green

No one knows how many composers or poets wrote topical ballads or elegiac poems about the Homestead Strike—its promise, trauma, and aftertones. No one knows where or when these ephemeral memorials vanished. During Big Steel's triumphant years, few archives or libraries valued the creative expressions of working people, but fortunately some survived. Among the tributes that entered folk tradition, we find "A Fight for Home and Honor at Homestead, Pa." penned by John W. Kelly during the strike's first week. Chicago publisher Will Rossiter issued it in sheet music form, registering it at the Library of Congress Copyright Office, July 16, 1892.

Literally, only ten days elapsed between the strikers' battle with Pinkertons and the song's copyright entry at the nation's capital. In retrospect, this short interval seems especially remarkable in that Kelly composed his ballad while working at Tony Pastor's Bowery "Opera House" in Manhattan, America's leading variety show and vaudeville center. Somehow, between July 6 and July 16, the song traveled by mail from New York City to Chicago to Washington, DC.

Born about 1858 in Philadelphia, Kelly, as a young man, moved to Chicago to work in an iron mill. After entertaining fellow millhands, he took to the minstrel stage, where he became known as the Rolling Mill Man. With Irish comic humor, fresh songs, and wry monologues, he scored two Tin-Pan-Alley hits: "Throw Him Down McCloskey" and "Slide, Kelly Slide." Kelly died in 1896 of Bright's Disease. His grave's location remains uncertain.

It is unlikely that Kelly anticipated the longevity of his Homestead ballad. Initially, Rossiter had offered "A Fight for Home and Honor" in sheet music and pocket songster (containing lyrics but no music). Kelly's Homestead sheet music does not seem to have survived, but, fortunately, we do have the ballad text in that it circulated in print and by word of mouth.

With or without Rossiter's permission, Kelly's text appeared in Delaney's Song Book No. 3 (1892). The strike song also moved from one friend to another as it struck a sympathic chord among working people. We sense how early the ballad entered oral tradition by noting a small broadside, "The Homestead Strike," on cheap newsprint (found in the Brown University Library). This printing carries a "bug," an International Typographical Union label, from Sharon, Pennsylvania. The undated broadside does not credit Kelly. Perhaps a local partisan in the Amalgamated Association paid for its printing and distributed copies while Homestead's spirit soared.

In 1942, Douglas Gilbert "rescued" Kelly's text and printed it in Lost Chords, an anecdotal popular-music history. Sadly, Gilbert did not specify his source and his research notes have not been found. Without the original sheet music, a Rossiter songbook, or Gilbert's material, how do we account for the fact that "folk revival" singers and labor educators know and perform Kelly's song?

The answer lies in the ways of oral tradition. In May 1940, George Korson recorded a full version of the "Homestead Strike" from Peter Haser at New Kensington, Pennsylvania, and included its text in Coal Dust on the Fiddle (1943). Coal miner Haser had presented the strike song at Labor Day rallies of the United Mine Workers of America. In previous decades, other unionists had performed Kelly's song on celebratory occasions.

During 1947, Jacob Evanson also netted the ballad from John Schmitt, a Pittsburgh steelworker. A fine musician himself, Evanson transcribed its tune, without the aid of of a recording. He spliced Schmitt's tune to Haser's text for printing in "Folk Songs of an Industrial City" within Korson's Pennsylvania Songs and Legends (1949). Thus Evanson made the melody of Kelly's "old" song available to modern performers and audiences.

Both Haser and Schmitt had learned the strike ballad as young men, cherishing it over the decades for its evocative rhetoric and plebian values. Like other carriers of trade-union tradition, these workers responded to "true" songs. Homesteaders, indeed had defended home and honor. Kelly could not have known in 1892 that "Baron Carnage-y" would win—that brave artisans would be forced away from mill gate and hearth into exile.

Present-day singers are indebted to Korson, Evanson, Haser, and Schmitt for Kelly's composition. After 1892, it had spread beyond the Monongahela to loggers and coal and metal miners. In some cases, they localized the ballad to different strikes or natural disasters. Although Kelly lost possession of his song to steel millhands and their fellow workers, the folk inadvertently honored him by internalizing the ballad's message, and by keeping it alive until collectors could place it in available print. Ellen Stekert, Joe Glazer, and Pete Seeger have recorded the ballad on LP albums. We can anticipate that it will also appear in CD form.

Like other songs in folk tradition, "A Fight for Home and Honor" shows changes in language from singer to singer. Musically, the chorus has remained stable, while the verses have acquired different melodies. Most of the collected tunes retain the lilting 6/8 meter that reminds listeners of the Irish-influenced musical stage in the 1890s.

Over the years, Pittsburgh collectors have found other Homestead songlore. During the 1960s, George Swetnam noted a ballad from an elderly doorman at the Elks Club on the North Side. It recounted events unrelated by Kelly, indicating that local poets had circulated strike pieces after July 1892. In 1990, folklorist Doris Dyen unearthed another Kelly variant from the John Hubenthal family, steel men at the Jones & Laughlin South Side mill. These finds by Swetnam and Dyen suggest that attics, scrapbooks, and memories in nearby communities may hold additional musical treasures memorializing one of America's watershed strikes.

Today, "A Fight for Home and Honor" serves various purposes as a steel-strike requiem, a social text, a laborlore memento, or an oral/aural complement to a historic site. During the 1890s, puddlers, rollers, heaters, miners, loggers, and other toilers across boundaries of skill, region, and ethnicity learned Kelly's ballad and carried it along a century's journey. How long will this composition—born in Tin Pan Alley, matured in Homestead's shadow—live? As Homestead adds symbolic meaning to itself in decades ahead, and as American workers adopt preservational strategies, J.W. Kelly's ballad will continue to be treasured. ❖

From Lost Chords, Douglas Gilbert, Doubleday, New York, 1942.

A FIGHT FOR HOME AND HONOR
(Sometimes called "The Homestead Strike")

We are asking one another as we pass the time of day,
Why men must have recourse to arms to get their proper pay;
And why the labor unions now must not be recognized,
While the actions of a syndicate must not be criticised.
The trouble down at Homestead was brought about this way,
When a grasping corporation had the audacity to say;
You must all renounce your unions and forswear your liberty,
And we'll promise you a chance to live and die in slavery.

Chorus:
For the man that fights for honor, none can blame him;
May luck attend wherever he may roam;
And no song of his will ever live to shame him
While liberty and honor rule his home.

When a crowd of well armed ruffians came without authority,
Like thieves at night, while decent men were sleeping peacefully,
Can you wonder why all honest men with indignation burn,
Why the slimy worm that crawls the earth when trod upon will turn?
When the locked out men at Homestead saw they were face to face
With a lot of paid detectives then they knew it was their place
To protect their homes and families and that was nobly done,
And the angels will applaud them for the victory they won.

See that sturdy band of working men start at the break of day,
Determination in their eyes that surely meant to say;
No men can drive us from our homes for which we've toiled so long,
No men shall take our places now for here's where we belong.
A woman with a rifle saw her husband in a crowd;
She handed him the weapon and they cheered her long and loud.
He kissed her and said, "Mary, you go home 'til we are through."
She answered, "No, if you must fight, my place is here with you."

The building behind the wall that enclosed the Homestead Works no longer stands. At the center is what was popularly known as "the hole in the wall," where the pay line formed.

JULY 27, 1986 —Excerpted from The New York Times.

A Chapter of Industrial History Closes With the Homestead Steel Works

Special to The New York Times

HOMESTEAD, Pa., July 25 —Red Hrabic, not so red anymore, was one. Ed Buzinka, Bill Evans and Ray MaGuire were others. So was Bob Todd, a large, outgoing man. . . .

These men were among the last 23 workers today at the Homestead Works, for a century one of the great centers of American steel making.

The plant, where manufacturing began in the early 1880's, rolled its last steel in late May. But the USX Corporation, formerly United States Steel, continued to bring in some production workers to ship remaining steel, tear down and cannibalize equipment for sale, and do the other chores of closing the works.

These men and a few supervisors were the only ones left in the huge, rusting, abandoned plant, which employed 20,000 workers in World War II and several thousand as recently as the late 1970's.

Their job was finished today.

Again, a Revolution

The vast production, the organization of work and the manufacturing techniques that occurred here and in other great steel works represented a revolution in American industry. So this day surely marks a revolution, too, for the Homestead works, like many other steel works and many other manufacturing plants, are being closed, as the economy continues to change and more and more manufacturing is done abroad.

The Homestead epic ended in a bittersweet manner, largely unnoticed outside this town just up the Monongahela from Pittsburgh. Plant closings are numerous in industrial areas, and USX, by closing sections piecemeal over the last several years, avoided the attention that closing a large facility at one time would have brought.

In a parking lot outside the plant, when the shift ended about 2 P.M., men chatted briefly about their days at the mill and their futures.

. . .

Inside the works, which stretch over three miles and 500 acres, building after building sits empty today. The Carrie furnace, closed. The 45-inch slab mill, closed. The 100-inch rolling mill, closed. The 160-inch rolling mill, closed. The works' huge steel lathe, once one of the largest in the world, capable of shaping steel pieces 92-feet long. Closed.

Already weeds and trees—lamb's quarter, sumac, cottonwood, ailanthus—have begun to grow in the works, once so immaculately maintained.

Gone too are the sights and sounds of steel making. Flames. Sparks. Steam. Smoke. Whistles. Shrieks. Bleats. Pounding. Throbbing. . . . *William Serrin*

A F T E R W O R D

by David Montgomery

*T*he battle against the Pinkertons and the subsequent military occupation of Homestead were not uncommon or isolated events. Commanders of national guard units around the country reported 23 instances in which their troops had been called out during 1892. In addition to patrolling the streets of Homestead for three months, state military forces had suppressed striking iron miners in Soudan, Minnesota, as well as silver and lead miners in Coeur d'Alene, Idaho, escorted strikebreakers through crowds of defiant railroad switchmen in Buffalo, New York, occupied Coal Creek and Oliver Springs, Tennessee, where miners had released convict miners from their stockades, and forced the Workingmen's Amalgamated Council of New Orleans to end a city-wide general strike, in which more than 20,000 white and black members of 42 local unions had stood together. Nor was the year 1892 exceptional: there had actually been more strikes and more use of armed force against them during the two preceding years, and the crescendo of violence was not to be reached until the Pullman boycott and coal miners' strikes of 1894.

In all these confrontations the military force of state or federal governments was mobilized to protect the claims of business enterprises to undisturbed use of their property in their pursuit of private gain. Local authorities manifested clear sympathy for the strikers, and even the governors of Pennsylvania and Tennessee complied only with obvious reluctance to the companies' demands for troops. Once those troops had been sent into action, however, the power of the local citizenry was irrevocably curtailed. Consequently, the military patrols in the streets of mining and mill towns during the 1890s constituted one critically important element in a structural transformation of American political life, which accompanied the consolidation of modern corporate power.

By the 1890s the United States was already a highly industrialized country. In fact, during the previous decade its total manufacturing output had outstripped that of Britain, to achieve a position of world dominance. Iron and steel production in western Pennsylvania typified this development, expanding from the first little Pittsburgh rolling mill of 1811 to an 1899 output in Carnegie's furnaces alone which surpassed the ingot steel production of any other *country* in the world. The vast Carnegie mills of Homestead, Braddock, and Duquesne made use of the latest technology to fabricate the steel beams, sheets, and plates with which the physical structures of 20th-century urban life were built. Like the Westinghouse Works in nearby East Pittsburgh, they provided the industrial revolution with what historian David Landes has called its "second wind."

For almost 20 years before 1892, however, the expansion of industry and agriculture had been stalked by chronically falling prices, a major depression (1873-1878) and intermittent sharp recessions. In 1890 markets for both minerals and railroad equipment had contracted sharply, and three years later a bank panic triggered the most severe depression of the 19th century. Employers' efforts to secure their profits by reducing wages were frequently challenged, and sometimes defeated, by the solidarities workers exhibited within their crafts and their communities. Although the effort of the Knights of Labor to bring all working people into a a single multipurpose organization was collapsing by the late 1880s, trade unions continued to grow, to direct a steadily increasing proportion of the country's strikes, and to provide each other with effective support.

When the delegates of the Amalgamated Association of Iron and Steel Workers assembled in Pittsburgh for their June 1892 convention, the *Pittsburg Post* called it "the most powerful independent labor organization in the world." (See page 32.) Although the union had been effectively excluded from such large mills in rustic settings as those in Danville, Bethlehem, and Johnstown, in Allegheny County throughout "the decade from 1880 to 1890," John Fitch later wrote, the "list of [iron] manufacturers who signed the [union] scale was practically a list of those engaged in the business." To be sure, bargaining over that wage scale was often intense, and strikes and lockouts occurred frequently, but so many puddlers and skilled rolling mill hands adhered to the union that even the strikes ended in negotiated settlements. In uncanny ways, the relationship between the iron masters and the Amalgamated resembled that which would exist in the 1950s between the steel industry and the United Steelworkers of America.

Joseph D. Weeks, a founder of the Western Iron Association and editor of the industry journal, *Iron Age*, promoted joint wage conferences, sliding scales (linking craftsmen's tonnage rates to product prices), employers' associations to stabilize prices, and protective tariffs to keep those prices high. In 1892 Weeks was secretary to the Republican National Committee. President William Weihe of the Amalgamated was by then also a Republican, as had been his predecessor in office John Jarrett.

So influential was the union in western Pennsylvania that Andrew Carnegie not only negotiated with it in his Bessemer and open-hearth steel mills, but also proclaimed his own sympathy for the aspirations of union workers. (See pages 2-3.) Nevertheless, his success in breaking a strike at the Edgar

(Afterword, continued)

Thomson works, after the workers had repudiated concessions negotiated by their union, not only encouraged him to challenge the Amalgamated in its Homestead stronghold, but also inspired some owners of older iron mills to demand concessions (sometimes under the threat of closing the business). In the summer of 1892 the union faced simultaneously a lockout at Homestead and a wage strike against the whole Western Association.

Community solidarity sustained the Homestead strikers. The support offered by the predominantly Slovak laborers, who were not themselves eligible for union membership, the townspeople's respect for the Advisory Committee, the rallying of men and women alike against the invading Pinkertons, the sympathetic strikes in Braddock, Duquesne, and Beaver Falls, and the arrival of a "company of millworkers from the Southside, Pittsburgh, . . . marching into 'Fort Frick' headed by the United States flag and a tenor drum," revealed strong bonds among local men and women as fellow workers, family members, and neighbors. (See pages 33, 39, 41, 61, 63-4, 76, 85.) What conquered that community was military force brought in from the outside—first unsuccessfully in the form of hired armed guards, and then irresistibly in the form of soldiers ordered in by Governor Robert Pattison.

The residents of Homestead expected local officials, and even Governor Pattison, to side with them against the importation of armed force. (See page 115.) Their expectation suggests a great deal about the relationship between working people and party politics at the time. From the late 1850s to the late 1920s western Pennsylvania was Republican terrain. Nowhere else in America was the Republican doctrine that the tariff kept business prosperous, jobs plentiful, and wages high more widely believed. In February 1878—scarcely six months after Pittsburgh's working people had driven from the city the Philadelphia troops who had come to restore the struck Pennsylvania railroad to operation and then burned the company's property—local workers turned out en masse to join their employers in a parade in favor of high tariffs.

Homestead's Republican burgess, John McLuckie, repeatedly attributed the 1892 strike to a conspiracy which had *reduced* the duty on 4 x 4 steel billets, after the union and the Carnegie company had agreed to base the sliding scale of wages on their price. (See pages 28-9.) As we have seen, both the editor of the iron industry's journal and the presidents of the Amalgamated were active Republicans. The Allegheny County organization headed by Christopher Magee and William Flinn used municipal contracts to link building and traction companies to the party, while it kept at arm's length the Protestant moral reformers, who drove so many workers in other cities into the Democratic fold. If the stark absence of municipal services kept workers' neighborhoods desolate, it also made taxes low.

Nevertheless, Allegheny County was not then under one-party rule. Between 1876 and 1890 the aggregate nationwide votes of the Republicans and Democrats were very close, and the balance shifted often in national elections and in those of

northern states. Even in Allegheny County, Republican votes for governor and for president averaged no more than 53 per cent during those 14 years, and third parties, like the Greenback-Labor party, often held the balance of power. In 1890 even Homestead had followed the national trend and cast a slim majority of its gubernatorial votes for Robert Pattison, though borough offices remained in Republican hands. (See page 42.)

Governor Pattison appointed the secretary-treasurer of the United Mineworkers of America, Robert Watchorn, chief factory inspector for the state. Watchorn has written that his own efforts to enlarge his staff of factory inspectors was effectively supported in the state legislature by both Governor Pattison and the Republican state boss, Senator Matthew Quay, over the opposition of Secretary of State William Harrity, who, Watchorn recalled in his autobiography, was the "intimate associate of very large financial groups" and national chairman of the Democratic party.

Even more important to the daily lives of Homestead's residents than the influence they gained in state legislatures as a result of the close competition between the major parties was the direct control they exercised over their burgesses, councilmen, and justices of the peace. This control was visible during the strike itself. Before the town was placed under military rule, the Advisory Committee elected by the strikers patrolled the streets with Burgess McLuckie's approval, cut down effigies, obtained pledges from saloon keepers to prevent excessive drinking, and escorted deputy sheriffs out of town. Recent immigrants were incorporated into strikers' patrols through what Advisory Committee chairman Hugh O'Donnell described as a "brigade of foreigners . . . under the command of two Hungarians and two interpreters." A striker who was beaten by two company watchmen was able to prosecute his assailants before a justice of the peace, and another squire jailed a stranger who appeared in town carrying a revolver. (See pages 33, 48, 55, 61.)

Contrast that scene with the same town in 1919. During the recruiting drives of the AFL's National Committee for Organizing Iron and Steel Workers, Burgess P.H. McGuire (who had participated as a youth in the strike of 1892) denied the union permits to hold meetings, insisted constantly that "no foreign speakers" would be allowed to make public addresses in the borough, and, when a court order did make meetings possible, had state policemen present on the platform to warn speakers against inflammatory remarks or criticism of local or national authorities. Residents accused the police of breaking into homes during the night to arrest people and of beating workers they had in custody. In 1919, mill guards brought strike supporters before Burgess McGuire for prosecution. McGuire asked defendants if they were on strike. Those who answered yes were fined under the vagrancy laws for not working.

The defeat of the union in 1892 had not only forced steel workers to toil the next 45 years without union protection on the job, it had also sharply curtailed townspeople's civil liberties and their influence upon government. By the end of the 1890s residents agreed, "If you want to talk in Homestead, you talk to yourself." Despite the Democratic electoral victory two weeks after the end of the strike, Homestead quickly settled into a virtually uncontested hegemony of the Republican party, with no organized voice of workers to influence that party. The borough joined the rest of Allegheny County in giving 70 percent of its votes to William McKinley in 1896, and thereafter experienced open political debate only in 1912, when, as novelist Thomas Bell wrote: "[Theodore] Roosevelt's rebellion provided timorous voters with a unique opportunity to get passionate about politics without having their Republicanism impugned." By the presidential election of 1924 fewer than 2,500 people cast ballots at all, and of those only 190 voted Democrat.

The commitment of government support to business' needs, the diminution of voting participation and of partisan competition for the labor vote, and the denial of public spaces and public institutions to use by working people were not confined to Homestead, nor can they be explained simply as consequences of one lost strike. On the contrary, they revealed an accommodation by government to the requirements of nascent corporate enterprise. Between 1894 and 1932 the Republicans enjoyed an unprecedented and continuous mastery of the federal government, and they guided national policy toward securing the prosperity and autonomy of the business enterprises which spearheaded the period's rapid economic growth.

Effective efforts at political reform in Allegheny County, as in most other urban areas during the early 20th century, were sponsored by non-partisan associations of people from society's managerial and professional strata. New registration and residency requirements for voters, designed to reduce political corruption, seriously reduced the size of the electorate, especially in the South, where electoral reforms systematically disfranchised African Americans, while they also kept large numbers of poor whites away from the polls.

A decisive role in the process of restructuring the relations between government and the economy was played by the judiciary. In 1893 the Supreme Court of the United States ruled that the unions of New Orleans had violated the Sherman Anti-Trust Act by their general strike of the previous year. Two years later the court declared that concentration of control over manufacturing did *not* violate the Sherman Act. In the same session (1895-6) it also declared a federal income tax unconstitutional, approved the government's use of injunctions against the American Railway Union, and gave its assent to racial segregation by law.

The industrial growth that followed this restructuring was formidable. By the 1920s at least 45 percent of all the value added by manufacture in the entire world was generated in the United States. The vigorous economy both attracted tens of millions of immigrants, and was in turn further stimulated by the initiatives of those immigrants. Most of the newcomers came from non-industrial parts of Europe. Their numbers were augmented by black and white Southerners, who left farming,

first for the mines and manufacturing towns of their region, and later for northern cities, as well as by hundreds of thousands of men and women who left Quebec and Mexico in search of jobs. Whatever their origins, the migrants dared to take charge of their own destinies by moving to strange and distant places.

Mill towns became divided into so-called "American" hillsides and "immigrant" hollows. The newcomers fashioned their own lives around their churches, their fraternal lodges, and their families. Although a politician might solicit the votes of those immigrants who had applied for citizenship, few government offices came their way. Justices of the peace appear in immigrants' recollections not as sympathetic neighbors, but as avaricious officials, quick to use "drunk and disorderly" charges to fleece the laborer of his week's earnings.

During the 1880s, when Homestead had been a union town, the disdain which skilled workers expressed often and openly toward laborers who had recently arrived from the kingdoms of Hungary and Italy, had not prevented the newcomers from involving themselves in community organizations and unions established by earlier arrivals. Slovaks suffered especially heavy casualties in the fight against the Pinkertons, and at the funeral of one of them, the Reverend J. Cedochi preached on the text: "All Reforms Are Brought About by Bloodshed." One poet, denouncing "Tyrant Frick," saluted them as "brave Hungarians, sons of toil, . . . seeking which was right." (See pages 63-4, 118, 124.) Such praise from "American" workers was seldom heard after 1900.

It was, however, the immigrant laborers who provided the driving force behind the steel strike of 1919 in western Pennsylvania. The words spoken by a Polish worker at a union meeting and recorded by a reporter captured their determination to take action, so that their lives and their children's lives might become something better than an endless round of toil for the mills:

Mr. Chairman—just like a horse and wagon, work all day. Take horse out of wagon—put in stable. Take horse out of stable, put in wagon. Same way like mills. Work all day. Come home—go sleep. Get up — go work in mills— come home. Wife say, "John, children sick. You help with children." You say, "Oh, go to hell"—go sleep. Wife say, "John, you go town." You say, "No"—go sleep. No know what the hell you do. For why this war ? For why we buy Liberty bonds? For the mills ? No, for freedom and America—for everybody. No more horse and wagon. For eight-hour day.

Many historians agree that it was the children of these immigrants whose votes made possible the New Deal in Washington, whose struggles brought the CIO to the steel and other basic industries, and whose vision of "freedom and America" redefined for the whole country the meaning of both. Once again the establishment of rights at work through union recognition and the reawakening of democracy in political life appeared hand in hand. As early as 1928 the borough had signalled its political reawakening by giving Al Smith a vote

68 percent greater than the town's total turnout in the presidential election four years earlier.

The next year the economic boom stimulated by the policies of the 1890s collapsed. By 1932 the nation's manufacturing output had fallen back to the level of 1885, and hunger stalked the streets of Homestead. In response the borough's residents mobilized to demand "work or wages," and began enrolling in unions once again (often secretly at first). The New Deal, which enjoyed their ardent support, sought to unclog the sclerosis built up in the arteries of the economy by 40 years of unimpeded corporate power, and to stimulate economic revival by increasing the earnings of ordinary people. The Wagner Act of 1935 explained the new public policy by arguing that the "inequality of bargaining power between employees who do not possess full freedom of association or actual liberty of contract" and corporate employers who depressed "wage rates and the purchasing power of wage earners," prevented "the stabilization of competitive wage rates and working conditions within and between industries," and thus "aggravate[ed] recurrent business depressions."

A huge meeting convened by the Steelworkers Organizing Committee in 1936 on the anniversary of the beginning of the 1892 strike carried a message of hope. It was addressed by Lieutenant Governor Thomas Kennedy, former secretary of the United Mine Workers, who had been made commander of the state constabulary, and used the police to facilitate, rather than impede public gatherings. Three months later, when some 500 delegates from various fraternal orders gathered in Slovenian Hall to rally behind the CIO, they were not only permitted to meet, but welcomed by Burgess Lawry with the words: "Everybody into the union. One for all and all for one."

Although more and more of the country's steel products were fabricated outside of western Pennsylvania during the 1940s and 1950s, for residents of Homestead prospects for the future appeared as secure as they had in the 1880s. The pattern bargaining made possible by the growth of industrial unions placed a reliable and rising floor under the incomes of millions of Americans.

By the late 1970s, however, popular hopes for sustained prosperity based on good earnings had evaporated. Furnaces were shut and factories closed throughout the region. At times it seemed as though the only sound coming from the Monongahela Valley was that of the wrecking ball. No longer did the United States lead the world in steel production. Its output was surpassed by the Soviet Union in 1971, and within another decade the second place was taken by Japan. While eastern European state planners clung to heavy industry until their economies collapsed, Western business executives secured the vitality of their enterprises at the expense of mill towns. All over the world regions which had once transformed 20th-century life with their coal and steel now lie in shambles.

The economy shaped by multinational corporations has knocked the props out from under the economic and political order forged by the New Deal and industrial unionism, as effectively as the defeat of 1892 destroyed the community and politics which had produced the Battle of "Fort Frick." The relocations of industrial activity, devastation of communities, and downward pressure on workers' earnings have also brought reawakened community initiatives. During the 1980s the Monongahela Valley produced important coalitions of local residents, unions, clergy, and business people, who sought to keep threatened plants and furnaces open under local auspices. Their proposals for new public authorities and policies that would reinvigorate regional production of socially useful goods and services have produced viable alternatives to resignation and despair.

These developments suggest that commemoration of the Homestead strikers entails more than just romantic nostalgia. The men and women who fought for hearth and home in 1892 provided a lesson as important for our age as it was for their own. A society which celebrates economic growth at the expense of community values and decent standards of life for all not only produces unseemly contrasts of wealth and poverty in its midst, but also makes its people the victims, rather than the beneficiaries, of whatever prosperity it experiences. People work in order to provide their own material needs, but that everyday effort also builds a community with purposes more important than anyone's personal enrichment. The last 100 years have shown how heavily the health of political democracy in a modern industrial society depends on the success of its working people in overcoming personal and group differences to create their own effective voice in the shaping of their own futures. The fight for hearth and home is still with us. ❖

Workers leave the U.S. Steel Works by the "Amity Gate" in the early 1950s.

SOURCES & SUGGESTED READINGS

Adamic, Louis. *Dynamite: The Story of Class Violence in America.* New York: Viking Press, 1931. Reprinted: London: Rebel, 1984.

Attaway, William. *Blood on the Forge.* New York: Doubleday, Doran and Co., 1941. Reprinted: New York: Monthly Review, 1987.

Bell, Thomas. *Out of This Furnace.* Boston: Little, Brown and Company, 1941. Reprinted: Pittsburgh, PA: University of Pittsburgh Press, 1976.

*Berkman, Alexander. *Prison Memoirs of an Anarchist.* New York: Mother Earth Publishing Association, 1912. Reprinted: New York: Schocken, 1970.

Bernstein, Irving. *The Desperate Years.* Boston: Houghton Mifflin, 1970.

Bodnar, John E. *Immigration and Industrialization: Ethnicity in an American Mill Town, 1870-1940.* Reprinted: Pittsburgh, PA: University of Pittsburgh Press, 1977.

Bowman, John. *Andrew Carnegie: Steel Tycoon.* Englewood Cliffs, NJ: Silver Burdett, 1989.

Boyer, Richard O. and Herbert M. Morais. *Labor's Untold Story.* New York: Cameron, 1955. Reprinted: New York: Electrical, Radio and Machine Workers of America, 1986.

Brecher, Jeremy. *Strike!* Boston: South End Press, 1972.

*Bridge, James Howard. *The Inside History of the Carnegie Steel Company: A Romance of Millions.* New York: The Aldine Book Company, 1903. Reprinted: Pittsburgh, PA: University of Pittsburgh Press, 1991.

Brody, David. *Labor in Crisis: The Steel Strike of 1919.* Philadelphia: Lippincott and Company, 1965. Reprinted: Champaign, IL: University of Illinois Press, 1987.

Brody, David. *Steelworkers in America: The Nonunion Era.* Cambridge, MA: Harvard University Press, 1960.

*Burgoyne, Arthur G. *Homestead.* Pittsburgh: Rawsthorne Engraving and Printing Company, 1893. Republished as *The Homestead Strike of 1892.* Pittsburgh, PA: University of Pittsburgh Press, 1979.

*Byington, Margaret Frances. *Homestead: The Households of a Mill Town.* New York: The Russell Sage Foundation, 1910. Reprinted: Pittsburgh, PA: University of Pittsburgh Press, 1974.

Clark, Paul, et al. *Forging a Union of Steel: Philip Murray, SWOC and the United Steelworkers.* Ithaca, New York: ILR Press, Cornell University, 1987.

Davis, James. *The Iron Puddler.* New York: Grosset and Dunlap, 1922.

Davis, Rebecca. *Life in the Mills.* New York: Feminist Press, 1972. Republished as *Life in the Iron Mills.* New York: Feminist Press, 1985.

Davenport, Marcia. *The Valley of Decision.* New York: Charles Scribner's Sons, 1942. Reprinted: Pittsburgh, PA: University of Pittsburgh Press, 1989.

Demarest, David P. Jr., ed. *From These Hills, From These Valleys.* Pittsburgh, PA: University of Pittsburgh Press, 1976.

Dickerson, Dennis. *Out of the Crucible: Black Steelworkers in Western Pennsylvania, 1875-1980.* Albany, NY: State University of New York Press, 1986.

Eggert, Gerald G. *Steelmasters and Labor Reform, 1886-1923.* Pittsburgh, PA: University of Pittsburgh Press, 1981.

*Fitch, John A. *The Steel Workers.* New York: The Russell Sage Foundation, 1910. Reprinted: Pittsburgh, PA: University of Pittsburgh Press, 1989.

Fogelson, Robert M. *America's Armories: Architecture, Society, and Public Order.* Cambridge, MA: Harvard University Press, 1989.

Foster, William Z. *The Great Steel Strike.* New York: B.W. Huebsch, 1920. Reprinted: New York: Arno Press, 1969.

*Gilbert, Douglas. *Lost Chords.* New York: Doubleday, Doran and Co., 1942.

*Goldman, Emma. *Living My Life.* 2 vols. New York: Alfred Knopf, 1931. Reprinted: New York: Dover, 1970.

Goldman, Emma. *Anarchism and Other Essays.* New York: Dover, 1970.

Goldman, Emma. *Nowhere at Home: Letters from Exile of Emma Goldman and Alexander Berkman.* New York: Schocken Books, 1975.

Harvey, George Brinton McClellan. *Henry Clay Frick: The Man.* New York: Charles Scribner's Sons, 1928.

Hays, Samuel P., ed. *City at the Point: Essays on the Social History of Pittsburgh.* Pittsburgh, PA: University of Pittsburgh Press, 1989.

Hessen, Robert. *Steel Titan: The Life of Charles Schwab.* New York: Oxford University Press, 1975. Reprinted: Pittsburgh, PA: University of Pittsburgh Press, 1990.

Hoerr, John P. *And the Wolf Finally Came: The Decline of the American Steel Industry.* Pittsburgh, PA: University of Pittsburgh Press, 1988.

Ingham, John. *Making Iron and Steel: Independent Mills in Pittsburgh, 1820-1920.* Columbus, OH: Ohio State University Press, 1991.

Ingham, John. *The Iron Barons: A Social Analysis of an American Urban Elite, 1874-1965.* Westport, CT: Greenwood, 1978.

Kleinberg, S.J. *The Shadow of the Mills: Working-class Families in Pittsburgh, 1870-1907.* Pittsburgh, PA: University of Pittsburgh Press, 1989.

Books excerpted in this volume.
Other Sources: Newspaper and periodical sources are cited in the text. The source for testimony from U.S. House of Representatives Report No. 2447 *(published February 7, 1893) and* U.S. Senate Report No. 1280 *(published February 10, 1893) is:* U.S. Detectives Committee to Investigate Employment: Report, *Washington, D.C.: Government Printing Office, 1893.*

Krause, Paul. *The Battle for Homestead 1880-1892*. Pittsburgh, PA: University of Pittsburgh Press, 1992.

Lens, Sidney. *Left, Right and Center: Conflicting Forces in American Labor*. Hinsdale, IL: H. Regnery Company, 1949.

Lens, Sidney. *Strikemakers and Strikebreakers*. New York: Penguin, 1985.

Levinson, Edward. *Labor on the March*. New York: University Books, 1956.

*Lichliter, M.D. ed. *James Jackson McIlyar–Preacher–Evangelist–Freemason*. Pittsburgh: n.d.

Livesay, Harold C. *Andrew Carnegie and the Rise of Big Business*. New York: Harper Collins, 1975.

Long, Haniel. *Pittsburgh Memoranda*. Santa Fe, NM: Rydal Press for Writers' Editions, 1935. Reprinted: Pittsburgh, PA: University of Pittsburgh Press, 1990.

Lorant, Stefan. *Pittsburgh: Story of an American City*. Garden City, New York: Doubleday and Company, 1964. Reprinted: Lenox, MA: Author's Edition, 1975.

*McGovern, Michael J. *Labor Lyrics and Other Songs*. Youngstown, OH: Vindicator Press, 1899.

*Martin, George. *Madam Secretary, Frances Perkins*. Boston: Houghton Mifflin, 1976.

*Meltzer, Milton. *Bread and Roses*. New York, Facts on File, Inc., 1991.

Miner, Curtis. *Homestead: The Story of a Steel Town*. Pittsburgh, PA: Historical Society of Western Pennsylvania, 1989.

Montgomery, David. *The Fall of the House of Labor*. Cambridge: Cambridge University Press, 1987.

O'Connor, Harvey. *Steel Dictator*. New York: John Day, 1935.

*Parton, May Field, ed. *The Autobiography of Mother Jones*. Chicago: Charles H. Kerr and Company, 1925. Reprinted 1972.

Powers, George. *Cradle of Steel Unionism*. East Chicago, IN: Figueroa, 1972.

Serrin, William. *Homestead: The Glory and Tragedy of an American Steel Town*. New York: Random House, 1992.

Sheppard, Muriel. *Cloud by Day: The Story of Coal and Coke and People*. Chapel Hill, NC: University of North Carolina Press, 1947. Reprinted: Pittsburgh, PA: University of Pittsburgh Press, 1991.

Shergold, Peter R. *Working-Class Life: The "American Standard" in Comparative Perspective*. Pittsburgh, PA: University of Pittsburgh Press, 1981.

*Spahr, Charles B. *America's Working People*. New York: Longmans, Green and Co., 1900. Reprinted as *An Essay on the Present Distribution of Wealth in the United States, America's Working People*: New York: Johnson Reprint Corporation, 1970.

Steel, Edward M., ed. *The Correspondence of Mother Jones*. Pittsburgh, PA: University of Pittsburgh Press, 1985.

* Steel, Edward M., ed. *The Speeches and Writings of Mother Jones*. Pittsburgh, PA: University of Pittsburgh Press, 1988.

*Stowell, Myron R. *"Fort Frick" or The Siege of Homestead*. Pittsburgh, PA: Pittsburgh Printing, 1893.

Van Dyke, John C., ed. *The Autobiography of Andrew Carnegie*. Boston: Houghton Mifflin, 1920. Reprinted with special arrangement with Houghton Mifflin: Boston: Northeastern University Press, 1986.

Wall, Joseph Frazier. *Andrew Carnegie*. New York: Oxford University Press, 1970. Reprinted: Pittsburgh, PA: University of Pittsburgh Press, 1989.

Wall, Joseph Frazier, ed. *The Andrew Carnegie Reader*. Pittsburgh, PA: University of Pittsburgh Press, 1992.

Warren, Kenneth. *The American Steel Industry, 1850-1970*. Oxford: Clarendon Press, 1973. Reprinted: Pittsburgh, PA: University of Pittsburgh Press, 1988.

Wexler, Alice. *Emma Goldman in Exile: From the Russian Revolution to the Spanish Civil War*. Boston: Beacon Press, 1989.

*Wexler, Alice. *Emma Goldman in America*. Boston: Beacon Press, 1984.

Yellen, Samuel. *American Labor Struggles, 1877-1934*. New York: Monad, 1974.

CREDITS

ILLUSTRATIONS
Institutions
Allegheny County Coroner's Office: p. 108.

The Carnegie Library of Pittsburgh: p. 11; p. 12; p. 14; p. 42 left; p. 53; p. 58; p. 66-69; p. 104 bottom; p. 110; p. 133, Underwood & Underwood stereograph; p. 135; p. 137; p. 154; p. 177, *The Pittsburgh Post*, July 27, 1892.

The Carnegie Library of Homestead: p. 5; p. 24; p. 138; p. 207.

Carnegie Mellon University: p. 2; p. 121.

Chicago Historical Society: p. 70; p. 71 bottom; p. 214.

Clayton Corporation Archives: p. xii; p. 6 top and bottom; pp. 96-97; p. 160.

Hagley Museum and Library, Wilmington, DE: p. 20 bottom and p. 36 top, H.C. White Co., stereograph, 1907.

Hillman Library, University of Pittsburgh: p. 34; p. 102; p. 199; p. 204; p. 205 top and bottom; Archives of an Industrial Society, p. 209.

Hirshhorn Museum and Sculpture Garden, Smithsonian Institution: p. 210, Lee Stalsworth photographer.

Historical Society of Western Pennsylvania: p. 50 bottom.

Illinois State Historical Library: p. 119; p. 123; p. 126 top.

Homestead, Borough of: p. 28.

International Institution of Social History, Amsterdam, Netherlands: p. 162 left and right.

Library of Congress: p. xi, H.C. White Co., stereograph, 1907; p. 45, H.C. White Co., stereograph, 1907; p. 71 top; p. 146, Underwood & Underwood stereograph; p. 161, Underwood & Underwood stereograph; p. 201; p. 202, H.C. White Co., stereograph, 1907; p. 211, H.C. White Co., stereograph, 1907; p. 212.

The George Meany Memorial Archives: p. 215.

National Museum of American Art, Smithsonian Institution, Peter A. Juley & Son Collection: p. 218.

New York Public Library: p. 46; p. 48; p. 49; p. 59 bottom; p. 62; p. 104 top.

New York Society Library: pp. 32-33; p. 38; p. 41; p. 42 right; p. 50 top; p. 51; p. 57 top; p. 59 top; p. 72; p. 74 top and bottom; p. 78; p. 79; p. 87; p. 89; p. 90; p. 91; p. 99; p. 100; p. 139; p. 142; p. 143; p. 150; p. 164; p. 167; p. 168; p. 170; p. 171; p. 172; p. 173; p. 174; p. 179; p. 182; p. 208.

Pittsburgh History and Landmarks Foundation: p. 180.

St. Mary Magdalene Church, Homestead: p. 116 top.

Swissvale Historical Society, Melvin Wach Collection: p. 131; p. 132; p. 136.

United Steelworkers of America: p. 217.

USX Corporation, Resource Management: p. 7.

Warren County Historical Society, Capt. Fred Windsor Collection: p. 148.

Individual Collections
William Baisely: p. 8.

William Gaughan Collection: p. 3; p. 220.

John K. Gates: p. 9.

James Getsy: p. 63.

David Hahner: p. 82; p. 84 top; p. 157.

Randolph Harris Collection: half title page; p. vii; p. 20 top; p. 109; p. 116 bottom; p. 126 bottom; p. 159; p. 221, Randolph Harris photographer; p. 222, Anthony Kambic photographer; p. 224, Randolph Harris photographer; p. 228.

Lawrence Levine Collection: p. 23.

John Schulman Collection: p. 158.

Edward Szerbin: p. 65.

Private Collection: p. 19; p. 27.

Marge Rybar: p. ix; p. 189.

Pat Varley: p. 36 bottom.

Reproduced from Books (See Sources)
Arthur G. Burgoyne, *Homestead*, 1893: p. 77; *The Homestead Strike of 1892,* reprinted 1982: p. 113.

James Howard Bridge, *The Inside History of the Carnegie Steel Company*, 1903: p. 52; p. 195.

John A. Fitch, The Steel Workers, reprinted 1989: p. 30.

M.D. Lichliter, ed., *James Jackson McIlyar: Preacher–Evangelist–Freemason*, n.d.: p.111.

Myron R. Stowell, *"Fort Frick" or The Siege of Homestead*, 1893: p. 54; p. 80; p. 84 bottom; p. 175; p. 184; p. 186; p. 190; p. 193.

Copy photography provided by: Caroline Borle, Mon Valley Media; The Carnegie Library of Pittsburgh; Jeffrey Cepull and staff, Photographic Services, University of Pittsburgh; Chicago Historical Society; Ray Fleming; Randolph Harris; Illinois State Historical Library; New York Society Library; New York Public Library; University Microfilm International, Ann Arbor, Michigan.

TEXT
Reprinted by permission of Clayton Corporation Archives: cable and letter, p. 57; cable, p. 88.

Reprinted by permission of Houghton Mifflin Co., New York: excerpt on page 215 from *Madam Secretary* by George Martin. Copyright © 1976 by George Martin.

Reprinted by permission of Joseph G. Jackel, West Mifflin, poem on p. 103.

Reprinted by permission of Charles H. Kerr Publishing Company, Chicago: excerpt from *Autobiography of Mother Jones*.

Reprinted by permission: excerpt on p. 224. Copyright © by The New York Times Company.

Reprinted by permission of Pantheon Books, a division of Random House, New York: excerpt from *Emma Goldman* by Alice Wexler. Copyright © 1984 by Alice Wexler.

Reprinted by permission of *Pittsburgh Post-Gazette*: excerpt from article on pp. 219-20.

Reprinted by permission of *Pittsburgh Press*: excerpt from article on p. 217.

Any omissions or misattributions are entirely unintentional.

THE CONTRIBUTORS

ROBERT S. BARKER teaches constitutional law, civil procedure, and comparative law at Duquesne University Law School. He has written extensively on constitutional topics.

JO BUTZ designs books and other publications. She has served as art director for D.C. Heath & Co., Lexington, Massachusetts, and for Herbick & Held Design Center in Pittsburgh, where she now lives.

DAVID P. DEMAREST, JR., who teaches English at Carnegie Mellon University, was responsible for the re-publication of Thomas Bell's *Out of This Furnace* and Arthur G. Burgoyne's *Homestead.*

STEFFI R. DOMIKE, a former steelworker, is a television and film producer whose programs include the prize-winning "Women of Steel." In 1987-90, she produced Labor's Corner, a weekly program about working people and their unions, for public TV station WQEX.

DORIS J. DYEN is a folklorist who documents traditional culture in southwestern Pennsylvania and develops interpretive programming. She directs the cultural conservation efforts of the Steel Industry Heritage Task Force.

NICOLE FAUTEUX, a television and film producer, won a 1990 Emmy award for her work on WNET's nightly current affairs program. With Domike, she is co-producing a film about the Homestead Strike, "The River Ran Red."

RUSSELL W. GIBBONS was communications director of the United Steelworkers of America for 24 years. Currently he is with the Philip Murray Institute for Labor Studies at the Community College of Allegheny County.

ARCHIE GREEN, a folklorist retired from the University of Texas, is especially interested in the traditions of working people. His book W*obblies, Pile Butts, & Other Heroes: Laborlore Explorations* is forthcoming from the University of Illinois Press.

RANDOLPH HARRIS is a photographer, photo archivist, and community organizer for the Steel Industry Heritage Task Force. His presentations on social and industrial history in the Monongahela Valley include "Homestead Heritage," a video aired on PBS.

PAUL KRAUSE is Associate Professor of History at the University of British Columbia and author of *The Battle for Homestead* (University of Pittsburgh Press, 1992).

EUGENE LEVY, who teaches history at Carnegie Mellon University, has written articles on the photographic depiction of the industrial era in western Pennsylvania.

IRWIN MARCUS, a professor of history at Indiana University of Pennsylvania, co-edited *People, Power and Profits: The Struggle of U. S. Steel Workers for Economic Democracy, 1882-1985.*

CHARLES McCOLLESTER, Associate Director of the Center for the Study of Labor Relations at Indiana University of Pennsylvania, has written and spoken extensively on the labor and industrial history of Pittsburgh.

DAVID MONTGOMERY is Farnum Professor of History at Yale University. His book *The Fall of the House of Labor* includes an analysis of the 1892 Homestead Strike.

KAUSHIK MUKERJEE is studying economic and social development at the University of Pittsburgh's Graduate School of Public and International Affairs.

THEODORE B. STURM, a social historian at Robert Morris College, has written on the Social Gospel Movement in the Protestant churches of Pittsburgh, as well as on other subjects.

SHARON TRUSILO has written on William Martin, the first national secretary of the Amalgamated Association of Iron & Steel Workers from 1876 to 1890. She teaches at the Community College of Allegheny County.

JOSEPH FRAZIER WALL, a professor of history emeritus at Grinnell College, is the author of A*ndrew Carnegie*, a biography that won the Bancroft Prize in American History in 1971.

FANNIA WEINGARTNER has edited and produced books, magazines, and catalogues for academic and trade publishers and museums in New York, San Francisco, and Chicago. She now works in Pittsburgh.

DON WOODWORTH teaches English at Indiana University of Pennsylvania. His interest in local and family history has led him to work with photographs and literature of the region.

RINA YOUNGNER, an art historian who has co-curated at both The Carnegie and the Frick Fine Arts Gallery, wrote *The Power and the Glory: Pittsburgh's Industrial Landscapes,* a catalogue of Aaron Gorson's paintings.